Between the Lamp Posts

Praise for Between the Lamp Post

We personally enjoyed this devotional. It is thoughtful
provides practical and applied Biblical principles for ever
living. It speaks very descriptively and eloquently about
challenges of life and how we are to face and respond to tl
We found the book very inspiring and encouraging and hi
recommend this read to anyone.

—**Barry and Cheryl Wi**
Barry Wissler, P
Presi
HarvestNet Internati

Walking is my favorite form of exercise. You might sa
an avid walker. I have discovered that the most effective w
walk is one stride at a time. Sounds pretty simple, but i
that simplicity is often clouded by fear and circumstance. P
119:105 declares "Your Word is a lamp unto my feet and
unto my path." In her engaging style, my friend and colle
Becky Toews walks with us in this series of practical devoti
that remind us the Light illuminating our path comes bu
step at a time. It is not a beacon that eliminates all dark
but a series of faith-filled luminaries that give life purpose
navigate stride by stride, one lamp post at a time guiding
of us through our respective faith journeys.

—**Dr. Peter W. Te**
Pres
Lancaster Bible Co

Between the Lamp Posts

365 Devotions for God-Seekers

By Becky Toews

Scripture quotations marked (NIV) are taken from the Holy Bible, New International Version®, NIV®. Copyright © 1973, 1978, 1984, 2011 by Biblica, Inc.™ Used by permission of Zondervan. All rights reserved worldwide. www.zondervan.com The "NIV" and "New International Version" are trademarks registered in the United States Patent and Trademark Office by Biblica, Inc.™

Scripture quotations marked ESV are taken from the ESV® Bible (The Holy Bible, English Standard Version®), copyright © 2001 by Crossway, a publishing ministry of Good News Publishers. Used by permission. All rights reserved.

Scripture quotations marked NIRV are taken from the Holy Bible, New International Reader's Version®, NIrV® Copyright © 1995, 1996, 1998, 2014 by Biblica, Inc.™ Used by permission of Zondervan. All rights reserved worldwide. www.zondervan.com The "NIrV" and "New International Reader's Version" are trademarks registered in the United States Patent and Trademark Office by Biblica, Inc.™ Used by permission. www.Lockman.org"

Scripture quotations marked NASB are taken from the New American Standard Bible® (NASB), Copyright © 1960, 1962, 1963, 1968, 1971, 1972, 1973, 1975, 1977, 1995 by The Lockman Foundation

Scripture quotations marked MSG are taken from THE MESSAGE, copyright © 1993, 1994, 1995, 1996, 2000, 2001, 2002 by Eugene H. Peterson. Used by permission of NavPress. All rights reserved. Represented by Tyndale House Publishers, Inc.

Scripture quotations marked KJV are taken from the King James Version Bible, published 1611. The KJV is public domain in the United States.

1 3 5 7 9 10 8 6 4 2

Printed in the United States of America

To Chip,

You are the best gift God has ever given to me

Acknowledgments

I'm so grateful for my family and friends in their love and support, and for the faithful prayers of my spiritual family at New Covenant Christian Church, in the writing of *Between the Lamp Posts*. Your lives have inspired many of the thoughts on these pages.

Thank you, Bethany, for helping to clarify my thinking, and Josiah and Lauren for your creativity and skills in getting the message out beyond my sphere.

Marty and Lisa, thank you for your continued generosity in allowing me a place to write where lamp posts inspired me every day.

A special thank you to Joanne Williams for your insight, suggestions and enthusiastic encouragement. And to all those who offered to be a second pair of eyes—Carla Reed, Janice Kaufman, Ann Mellott, Amber Mellott, Theresa Discavage and Gary Schmidt—thank you, thank you, thank you.

I asked the Lord to send me a midwife to help me birth this project. He sent me two. Thank you, Amy Deardon, for walking me through the publishing process and getting my book into print. And Marlene Bagnull, thank you for your excellent editing skills. What a blessing you have been. Perfect timing! A shout out also to Dara Stoltzfus for the beautiful cover design.

Chip, it would take another book to express my gratitude for all the support you have given me, from the beginning stages when writing a 365–page devotional existed only as a faint idea to bouncing around ideas at every step of the process. You believed in me more than I believed in myself. I am so grateful God purposed for us to walk together *between the lamp posts*.

And thank you, Lord Jesus, for presenting another opportunity for this poor vessel to express thoughts from you. *What is man that you are mindful of him?*

Note: *The material discussed in some of the readings is referenced at the back of this book.*

"It will not go out of my mind that if we pass this post and lantern, either we shall find strange adventures or else some great changes of our fortunes."

—Lucy Pevensie
The Lion,
the Witch and
the Wardrobe
by C.S. Lewis

Introduction

One morning I woke up with the word *penumbra* on my mind. I had actually dreamed about the word. What made it even stranger was I had no idea of what *penumbra* meant. After looking it up, I discovered it meant partially shaded or obscure. Technically, it's the glow around the sun occurring during a solar eclipse, like the one we recently experienced. Although the moon filters the brightness of the sun, an outer radiance remains so total darkness doesn't cover the earth.

I realized situations in my life seemed much like a penumbra—kind of vague and undefined. It's not that I doubted God's existence. Like the sun, his light remained fixed. But converging circumstances were overshadowing his presence. I wanted to see him more clearly, yet I found myself suspended between darkness and light. At the same time, the devotional I was reading that year, *Streams in the Desert,* advised this: "Do not try to get out of a dark place except in God's time and in God's way.... Premature deliverance may frustrate God's work of grace ... be willing to abide in the darkness as long as you have His presence."

The reading of that entry didn't solve all my problems, but it shed enough light to keep me pressing on. I believe much of our Christian journey is similar. God, by his grace, reveals enough of himself to carry us to the next mile marker. Those moments are like *lamp posts of grace*. Without them, we couldn't take another step. They illuminate the path ahead, keeping us from turning back. They lessen the darkness between each ray of light.

Lamp posts stand like sentinels dutifully at watch over their city streets and houses. When the sun begins to set, they begin their work. As light beams from their stately lanterns, travelers find both comfort and direction. In the *Chronicles of Narnia,* the lamp post shines as the entrance into an enchanted country as well as pointing the way back home. Lamp posts represent adventure. They represent stability.

Daily entries from *Between the Lamp Posts* use illustrations from everyday life to illuminate some aspect of our walk with Christ. They'll show you what Screamo concerts, Bonsai trees, Swiss chocolate bars, trash collectors and speeding tickets have to do with faith. Devotionals like "Stubbornness of Hope" and "What Do You Do with Doubt?" as well as seasonal devotionals like "Not Your Typical Messiah" and "Tunnel Vision Christmas" will broaden your perspective on issues vital to Christianity. Themes touching upon trust, faith, truth and love run throughout the year, but also insights on gratitude, perseverance, prayer and redemption. Each devotional helps the reader apply some biblical principle.

So, fellow God-seekers, I pray *Between the Lamp Posts* will shed light on your adventure with Christ. I'm praying it will stretch your thoughts on some days, stir up your passion on others, and rekindle your missional call throughout the year. As you move forward, may the insights from these personal entries shine light on your own life journey. I pray your light will intensify as well, for as the Lord encourages us: "Let your light shine before others, that they may see your good deeds and glorify your Father in heaven." (Matthew 5:16)

January 1st

I press on toward the goal to win the prize for which God has called me heavenward in Christ Jesus.   *—Philippians 3:14 NIV*

Soul Goals

For many of us, a new year denotes a fresh start, a new set of resolutions, some new goals.

A cup of coffee and cookie after grading papers. Watching an episode of *Blue Bloods* after a full day. Taking a walk after a morning of writing. These make up some of the small rewards I give myself upon completing my goals. Goals—and the rewards that follow—foster my discipline. Without the small, temporary goals, I would accomplish little, and what I did carry out would be far less satisfying without some semblance of celebration upon their completion.

But other kinds of goals show the source of my real treasure. I call them "soul goals." Soul goals reveal whether I'm striving for earth or heaven, whether I'm pursuing man's applause or God's. Jesus says if we do our works so men will see how righteous (or compassionate or talented or smart) we are, then we have won our reward. However, in so doing, we forfeit any reward from our Heavenly Father (Matthew 6:1). We evidently have an option.

We mine for what we prize most. If the treasure we seek lies buried in the accolades of others, we will find some way to let them know—even if we don't have a Facebook account. But no matter how gratifying the praise of people feels now, it evaporates quickly and never truly satisfies.

Paul knew this. He was not about to settle for some puny, temporary goal that yielded a puny, temporary reward. He set his eyes on the highest prize—a prize so invaluable not one thing on earth could come close. Not. One. Thing. Nothing compared to the soul goal of knowing Jesus. *Everything* else, from his successes to his sacrifices, lagged far, far behind.

Soul goals do that. Not only do they touch earth, they reach heaven. They teach us how our "momentary struggles" are just that, momentary, and our fleeting pleasures hint of sweeter joys around the bend.

So, as you consider new goals this year, make sure to remember your soul goals. Don't substitute temporary rewards for the eternal one. Always press on toward the highest treasure. The one for which God has called you.

January 2nd

Cast your bread upon the waters, for you will find it after many days.
—Ecclesiastes 11:1 ESV

Message in a Bottle

In response to someone admiring his work, C. S. Lewis once wrote, "It is always cheering to know one's bottle with a message in it has found land." I couldn't help but think what an apt description for those who write! We put our words in bottles of books or blogs, and in faith pray our communiqué finds fertile soil. But "bottles" come in as many shapes and sizes as the messages they contain

Musicians compose their opuses; photographers snatch life glimpses; painters make a blank canvas come alive. Beyond artists, mothers and fathers train children. Teachers impart their expertise; contractors bid jobs; preachers deliver sermons. All hope their message will "land."

Yet, isn't each individual life a message in a bottle? We have been cast from our mothers' wombs, custom-made, to tell a unique story. Yours. Mine. No matter how far the culture trends, our lives cannot be squeezed into a hash tag. We were made for so much more. What we do with our message matters.

Don't be deceived into thinking your life is insignificant. The power of your story—your bottled message—cannot be measured by the opinion of others. Our job is to live up to what we have already attained and to keep pressing on. We continue writing the story, casting our bread on the water, until the Author says it is done.

God has created you with a purpose. Max Lucado writes in his book, *Fearless*, "The Amazon River out of which a thousand fears flow [is] do we matter? We fear we don't." My friend, be assured that you do matter. You matter more to God than you can possibly imagine. Don't shrink back from letting him form the message he has designed for you to live. Send it out in faith, and when it returns after many days, you will find it to be, in Lewis' words, quite "cheering."

January 3rd

See to it that no one falls short of the grace of God.
—Hebrews 12:15 NIV

Before There Was Grace

Picture a mountain of doom, one more ominous than anything conceived in the imagination of J.R.R. Tolkien or the artistry of Peter Jackson. This mountain radiates darkness, gloom and storm. It burns so fiercely, that even if an animal touches it, immediate death follows. Words spoken from this mountain emit such terror that people beg for silence. They can't bear the weight of its commands. The sight of it so terrifies, it causes even mighty men like Moses to melt with fear and trembling. This is how the writer of Hebrews depicts life before grace.

This looming mountain of judgment causes even us twenty-first century sophisticates to cower in its presence. It exposes our profanity. It reveals how we, like Esau, have carelessly thrown away our birthright for momentary pleasures. No amount of begging can bring it back. The door to mercy is marked CLOSED. And all our attempts to open it end in futility.

Life before grace.

Now picture another mountain, a heavenly one. The judge of all men lives here along with thousands upon thousands of exuberant angels. It emanates light, joy and peace. Jesus stands at the door of this mountain. Because of his slain life, he has the authority to arbitrate on our behalf, to become our defender, to reconcile us with pure goodness, to make us straggling beggars righteous men and women. All who wash in his blood bathe in forgiveness. They discover he has turned the CLOSED sign to OPEN. That describes life after grace.

Grace brings us an earth-shattering sigh of relief. Yet the writer of Hebrews warns us not to miss it. Before grace, we had no hope of changing the direction of our hell-bent souls. Now, in the light of grace, we can anticipate a destiny filled with unending goodness and unfathomable love. Grace reminds us of where we were before it wrapped us in its shelter.

Let's never forget our great escape from that mountain of doom. Let's embrace our freedom and grow in grace. Let's not miss it!

January 4th

Don't be deceived, my dear brothers and sisters.

—James 1:16 NIV

Fake News

Do you know how easy it is for "fake *news*" to become "fake *views*"?

"I'm not sure about God anymore." Sadly, I've heard this more than a few times over the years. People who once seemed to have a solid relationship with the Lord suddenly find themselves questioning whether or not he even exists. Digging a little deeper, I've found a frequent commonality among them. They want to sin. And it's a lot easier to sin when we dismiss moral authority that differs from our desires.

Don't get me wrong. Many people have honest questions about God. They deserve honest answers. But when God becomes an "inconvenient truth" who gets in the way of our sinful pursuits, our "confusion" becomes the first step on a slippery slope to destruction.

It's like "fake news." A lot is currently being reported that has no basis in the truth. Since we tend to gravitate toward news that favors what we want to think, we become easy targets for believing things that fit our grid, whether true or false. The danger—fake news produces fake views. The further we move away from truth, the likelier we are to believe "fake news" about God, fake news which inevitably creates a fake view about him, making him easier to reject.

James warns the church to guard against being deceived. He cautions that once we allow a little deception to enter our thinking, it will take over. So, how do we guard against it?

We begin by taking a cue from counterfeit experts. Know how they spot the fakes? They diligently study the real thing. The more we immerse ourselves in the truth, the harder it will be to justify actions countering it. When tempted, we let what the Bible says bring us back to reality.

God is who he says he is. No amount of fake news about him will ever change his love, faithfulness and power. Let's be on guard not to allow thinking that contradicts what the Bible says about him. Let's not feed fake views of our Sovereign God even if the truth calls us to repentance.

January 5th

I am like an olive tree
flourishing in the house of God;
I trust in God's unfailing love
for ever and ever.

—Psalm 52:8 NIV

From Black and White to Technicolor

So how does God change a somewhat colorless existence into one bursting with vibrant life? And why would he want to?

I didn't know quite what to expect when the Lord led me to a quaint little town on Lake Erie to spend an uninterrupted week of writing. I would be alone. Just God and me. What emerged was the genesis of a book and more importantly, a deepening connection with my Creator.

When I first arrived, it seemed like every inch of Lakeside oozed beauty and creativity. The waters of Lake Erie beat on the rocks at the lake's bank. The stately peer stretching into the lake welcomed visitors to sit and admire the view to Put-In-Bay.

The cottages with their screened-in porches of wicker furniture and flower-filled window boxes graced names like "Almost Free" and "Lady of the Lake." And the lamp posts lining the footpath by the water seemed, well, *Narnian.*

Although the beauty of Lakeside captivated me, something more caused the deeper attraction. My brother and sister-in-law own the cottage where I stayed. Her parents had the foresight years ago to invest in a place for their young family to find a respite from the busyness of life. The memories created there fostered a sense of security and belonging, of a legacy now being passed on to their children. It is in this relational connectedness that the secret of Lakeside's deeper beauty rests.

I believe it's much the same with all of life. It is the *connectedness* to God we experience through Christ that changes a black and white world into Technicolor. We become, as the psalmist put it, like olive trees flourishing in his presence. When we risk connecting with him, we emerge with renewed trust in his "unfailing love." It is through such trust that new colors emerge.

You don't have to visit Lakeside to find the kind of connectedness I'm talking about. God wants you to flourish because you are his child. He will provide experiences and opportunities that lead you into his presence and foster trust. When that happens, don't be surprised when the life around you begins to soar with vibrant color.

January 6th

As she stood behind him at his feet weeping, she began to wet his feet with her tears. Then she wiped them with her hair, kissed them and poured perfume on them.

—Luke 7:38 NIV

Don't Miss the Trees for the Forest

I wonder what was running through the mind of that "sinful woman" who crashed Simon the Pharisee's dinner party. It took a lot of courage. Everyone at the table looked down on her, due, no doubt, to her immoral profession. It took a degree of recklessness. While Jesus was reclining at the table as the invited guest, she—the uninvited one—threw herself at his feet, washing them with her tears, wiping them with her hair, kissing them with her affection. It took love.

Jesus said her actions were motivated by her great love for him. Her overwhelming gratefulness prompted her to respond—right then—in the only way she knew. She didn't wait for the perfect time or the perfect place. She seized the opportunity to show Jesus her devotion.

Sometimes I miss the trees for the forest. Nope. That's not a typo. I get so focused on the long-term goal I can miss what's right in front of me. I set out to write about being more merciful or kind. While I'm crafting my thoughts, I scroll through Facebook and am surprised to see a post from someone who had come down with an unexpected illness while on a mission trip. It strikes me that I had been prompted to pray for this very person that morning. Rather than getting back to my "important work," I sense a nudge. *Take the time to send him a note, telling him you've been praying for him.* Since it's someone I rarely communicate with, I feel a bit awkward; I hesitate. Then I think of that "sinful woman." Her situation was far more awkward and inconvenient than mine. Yet she embraced the moment. She missed neither the trees nor the forest.

On the way to writing about being kind, God gave me the opportunity to put it into practice. And isn't that what's it's all about? The big picture for all of us is to become more like Christ. I don't want to miss the little saplings he puts in my path to get me there. How about you?

January 7th

Be strong and courageous. Do not be afraid or terrified … for the LORD your God goes with you; he will never leave you nor forsake you.
—Deuteronomy 31:6 NIV

Befriend It

I dreamed Ray and I were in a kayak floating down a stream when a shark surfaced. He kept bumping our boat, consistently bumping, bumping. We didn't know how to deal with its annoying, threatening presence. Then I heard the words, "Befriend it."

My friend relayed this story soon after her husband was diagnosed with the early stages of Alzheimer's. She readily identified the persistent shark as his debilitating disease. She knew the Lord was showing her—through the dream—how to move forward. Instead of continuing to fight a losing battle, they began to embrace Ray's illness. Their changed mindset catapulted them into a place of peace. So, how does befriending something as pernicious as Alzheimer's lead to peace?

Once they stopped fighting the diagnosis, they began to recognize an unprecedented flow of God's mercies. When Ray couldn't remember where he'd placed certain items, God consistently directed them where to look. Where before the little pleasantries of life were taken for granted, they were now cherished, from enjoying the beauty of snowcapped mountains out their window to watching *Jeopardy* and playing *Uno* together. My friends are learning to laugh, even through tears.

The Alzheimer's has led them into a deeper reliance on God and a richer spiritual life.

Far from denying reality, they know what lies ahead. They experience frustration, sadness and fear. But their lives resonate with more joy than sorrow, with more victory than defeat. Yes, Ray is walking into unknown territory, but as Joshua encouraged Israel upon entering a new land, they have the assurance there is One holding their hand through the hazy path. One who promises to never leave them or forsake them. One who is making them "strong and courageous."

We're not always called to fight the giants in our lives. Sometimes we must embrace them. But embedded in our surrender, we discover God's peace. God's presence. Whatever you are facing today, or in days to come, I pray you will discover, like my friends, that you are not alone. You don't have to be afraid of the sharks. You serve a God who promises to be with you. Always. No matter what.

January 8th

There has never been a day like it before or since, a day when the LORD listened to a human being.

—Joshua 10:14 NIV

Here Comes the Sun Again

No way! Impossible! Never gonna happen!

That's what most people would have concluded had they calculated Israel's odds as they began their conquest of the Promised Land. In Joshua 10, five Amorite kings joined forces to stop Israel's advancement. How in the world could this band of unseasoned warriors ever defeat this coalition of ruthless, war-savvy Canaanites? With something out of this world.

The Lord not only gave Joshua a strategy for winning, he also intervened with supernatural finesse. As Israel marched through the night to take the coalition by surprise, the Lord threw the five armies into so much confusion they had no other option than to retreat. In their desperate flight, the Lord intervened again. He hurled so many hailstones on them that more died from the barrage of ice than from the swords of the Israelites. But the battle raged on and Joshua (with a boldness I can't even imagine) asked the Lord to cause the sun to stand still until they completely avenged their enemies. And so, "The sun stopped in the middle of the sky and delayed going down about a full day" (Joshua 10:13).

God revealed his power through the confusion, the hailstones and the postponed sunset. But look at what the writer of Joshua referred to as the real miracle: "when the Lord listened to a human being."

Do we get that? The Lord God Almighty, creator of the universe, hears the outrageous request of his servant. I think our senses have become so dulled, that we no longer realize how we can tap into the power of God. In Annie Dillard's words from *Teaching a Stone to Talk*, "It is madness to wear ladies' velvet hats to church; we should all be wearing crash helmets. Ushers should issue life preservers and signal flares; they should lash us to our pews. For the sleeping god may wake someday and take offense."

The spiritual forces arrayed against you and me are more powerful than the five Amorite kings. But they are no match for our God. Remember that the next time you think, No way! Impossible! Never gonna happen! Call on God and put on your crash helmet.

January 9th

Provide for those who grieve in Zion—to bestow on them a crown of beauty instead of ashes, the oil of joy instead of mourning, and a garment of praise instead of a spirit of despair. They will be called oaks of righteousness, a planting of the LORD for the display of his splendor.
—Isaiah 61:3 NIV

Out of the Fire

Sometimes God turns up the heat to make us holy.

In 2001, our family visited Yellowstone National Park. We were stunned to learn that in 1988 almost 800,000 acres of the park—36 percent—had been ravaged by a forest fire. No tree was affected more than the lodgepole pine, the primary tree at Yellowstone. This tree reproduces in one of two ways, either by typical male/female reproduction, or by having its hard outer coat of resin melt. As the resin dissolves, the seeds are released and dispersed throughout the rich soil.

The resin that surrounds the lodgepole pine seeds only melts at extremely high temperatures, like those associated with fire. In the inferno of 1988, it is estimated that as many as one million seeds *per acre* were released from the cones, paving the way for prolific new growth. Without the fire, it would never have happened.

I believe God at times "turns up the heat" in our lives to deepen our holiness. Like those lodgepole pines, the hard resin of our sinful nature can trap our seed and hinder its release. That seems to be what happened with Israel. They had let their

12

hearts grow hard toward God. Their rebellion resulted in barren lives and the devastation of their cities. Defeat by their enemies covered them with shame. They needed some intense heat in their lives. God provided it.

But God didn't leave them. He redeemed them. The heat brought them to repentance, transforming their ashes into something beautiful. He turned their mourning into joy, their despair into praise. Without the heat, the prolific growth would not have happened.

So, the next time "heat" comes in your life, don't be afraid. Remember Israel. Remember those lodgepole pines. Have confidence the Lord will use the fire of your sufferings to burn up the bad and make way for the good. Have no fear. The day will come when your ashes will be turned into beauty.

January 10th

A happy heart makes the face cheerful.

—*Proverbs 15:13 NIV*

When You're Smiling

People. All kinds of people live in the world: People who feel lonely and displaced. Beautiful people. Weird people. But what about friendly people? We too easily overlook the impact of friendliness. A man waves you to go in front of him in a line of traffic. You receive a compliment on how you look. A stranger strikes up a conversation. Small incidents that won't alter the course of our existence, but they make life more pleasant and cost us NOTHING.

Friendly people aren't necessarily church people. Christians have no corner on the market when it comes to friendliness. There is no 11th commandment that says "Thou shalt be friendly," but Proverbs reminds us happy hearts create cheerful faces. Verses that exhort us to be kind and compassionate flood the Scriptures. And the greatest commandment of all is to love. I think of friendliness as a second cousin to love. So maybe it's to our discredit believers aren't distinctly known more for being friendly.

Of course, I'm not talking about the kind of "fake friendly" that occurs so commonly. The "have a nice day" from the cashier who doesn't even make eye contact. The girl who smiles during your conversation but whose eyes dart around the room. The forced grins of salesmen whose only motivation is to make a buck.

No one is drawn to that kind of "friendliness." But people are drawn to the real thing. True friendliness, even if momentarily, alleviates some of the stress in life. It makes a brief connection, and for some folks a brief connection may be all they experience in a day. We all have a yearning to live a significant life, to make a difference. Typically, we think in terms of doing something "big." But why not nurture a culture of kindness by practicing friendliness on the smallest level? Like with a smile.

My grandpa used to tell me God must have created us to smile because it takes a lot more muscles to frown than to smile. Maybe if we simply smiled more, we really could make the world a better place. Maybe the old song was spot on when it said the whole world will join us when we smile.

Why don't you try it?

January 11th

By the rivers of Babylon we sat and wept when we remembered Zion. There on the poplars we hung our harps.

—Psalm 137:1-2 NIV

Unstrung Harps

Discouragement. It stops us in our tracks. It locks us in limbo. It deafens us to hope. Israel was well acquainted with it. After four hundred years of cruel Egyptian bondage, the nation became so steeped in discouragement that when God sent Moses to them with the promise of deliverance, they refused to listen (Exodus 6:9). The loudness of their pain silenced any other message.

Years later, when the Israelites once again found themselves enslaved in a foreign land, their discouragement became so severe that they "hung their harps" on the poplar trees. They would allow no melody of hope to sing its song. They literally chose not to listen.

None of us can escape discouragement. We would not be human if we didn't encounter discouraging situations. The question is not whether we meet discouragement, but how long we keep its company.

For some of us, as soon as disappointing circumstances rise, we flip on a "surround sound system" of pessimism. It takes less energy and a lot less risk of future disappointment. However, in all the gloomy clamor, we miss the whispers of hope. Whispers assuring us help is on the way. Whispers reminding us God remains in charge.

In spite of Israel's paralyzing discouragement, God kept his promises. He delivered them from Egypt and again from Babylon. His faithfulness did not depend on their feedback. "If we are faithless, he remains faithful, for he cannot disown himself" (2 Timothy 2:13). God's unwavering faithfulness provides a starting place for us to snap the grip of discouragement.

When writers suffer from writer's block they often break through by starting to write—about anything and everything—they just write. It eventually "primes the pump" until the words they're searching for begin to flow. Meditating on God's faithfulness has a similar effect in helping us break through the block of discouragement. As we specify his goodness in the small details of our lives, we begin to be thankful and the pump of faith is primed. Hope returns and what once overwhelmed us begins to shrink.

If discouragement is getting the best of you, don't hang up your harp. In faith, string that harp and start to sing.

January 12th

He replied, "Because you have so little faith. Truly I tell you, if you have faith as small as a mustard seed, you can say to this mountain, 'Move from here to there,' and it will move. Nothing will be impossible for you."
—Matthew 17:20 NIV

Plant Those Seeds

Faith, even small faith, can make a difference.

In 1973, I had just gotten married and was living in Florida. That fall, I got the call my dad had suffered a very serious heart attack. His condition was so critical that I was advised not to come home because the shock of seeing me could have made it worse. There was nothing to do but pray. At the time, I worked as a speech therapist in a clinic about an hour away from home so my surroundings were somewhat unfamiliar. But on this particular day, I felt compelled over my lunch hour to search for a church to pray on Dad's behalf.

I started driving through the streets of Melbourne. Eventually, I spotted a church and made my way up to the front door, not really expecting it to be unlocked. Even back in 1973 not many churches left their doors unlocked. But to my grateful surprise, it was open! That in itself began to stimulate my faith. As I knelt before the altar in that little chapel, not knowing whether Dad would live or die, I found the assurance that it was God's will for him to be saved. I prayed, "Father, I believe you are speaking to me that you want to save my dad, so I'm asking in faith that you spare his life until he finds you." That was my only point of faith—believing God wanted my dad to be saved. So, I planted that seed in faith.

Well, my father recovered from the heart attack. It would be another seventeen years before he accepted Christ, but from that day on, in my mind it was a done deal. At sixty-five years old, my dad accepted Jesus and experienced one of the most dramatic conversions I have ever witnessed. For the next twenty years, until my dad's death, that seed of faith stood like a mighty oak. Even now, it continues to bear fruit in the lives of those who knew him.

Jesus told us we don't have to possess extravagant faith to move mountains. Mustard-seed size will do just fine. Friend, let those seeds in you germinate. Exercise your faith and watch them produce more fruit than you can imagine.

January 13th

Therefore we do not lose heart.

—2 Corinthians 4:16 NIV

Don't Lose Heart

Stress, so heavy it feels as if life itself is being squeezed out. Thoughts swimming in a sea of uncertainty. Feelings of rejection, ridicule and defeat threatening on every side. Ever feel like this? Paul certainly did. Yet he sends a clear message to struggling believers of every age—the pressure will not crush us; our confusion will not destroy us; and no matter how severe the persecution, the Lord will not abandon us. Because Paul had experienced countless rescues by the hand of God, he is able to encourage fellow believers going through such troubled times with an amazing message of hope: don't lose heart.

I have to admit, I'm tempted to lose heart over circumstances much less taxing than the ones Paul describes. When I focus on the seen rather than the unseen, I give too much power to people and situations which by nature are passing. When I allow the "temporary" to become the "eternal," I forget that in this jar of clay resides the unending power of God. A power that transforms my greatest crises into "light and momentary troubles."

Those sweet yet powerful words—*don't lose heart*—are being spoken to you today. To me. We have the opportunity to let go of despair and grab the gospel ... a gospel which reminds us that when the world was at its darkest, hope rose from the tomb. And because Christ's greatest trial became the source of his greatest triumph, so it is for us. Our problems "are achieving for us an eternal glory that far outweighs them all" (2 Corinthians 4:17).

But don't take my word for it. If you are struggling, it's time to give your faith a little boost by hearing the Word of God. I can't think of a better place to start than the fourth chapter of 2 Corinthians. Read it. Consume it. Draw inspiration from its timeless message.

Let the infallible word of God cause you *not to lose heart.*

January 14th

The woman came and knelt before him. "Lord, help me!" she said.
He replied, "It is not right to take the children's bread and toss it to the dogs."
"Yes it is, Lord," she said. "Even the dogs eat the crumbs that fall from their master's table."

—Matthew 15:25–27 NIV

Ain't Too Proud to Beg

Wow! This mother was desperate. The disciples urged him to send her away. Her cries annoyed them. Her audacity probably did too. But she kept pursuing Jesus even when he seemed to ignore her. "Lord, help me! My daughter is suffering terribly." When he finally responded, he told her what she already knew ... he was here for the lost sheep of Israel, not Gentiles. You would think that would have caused her to slink away, red-faced. Not this woman! She got on her knees and begged. She begged like a dog.

She knew she had no place at the table. She was a Greek, for goodness sake! She had no illusion she deserved a miracle. But somehow, she was convinced Jesus might break through all the social and religious barriers to heal her daughter. So, she begged for a crumb. And she got it.

I can't imagine what must have been going through Jesus' mind as he witnessed such a display of humble belief. "Woman, you have great faith! Your request is granted" (v. 28).

Contrast this with the encounter Jesus had just experienced with the Pharisees. No way would they even think about breaking through social or religious barriers. Their man-made rules far outweighed God's commands. Even the *thought* of breaking one of their traditions was intolerable. They clung to their laws because laws made them feel superior to other people. And they were all about pride. I can hardly picture them begging anyone for anything. Jesus called them out on their blatant hypocrisy. "Leave them; they are blind guides" (Matthew 15:14).

Sometimes we need to be reminded not to fall into the Pharisee camp. Not to be blinded by *Christianese*. None of us acquire immunity from pride. We limp through life as a fallen, rebellious people who have no more right to sit at the table than that desperate Gentile mother. Jesus paid an exorbitant price to secure a place for us. Let's not take it for granted.

I want always to remember I'm a lot like that Gentile woman. I'm desperate. I'm unworthy. And I ain't too proud to beg.

How about you?

January 15th

For you know the grace of our Lord Jesus Christ, that though he was rich, yet for your sake he became poor, so that you through his poverty might become rich. —2 Corinthians 8:9 NIV

Louder than Screams

When my husband and I took our son back to school in Nashville after spring break of his freshman year, he was excited about showing us "his town." But no more than we. We wanted to see everything that was a part of his new life—where he ate, slept and studied. We wanted to meet his friends and worship at his church. We explored every inch of the Belmont campus.

When he asked if we wanted to go to a concert, we jumped at the chance—even when he warned us we might not "exactly" like the music. After all, he was studying music business. If we could manage to get a closer look at his interest, we were all for it. But we were about to learn it "wasn't your mother's rock and roll."

In a crowd of over a thousand, my husband and I had to have been the only ones over forty-five years old. I never saw so many piercings and so many tattoos in so many places. When we finally entered the hall, we found our "spot" on an overlooking balcony. This proved to be a wise decision because as the band started playing, the crowd below emerged into two sections—the shove pit and the thrash pit. My words could never do it justice. I anticipated the music would be loud, but I didn't expect that the lead vocalist didn't have to know one melody line! It turned out to be our initiation into the venue of *screamo*.

I would do it all over again. Why? Because I love our son and I just wanted to be with him. I think that's a glimpse of God's love. He wants to be with us. He wants to walk where we walk, see what we see, hear what we hear. So much so that he left the splendor of heaven to do it. He subjected himself to all the things we face to save us from ourselves so we could be with him forever. Such love says a lot about who we are.

It speaks even louder than *screamo*.

January 16th

But the greatest of these is love.

—*1 Corinthians 13:13 NIV*

Are You an Extremist?

We hear a lot these days about extremist groups—Islamic extremists, right-wing extremists, environmental extremists— over 250 separate groups, worldwide, have been accounted for. Although characterized by passion for their various causes, their radicalism is most often defined by hatred. In fact, most searches equate extremists with hate groups.

But there's another definition of extremist I want to consider. In 1963, Martin Luther King, Jr. penned his now famous *Letter from a Birmingham Jail.* Countering those opposed to the Civil Rights movement for fear of the violence it might spawn, King implored them (many of whom were church leaders) to action with these haunting words: "The question is not whether we will be extremists, but what kind of extremists we will be. Will we be extremists for hate or for love?" He pointed to Calvary as a demonstration of the latter.

There remains no greater distinguishing mark for the Christian than love. Paul describes what this love looks like in 1 Corinthians 13. It's radical. It's costly. It's attainable. It's the way God calls us to live. Will we get hurt in the process? Most certainly. As Henri J. M. Nouwen writes in *Bread for the Journey*

"Every time we make the decision to love someone, we open ourselves to great suffering, because those we most love cause us not only great joy but also great pain." Yet he concludes that the "risk of loving is always worth taking."

Why don't we renew our commitment to take that risk? How about we accept MLK's challenge and become extremists for love? To show the world we serve a God who teaches us "the greatest of these is love." Now that's an extremist group I'd like to join. Are you with me?

January 17th

And I am sure of this, that he who began a good work in you will bring it to completion at the day of Jesus Christ.

—Philippians 1:6 ESV

Completion

Most of us don't like the feeling of incompletion. Much of our sense of security comes from knowing a task will be finished and a job will not be left undone. Incompleteness can make us feel restless at best and frustrated at worst. I believe this God-driven need for completeness is yet another manifestation of being created in God's image. He is a God of completion.

This is evident from the first pages of Scripture. Genesis 2:1 says, "Thus the heavens and earth were completed in all their vast array." God was so satisfied with the completion that he blessed the seventh day with the holiness of rest.

When God instructed Moses on how to build the tabernacle, every minute detail was followed exactly as God commanded. "So all the work on the tabernacle, the tent of meeting, was completed. The Israelites did everything just as the LORD commanded Moses" (Exodus 39:32). The finishing work was capped with the glory of the Lord filling the sanctuary, for now it would stand as the place of his presence.

The work of redemption was completed on the cross. "When he had received the drink, Jesus said, 'It is finished.' With that, he bowed his head and gave up his spirit" (John 19:30). Nothing was overlooked that would need to be added, no matter how hard we humans try at times. It is a finished work—no amendments! Nothing in the fine print exacts future payments.

And so it is in our lives. When you are tempted to give up or give in to thoughts that your work is going nowhere, remember this: The God you serve is the God of completion. He will not leave you stranded or half-baked. In fact, he wants to finish the work in us more than we do! And that's something you and I can declare with confidence to ourselves and to one another.

January 18th

At that point Peter got up the nerve to ask, "Master, how many times do I forgive a brother or sister who hurts me? Seven?" Jesus replied, "Seven! Hardly. Try seventy times seven."

—Matthew 18:21–22 MSG

Forgive How Many Times?

No matter how long we live on the earth, we will never reach a quota on forgiveness.

I recently read the inspiring story of Abbot Iscu, sentenced to prison and tortured in 1951 in what was then Communist Romania for preaching Christ. One lonely night a new inmate was placed in the adjoining cell block. Providentially, he had been the one who as a faithful Communist officer had tortured the abbot. Now a prisoner himself by the system he had defended, he lay awake ... begging for prayer. Without hesitation, Abbot Iscu laid his hand on his former torturer's head and spoke forgiveness. Abbot Iscu was prepared for that moment. He had invested in forgiveness all his life. When he had to make a withdrawal, there was no shortage of the love and unbounded grace needed to meet the test.

Cultivating forgiveness begins long before we are asked to extend it to our enemies. We learn to forgive as we release minor offenses. Our boss disrespects our work, a friend makes an insensitive remark, our spouse overlooks something important to us. Jesus set a baseline of seventy times seven when Peter asked him how often we were to forgive. I guess he knew we needed a lot of practice. Forgiveness does not come naturally for most of us. In fact, at the moment, it may seem an impossibility. Yet as Christians, it is what we are called to do. Jesus says we have no excuse for unforgiveness because of the forgiveness we've received from our Father. He will help us. And the relief that follows makes us wonder why we didn't forgive sooner.

Don't overlook the command to forgive on whatever level the challenge arrives. A wise man once said, "what you do not forgive, you are doomed to live." That alone should motivate us. Even seventy times seven! Are you cultivating forgiveness?

January 19th

The LORD blessed the latter part of Job's life more than the former part.
—Job 42:12 NIV

A Christian Bucket List

How do you plan to spend the rest of your life? That was a question posed at a conference we recently attended. I had to push the pause button and think about it. It was a relevant question, not only because I have obviously entered my latter years, but because living with intention seems to be timely no matter what stage of life we're in.

If I were to construct a "bucket list," there's no lack of ideas. But I think the speaker was challenging us to address our most important priorities and commit to pursuing them. So here are a few things I would put on my "Christian bucket list."

First, I want to spend the rest of my life knowing God more. Paul said he considered "everything a loss compared to the surpassing worth of knowing Christ Jesus" (Philippians 3:8) and I think he knew a few things about priorities. Nothing increases my knowledge of God more than obedience. Every time I say *yes* to his direction, I learn something more about his character attributes like kindness, patience, justice.

Next, I want to "excel in this grace of giving" (2 Corinthians 8:7). Few things communicate God's pleasure to me as clearly as when I'm giving. I don't want to be stingy with my money, talents, time or even gratitude. I don't want to look back on my life and wish I would have given more—in any area.

Finally, my bucket list includes loving people more ... my family and friends, but also those who don't like me or disagree with me. It's a waste of time to nurse petty resentments or feed silly grudges. We have access to the inexhaustible love of God, and I don't want to waste a drop of it.

Scripture says the latter part of Job's life was better than the first. I think his blessings included more than material things. His understanding of God grew, and it positioned him for the finish line. How about you? Are you positioning yourself?

Who knows but that the best is yet to come in your life?

January 20th

We do not want you to become lazy, but to imitate those who through faith and patience inherit what has been promised.
—*Hebrews 6:12 NIV*

Keep Fit

A few years ago, I began experiencing pain in my upper right arm. I was told, among other things, to do stretching exercises every day. I followed these instructions diligently and eventually my arm came back to normal. Normal ... until my recent illness.

My stretching routine took a hiatus while I recovered. It wasn't long until I realized—much to my surprise—the same old arm ache had returned. I could hardly believe how quickly I grew out of shape. When I began exercising again, the pain dissipated.

But it started me thinking about how important it is to keep our spiritual lives fit. After a while, we can begin to take the changes God has made in us for granted. We stop growing. Old flabby patterns start to creep back. We resist forgiving, shorten our prayer time, neglect the Word, ignore warning signs. The writer of Hebrews was well aware of this tendency, and he cautions us not to become lazy lest we fall away. He encourages us to keep exercising the spiritual disciplines.

But he also assures us of God's grace in our weakness. No matter how many times we slack, the Lord presents us with the opportunity to get back up and try again. Ours is a God who wants us to succeed. He remembers our work and love (Hebrews 6:10–11). When we fail, he encourages us to get back on the treadmill. When we become apathetic, he says, "Start stretching again!"

Both laziness and diligence are creatures of habit. It was hard, once I stopped, to get back into the routine of stretching although the pain served as a great motivator. I don't think God wants us to experience unnecessary hurt to get us moving again. So, let's heed the warning in Hebrews. Let's be diligent *to the end*. Let's imitate the faith and patience of those who have gone ahead. Let's embrace our inheritance by keeping fit!

January 21st

Do this in remembrance of me.

—Luke 22:19 NIV

Try to Remember

Have you ever been in the place where your hurt penetrates so deeply that it causes you to withdraw into yourself and miss the big picture?

I'm reminded of a scene from the movie, *The Patriot*. Benjamin Martin's sons had been ruthlessly killed by a British commander. Now, in the midst of battle, Martin spots the officer. Filled with the desire for revenge, Martin takes after him, but then he realizes that without his leadership, his troops are retreating. At that moment, his dilemma crystallizes. Does he go after the British commander and avenge his sons' deaths, or does he return to his troops and rally them to stand their ground?

As strong as the draw to vengeance must have been, he *remembered* the battle wasn't about him, about his sons, or about revenge. It was about liberty from British tyranny. He was able to let go of his agenda and embrace the bigger picture. He grabbed the American flag and selflessly charged into battle, rallying his troops, inspiring them to not retreat and eventually taste victory.

It takes something powerful to pull us away from our hurts in life and open our eyes to the greater battle. But God has shown us how in Luke 22.

Scripture says we are to participate in communion in remembrance of Christ. Each time we partake of the wine and bread, we actively recall the price Jesus paid for our sins. We replace remembering ourselves and the hurts we've encountered with remembering what the Lord has done. His body. His blood. His sacrifice. His cross overshadows whatever cross we've been called to bear. As we replace remembering our hurts with remembrance of him, we're drawn to the bigger picture, the glue that stuck us to our pain loses its adherence.

May you always remember what this short span in life is about. Let God replace any dwarfish perspective with a boundless picture of a gigantic purpose woven throughout life. In remembrance of him.

January 22nd

My grace is sufficient for you, for my power is made perfect in weakness.

—2 Corinthians 12:9 NIV

Need Super Hero Power?

It was my last public speaking class of the semester, and the assignment was a graded impromptu. Students were asked to list three potential topics on a sheet of paper. After turning in their folded lists, they had to pick a paper and chose their speech topic from one of the three listed. They had ten minutes to prepare.

One of my students was in a wheelchair. He also had limited control over his arms and hands, so I helped by writing down the thoughts that came to him. As it turned out, only one of the potential topics suited—what power would you choose if you were a superhero? His first thought, of course, was that he'd be able to walk. But as he began to construct his speech, he realized the enormity of the task. He had so trained his mind to accept the fact that he would never walk, that he struggled to come up with the benefits! In the end, he told the class that he really didn't need to have a superhero power at all. He had God. And that was all the power he would ever need.

It was one of those gut-wrenching moments that occurs when you come face-to-face with true courage. Here was a young man who had learned to accept his limitations and work within them. He knew—really knew—that it could not keep the purposes of God from being fulfilled in his life.

Scripture assures us God's grace remains adequate no matter what we face. In fact, our weaknesses display his boundless power. They move us from self-sufficiency to God-sufficiency. We all have limitations in one form or another. Sometimes God removes them. We experience a miraculous healing, either physical or emotional. Money to pay those outstanding bills appears "out of the blue." But when our constraints are not taken away, I pray we would have a mindset like my student. I pray that we, too, would know that nothing can keep God from finishing his plan in us and through us.

January 23rd

Well done, good and faithful servant!

—*Matthew 25:21 NIV*

It's All About... "Me"? Part 1

We live in a society embroiled in self: self-fulfillment, self-realization, self-help, self-sufficiency, self-esteem. It's hard to escape the "me" mindset. A book by Gary Thomas entitled *Authentic Faith* describes his experience when asked to write an article on selflessness. The magazine editor responded to his article by saying how much he liked it, but could he expand more on the rewards of selflessness?

It can be shocking when we realize how easily we succumb to looking at the world through the lens of self. One day while sitting in a beauty salon, preoccupied over a situation, I was so desperate to hear something from God that I cried out, "Lord, please speak to me! Tell me what's going on!" Right then my eyes fell upon a hair product sitting on the shelf. The name of the product was Self-absorption. Ouch! *I* was the problem, and I was so absorbed with myself that I didn't recognize it.

Because self-centeredness reflects our natural fallen tendency, it takes effort to overcome. Self-centeredness may say something like, "I've served all these years. Let someone else teach Sunday School or take a meal to that new mother or mow the lawn for my elderly neighbor. I deserve a break." The focus isn't on the need, but on whether we feel like giving. Too often, we get to a place where we think we don't have to sacrifice any-more. We've done our part. We're through. But it's up to God—not us—to determine when we finish giving beyond our self.

Believers who remain faithful to the end reject the *"me"* mindset. They live for something higher, considering themselves dead in order to let the Lord live through them. They seek to satisfy God rather than their own agenda. They exchange me, me, me, with Thee, Thee, Thee. They remain confident they will stand before the Lord on judgment day and not hear the echo of their own voice saying, "I'm done," but will hear God say, "Well done."

Let's emulate those believers!

January 24th

For I am already being poured out like a drink offering, and the time for my departure is near. —2 Timothy 4:6 NIV

It's All About… "Me"? Part 2

Self-centeredness usually succeeds because it causes us to center more on what we don't have than what we have. One of its most insidious manifestations erupts in self-pity. Oswald Chambers writes in *My Utmost for His Highest*, "No sin is worse than the sin of self-pity, because it obliterates God and puts self-interest upon the throne. It opens our mouths to spit out murmurings and our lives become craving spiritual sponges, there is nothing lovely or generous about them."

Nothing about feeling sorry for ourselves inspires others. In fact, it sucks people dry because self-pity refuses to be comforted. Self-pity faces defeat every time we make conscious decisions to keep pouring out. In spite of our circumstances, we choose to empty self rather than be absorbed by it.

Scripture encourages us in this mindset. Paul wrote to Timothy with the realization he did not have a long time left on the earth. And what was he doing? Complaining that he was finishing in prison? Lamenting that he had nothing left to give? No way! He was continuing to give instruction and encouragement not only to Timothy but, unbeknown to him, to future generations.

How many of us today have found strength in his admonishment from that lonely prison cell to fight the good fight, finish the race and keep the faith (2 Timothy 4:7)? What if we didn't have those recorded words? What if Paul would have focused on himself rather than remaining fixed on God's plan? The world would be poorer.

So, my friend, if you struggle with self-pity, keep resisting its nasty pull. No matter what you are facing, refuse to feel sorry for yourself. Instead, reach out to others. Embrace the kind of giving that slices through our self-centered natures like a laser beam disintegrating a tumor.

Don't waste another minute on the "worst of sins."

January 25th

In addition to what you vow and your freewill offerings, offer these to the Lord at your appointed festivals: your burnt offerings, grain offerings, drink offerings and fellowship offerings.

—Numbers 29:39 NIV

What's in Your Wallet?

God is an extravagant giver. In our quest to reflect his image, it's hard to overestimate the importance of giving. Not only does generosity help others "see" God, but it has the added benefit of heightening our own awareness of his benevolence.

I once had a student in my public speaking class who, for his demonstration speech, showed us how to use his most precious possession, his high-tech computer. But more interesting to me than how the computer worked was how he got it. He told the class he had been saving and saving until he had accumulated almost enough for the purchase. Then at church one night he heard a missionary speak. Convicted about the needs presented, he felt the Lord tell him to give all the money he had painstakingly set aside—over $800—to the missionary. He relinquished the cash as well as his dream and started the saving process all over again.

A few weeks later I ran into a former student at Barnes & Noble. Now enrolled in a nursing program, I knew she was planning to soon leave for a medical mission trip. When I asked how her fund-raising was coming along, she cheerfully replied, "I still have a long way to go." Immediately I thought of the computer speech. I opened my wallet and gave her all I had. It was only $20, a small measure of sacrifice, but I was spurred to give because of my public speaking student's testimony. I had been given a "glimpse" of God's generous nature, and it made me want to give in turn.

In Numbers 29, the Israelites are instructed repeatedly to give "in addition to" their required offerings. They were to go beyond the expected. It set the foundation for us if we hope to live the way God purposes us to live. God has created you to be a giver. So, give, give, give. Don't confine yourself to tithes and offerings. Let the Lord's bounteous nature flow through you so that as the world sees your generosity they will see what a good Father he is.

Like the commercial says, "What's in your wallet?"

January 26th

So then, those who suffer according to God's will should commit themselves to their faithful Creator and continue to do good.

—1 Peter 4:19 NIV

Our Finest Hour

The Battle of France in WWII had been lost. British Prime Minister Winston Churchill knew England would be the next target in Hitler's relentless pursuit. The stakes couldn't have been higher. Churchill believed if England failed, the whole world would enter into a sinister era of darkness. So, he called upon his fellow citizens to stand firm in duty. Anticipating the inevitable bombs that would explode in London streets, Churchill forewarned the people to brace themselves so that in years to come, men would look back at England in this time of turmoil and mayhem and say, "This was their finest hour."

I've been thinking lately about the "bombs" that burst in our emotional landscape. "Clear out your desk by noon." "I'm leaving you." "Your teenage daughter is pregnant." "You have stage-four cancer." The most insidious bombs seem to be the ones we're not expecting. One minute life feels safe, secure. The next minute we find ourselves desperately aching to turn back the hands of time. We weren't prepared to have our faith torpedoed in an instant.

Perhaps we could face the "bombs" more bravely if we weren't caught off guard, if we remembered we live in a fallen world—a world, as it were, under siege. We face a foe who thrives on using our weak flesh against us and against each other to wreak as much destruction as he possibly can.

Perhaps we could face the "bombs" more bravely if we remembered who and whose we are. We belong to One far stronger and greater than the enemy. A Redeemer who promises to turn all things into good. One writer has remarked that God "never wastes his children's pain." Embedded in our troubles we can, as Peter encourages, connect with our faithful Creator and keep doing good.

Remember that the bombs exploding in your life today—or tomorrow—don't signify the end. How you respond will be recorded in eternity. May it be said of you and of me, "This was their finest hour."

January 27th

All have sinned and fall short of the glory of God.

—*Romans 3:23 NIV*

Irrefutable Good Guilt

It makes us uncomfortable. Like gum-soled shoes on a pavement, it stops us in our tracks. It gnaws away at our peace and disrupts our direction. Yet it stands as the force behind all repentance and hope for recovery. Guilt.

Some guilt results from an oversensitive conscience. We feel guilty if we forget a friend's birthday. We feel guilty for not praying enough, reading the Bible enough, giving to the poor enough. And on the rare occasions when we sense no guilt, we feel guilty about not feeling guilty! No matter how hard we try, bad guilt hangs on like an annoying song we can't get out of our mind.

But there's another kind of guilt: "good guilt." Good, because it stems from reality. The most succinct description of the valid base for guilt resounds in G.K. Chesterton's oft quoted response to a journalist who asked the question, "What's wrong in the world today?" Chesterton simply stated, "I am."

He derived his humble assessment from a clear understanding that human nature is corrupt. "All have sinned and fall short of the glory of God" (Romans 3:23). We don't have to look far to verify the mark of sin in ourselves and in others. Irrefutable evidence exists that we indeed have much to feel guilty about. But God never intended for guilt to overwhelm us. He meant it to save us. And he has provided more irrefutable evidence to prove it.

The cross unveils the high price God paid to rescue us from guilt. Calvary proves God's love beyond any and every shadow of doubt. This truth leads our guilty hearts to repentance. Through repentance we find forgiveness, and with forgiveness comes freedom from all that pesky guilt.

We no longer have to be stuck in guilt for even a nanosecond. Every day offers the opportunity to bring our guilt to Jesus and repent. He declares us innocent not because we deserve it, but because he has it covered. With his blood.

And that is *irrefutable*!

January 28th

So the last will be first, and the first will be last.
— Matthew 20:16 NIV

Underdogs No More

Underdogs have no greater champion than Jesus. He delights in seeing the "last" made "first." If you don't believe me, just look at Luke 18.

Who did Jesus choose to illustrate the importance of persistent prayer? A vulnerable, helpless widow who was being treated unfairly. She relentlessly pursued the unjust judge until he finally responded to her request for justice. Jesus praised her tenacity and said when we pray, we should be like her (vv. 1-8).

Who did Jesus choose to depict the virtue of humility? He described the prayers of two men. One self-righteous Pharisee and one lowly tax collector. If ever there was an underdog, the tax collector fit the bill, yet Jesus exalted him over the prideful Pharisee because of his humbleness (vv. 9-14).

And who did Jesus choose to describe the type of people who belonged in the kingdom of God? Children. Not the accomplished, not the popular, not the ones who had it all together. Children. (vv. 15-17).

I grew up in southern Ohio, on the outskirts of Appalachia. Due to a combination of grants, scholarships and loans, I somehow made it to college. That's when I realized, relatively speaking, I'd achieved "underdog" status. People would ask me to pronounce certain words just to hear my "hick" accent. One girl told me I was the most unsophisticated person she had ever met. But you know what, it didn't bother me. In fact, I kind of wore my position like a badge of honor. I look back and realize why. Although I was young in my faith, Jesus had laid a foundation of affirmation and acceptance in me that no one could strip away. I didn't understand it at the time, but my confidence came from God's approval, not others. It was enough to carry me through. Still is.

No one stands outside the love of Jesus. If you've ever felt like you're on the outside looking in, be assured there is Someone on the outside of the crowd with you. He wants to elevate you as he does all who come to him. He wants to transform you into a champion. We are underdogs no more!

January 29th

Let us, therefore, make every effort to enter that rest, so that no one will perish by following their example of disobedience.

—Hebrews 4:11 NIV

The Power of the Pause

I've recently added a new element in my public speaking classes called "the power of the pause." Most experts in public speaking explain how important it is, when speaking, not to offer a long uninterrupted flow of speech when presenting. They understand that it's in the pause that people have the opportunity to actually think about what you're saying.

But all too often pauses—whether in public speaking or in life—seem to be unnecessary add-ons. When speaking, we'd much rather plow right through, or fill the spaces with *uhs* and *you knows*. In similar fashion, the essence of our lives becomes filled with endless to-do lists. We don't want our minutes and hours falling on unproductive soil, so we navigate from task to task, filling our insecurities with activity upon activity, until even our "leisure" time leaves us exhausted and unfulfilled.

It never ceases to amaze me how a book written thousands of years ago continues to be so relevant. The Bible has always called us to pause, to rest. In fact, it commands us to spend one whole day out of seven at rest. And that was long before texts, tweets, Instagrams and other components of multitasking. God invites us to put commas of rest in our lives not as distractions, but as enhancers and empowerers to make our communication with others—and more importantly with him—more effective.

We must learn to "pause" to hear God. For it is there, in the trenches of pause, a life free from anxiety and full of trust is created ... a life of rest.

For many of us, this doesn't come easy. The author of Hebrews says we should make every effort to enter rest. We must work to stop working. But I suspect if we consistently choose "the power of the pause," we'll find out the author of Hebrews was right.

A new strength to resist the pulls and pressures of fallen life will emerge. So, why don't you today begin to enter that rest?

January 30th

When the chief priests had met with the elders and devised a plan, they gave the soldiers a large sum of money, telling them, "You are to say, 'His disciples came during the night and stole him away while we were asleep.'"
—Matthew 28:12–13 NIV

All Lies Matter

Unbelievable! The chief priests bribed the soldiers to lie about Jesus' resurrection. The greatest event in human history had just occurred and they wanted more than anything to deny it happened. Even to the point of promulgating a bold-faced lie. Here I thought such twisting of the truth was birthed in present-day politics.

Not really. It is clear deception has marked human nature since the fall of man. But the terrible consequences of loving lies more than truth may not be as clear. After a while, we can't distinguish what's true and what's not (2 Thessalonians 2:10–12). The amazing gift of discernment God gives us as a means of protecting ourselves atrophies from lack of use. And without truth we become defenseless.

The shriveling up of truth doesn't happen all at once. Who would choose to defend something that can only be maintained by lies? For most, it's probably a slow journey into darkness. We hedge a little here, fudge a little there, thinking our mini-deceptions harmless. Eventually we buy into the idea the end justifies the means. We reason if our goal is important enough, any means of achieving it is acceptable—even if those means include lying.

"Oh, what a tangled web we weave when first we practice to deceive." Sir Walter Scott's sentiment remains one of the most quoted lines in Scottish poetry. Lies trap us. They cause us to compromise and veer from the truth until truth becomes no longer recognizable. Truth offers the blade we need to cut through the tangled web.

All lies matter, even small ones, even ones we cling to for self-preservation. As believers in truth, we must resist deception in whatever form it raises its ugly head. Don't let people willing to kill the truth drag you down with them.

January 31st

So I did as I was commanded. —Ezekiel 12:7 NIV

True Success

The idea we are called to faithfulness more than success poses a hard sell in our goal-driven society.

It's far too easy for us to jump on the cultural treadmill and conclude the chief end of man, rather than to glorify God and enjoy Him forever, is to succeed. There's nothing wrong with accomplishment. Who wants to be a failure? The problem lies more in the definition of success than its pursuit. God's view of it appears to differ sharply from man's.

When the Lord directed Ezekiel to warn Israel they would soon be exiled because of their rebellion, he gave him some outlandish instructions. Ezekiel was to pack a bag for exile, then each night dig through a wall, carrying his belongings. He then covered his face to prevent him from any longer seeing his "homeland." How did Ezekiel respond to being a living metaphor? He did as he was commanded.

He remained faithful to God's call.

Ezekiel didn't just arrive at faithfulness. Scripture tells us he who is faithful in little will be faithful in much (Luke 16:10). Cultivating it begins in the everyday. After my dad's death, I discovered the diary he kept in 2008, the year after his wife passed. Since I lived over four hundred miles away, concern over his aloneness evidently prompted me to call him regularly. For as I read the pages of his diary, I found recorded day after day, Becky called. Month after month, Becky called. Throughout the whole year, Becky called. I hadn't even remembered. But my father did.

And so, we have a Father in heaven who records all our phone calls, all our deeds. He's writing down every act of kindness, every instance where we forgive, every single moment we choose to live for him. He notices our faithfulness even when others don't. Someday, he'll go over that record book with us. I don't think God will be impressed with our honors, our degrees, or the wealth we accumulated. What will matter to him will be reflected in the words, "Enter good and faithful servant."

That is *success* in God's eyes.

February 1st

Neither do people pour new wine into old wineskins. If they do, the skins will burst; the wine will run out and the wineskins will be ruined. No, they pour new wine into new wineskins, and both are preserved.

—Matthew 9:17 NIV

Stretch

I believe it is in the small setbacks we face in life where we learn to align ourselves increasingly with God's character. Where we choose either to shut down and refuse to let anything change our wineskin or grasp the opportunity to be enlarged.

There we were unloading the car outside of State College, PA, when we realized my suitcase remained quietly reposed on the bed at home. All I had with me was a book bag with my Bible, journal, and reading material, but other than that, not even a hairbrush. Not even my laptop. My thoughts were frozen in *what do we do now* mode, while my spirit whispered *make the best of it*. My husband offered to drive the two and a half hours back to retrieve it, and although I was touched by his sensitivity, somehow that didn't seem right. But the options were limited: either let frustration immobilize me, or allow my set expectations to bend.

Little by little, my inflexibility started to give, and ideas began to surface. My flash drive (which I had inadvertently dropped into my bag) would work on my husband's Netbook so I could still complete some work. A quick run into town would provide the lacking necessities. I could make-do for the rest.

As we ate Chinese takeout later that night on the front porch, I was struck with how God had not only turned the circumstances around, but how he had so meticulously adjusted my "wineskin." He had stretched my capacity for "being content" and deepened my trust in his faithfulness to "work all things together for good."

In one of Paul's last recorded messages, he wrote he was "being poured out like a drink offering" (2 Timothy 4:6). When I reach that time in life where I am called to be "poured out," I hope the choices I've made will evidence more than a few drops. I pray that my life's challenges would have caused my wineskin to have been expanded, not shrunk.

How about you?

February 2nd

Have this mind among yourselves, which is yours in Christ Jesus, who emptied himself, by taking the form of a servant, being born in the likeness of men. —Philippians 2:5–7 ESV

Gotta Serve Somebody

Why does serving make people happy?

A few months after my dad's wife died, hospice contacted him and asked if he would be interested in volunteering with their patients. Before long he was visiting up to thirty, sometimes forty, people a day! My dad was eighty-five years old; he had suffered a heart attack, leukemia, a broken leg, and a garden variety of other ailments. But I had not seen him as healthy or as fulfilled in years.

There's actually a physiological explanation for his health. Researchers have found that endorphins are released in the brain that cause pleasant sensations when people give. As Arthur Brooks writes in his book *Gross National Happiness,* a direct link exists between giving and happiness across the board. He cites studies that show teenagers who volunteer have higher degrees of self-esteem than those who don't. One study of senior citizens in the Detroit area actually measured subjects' happiness levels before and after a set of volunteering activities. After six months of volunteering, researchers discovered an increase of seniors' "morale, self-esteem, and sense of social integration."

Sometimes I find studies like those hard to trust. But after seeing my dad, I'm a believer. Created in God's image, we were designed to give. For it's through giving—whether in small acts of kindness or in making sacrifices that are dear—that we fulfill our true purpose in life and write a better story.

Paul encouraged the Philippians to emulate the attitude of Christ. Jesus didn't have to serve; he chose to serve. In fact, his whole life was one great expression of serving. The creator of the universe and everything in it, became "nothing" in order to serve you and me.

In response, how about we embark on a new season of serving others. Let's not let the hustle and bustle of everyday life distract us from our call to imitate the servant nature of Christ. Let's serve somebody!

February 3rd

That is why, for Christ's sake, I delight in weaknesses, in insults, in hardships, in persecutions, in difficulties. For when I am weak, then I am strong. —2 Corinthians 12:10 NIV

The Power of Helplessness

C.S. Lewis writes that security is mortals' greatest enemy. I hate to admit it, but I think he's right. Nothing keeps me on the edge more than a sense of desperation. If my life had no tension, no drama at all, I would no doubt become restless and lazy. I would probably be sucked into a life of self-indulgence in my quest for fulfillment. But indulgence always leads to emptiness. We were made for something more. Actually, for Someone more.

Living "for Christ's sake," as the Apostle Paul puts it, requires us to jump into the fray. There we realize an ongoing battle rages within us between the Holy Spirit and our sinful nature. It can be agonizing, especially when we keep seeing the same weaknesses. But each time depression or insecurity or pride surfaces, we have the opportunity to meet it head-on and discover, once again, that we simply can't do life on our own. We were never meant to.

Helplessness drives me to prayer. It humbles me. It carries me from wanting to "be *like* God" to wanting to "be *with* God." Ultimately it opens the door to the Holy Spirit's power. It leads me to the ultimate discovery—that life is not about me after all; it's about him, about walking close to him.

I imagine some of you reading this feel battle-worn. You think you'll never overcome the difficulties in your life. But you can learn, as did Paul, to delight in the very weaknesses that thrust you into God's mercy. He discovered every insult, every hardship, even persecution served the higher purpose of finding strength in God. True strength. We can too.

There is nothing coming against you—or rising within you—that God can't use for good. It's a promise he gives to all those who love him. So, don't balk at being desperate. Say goodbye to your control.

Let helplessness be your new BFF, your best friend forever.

February 4th

But this I call to mind,
and therefore I have hope:
The steadfast love of the LORD never ceases;
his mercies never come to an end;
they are new every morning;
great is your faithfulness.
—*Lamentations 3:21–24 ESV*

Spiritual Alzheimer's

How do we remain faithful in a culture where almost every sphere of life has been affected by unfaithfulness? When our present injustices, sorrows and disappointments threaten our concept of God's faithfulness to us? When we find ourselves asking the Lord questions like, "Why did you let this happen? Where is your love now? Don't you hear me?" Perhaps even, "Why have you forsaken me?" How do we keep those thoughts from becoming excuses for our own disloyalty?

Jeremiah's predicament in the third chapter of Lamentations may shed some light. At first, his thoughts are consumed with his affliction. He feels God has shut him out. He's forgotten what prosperity is. All he had hoped from the Lord is gone. He's bitter and depressed. But then, he intentionally shifts his focus and begins to remember the Lord's track record of faithfulness. Jeremiah's circumstances didn't change. But his perspective did. He remembered God's character—his love, mercy, faithfulness—and it lifted him out of his despair.

Remembering God's faithfulness stimulates our own. No wonder we are exhorted throughout Scripture not to forget what he has done. Forgetting feeds unfaithfulness. Remembering God's love and faithfulness helps us meet whatever pressure we're facing with the truth. One author suggests remembering the truth works like a tourniquet to stop the bleeding.

Forgetting reminds me of when my grandma got Alzheimer's. Early signs of confusion and simple forgetfulness grew into that vacant stare and inability to recognize anything once familiar. In the end, she was suspicious of everyone, her actions at times bizarre. Although she obviously had no choice, when it comes to warding off spiritual Alzheimer's, we do. We can choose to remember who God is and what he's done and avoid becoming untrusting, suspicious and eventually unable to even recognize the Lord.

Are you feeling down today? Why not intentionally recall the goodness of the Lord? Let's avoid getting spiritual Alzheimer's.

February 5th

And pray in the Spirit on all occasions with all kinds of prayers and requests.
                                                                    —Ephesians 6:18 NIV

They Don't Have a Prayer?

They don't have a prayer! I think it's a claim that should be stricken from the Christian's lexicon.

Paul exhorts the church to be praying all the time—in all kinds of situations with all kinds of requests. We wouldn't be encouraged to pray so much if it didn't make a difference. God planned to let us participate with him in affecting the universe. As Max Lucado puts it in *Out Life Your Life,* "God has wired his world for power, but he calls on us to flip the switch." Prayer is the switch.

Once my mom was shopping in the mall. She found a seat in the crowded food court and sat down to enjoy a moment of rest. Not long after, a harried woman asked if she could sit down in the unoccupied chair at her table. Mom welcomed her, and before long they were in a conversation. The woman began pouring out her troubles, and Mom became a bit overwhelmed with the difficult circumstances her new acquaintance was experiencing. Finally, my mother asked if she could pray for her. Right there in the middle of Auntie Anne's, Subway and a couple hundred people, they bowed their heads and Mom called on God for help. The woman's tear-stained face of gratitude was the "amen."

You should know that my then eighty-six-year-old mother was not a bold, evangelistic type person. She was quiet about her faith. But when confronted with the enormity of the woman's difficulties, she knew she had access to the power that was needed. Rather than thinking, her situation doesn't have a prayer, she "flipped on the switch" and teamed up with God to bring relief.

Each of us can do the same. No matter who we are or what we face, no problem is too small, no challenge too great to talk about with God. He wants us to pray fervently, persistently and confidently. He is delighted when we unceasingly call upon him for all kinds of people and all kinds of situations.

May God help us to pray, pray and pray. Pray as if it were our only hope.

February 6th

Search me, God, and know my heart;
test me and know my anxious thoughts.
See if there is any offensive way in me,
and lead me in the way everlasting.
—Psalm 139:23–24 NIV

The Realness of Repentance

People today are looking for authenticity.

Author Brett McCracken reports in *The Wall Street Journal,* "Seventy percent of Protestant adults stop attending church regularly after they leave home. This has caused many in the evangelical church to try and be more cool. As a twenty-something, I can say with confidence that when it comes to church, we don't want cool as much as we want real."

There has never been a more "real" person to walk the face of the earth than Jesus Christ. He knew where he came from, where he was going, and why he was here. He wasn't threatened by injustice, man's scrutiny or imposing expectations. He didn't try to make himself look better by hiding his sins—there were none to hide! Although fully human, he was perfect.

So how do we, far-from-perfect followers of Christ, become more real? It begins with realizing that God is also looking for real. The psalmist cries out for God to search his heart. He didn't trust his own assessments, so he asked his Creator. Expose anything hiding in me, Lord! And that is how God wants us to come—with our good, our bad and our ugly—even our very ugly. Pretending to be something we're not brings shame to his name. It's simply "un-Christ" to be phony. Further, we can't get rid of something we don't see.

It takes pure courage to look at ourselves honestly. And it takes guts to repent. But at the heart of repentance lies realness. In fact, it is repentance that leads to authenticity. My favorite part in *The Voyage of the Dawn Treader* comes when Aslan pulls the scales from Eustace's dragon-body. The pain of extracting from Eustace all that was "un-real" to uncover the "real" was excruciating, but necessary. And so, it is for us.

Like Eustace, we can't get rid of our "scales" by ourselves. But, if every time we mess up, we fall at the cross and repent, the forgiveness of the Lord will wash over us and we'll discover a realm of grace that has the power to change us.

A power that makes us *real.*

February 7th

Have salt in yourselves, and be at peace with one another.
—Mark 9:50 ESV

Sin, Salt and Peace

An argument ensues among the disciples as to which one of them is the greatest. Someone driving out demons in Jesus' name offends them because he is not in their circle. They have to be warned not to let their attitudes and actions cause younger believers to stumble. Pride. Exclusivity. Legalism. Sin hasn't changed much in the last two thousand years, has it?

Each of these situations is recorded in the Gospel of Mark, chapter 9. Immediately after these blatant displays of human nature the Lord warns the disciples they must treat sin radically. He uses hyperbole to illustrate. "If your hand causes you to sin, cut it off. It is better for you to enter life crippled than with two hands to go into hell" (v. 44 ESV). Why such severity? Pride, exclusivity and legalism split believers from one another and from the body of Christ. Jesus wanted to show them that behavior which cuts off fellow believers mirrors dismembering their own bodies.

But Jesus doesn't stop there. He presents them with the remedy. He tells them "everyone will be salted with fire" (v. 49 ESV). No exceptions. Every individual who truly follows Christ will experience a fiery purification. Only the cleansing salt of the Holy Spirit can eradicate the deeply hidden sin that separates us from others.

Painful as the process might be, it leaves within us a deposit—a salty residue that emanates peace. Elsewhere Scripture says, "If it is possible, as far as it depends on you, live at peace with everyone" (Romans 12:18). We can more graciously follow that command when we've been "salted with fire." The fire produces peace that prevails even if others don't extend it back. In fact, when we offer this peace to our enemies, some of the coals from our fire end up landing on their heads (Romans 12:20)!

So, don't lose your saltiness. Don't let your heart be "flame-resistant" to the sanctifying fire of the Holy Spirit.

February 8th

Come, see a man who told me everything I ever did.

—John 4:29 NIV

Individually Yours

Republicans, Liberals, Americans, Blacks, Presbyterians, Catholics, the 2 percent. Our culture is plagued with viewing others through categories. And although labels might help us put people into nice neat boxes, they all too often blind us to seeing people as individuals. But Jesus never viewed people this way.

Consider when he traveled through Samaria and met the woman at the well. Local custom dictated that he would have ignored her. Would have written her off because she was both a Samaritan and a woman—and a sinful one at that. But he didn't. He looked deeper and discovered one unique personality thirsting for true life. She just didn't know it. He met her with precision and compassion: "Come, see a man who told me everything I ever did" (John 4:29). It was enough. Her single testimony reached the whole town, "and many more became believers" (v. 41).

From Samaria, Jesus traveled to Galilee. He knew the folks there only welcomed him because they wanted to see a miracle. Not what we would consider a noble people-group. Sure enough, right off the bat, an official came to Jesus and asked him to heal his dying son. In spite of the spirit of the town, Jesus spoke the word of healing to this solitary man and his son recovered (John 4:46–53).

What a God who looks beyond our cultural surroundings and treats us as individuals! Truth came and met the immoral woman. It embraced the grief-stricken father. Truth plucked both of them out of their respective crowds and said *I know you.*

He knows you too. He looks beyond every label you carry. Beyond how everyone else views you—whether they admire you or despise you. He doesn't treat you exactly the same as he does the person next to you; he understands what makes you, well, *you.*

There are few things in life more precious than being known. Maybe Jesus wants us to start looking past the labels and see people like he did. Maybe he wants us to recognize there's a you—*a unique, hand-crafted individual*—living behind all those outward identifiers. Maybe it would cause some labels to fall, some common ground to surface.

February 9th

And who is my neighbor? —Luke 10:29 NIV

Samaritans on the Loose

Oh no! We were ten miles away from the Allentown airport when the battery light on the car started to flash. We literally coasted into a gas station directly across from the airport before it died completely. My husband offered to pay a man at the gas pump to take my mom to the gate where she was to catch her flight. "No problem. My wife is headed there right now to return a rental car," he replied. That was only the beginning.

For the next two hours that family (husband, wife, son and cousin) stuck by our side—in the cold, icy rain—trying to help us. It soon became obvious we would have to get towed seventy miles back to our mechanic's garage. But rather than leaving us, the family insisted on staying until the tow truck arrived. So there, in the warmth of their running car, we waited and exchanged stories. All I could think of was, *How do they have the time to do this? We're strangers. We barely speak the same language (they were Hispanic), yet here they are showing us such kindness.*

I've thought a lot about the parable of the Good Samaritan since that night. The priest and Levite passed by the man who had been robbed, beaten and left on the road to die. Life was about them. They had places to go and people to see. I bet they were busy. I bet their lives were full of sentences with no commas, too full to be interrupted. Probably not a lot different from mine.

Not so, though, with the Samaritan. And not so with these dear folks. Because of the time they took for us on that cold wintry night, our lives were touched. Changed. Challenged to slow down and consider God's undeserved mercy. Mercy reflected by those Samaritans on the loose.

February 10th

Dear children, keep yourself from idols. —*1 John 5:21 NIV*

Idol Detection

I recently heard an interesting comparison taken from the movie, *Rocky Balboa*. Being almost sixty years old, Rocky is asked why he wants to fight again. He responds, "If I can go the distance, I'll know I'm not a bum." I doubt many would put it in those words, but I suspect some of us share Rocky's sentiments. We look at life and think, *If I just had **that**, I wouldn't be a bum.* Or—

- If someone really loved me …
- If everyone thought well of me …
- If my children were successful …
- If I didn't have to worry about money …
- If I escaped this addiction …

None of these desires are bad in and of themselves. In fact, they are worthy aspirations. But if our drive for meaning causes us to seek them more than God for our sense of significance, they can turn into idols. Tim Keller writes in his book *Counterfeit Gods,* that an idol is basically anything that becomes more important to us than God. Most of our idols consist of good things gone bad. They, rather than God, become the source of our identity, the means to keep us from feeling like a bum.

The apostle John, in one of his last letters, warns us to beware of idols. He's written about the importance of walking in love, of believing in God and obeying all his commands. Then he ends with this simple instruction of keeping ourselves from idols. It at first seems out of context. But John wants us to realize that although the issues he has instructed us in are vital, if we break the first commandment (Exodus 20:3), we will lose it all.

These idols don't replace God—at least not in the beginning. They simply co-exist with him. That's what makes them so difficult to recognize. But if we hope to find the security we crave, recognize them we must—and repent. We are to have "no other gods," whether those "gods" are exalted above the Lord, slink alongside him, or are hidden in our hearts. We must ask the Holy Spirit to expose them and root them out.

Detecting any idols in your heart? Don't forget that only God can keep you from "feeling like a bum."

February 11th

Jesus replied, "Very truly I tell you, no one can see the kingdom of God unless they are born again."
—John 3:3 NIV

Extreme Makeover

Anyone who has watched the TV show, *Extreme Makeover,* knows we're not talking about a little touch-up here and there. The redo brings drastic change. Normal looking women become drop-dead gorgeous, and once barely sufficient houses turn into covers for *25 Beautiful Homes.*

Jesus was pointing to our spiritual need for an *extreme makeover* when he said in order to participate in the kingdom, we must be *born again.* No one has described it better than C. S. Lewis in *Mere Christianity:*

> Imagine yourself as a living house. God comes in to rebuild that house. At first, perhaps, you can understand what He is doing.... But presently he starts knocking the house about in a way that hurts abominably and does not seem to make any sense....You thought you were being made into a decent little cottage; but he is building a palace. He intends to come and live in it Himself.

God has always been in the makeover business:

- Moses went from murdering an Egyptian to being the meekest man on earth.
- Gideon was transformed from being a man of insecurities to a mighty man of valor.
- Abraham lied about Sarah being his wife twice but became the father of our faith.
- Peter changed from an impulsive, unsteady denier of Christ to the Rock.
- John, the "Son of Thunder" who wanted to bring down judgment on unreceptive towns, grew to be the apostle most known for his love.

We are contaminated with sin more than we realize. We may think we need slight changes here and there, but the reality can't be ignored: we are totally corrupt. Each and every one of us without exception. So, don't be discouraged in whatever part of the makeover process you are presently undergoing. Let God finish the construction. Something drastic must happen to alter our situation.

Something as extreme as being born again.

February 12th

When you see the ark of the covenant of the LORD your God, and the Levitical priests carrying it, you are to move out from your positions and follow it. Then you will know which way to go, since you have never been this way before.
                                                                  —Joshua 3:3-4 NIV

Bonsai Christians

Do any of you experience a "sick-in-the-stomach" reaction when challenged with circumstances that force you out of well-defined boxes? God desires to replace the anxiety that accompanies new encounters with a deeper level of trust. He wants to pry us away from our incessant need for certainty to make room for creativity and new growth. To accomplish this he will, from time-to-time, present us with unfamiliar experiences to rescue us from eventual stagnancy and stunted development.

We all have I've never been this way before experiences. We leave home, marry, have children. We start a business, take a new position, enter the mission field. Like Israel, our victory over the accompanying apprehension will depend on whether we have allowed ourselves to follow the ark —the ark of trusting that God goes with us.

Taking the Promised Land required a level of trust the Israelites had never known. Everything from marching around Jericho seven times and literally shouting the walls down, to each man possessing his own "vine and fig tree" necessitated the assurance that God was with them. The fledgling nation would have to trust God in a greater measure if they hoped to survive. They had never been this way before.

When God leads us to places we have never been before we, too, can go confidently if we maintain our trust in his guidance. When a situation looms before us and we don't know what to do, we have to stretch our roots to find the life-giving streams of wisdom. The level our roots went before no longer suffices because God wants us to go deeper and stand taller.

Bonsai trees are lovely to look at, but they produce little fruit due to severe pruning of their roots. And neither will we if we don't learn how to embrace new circumstances with trust in the God who leads the way. We were made to go, and to grow—not become bonsai Christians.

February 13th

Every good and perfect gift is from above.

—James 1:17 NIV

Eat the Whole Thing

In the late seventies my husband and I had the opportunity to study at L'Abri in Switzerland with noted theologian Francis Schaeffer. We had been saving our money to go for quite a while, but between the cost of our flight and our stay, to say our budget was tight would be an understatement.

One "day off" we were hitchhiking to Lausanne when a man in a small truck picked us up. We rode with him until he reached his destination, a small grocery store which he owned. As we got out of the truck, my husband naturally began helping the man unload his boxes. After finishing, the man came running out of his store with a chocolate bar. He was so grateful for the assistance that he insisted my husband take it as a thank you.

Well, this was no ordinary chocolate bar. This was Swiss chocolate! We had discovered Swiss chocolate not long after we arrived—and we were hooked. Whenever we splurged to buy one, we always doled out the pieces, savoring every bite, making it last as long as possible. Now we had been *given* one, and we were as excited as two little kids at Christmas. We began planning how much we would eat; how much we would save for latter. Then, realizing the blessing the grocer had intended, I finally said, "Chip, why don't you just eat the whole thing!"

I've never seen anyone enjoy a chocolate bar like my husband did that day. It was one of those moments when you are fully aware of God's goodness.

James tells us every good gift we receive comes from God. Think of that! We have a Father who wants to give his children pleasures—real tangible things to bring us happiness. How much we miss when we fail to recognize the unmerited blessings of God.

That unassuming experience in Switzerland continues to remind us of the importance of receiving with gratitude God's countless gifts. How about you? Do you ever struggle seeing God as our generous Father? The next time you are unsure about receiving, why not simply enjoy his gift with thankfulness and "just eat the whole thing."

February 14th

And the two will become one flesh. So they are no longer two, but one flesh.

—Mark 10:8 NIV

Strengthening the "And"

"My wife just left me. She was my best friend. The love of my life." An acquaintance recently spoke those painful words to me. I knew this man viewed his marriage commitment as one for life; his wife didn't share his perspective. The raw devastation touched me deeply. I'm aware of other marriages in trouble. But I'm also aware of a lot more who have weathered the inevitable storms accompanying that most unique calling of two becoming one flesh.

Contrary to what we hear, marriage matters. God designed the love, sacrifice and unity in marriage to reflect the inestimable relationship between Christ and the church. Scripture calls it "a profound mystery" (Ephesians 5:32). Real marriage models the beauty of dying to self, just as Jesus died for the body. It exposes the vacant promises of life centered on *my* wants, *my* needs, *my* desires. It teaches us to press through immediate gratification for something larger than self.

We've all heard the statistics: half of marriages in our society end in divorce and Christian marriages fare no better. Do you know recent research from the National Survey of Family Growth proves those "facts" to be false? Turns out, most marriages, about 70 percent, do *not* end in divorce and the divorce rate for regular church goers is much less than that.

That is good news. News that needs to be heralded. Because the more marriage is viewed as irrelevant, the less likely we're apt to stand for its virtues.

So, these days I've been praying for the *and* in marriages to be strengthened. For Gary *and* Terry, Rich *and* Ann, Marty *and* Lisa ... Jesus is counting on us to show the world what the love it craves really looks like. If you are married, pray you *and* your spouse will grow more and more in love. May you have the courage to let no one—including your self—separate what God has joined together.

February 15th

In your anger do not sin: Do not let the sun go down while you are still angry, and do not give the devil a foothold.
—*Ephesians 4:26–27 NIV*

Heart Conditions: Hard Hearts

When Jesus prophesied that in the last days "the love of many will grow cold" (Matthew 24:12 ESV) he could have been talking about today's world. It seems we're becoming a people steeped in hate. Author Peter Wood, in his book *A Bee in the Mouth: Anger in America Now,* has concluded just that. He writes that our country has turned into an "angri-culture," one with a "hate-therefore-I-am" mindset. Hatred and rage are embraced as virtues, as new avenues to gain respect. And although anger may bring temporary relief, in the end, it spawns a binding hardness.

Ravi Zacharias writes in *The Grand Weaver,* "At the end of your life, one of three things will happen to your heart. It will grow hard, it will be broken, or it will be tender. Nobody escapes." Our hearts are made ready for hardening when we fail to move past the offenses of others. The ensuing hurt and continued focus on what they've done to us settles in on us like an invisible fog of resentment. Before long the ability to see things clearly becomes completely obscured. Once we allow that resentment to kindle into anger, it doesn't take long for that anger to lead us to sin.

Paul warns us to take our anger seriously. He doesn't say anger itself is sin, but it can become sin if we don't deal with it. Rather than coddling our offenses like a mother pampers a spoiled child, he exhorts us to see anger for what it is: a landing strip for Satan to get a foothold in our souls.

If we hope to keep our hearts from turning into stone, we must call on the grace of God to help us reject the slippery slope of resentment. And without delay! The longer we let anger brew, the greater the likelihood self-justification, rationalizations and other such devices will act as hardening forces. Forces that entrench "Satan's foothold." Let's not let the sun go down on an angry heart. As the author of Hebrews warns, "Today, if you hear his voice, do not harden your hearts" (Hebrews 3:7–8).

February 16th

The LORD is close to the brokenhearted and saves those who are crushed in spirit. *—Psalm 34:18 NIV*

Heart Conditions: Broken Hearts

From the man who after thirty years of faithful employment is told to "clean out his desk" to the piercing words of the oncologist, "there's nothing more we can do"; from the heartrending accounts of fallen soldiers to the sad, vacant faces of those who have been trafficked—the world at times seems awash in tragedy.

I imagine there are many of you, too, who have suffered great loss. The condition of your heart has not only been broken by sorrow but crushed by the threat of ongoing emptiness: empty promises, empty nest, empty pillow, empty womb, empty arms.

Broken hearts are empty hearts. What was once filled with faith, hope and love lies depleted, at risk of never risking again, for love always involves risk. Whether romantic love, parental love, friendship—hearts that are vulnerable are hearts that can break. When we meet the suffering part of love, we stand at one of those crossroads where our choices will determine whether we put our hurting heart in a lockbox and place it on a shelf like an artifact in a museum. *Look but don't touch.* Or whether we bring it to the Healer. A Healer who longs to bind wounds and restore our hope.

David declares the Lord's concern for the brokenhearted. He had experienced it. When his spirit was crushed, when he saw no way out and the waves of depression threatened to overwhelm him, he called out to the Lord, and the Lord heard him. God seems to have a special place for us when we hurt.

One of the distinguishing signs of the Messiah is that he would heal broken hearts (Isaiah 61:1).

He who was despised and rejected by men, who was familiar with suffering, who took up our infirmities and carried our sorrows extends triumphs over all emptiness.

The empty tomb looms large enough to swallow up whatever our empty might be. It declares victory over death. It fills us with hope—hope for a new beginning, hope that life can come from death. If your heart has been torn and you are facing the threat of ongoing emptiness, remember that the God of love is the God of redemption. He stands ready to heal, to fill, to restore.

February 17th

Blessed are the poor in spirit, for theirs is the kingdom of heaven.
—Matthew 5:3 NIV

Heart Conditions: Tender Hearts

The tender heart is the heart that has been massaged with grace. Rather than allowing the difficulties in life to either harden us or break us, we view our troubles, as Francois Fenelon writes, like "cures to the poison of [our] old nature."

This has certainly been true in my own life. Every time I've allowed God to carry me through my deepest disappointments and discouragements, some residue of my old nature is extracted and left behind. Were it not for the trouble, the "poison" might not be exposed. Insight into the hidden idols of my heart and the depth of my sinful nature is simply a part of the maturing process. Albeit, an uncomfortable part.

Paradoxically, the more I have longed to be like Christ, the greater the realization of how far I fall short.

We shouldn't be surprised at such revelation of ourselves. If we hope to be like Christ, areas in our hearts that are unlike him will have to go. The piercing awareness of our shortcomings initiates the softening. It prepares us for grace. Like the skilled hands of a masseuse, grace locates those points of tension—those knots of stubbornness—and works to release us from the pride and self-reliance that would hinder us from entering the kingdom of heaven. It's why Scripture tells us that the poor in spirit are blessed. They are blessed because they know their spiritual poverty.

I pray you will be diligent in checking the condition of your heart. If you discover areas of hardness or brokenness, please don't give up. Let the warmth of his compassion melt the coldness; let the immensity of his goodness fill the fractures. Let the gift of his grace help you resist every pull toward resentment or isolation so you can keep your heart tender.

February 18th

For the grace of God ... teaches us to say "No" to ungodliness and worldly passions, and to live self-controlled, upright and godly lives in this present age. —Titus 2:11–12 NIV

Grace Happens

Grace happens in the most unexpected ways.

Busted! I knew he was coming after me as soon as I saw him turn on the flashing lights and pull up behind my car. Although the cruise control had kept me close to the speed limit for most of the trip, I somehow managed to fly past the state trooper fifteen miles over the speed limit. "Mam, do you know how fast you were going? May I see your driver's license and registration?" It's interesting how such simple questions can cause a near heart attack. We both knew I was guilty.

Waiting in my car for the officer to write up the ticket, I prayed, cried and almost vomited. I was without excuse. *How could I be so stupid?* The longer he delayed, the lower my spirits sank. Yet when he finally returned, I could hardly believe my ears. "I'm going to cut you a break and give you a warning. Drive carefully now."

I didn't deserve the grace he gave me that day. I should have gotten a fine, and a hefty one at that. But his words did not go unheeded. I bet I was the safest driver on Interstate 80 that afternoon. Whenever the cruise control kicked off and the speedometer started to creep up, I immediately slowed down. Sure, I had no desire to get stopped again, and I wanted to be safe, but you know what really motivated me? It was that state trooper giving me a second chance. Even though he would never know, I wanted to "live out" my gratitude.

The Bible teaches it is grace that teaches us to say no to ungodliness. I believe it. It's not that laws aren't necessary. But the law can't really change us. It serves to keep us in line, to *protect* us. Grace, however, moves from the inside out. It's fueled by gratefulness. We don't *want* to let down the one who "cut us a break." Not if we really know how guilty we are.

So how about you? Are you, like me, thanking God today that you're not receiving what you deserve?

February 19th

Not looking to your own interests but each of you to the interests of the others. —Philippians 2:4 NIV

Sticks and Stones and Names

One of the students at the college where I teach was asked whether he believes "God causes suffering for our growth." The student wisely answered, "I'm only twenty years old. Honestly, I don't know a lot about suffering, so I don't think that I'm qualified to answer." I found his humility refreshing.

We live in a competitive world. One-upmanship and the drive for power seeps through every aspect of life, from the school-yard playground to the halls of Congress. To admit we don't have an answer or that we are wrong or weak makes us feel vulnerable, and in our culture vulnerability just doesn't play well. Defensiveness comes so *naturally*. Yet, shockingly, Scripture tells us we should consider others better than ourselves! We're called to look out for their interests as well as our own.

Sundar Singh, the great Indian convert who was so instrumental in bringing Christianity to India, presents a beautiful picture of a life free from defensiveness: "When I throw a stone at the fruit tree, the fruit tree throws no stone back, but gives me fruit.... Should we not be like the sandalwood, which imparts its fragrance to the ax which cuts it." Singh wasn't just philosophizing. His profession of faith met the ax of persecution throughout his life. But the greater the injustices hurled at him, the stronger the fragrance of Christ became.

I don't like getting hit by axes or stones any more than you do. But being our own defense attorney is both exhausting and futile. Why not cultivate the mind of Christ and decide not to cling to our *rights*? Why not humble ourselves and put another's interest ahead of our own? The next time someone tosses an insult our way, why not do something radical? Why not give back the fruit of the Spirit—love, joy, peace, patience, kindness.

Let's defuse the sticks and stones and names that really hurt us by taking on the attitude of Christ.

February 20th

Do not drag me away with the wicked,
with those who do evil,
who speak cordially with their neighbors
but harbor malice in their hearts.

—Psalm 28:3 NIV

With Malice Toward None

The immortal words from Abraham Lincoln's Second Inaugural Address, "with malice toward none, with charity for all," remind me of the great civil war that rages within our souls in the aftermath of hurt and deception. The pain we experience forces us to make a choice. We can trust God for healing, "My comfort in my suffering is this: Your promise preserves my life"

(Psalm 119:50). Or we can rely on ourselves and seek comfort in thoughts of revenge.

Malice doesn't make its initial appearance in a hard, judgmental form. *So, what if I indulge in a little resentment? So, what if I ruminate on how I've been treated unfairly?* But the more we feed it, the larger it grows until our once thriving confidence in God is consumed by the never-satisfied appetite of malice. Before we know it, our bloated bitterness squeezes out the Holy Spirit.

Countering malice, as Lincoln penned, lies in cultivating charity. The magnanimous nature of God's grace offers believers an entrance to generous, forgiving love. We access it every time we decide to entrust our hurts to the Lord. It will protect our soul, if not our body.

Ironically, Lincoln—whose highest goal reached to help a torn nation reunite—became a victim of the malice he sought so tirelessly to abolish. The bullet that penetrated Lincoln's brain was fired by a man consumed with hatred and misguided egotism. History reports the comfort John Wilkes Booth thought he would find in revenge was short-lived. It always is. Only charity—only love—lasts.

When malice invites you to sit at his table, refuse! Don't risk being dragged away with the wicked! Nothing anyone does to you warrants surrendering to malice. As we commemorate Abraham Lincoln's birthday this month, be inspired by his example. He was bigger than malice.

And so are you, dear child of God.

February 21st

But make up your mind not to worry beforehand.

—Luke 21:14 NIV

Don't Worry, Be Happy...In God

Worry. Worry. Worry. We worry about everything from what we're going to wear, to how we'll pay the bills, and to threats of terrorism. We can get to the point where we feel irresponsible if we're not worrying about something! But worry is toxic. It robs us of God's peace and accomplishes absolutely nothing. It reveals how we rely on ourselves rather than God to fix things in our own desperate search for understanding.

Irresistible as it may appear, we actually have a choice not to worry. As this passage in Luke testifies, we can decide ahead of time not to give in to anxious thoughts. Jesus exhorts his disciples to replace worry with reliance on his words and his wisdom. He warns them that they are about to face betrayal, rejection, even death. Yet he promises that no matter what they face, he will help them. That's all they needed to know. It's all we need to know as well.

I don't know if you're like me, but when a trial comes, it's usually accompanied by a relentless mental pursuit to "figure it out." I want to make sense out of my suffering, so I try and try to connect the dots. But it never helps and usually makes things worse. What has helped is the discovery that I don't have to fret. Worry can be replaced with a quiet, confident declaration: Jesus, I trust you.

Much of my worry centers around people I care about. But even then, the realization I can make up my mind not to worry has been quite freeing. When I remember he cares about them far more than I do, and has the power (unlike me) to affect change, I can release the worry and receive the peace. God is bigger than me, bigger than the circumstance, bigger than any terrible outcome I fear. And I can make up my mind to choose truth over worry. Who knew?

How about you? Are you stuck in the worry pit? You don't have to be. Make up your mind not to worry. Be happy in the God who loves you.

No man's life lasts longer than a breath.   —*Psalm 39:5 NIRV*

In the Middle of the Mess

As we stopped at the head of our driveway coming home from the hospital, my eyes welled with tears. It had been six days earlier, at 3:30 a.m., when we raced out the lane headed for the emergency room. We had no idea I was on the edge of septic shock and a dangerous threat to my life. We didn't know. But God did.

The doctor told my husband had we gotten to the hospital twenty minutes later, my hopes for recovery would have been cut in half. If you knew how prone our family is to "doctor" ourselves, you would realize the fact we drove to the ER in the middle of the night was a miracle in itself. Moments after being admitted, my fever spiked and blood pressure plummeted. I was rushed to the ICU and the doctors and nurses went into action. They discovered a kidney stone blocking my right kidney, diverting all the poison to my bloodstream. The ensuing sepsis plunged me into a sickness like nothing I'd known before.

I've always been graced with good health. I even took a bit of pride whenever I had to fill out routine medical history forms. I loved marking no to all the listed ailments. It's not that I took my health for granted; I just wasn't expecting something so severe to mess up my formerly pristine medical history.

Life gets messy at times, doesn't it? Unpredictable. We all experience marred medical history forms in one way or another. Yet, in the unpredictable messiness we have opportunity to experience deeper grains of grace. Of redemption.

For me, that redemptive grace appeared through God-appointed doctors and nurses being at the right place at the right time to save my life. It took shape in the prayers, love and kindnesses of family and friends. It brought me extraordinary comfort through my husband's tender care. Most of all, it produced in me an overwhelming sense of gratitude.

The psalmist tells us life is but a breath. Our short span on earth will never be immune from its messiness. But whatever might splatter over our allotted time, we can find peace in knowing God is right in the middle of our mess, and he promises to use it for our good.

February 23rd

He will come to save you.   —*Isaiah 35:4 NIV*

Will He Come?

With pointed alliteration, Max Lucado, in his book *Great Day Every Day,* poses the three questions we ask about God when trouble overwhelms us:

- Do you think he can?
- Do you think he cares?
- Do you think he will come?

If we believe the Bible at all, we can't help but acknowledge he is the all-powerful, almighty creator of the whole universe. He fashioned everything—from the DNA polymers that determine the makeup of every living being to the stars in the Milky Way. Nothing lies beyond his reach (Luke 1:37).

Of course, he can.

But does this supreme, omnipotent God really care about the struggles we face? "What is man that you are mindful of him?" inquires the psalmist (Psalm 8:4 ESV). Is the God "who did not spare his own Son, but gave him up for us all" concerned over our concerns? (Romans 8:32). Is it perhaps no accident that the most quoted passage of Scripture through the ages has been John 3:16, "for God so loved the world"?

Of course, he cares.

But will he come? That question challenges me the most. Doubts start to cloud my mind when my timing clashes with God's. Because God doesn't show up when I determine he should, I think he has somehow gone AWOL. I think I can't stand the situation another minute, and I cry out in desperation, "Where are you?" Sometimes that "minute" turns into days, months, even years. And you know what? I find I can "stand" more than I thought I could. Not because I'm necessarily strong or faith-filled. But because of what our powerful, loving God has promised.

When Israel was experiencing a low ebb, Isaiah assured the disheartened nation God had not forgotten them. His confidence rings like music to my ears. "He will come to save you."

Will he come? Nope. He doesn't have to. He is already here.

February 24th

But whoever drinks the water I give them will never thirst. Indeed, the water I give them will become in them a spring of water welling up to eternal life.

—John 4:14 NIV

Dehydrated Christians

Did you know 75 percent of Americans suffer from "chronic dehydration"? Most of us are unaware our bodies aren't receiving adequate water intake. Symptoms range from fatigue and dizziness to seizures and in rare instances death. Some reports claim by the time we feel thirsty, our bodies have already begun to dehydrate!

There's another type of dehydration that similarly can go unnoticed: spiritual dehydration. Symptoms include wilting faith in the heat of trials, droopy hope, and sagging passion for God. If we find ourselves lacking spiritual vitality, perhaps it's time for a water level check! The "living water" kind.

Israel knew something about dehydration. Jeremiah exposed the source of their arid spiritual condition. They had polluted their worship of God with idolatry. "My people have committed two sins: They have forsaken me, the spring of living water, and have dug their own cisterns, broken cisterns that cannot hold water" (Jeremiah 2:13).

Could the root of our spiritual dehydration flow from a similar spring? Are we digging our own wells? Looking to other sources to satisfy our thirsty souls? Maybe we've been sipping in the culture a bit too much. Downing people's approval more than God's pleasure. Imbibing in hectic lifestyles that eventually leave us parched, exhausted and unfulfilled. Only the living water found in Christ can hydrate our spirit.

When Jesus met the Samaritan woman at the well, he assured her those who drink from him never thirst again. In fact, he said a spiritual artesian well would erupt! His Spirit within us provides a steady stream of life that keeps hearts from becoming dried out and hardened. There's no "run-off" with living water.

I'm told dehydration can be cured 100 percent by simply drinking more water. I suspect the same might be true with spiritual hydration. For some of us, it's time to start drinking in more Jesus. More Holy Spirit. Let's get saturated in his Word and soaked in prayer. We don't have to be living as dehydrated Christians. In fact, dehydrated Christians aren't living at all.

So, get your thirst on. Drink up!

February 25th

Go in peace.

—2 Kings 5:19 NIV

God Meets Us

God meets us. Right where we are, he meets us. To me, that's one of the most profound truths of the Christian faith. We don't have to go through years of self-abasement to catch a glimpse of him. We don't have to kill infidels to please him. We don't have to rigidly follow a set of rules to make him love us. Even the Old Testament whispers this truth. The story of Naaman recorded in the fifth chapter of 2 Kings shouts it.

Naaman, commander of the Aramean army, was healed of incurable leprosy through the prophet Elisha. The miracle had broken Naaman's pride and arrogance, causing him to proclaim, "Now I know that there is no God in all the world except in Israel" (2 Kings 5:15). Naaman had thought Israel's God was just like all the others. When he went for healing, he expected a great "show" or some valiant sacrifice on his part to appease God and garner his favor. Whoops! Wrong god! This God's cure went further than skin-deep.

As a result of his healing, Naaman vows that he will never again worship any other god than the Lord. But he asks the Lord to forgive him when he returns to his country and has to accompany his master to the temple, bowing to gods he now realizes aren't gods at all. What? Bow to pagan deities? How does Elisha respond to that? Does he express outrage and demand Naaman make a public denunciation of the false gods? Does he insist he leave his idolatrous culture and move to Israel? Does he chastise him for being "afraid to witness?" Astonishingly, Elisha's words are as soft and tender as Naaman's new skin: "Go in peace."

That kind of grace moves me to tears. It tells me about a God so rich in mercy that he heals in spite of our pride, our half-baked ideas, our many misperceptions and our legalisms. It tells me of a God who wades through all the muck and mire of our sin to meet us right where we're at. And gives us *new skin*.

February 26th

Peace I leave with you; my peace I give you. I do not give to you as the world gives. Do not let your hearts be troubled and do not be afraid.
—John 14:27 NIV

An Unexpected Visitor

My grandma, Ocie Adloff, died when I was young so I don't remember her well, just her sweet fragrance and how she would kiss me in my ear. I also remember she was a gentle woman who exuded a "holy disposition" if there is such a thing. And there's one story about her I have always remembered.

Grandma had her first heart attack when she was in her early 30s. She suffered from congenital heart disease, so she was in and out of hospitals the last years of her life. One time, about four years before she died, she had a visitor at her hospital bed. Given her quiet temperament, her Jewish agnostic doctor said had it been anyone but Mrs. Adloff, he wouldn't have believed it.

She experienced a visitation from Jesus. He stood at her bed and undisturbed, they had a twenty- minute conversation. Afterwards, when she told of it, she insisted it wasn't a vision. He was really there. The incident was so powerful that years later, when Mom ran into one of the nurses who had worked there and asked if she remembered the incident, the nurse didn't hesitate, "I will never forget it."

Why? Why would Jesus appear to Grandma like that? She had always been a devout woman; she attended church regularly and served faithfully in her quiet way. Now, she was confined pretty much to her home. At one point, she was on bed rest for a whole year. If anyone's circumstances could engender discouragement and fear, Grandma's would qualify. Jesus came to give her peace in the greatest battle of her life.

He does that, you know. He spoke peace to the disciples in the Upper Room right before his death and resurrection. He assured them that although he was leaving, they would someday be reunited. Although they were going to experience grief, trouble and confusion, he offered them something the world knew nothing of. His peace.

He continues to offer it to you, to me. Don't be afraid.

February 27th

Then Satan entered Judas.... And Judas went to the chief priests and the officers of the temple guard and discussed with them how he might betray Jesus.
—Luke 22:3-4 NIV

Betrayal

Betrayal. It's an ugly word. Eight small letters united to form an act so strong that it can dissolve marriages, friendships, even countries. No one admires a betrayer. Parents don't typically name their children *Benedict Arnold.* Betrayal steals the petals from the flower and leaves it naked, misshapen. It tramples hope. It dismantles the most sacred of trusts.

I believe it begins with disappointment. We anticipate a certain action or response but get something different. Our failure to deal with it causes more and more discontentment with the one who has "let us down," so much so that we begin to look for occasions that justify our misgivings. Rationalization validates our bitterness until finally our hearts become a bed for Satan to sow seeds of betrayal. That seems to be what happened with Judas.

Jesus didn't meet Judas' expectations. He thought Jesus would deliver Israel from the Romans. When it became clear this was not his intention, all the miracles Judas had witnessed—the healings, the multiplication of bread and fish, the calming of seas, even raising the dead—weren't strong enough to alleviate his disappointment. The purity of Jesus' life, the depth of his compassion, his devotion and sincerity, his goodness—nothing could counter what Judas wanted. It made Judas the perfect candidate for the role of betrayer. So, he fell into Satan's hands.

I don't know whether you have experienced the kiss of betrayal. If so, no one understands your pain more than Jesus. And no one can heal you like he can. Disappointment, however, is familiar to us all. Be on guard when it comes. Take it to the cross. Don't let Satan use it to sow seeds of betrayal either toward God or toward your fellow man—your fellow fallen man.

February 28th

Against all hope, Abraham in hope believed.

—Romans 4:18 NIV

The Stubbornness of Hope

I'm thankful hope is so stubborn. If it wasn't, I think I'd be a goner. In spite of how many times circumstances tempt me to throw in the towel, I find that entity of hope popping to the surface and eventually taking over.

Oh, I've tried to resist. I've let discouraging thoughts smother the "noble, lovely and praiseworthy" (Philippians 4:8). I've listened to the whispers of failure and the voice of disappointment. But I find after all my rants and raves, hope stands there quietly waiting. She penetrates my protests with undeniable assurance that everything will be okay.

It's a God-thing, of course. Scripture compares hope to an anchor (Hebrews 6:19). It attaches us to what is really real. To what is solid. It causes hearts that would otherwise go adrift in life-crushing breakers to dig in to the truth.

Abraham learned this. Although he didn't start out that way, he somehow arrived at that place which required him to "hope against hope." He had been given big promises—promises accompanied by big delays. Delays that stretched him, that pushed him to the edge, that most certainly disheartened him. But despite all the waffling doubts, he kept hoping.

The stubborn nature of hope arose every time he looked at the brilliance of the night—a night that echoed what God had spoken to him, "I will make your descendants as numerous as the stars in the sky" (Genesis 26:4). When he walked in the endless desert sand, he was reminded that God said, "I will make your offspring like the dust of the earth, so that if anyone could count the dust, then your offspring could be counted" (Genesis 13:16). Whenever he heard his new name, "Abraham," hope took him back to the time when God told him he would be the "father of many nations" (Genesis 17:5). Hope bound him so tightly to the word of God that it yielded the indomitable substance we call faith.

It will do the same for us. Don't be afraid. Give in to the stubbornness of hope.

February 29th

Before I formed you in the womb I knew you.

—Jeremiah 1:5 NIV

God Rocks!

Before we were born, God made us with a plan in mind.

Oh no, what did he do this time? That was my common response during our son's teenage years. After being homeschooled through eighth grade, he entered high school filled with a sense of, well, *adventure.* It seemed like every month we got a call from the guidance counselor informing us of some near-disaster that had been averted. Like the time he wanted to demonstrate to his English class how he could insert the foil from chewing gum wrappers into an electrical outlet and cause a "mini explosion." Unfortunately, it also caused the breaker to go off, killing the lights as well as his teacher's computer.

Then there was the time after soccer practice he jumped on the trunk of a moving car right as the coach was coming out of the locker room. (*Mom, it was only going 5 miles per hour!*) And the day he took a dare to place himself in an empty garbage can and roll down the school ramp. We were thankful the damage was limited to a broken arm.

But one of the most classic examples is when someone on the morning school bus dared him to wax his hair. Now, we're not talking even mega-hold gel. But wax. The kind that has the potential of transforming a simple head of hair into a lethal weapon! The finished product consisted of hard, pointy spikes all over his head.

Upon arriving at school, his homeroom teacher suggested he visit the principal with his new look. On the way to the office, he suddenly got concerned his spikes might look a bit demonic. And because he didn't want the principal to think he worshipped Satan, he grabbed a marker and wrote across his forehead, God Rocks!

We've come a long way since high school, but my son still possesses that bold, adventuresome spirit. He'll take a risk, if necessary, to speak the truth. It's the way God made him. God knew him before he was formed in the womb. He knew you too. And he has a plan to use the way he made you for his glory. The more we all yield to our Creator, the more the world will see how, in my son's words, God Rocks!

March 1st

Jesus answered, "Unless I wash you, you have no part with me."
—John 13:8 NIV

Dusty Souls

Dust! It's everywhere! Everywhere! This was an accurate description of my home after workers came to install a new heating system in our two hundred-year-old farmhouse. The sawing and drilling left a gritty residue on everything from the keyboard on my computer to the clothes in my closet. And on top of that, the weather was calling for a dusting of snow, and I was reading through a student's research paper on the Dust Bowl. I was swimming in a sea of dust!

It was the kind of dust that's hard to pick up. I would wipe off a piece of furniture only to find it covered again minutes later. I vacuumed, mopped and scoured, wondering if my house would ever sparkle again. Evidently, disposing of plaster dust requires more than the light cleaning I was used to.

It's like what happens when our souls need scrubbing. God allows major upheavals in our lives as part of the reconstruction process when we are born again. We get hammered, hacked and shaken. And when the dust settles, like the sun streaming through a window, God makes visible all the dust particles we never knew were there. Particles like selfishness, jealousy, insecurity, pride, worry. We thought we needed a light cleaning. We needed so much more.

We still do. I don't know about you, but my soul continues to get dusty. My futile attempts to clean up never succeed in getting rid of all the scum. I need something bigger than me. Something purer. Something full of grace and truth.

When Jesus washed his disciples' feet at the Last Supper, Peter initially resisted. He didn't recognize his need. He must have thought his feet (and soul after three years with Jesus) looked pretty good. Left everything to follow the Lord. Walked on water. Drove out demons. Referred to as the rock on which the church would be built. With those kinds of creds, it would be hard for anyone to recognize the dust within!

But the Lord exposed Peter's lack, and he responded with unabashed abandon, "Then, Lord ... not just my feet but my hands and my head as well!" (John 13:9).

So how is your soul these days? Is it a bit dusty? I know the best Cleaner-upper.

March 2nd

Do not give a war cry, do not raise your voices, do not say a word until the day I tell you to shout. Then shout!   —*Joshua 6:10 NIV*

Wait for the Snap

Talk about needing self-control! Imagine how much self-control it must have taken Israel to obey God at Jericho. The army was full of confidence, ready to fight. Pumped to the max. Yet they were told to march—just march—around the city, not one day but six. It wasn't until the seventh day they were to shout the victory cry and then attack. The walls would fall and the city would be theirs.

Although Jericho proved to be a resounding victory, Israel did not fare as well in the next battle. In fact, they were completely routed. The cause of their defeat, however, was clear. One man did not exercise self-control. At Jericho, Achan couldn't resist. He wanted the forbidden spoils of war, and he wanted them now. So, he took some of the plunder and foolishly hid it in his tent. His lustful refusal to exercise self-control not only cost Israel the battle, it also resulted in the death of thirty-seven fellow soldiers and the stoning of his whole family. A high price.

But self-control is about more than learning to say *no* to our desires. It trains us to hear the *yes* of God's plans. It makes me think of two football teams in position before the ball is snapped. Full of passion, hyped, ready for the play to start, but similar to Israel at Jericho, they can't do what they feel like doing. They must stay in place, stretching their discipline to the nth degree because if they move too soon, they'll get penalized for a false start and lose five yards. But you can be sure that while they're waiting, they're alert. They're straining every part of themselves to be attentive to what's coming next.

And so, it is with us. Some of the battles we face require time and discipline. That's why we've been given the fruit of self-control. Failure to exercise it could be the deciding factor as to whether we win or lose. So, don't let lust take over. Wait for the snap, and then give it all you got.

March 3rd

A woman was there who had been crippled by a spirit for eighteen years. She was bent over and could not straighten up at all. When Jesus saw her, he called her forward and said to her, "Woman, you are set free from your infirmity."
—Luke 13:11-12 NIV

Boxed In

The woman had been crippled for eighteen years. Although her bones were fused together, her destiny was not bound to immobility. Jesus touched her, and as that once rigidly fixed body straightened, her whole life began to expand in new dimensions of freedom. Ah, but it was the Sabbath. Rigidity of another kind surfaced. The Pharisees hated what they saw. Their bones of legalism merged together so tightly that they allowed no movement in their view of God or man.

Although we disdain the mindset of the Pharisees, I must ask myself how many "boxed in" perspectives I allow to cripple me. I am apt to box-in myself. *I will never succeed. I have nothing to give. I'll never measure up.* If I'm not careful, my intricately constructed limitations become self-fulfilling prophesies.

Boxing in others may be subtler but no less devastating. How often do we bind people in their weaknesses? Sometimes, even after they've repented, we persist in confining them to old patterns. I knew a woman who confessed she liked her husband better when he was a drunk. Now that he was sober, she didn't know what to expect. She was forced to confront her own rigidity.

Yet the most limiting perspective of all happens when we try to box in God. We take a God whose love extends beyond the wildest of dreams—whose power, knowledge and wisdom surpasses the deepest of earthly understanding—and try to squeeze him into our puny framework. We feel more comfortable with a predictable God, safer when we maintain control. Just like the Pharisees.

But like the woman Jesus healed, we don't have to stay confined to our crippling views. His touch will liberate us again, and again and again. His ways are so much higher than ours that he can set us free from all our rigid notions about ourselves, other people and God.

I don't want to be in the Pharisee camp. Do you?

March 4th

For this is what the LORD, the God of Israel, says: "The jar of flour will not be used up and the jug of oil will not run dry until the day the LORD sends rain on the land." —1 Kings 17:14 NIV

Avoiding Bankruptcy

Rising unemployment. Fear of inflation. Businesses going bust. Mortgages underwater. Depleted savings. With all the talk of economic woes, it started me thinking of a far greater danger than the loss of money: the threat of *spiritual* bankruptcy.

Spiritual bankruptcy occurs for a variety of reasons. Often it creeps up on us when we experience a period of stagnancy or weariness. We wrongly conclude our usefulness is over and opt for some kind of premature retirement, not realizing that our most productive years may lie ahead. Winston Churchill led the free world against the ravages of Nazism in his late sixties, Ronald Reagan was reelected president of the United States at seventy-three, and Grandma Moses *started* painting at seventy-seven. Yet each one faced earlier defeats that could have derailed future fulfillment of God's purpose.

In order to avoid spiritual insolvency—keep investing, even when it seems you have nothing left to give. Remember the story in 1 Kings. A drought was ravaging Israel. A poor widow was about to use up her last bit of oil and flour to feed her family when Elijah asked her to first make him a loaf of bread. When she protested she didn't have enough, he promised if she gave what she had, she would have enough flour and oil to last throughout the drought. Her obedience resulted in a continual supply of food for her family.

What is God commissioning you to do right now? Maybe it's persevering through a rotten job. Maybe it's learning to be thankful that you have a job at all. Perhaps you have been assigned the care of an elderly parent or young child. You might be learning to forgive. Or your assignment may be trusting the Lord to be with you in the unexpected circumstance you are facing.

I don't know what it might be for you. But I do know this: the more you spend yourself completely, not only will you avoid bankruptcy, but you'll also find the riches of heaven.

March 5th

As long as it is day, we must do the works of him who sent me. Night is coming, when no one can work. —John 9:4 NIV

Missed Opportunities

The race you never ran. The book you never wrote. The old flame you never looked up. The exotic vacation you never took. All are examples of "missed opportunities in life," declares the luxury car advertisement in its appeal for you not to add *the car you never bought* to the list. The fear of "missing out" runs deep in the human psyche. Who of us wants to reach the end of life only to discover all the could-have-beens?

Sometimes the fear of living a mediocre life threatens me more than one of failure. At least if I fail, I know I've tried. I've married up, in a sense, with the universe and positioned myself for divine intervention when I reach beyond my limitations. John Piper has inferred believers' lives should be marked with radical risk. I think that's the way God designed us.

My son works for a music company in Nashville. One of the bands he manages consists of three young men who lost a close family member to an untimely death. For them, his death was a wake-up call to the brevity of life. It roused them to leave the confines of their once safe, predictable lives and take a shot at their dreams. Their willingness to take the risk and embrace the journey has already led them to places they once believed to be unattainable.

Jesus never missed an opportunity to heal, to teach, to serve. He told his disciples it was vital to work while it was day. A time of night was approaching when it would no longer be possible to accomplish his Father's work. So, he would keep healing, keep teaching and keep serving no matter how much resistance he got from the Pharisees. Nothing would stop his light from shinning in the time he was allotted.

God has significant works for you to do. Don't be afraid to cultivate the "risky radical" flavor you need to accomplish them. You don't want to wake up some day and lament all the missed opportunities.

March 6th

You are filled with grief.... But very truly I tell you, it is for your good that I am going away. —John 16:6–7 NIV

Thanks for the Memories

Ever since I heard Edith Schaeffer talk about the importance of creating memories, I've been on it. I think I have some kind of sentimentality gene in my DNA because of my penchant for wanting to make every occasion memorable. *"But Mom, it's cold and rainy." "Yes, but think of the great memory we're building!"*

Memories are purposed to foster security and stimulate faithfulness. They help us through tough times as we recall God's goodness in the past. Yet as much as I relish the sweetness memories bring, they also come with a caution: be careful not to pine for the past as a means of avoiding the present. We can long so much for what was that we miss the opportunity for what is and certainly for what will come. We don't want to be like the person who puts his hand to the plow and looks back.

I wonder if Jesus' disciples struggled with this. Did they long for the "glory days" when all the crowds were following Jesus? Did they wrestle with wanting to go back and relive what must have been extraordinary times of intimacy around evening campfires? We know they were filled with grief when he told them he was leaving. Yet he assured them his going was for their good. We don't know how long they may have lingered in the past, but thankfully for us, they took the torch and carried it forward. Had they refused, the world would be a much different place.

No matter how rich the past, it can never be relived. Loved ones pass away. Children leave home. Once tightly-knit relationships fray. As painful as change can be, God enables us to go forward by promising something new. It remains for us to take our torch and carry it to a different time, a different place.

So, the next time those misty water-colored memories come to mind, let them put a smile on your face. Enjoy them. Be thankful for the blessing of the good ones and the redemption of the bad ones. Just don't let them become a shrine that keeps you from the new adventures that lie ahead.

March 7th

If anyone would come after me, let him deny himself and take up his cross and follow me.
—Mark 8:34 ESV

En-ti-tle-ment

en·ti·tle·ment: the feeling of having a right to something.

There's been a lot of talk about "entitlements" and "entitlement reform" in our country. Most would agree that the "right to life, liberty and the pursuit of happiness" encompasses far more now than the founding fathers originally intended. Although some believe this reveals progress, others would argue the evolving "entitlement mentality" erodes both personal responsibility and individual initiative. It deceives us into thinking we're being cheated out of something we deserve if we're not provided with cell phones, contraceptives, and cable TV. When people make more money not working than working, something has gone seriously wrong. It's killing our spirit. It's also robbing our souls.

But there's a more serious kind of entitlement mentality. As believers, have we slipped into an "entitlement mentality" in our spiritual lives? Have we come to view hardship as something we don't deserve? When life gets tough, do we resent the interruption of our personal peace and affluence? Do we believe if we just do everything right, we merit a "get-out-of-pain" card? Have we forgotten that the world is, after all, fallen?

Martin Luther concluded in one of his final writings that we are all beggars. C. S. Lewis intoned that we are "jolly" beggars. We should bring our needs to Jesus not based on our rights, but on his goodness and mercy. The deeper our awareness of how much we're not entitled to, the fewer our demands, and the greater our contentment no matter what our circumstances.

Jesus left behind all his "entitlements" precisely so we would *not* get what we deserve. His sacrifice opened the door to all the riches of heaven for us self-seeking sinners. But entering requires from us the antithesis of entitlement thinking. Jesus warned if we hope to follow him, it requires we deny our self, take up the cross and follow. No clamoring for our rights. No I'm entitled attitude. Jesus paid it all; he did it all.

Let's choose not to let any mindset of spiritual entitlement rob us of becoming those jolly beggars.

March 8th

For no matter how many promises God has made, they are "Yes" in Christ. And so through him the "Amen" is spoken by us to the glory of God.
—2 Corinthians 1:20 NIV

The Age of Fickleness

How important is it to you to keep your promises? To always do what you say you will do? It used to be a given: A man is only as good as his word. Scripture refers to the godly as those who keep their word even when it hurts (Psalm 15:4). But today we live in the age of fickleness. People contradict themselves without a second thought if it benefits their cause or their convenience. As a result, broken promises lay scattered like debris after a celebration. But there's a better way.

When Paul altered his plans concerning an upcoming visit to the church in Corinth, he clarified the change was not due to planning in a "worldly manner" (2 Corinthians 1:17). He understood he represented a God who always keeps his promises, and he didn't want his actions to be misinterpreted.

Like Paul, we who follow Christ need to reflect a God who always keeps his promises by doing our best to keep ours. It begins with petty things. Do we call someone when we tell them we'll call? Do we pray for someone when we tell them we'll pray? Do we follow up with promises we make to our children? Our spouses? Our friends?

My parents divorced when I was young. My dad had a hard time following through on things he said he would do. His expected presence at birthdays and ball games was met most often with the empty bleachers of disappointment. Don't get me wrong. I believe Dad had good intentions; he simply got caught up in the moment and promised things he couldn't deliver. But it bled into my concept of God. Had it not been for Grandpa's consistent faithfulness, my image of God might have been irreparably diminished. And to sure up my views of reliability even more, God gave me a husband who would rather walk on hot coals than renege on a commitment.

Never underestimate the importance of being a person of your word. Show the world our God is one of "Yes" and "Amen."

March 9th

You have heard that it was said, "Love your neighbor and hate your enemy." But I tell you, love your enemies and pray for those who persecute you.

—Matthew 5:43–44 NIV

#Forgiveness: It's Never Out of Style

We show intolerance to those who are intolerant. We judge those who are judgmental. We readily dismiss the ideas of those who dismiss ours. Such is the state of a culture where being angry appears to be more en vogue than being charitable ... and often in the name of love. If one thing seems to be trending in today's world, it's #hatred. Hatred pollutes. It weakens our cause, no matter how noble.

When Israel entered the Promised Land, they were not to worship God in the same way the other nations worshipped their gods (Deuteronomy 12). He knew if they practiced what the surrounding culture practiced, they would soon be absorbed by its influence. It's a tricky business not to be "of the world" (John 17:16). Yet that is what every believer in Christ is called to do.

He has put you and me on the earth to mark a revolutionary path. A path edged with grace and truth. A path that refuses to be replaced with a trail of bitterness and victimization.

We will never win the world with the world's ways. We were never supposed to. Jesus established doing life a different way, a way that will always run counter to the culture. He said instead of hating our enemies, we should love them. Instead of retaliating against those who persecute us, we should pray for them. There's no room for hatred in his kingdom unless it's directed toward sin.

This doesn't mean we never get angry. Jesus, on more than one occasion, showed deep distress over sin's results. We should always be disturbed by injustice and suffering, by hypocrisy and callousness. But we need to fight it in a way that doesn't leave a residue of dirt in our hearts.

We don't have to wear the hashtag #hatred no matter how prevalent. Jesus' death and resurrection provides a hashtag for eternity. It's one that's always in style: #forgiveness.

March 10th

Truly I tell you, whatever you did for one of the least of these brothers and sisters of mine, you did for me. —Matthew 25:40 NIV

The Least of These

My brother-in-law serves as a great example of someone who sees the dignity and value of every individual. Despite living in our success-driven society, he's able to step out of the mode and recognize the source of true human worth.

He excels in seeing Christ in the "least of these." Everyone in the family loved the youngest of the siblings. But David had a special way of looking over the fact that Danny had Down syndrome. He painstakingly listened to his garbled speech and tried to make sure he understood every directive. When decisions had to be made, rather than just telling Danny what to do, he laid out the options and, if feasible, respected his choices. When their dad died, it was David who stood beside him when he took his last breath. He maintained his father's dignity—even in death—as he meticulously prepared his body for the undertaker.

Jesus' entire life stamped a mark of dignity on all people—poor shepherds, common fishermen, women, children, thieves. He didn't shy away from touching lepers, even ungrateful ones (Luke 17:17). He refused to join the legalists in condemning the sinful (John 8:11). His compassion extended to the hungry (Matthew 15:32), the self-seeking (Mark 10:21) and the unbelieving (Matthew 23:37). All "the least of these" types.

Mother Theresa famously said if we're to be with Jesus, we must touch him in his distressing disguise. That disguise may take many forms: The disfigured. The poor. The annoying. The hurtful. Maybe a spouse. A grumpy neighbor. When they look in our eyes, will they see mirrored back the dignity due them as image bearers of Christ? Will they detect warmth, tenderness and acceptance?

I don't know who the "least" in your life might be. But I pray that as you make the effort to find Christ in them, they will see Christ in you.

March 11th

By the grace of God I am what I am.   —*1 Corinthians 15:10 NIV*

What About Bob?

No one can be a better you than you. No one has had your set of life experiences to shape you into God's distinctive purpose. Everything from your accolades to your addictions comprise who you are and who, by God's grace, you are destined to become.

Nothing robs us from this truth more than the comparison trap so predominant in our culture. I'm not as successful as he is, not as pretty as she is, not as spiritual as ... You know what I mean. C. S. Lewis describes what life might be like among people in a less *bent* world in *Out of the Silent Planet,* the first of his Space Trilogy. The three "creature groups" who live on the fictional Mars—although vastly different in appearance, lifestyle and purpose—regard each other with genuine appreciation. They derive their security from knowing their creator has made them to be who they are, not someone else. And they thrive.

Comparison with others causes us to view life on a curve. How we see ourselves depends upon where we fit in relation to those who do better or do worse. Not a lot of liberty to fail. Or to walk in selfless love. Or to value our assignments. God did not intend for us to live such constrained lives.

After coming to Christ, Paul considered himself the "least of the apostles." In fact, he felt unworthy to be called an apostle at all! In his ignorance, he had persecuted the church. If anyone deserved to be disqualified from serving Christ, Paul's name should have been at the top of the list. But Paul found grace— a discovery that made it possible for him to boldly declare, "By the grace of God I am what I am." He didn't have to be like Peter or John or James. Jesus asked him to simply be Paul.

So, the next time you find yourself in the defeating throes of comparison, remember who and whose you are. Your Creator not only loves you, but he likes you or he wouldn't have made you in the first place.

Forget about Bob. Forget about Mary. Forget about your failures and successes. Go, by God's grace, about the essential work of just being you.

March 12th

Consider it pure joy, my brothers and sisters, whenever you face trials of many kinds. —James 1:2 NIV

Joy! Joy! Joy! Joy?

I've got the joy, joy, joy, joy, down in my heart.

Are you familiar with the refrain? Maybe you're a bit like me when it comes to joy. Rather than springing from the deep well of my heart, it comes and goes according to circumstances. I feel joy when Penn State wins its football game, when my classes go well or when someone compliments me. Doesn't always happen. When Penn State loses, my class is uninspired and no one notices my new haircut, my joy evaporates.

The kind of joy that comes in the morning and remains through the dark night reveals the fruit of the Spirit rooted in the wisdom of God. It enables us, as James exhorts, to face our trials without despair. James tells us to seek God's wisdom when our trials start to overwhelm us and we begin to doubt. When we ask God for wisdom to overcome, he assures us God will give us the understanding we need. We should consider that pure joy.

Godly wisdom takes the isolated parts of our life and puts them in the context of the whole story. It gives us a peek into God's sovereign plan and helps us recognize it often takes the "worst of times" for the "best" to ultimately occur. Joy flows from the understanding that everything in life—including those "trials of many kinds"—shapes our unique story for the kingdom.

Do you realize we face an opponent who tries to make us think of every trial and every loss as evidence of defeat? No wonder we lose our joy. But we don't have to. James uses Job as an example to spur us on. When Satan boasted to God he could make Job fall by unleashing trials of many kinds, God defended him. And Job's perseverance resulted in an increase of *joy*—as well as integrity. We're encouraged today by seeing "what the Lord finally brought about" (James 5:11).

I think God will defend me too. And you. I hope when life deals us blows and our landscape shakes we will let his wisdom guide us to the deeper reality. A reality where we draw from streams that bubble into inexpressible uncontainable joy! Joy! JOY!

March 13th

Continue to work out your salvation with fear and trembling, for it is God who works in you to will and to act according to his good purpose.
—Philippians 2:12–13 NIV

Buck Up

I recently re-watched the movie, *Prince Caspian,* second in the *Chronicles of Narnia* series. One observation particularly struck me. In previous battles, Aslan had run to the rescue of the Narnians. In the current conflict, however, he stood at a distance. The children were forced to "buck up" and to fight— on their own—an enemy much stronger and fiercer than they. But in the process, they became something they weren't before; they became heroes.

I sometimes forget that "God's ways are higher than our ways" (Isaiah 55:9). I get discouraged when he doesn't just step in and restore a broken relationship or provide work for someone who has lost his job. I fail to remember that God might be working something deeper and more substantial in them, that the struggles they encounter are necessary in making them into the man or woman he intends them to be.

In Paul's letter to the Philippians, he describes the process of how we become "new." As we work out our salvation with fear and trembling, the Lord works in us to complete his purpose. We don't just sit back and watch God solve all our problems. Prayer isn't a magic pill that makes the obstacles we face disappear. We learn how to tackle the trials. In so doing, we give God the access he needs to use those very difficulties to bring about the transformation of becoming "little Christs." It's a terrible, wonderful progression, and like any creative endeavor contains both agony and ecstasy. The saints call it sanctification.

If you are wondering where God might be in your present battle, why he's not rushing to the rescue, be assured he has not left you. He stands on the edge, using the conflict to turn you into something beyond nice, something with a good and holy purpose.

Buck up, my friend.

March 14th

The path of the righteous is like the morning sun, shining ever brighter till the full light of day. —Proverbs 4:18 NIV

Spring Break Perspective

What do a VW bus, a grandpa with his granddaughter and her best friend, the month of March and the beach have in common? If you guessed spring break in Florida—you would be correct. All four years of college Grandpa drove my friend and me to Daytona Beach to escape the cold weather and rigors of academia to bake in the sun with a few thousand other students. While Grandpa found a spot to camp, my friend and I pooled our money and got a motel. Grandpa was quite content to visit us on the beach each day. Little did he know, little did I know, of the enormous investment he was making in me.

As I look back on those years, it's only now I recognize how susceptible I was to influences of the world. Although I professed Christianity, my faith throughout those undergraduate years was beginning to be tested. I would soon face challenges to compromise around every corner. It wouldn't be until the end of graduate school that my faith became my own.

I've often wondered why I didn't fall away. I think it had a lot to do with those spring breaks. Oh, not the trips themselves, but their representation of my grandpa's unconditional love, and in turn, God's. It's a lot harder to reject God when you have seen him so clearly through one of his servants.

Proverbs tells us the righteous shine like the morning sun. That was my grandpa. If you're a grandparent, parent, aunt or uncle, it might be your righteousness that will light the way for them. God wants you to influence others by radiating his light. So always let your path shine ever brighter. Keep pouring out "till the full light of day."

March 15th

I praise you because I am fearfully and wonderfully made;
your works are wonderful,
I know that full well.

—*Psalm 139:14 NIV*

A Validated Parking Ticket

Validated! A word all human beings need to have stamped on their hearts.

I imagine at some point in your life, you've probably gone to a restaurant, movie or hospital and pulled into a parking garage. After parking your car, you take your ticket to the proper authority and get it stamped. That little imprint means free parking. As long as the ticket is validated, you don't have to pay.

I think many of us spend a major portion of our lives trying to "validate our parking tickets." We move from job to job or relationship to relationship looking for that elusive stamp of approval. Sometimes, even within our own families, we struggle to see where we fit. We search for something beyond ourselves to authenticate our right to be parked on the planet. Often our quest is fueled by past wounds. Powerfully depicted in movies from *Citizen Kane* to *Social Network,* it's clear that no amount of success or wealth can compensate for the need to "prove we're somebody" to those who have hurt us.

Sadly, our longing for validation can lead us into an ongoing preoccupation with self. We begin to feel unsatisfied unless we're influencing others, we get irritated with people who don't approve of us and we find discontentment with those who fail to recognize our work. It's all backwards.

Psalm 139 reveals the source of man's validation. It begins with a Creator who made us "fearfully and wonderfully." The One who wove us together in the womb, the One who knows our thoughts before we speak, the One familiar with all our ways—validates our life. God stamps us with his image, and it's all the validation we need. He is the One who "thought us up" so, of course, our life has meaning!

There's no sin in needing affirmation. Yet our identity lies in neither our failures nor our successes. So, no matter how many times we get our parking ticket validated by man, we will come up short unless we go to the real source of validation. To our Creator. Our Redeemer. He paid an incredible price to give us the authentication we crave.

March 16th

With man this is impossible, but with God all things are possible.
—Matthew 19:26 NIV

From Losing to Winning

Ever feel like you're in a lose/lose situation? You can't imagine how God could ever bring good out of this time. Finances have never dropped this low. The relationship has never been this broken. The future has never looked this gloomy. But it's often when circumstances are bleakest that God shines brightest. He can pull out a win even when it looks like a triple lose.

The Arameans had besieged the city of Samaria causing a famine that became so severe the women were even cannibalizing their children (2 Kings 7:3–9). Outside the city gate sat four men with leprosy. They, too, were starving and their options looked dismal. They could remain at the gate and die—first lose; they could go into the city and perish with the other starving people—lose/lose; or they could go to the Aramean camp and surrender where they had a chance of being spared but most likely would also die—lose/lose/lose. They decided on the third option. But a funny thing happened on the way to their deathbeds.

When they arrived at the camp, they found it to be completely abandoned! God had caused the Arameans "to hear the sound of chariots and horses and a great army" (2 Kings 7:6), They mistakenly thought Israel had hired extra forces to fight against them so they panicked and "ran for their lives." In their haste, they left everything behind—food, drink, gold, silver, horses, donkeys. The lepers reported the good news to the king of Israel and the city was saved—WIN!

Now who would have thought a miracle like that could happen? Not the citizens of Samaria. Not the lepers. They were so consumed with getting their next crust of bread that I doubt divine intervention was even considered. Although the famine occurred because of the people's rebellion, God had no intention of letting them starve to death. Such is his mercy. Such is his power.

So how about those impossible situations you are facing right now? Even those lose/lose/lose ones. Take heart. God has a WIN for you. He remains the God with whom all things are possible.

March 17th

Whom have I in heaven but you? And there is nothing on earth that I desire besides you.   —Psalm 73:25 ESV

It's No Wonder

"Christ with me, Christ before me, Christ behind me, Christ in me, Christ beneath me, Christ above me ..." You're probably familiar with St. Patrick's famously quoted prayer. But did you know there's more? He continues, "Christ on my right, Christ on my left, Christ when I lie down, Christ when I sit down, Christ when I arise, Christ in the heart of every man who thinks of me, Christ in the mouth of everyone who speaks of me, Christ in every eye that sees me, Christ in every ear that hears me."

I would guess St. Patrick desired a pretty intimate relationship with the Lord. But not just St. Patrick. Is there anything more desirous for a follower of Christ than to be surrounded by him? Yet all too often we let "fallen life" interrupt our pursuit.

In Psalm 73 Asaph looks at the world and concludes it's no use serving God. Those who reject God—the wicked, arrogant, and callous-hearted—keep winning while the righteous keep losing. The ungodly amass money; the godly amass pain. He perceived a world with an absentee God. A world devoid of any basis for hope, goodness and purity. But he wasn't seeing clearly.

He became so focused on the evil, he no longer recognized the good. It wasn't until he "entered the sanctuary of God" (Psalm 73:17) that his myopic eyes were opened to see the extent of God's presence. God had abandoned neither him nor the world. Asaph's heartfelt repentance rings through his song, "Whom have I in heaven but you? And there is nothing on earth that I desire besides you."

Have you ever been in Asaph's camp? I know I have at times. That's when I have to step back and remember. Remember all the times Jesus has been with me ... before me ... in me.... How he's been my companion in the shadows, letting me discover grace I never thought I'd need. How he's gone ahead of me, providing experiences beyond my wildest imagination. It makes me desire him even more.

How about you? Maybe this is a good time to remember all the times he's there, by your side, on your side ... like no other.

It's no wonder we want to be surrounded with Jesus, is it? It's no wonder.

March 18th

Nazareth! Can anything good come from there?

—John 1:46 NIV

Trash Collectors

One of my students was struggling to come up with a topic for her narrative speech when she remembered a high school art project. She had constructed a mural consisting of literal pieces of "trash," discarded items no one had further need of. Yet in the middle of her display, she fashioned the semblance of a cross. The message was subtle, yet powerful: Jesus stands in the middle of the broken, cast away pieces of our lives to create something beautiful. She told the story—her story—of how God had used her to reach out to the "discarded people" in her school. She befriended those whom others avoided. She embraced the lonely, the unpopular, the rejected. Like the cross on her mural, she offered hope to lives littered with the debris of pain.

Not many of us have the talent to artistically display God's call in our lives as my student. But I think most of us have encountered the blight of unwantedness, maybe in the eyes of a teenage girl begging for her father's affection, in the confused look of the elderly no longer deemed useful in our youth-driven culture, in the daze of people who've been thrown under the bus by one-time confidants. God wants us to bring them the good news of the gospel.

Do you know we're commissioned by our Redeemer to be his "trash collectors" on the earth? He commissions us to let people know how he can transform the rubbish of their lives to make them a masterpiece (Ephesians 2:10).

Can anything good come out of Nazareth? Iran? China? Venezuela? Is there anything that can be salvaged in New York City? Washington, D.C.? Lancaster, PA? Can restoration come from lives torn by addiction, abuse and poverty? My student's artwork reminds me God says *Yes!*

March 19th

We are not ignorant of his schemes.

—2 Corinthians 2:11 NASB

A Relentless Foe

Want to know the kind of enemy we believers face?

For a peek behind the curtain of spiritual warfare take a look at the sixth chapter of Nehemiah. Nehemiah returned to Jerusalem to help his countrymen rebuild its broken walls and repair its gates. But this did not sit well with his adversaries— Sanballat, Tobiah & Co. They sent word for Nehemiah to meet them in an isolated place. Four times (the enemy is persistent) Nehemiah was asked to and four times he refused. He knew they were scheming to harm him.

When the attempt on Nehemiah's life failed, they tried to kill his spirit. They sent out letters accusing Nehemiah of leading a revolt and seeking to make himself king over Judah. It wasn't true, but Sanballat hoped the false accusations would bring so much discouragement to Nehemiah that he would just give up. When Nehemiah didn't succumb to despair, the enemy tried a third ploy.

He tried to lure Nehemiah into moral and spiritual compromise. A false prophet urged Nehemiah to hide in the Temple because of the threat to his life. But Nehemiah was not authorized to enter the Temple. His entering would have been breaking the Law to save his own skin. Such sin would have discredited his reputation and undermined his authority. Nehemiah would have none of it.

Do any of these tactics sound familiar? Has Satan ever tried to literally wipe you out? Has he ever overwhelmed you with false accusations to make you feel like giving up? Has he ever tried to sneak things that don't belong there into the "temple" of your spirit to compromise your spiritual authority—things like grudges, pride, fear?

Don't be ignorant of his schemes. Satan's strategies don't change much. But neither do our opportunities to defeat him. Nehemiah prevailed not because he was particularly courageous or wise or strong. He knew his own fortitude waned against such a persistent adversary. So, with great consistency he turned to the One who was greater than any enemy he faced.

If we hope to meet a relentless foe with a resounding no we too must rely on God. Completely. The battle is too great and too much is at stake to depend on anything or anyone other than him.

March 20th

The whole assembly then agreed to celebrate the festival seven more days; so for another seven days they celebrated joyfully.
—2 Chronicles 30:23 NIV

Party Like a Christian

Have you ever heard the term "party like a Christian"? Neither have I.

But the very foundation of our faith reflects a God who calls for celebrations, and lots of them. Those Israelites knew how to party. When King Hezekiah called the people to celebrate the Passover, they were so filled with joy they decided to extend the celebration for another seven days. And God was pleased. He approved of his people celebrating his goodness for a full two weeks!

In the Old Testament, God commanded Israel to celebrate seven annual holidays amounting to thirty days a year. If weekly Sabbaths are included, the number rises to eighty! According to author Randy Alcorn in his book *Happiness*, the "main reason for celebrations is to help us recognize and enjoy God's goodness." I'd call that a pretty worthy purpose. Can you imagine that happening today?

I think we do the world a great disservice when we fail to incorporate God-centered celebration into our lives. Yes, sin and sorrow floods us. We live in a world wrought with injustice, suffering and heartache. All the more reason for believers to demonstrate, in spite of all the bad things surrounding us, good will not be eclipsed. God promises light will always overcome darkness. And's that's something that should cause us to click our heels and break out the wine of gladness.

The world describes those who "party hardy" as celebrating without restraint, of entering a type of self-indulgent free fall. I think it's about time for us to take back the definition of partying.

Let's party, my Christian friends. Celebrate God's goodness. Sing, dance, shout for joy. The world remains gloomy, but we look beyond its restrictions. Jump right in the "river whose streams make glad the city of God" (Psalm 46:4 ESV). Join with all of God's creation—heavens, earth, sea—and rejoice (Psalm 96:11). Be happy and full of joy, because the Lord has done a wonderful thing (Joel 2). Go ahead. Party with all your heart.

Party like a Christian!

March 21st

And if anyone gives even a cup of cold water to one of these little ones who is my disciple, truly I tell you, that person will certainly not lose their reward.

—Matthew 10:42 NIV

Tangible Compassion

People need to experience compassion in a tangible form.

Rod attended the church my grandpa pastored for as long as I can remember. Although he rarely missed a meeting, he had never confessed Christ as his Savior. It wasn't that he didn't know his condition; he was fully aware there was something he refused to release. Years before, his youngest son had been killed in a street fight. Rod could not let go of the revenge he harbored for his son's assailant. But he continued to be a regular at Rehoboth Mission.

As Grandpa and Grandma aged, they began to have trouble getting around. Rod and his wife loved my grandparents. They started picking them up for every church service. They took them to the grocery store and out to dinner. There was nothing Grandpa and Grandma had need of that Rod wasn't there to meet. He embodied the passage in Matthew that describes the person who gives a cup of cold water to one of Christ's disciples. And at long last, Rod received his reward. I remember it, because it's noted in the margin of my Bible next to Matthew 10:42: *Rod M., winter '88.* That's when Rod accepted Christ as Savior.

Although this passage may well be referring to rewards in heaven, I believe the Lord also enjoys granting earthly blessings to those who give to his children. Remember the Shunammite woman who prepared the room for Elijah; her barrenness was replaced with a son due to her kindness (2 Kings 4:8–17). Cornelius' gifts to the poor had "come up as a memorial offering before God" and as a result he became the first Gentile to hear the good news (Acts 10:4).

There are many people over the years who have given me "cups of cold water." Small acts of kindness, especially in hard times, have quenched my soul's thirst for concrete evidence of God's love. I pray for their reward. I pray, too, that the Spirit would give me opportunities to refresh other parched and weary pilgrims. How about you?

May you and I be vessels of tangible compassion in this very needy world.

March 22nd

You will be hated by everyone because of me, but the one who stands firm to the end will be saved.

—Matthew 10:22 NIV

Standing Firm

Early one morning, I was reading in Matthew 26 how Jesus stood firm during his arrest and trial. Judas betrayed him. The rest of his disciples deserted him. He stood alone before the Sanhedrin and endured one false accusation after another. It culminated with slimy spit, mocking slaps, sucker punches and demands for his death. Desecration.

After reading the passage, I happened to drive over to our church. I was sickened by what I saw. There, in the front lawn, I was greeted with deep cuts left by someone's four-wheeler activity. The ugly ruts crisscrossed the yard, leaving what seemed like a minor degree of the desecration against Christ's body I had just read about.

Today, Christ's body—the church—continues to be pummeled. Whether marred by tire tracks or graffiti, the target of vandals or an arsonist's torch—physical damage to the church occurs throughout the world. That kind of destruction can be repaired. It's not the attacks launched against wood and concrete structures but against the body of believers who comprise the church that poses the greatest challenge. Will we, like Jesus, stand firm no matter what flies against us?

Jesus warned identification with him would not win us popularity contests. He said if men hated him, they would hate us as well. But we live in a society that finds its security in how other people perceive us. We crave others' approval and admiration. If we're not careful, when someone demeans the body of Christ, we throw our hat in the ring to show how enlightened and, therefore, how relevant we are.

Our job as the body of Christ is to stand firm in following Jesus, no matter the repercussions—even if all men hate us. The church consists of imperfect people. We will always need a Redeemer to clean up the residue of tire tracks and graffiti in our lives, whether rising from within the church or outside its borders. But if we follow Jesus and "stand firm to the end," we will mark a path that leads others to salvation.

How about you? Will you stand firm to the end?

March 23rd

Then I heard the voice of the Lord saying, "Whom shall I send? And who will go for us?" And I said, "Here am I. Send me."

—*Isaiah 6:8 NIV*

What's in Store Today?

Do you ever feel stuck in your weaknesses? Sometimes the awareness of my inadequacies has a paralyzing effect on my outlook.

I was having one of those mornings when my Scripture reading took me to Isaiah 6. In the presence of the Lord Isaiah became so conscious of his unworthiness that he cried, "Woe to me! I am ruined!" (Isaiah 6:5). In response to his anguish, an angel took a coal from the altar of God and touched his "unclean lips," declaring him free from guilt and sin. It was then the prophet could say with utter abandon, "Here I am. Send me." His transformation inspired me.

Rather than continuing to focus on my inadequacies, I made an intentional decision to let the "coal" burn through my tainted thoughts. I asked, "Father, what great things do you have in store for us today?" A list of possibilities came to mind: invite some folks for dinner, send an encouraging note, cut a check for a missionary friend in need, treat someone the way I would want to be treated if I were in a similar situation. And that was just the beginning. It was amazing how, in the words of storybook Alexander, the beginnings of a *terrible, horrible, no good, very bad day* converted into *Great Expectations*.

How much time and opportunity do we squander because we dwell on our weaknesses? How long do we linger in shame and guilt when we ought to be about works created for us to do before the foundation of the earth? Don't hesitate, my friend. When the Spirit says to your heart, "Whom shall I send?" join with this fellow imperfect child of God and let's declare with Isaiah, "Here I am. Send me!"

March 24th

But they that wait upon the LORD shall renew their strength.
—Isaiah 40:31 KJV

Change by Degrees

We want change and we want it now! It's a sentiment we've all experienced at one time or another. Whether in recovering from sickness, struggling in a relationship, or in how we see the direction of the country, we abhor waiting. We long to "turn the corner," not shift by degrees. But most change in life occurs slowly, by degrees. And there is reason for it.

The waiting seasons give us opportunity to cultivate trust in God. And trust is vital, because without trust, we can never grow in the fullness of walking with him. According to Psalm 50:8–15, God prefers we trust him in our troubles over any sacrifice we might make. Trust indicates we love God more than we love our own thinking. It means we *believe* he knows best and has our best in mind. Facing "change by degrees" provides the perfect place for us to practice trust.

During my recent illness, I was struck by comments like, "You look a lot better." "Your voice sounds so much stronger." I wasn't feelin' it. Aside from the fact that a week in the hospital without washing my hair was a pretty low bar of comparison, I had a hard time thinking I looked better when I still felt bad. Although I knew I was gaining strength each day, my recovery was taking far longer than I anticipated. So, it felt like no progress was occurring.

Not recognizing the "degrees of change" pushes us into discouragement. Whether recuperating from a sickness or persevering in praying for what seems like a lost cause, we must learn to fully rely on God in the process. Are we going to trust him with the whole thing or delegate the timing part to ourselves?

Isaiah declared centuries ago, "They that wait upon the Lord shall renew their strength." That oft quoted passage reminds us our weariness is not permanent. He will revitalize us until we "soar like eagles" if we wait. Let's not get bogged down when our victories and changes come by degrees. Rather, let's embrace the opportunity to trust in God's way. In God's purpose. In God's time.

March 25th

Behold, I create new heavens and a new earth; And the former things will not be remembered or come to mind.   —Isaiah 65:17 NASB

Have a New Day

I recently received news that the chronic illness of a longtime friend is nearing its end. Her husband reported that although his wife is slipping away, the peace of God surrounds them. They both know the cancer consuming her life has no power to block the new body that awaits her. *New.*

Isaiah speaks a lot about the *new* coming our way. So much *new* that we won't even remember the "former things." In Chapter 65 he expounds on some of these things that will be forgotten:

- Untimely death: "Never again will there be in [his kingdom] an infant who lives but a few days, or an old man who does not live out his years" (v. 20).
- Unrewarded work: "No longer will they build houses and others live in them, or plant and others eat" (v. 22).

- Unrealized legacies: "They will not ... bear children doomed to misfortune" (v. 23).
- Unheard cries and unanswered prayer: "Before they call I will answer; while they are still speaking I will hear" (v. 24).

Dark devastating events that cause sleepless nights, anguished tears and overwhelming sadness—all vanish in the brilliance of the new. I think it's a perspective God wants us to develop now. Today. He desires his children to cultivate a view of the *new*.

We can receive new mercies every morning, no matter how badly we missed it the day before. We can walk in a new covenant that moves us from a relationship characterized by reading the manual to one where we are invited into the office. Each day offers the option to sip *new* wine, sing new lyrics and think new thoughts.

Prepare now for the new heavens and new earth. Go ahead. Go beyond having a *good* day. Have a *new day!*

March 26th

Blessed is the king who comes in the name of the Lord!
—Luke 19:38 NIV

What is Victory?

Hosanna to the Son of David!" shouts the crowd as Jesus enters Jerusalem. He's riding on a colt, just as it was prophesied centuries before the Messiah would do (Zechariah 9:9). Some lay their cloaks on the road before him; others wave tree branches as a way of showing him honor. We refer to Palm Sunday as the "triumphal entry." But the joy of the "triumphal entry" lasted only a moment. Although the oblivious crowd seemed to be going crazy with praise and adoration, Jesus knew better.

It would be another seven days before the actual victory—the final one—the costly one—occurred. He literally had to go to

Hell and back to secure it. But secure it he did. No shortcuts. No altered goalposts. How about us? How do we define victory?

Is victory having a good church or a God church? Is it landing a book on the *New York Times* bestseller list or knowing one's writing makes a difference? Is it basking in our goodness or dying to our self so God's goodness can be revealed through us? On a broader scale, is victory winning an election or governing well? Although our culture increasingly favors image over reality, the success it guarantees eventually falls short.

The rush to declare victory may promise a bypass around the challenges we face, but it can't deliver. Before the sigh of relief leaves our mouth, the win starts to wane. The kind of victory Jesus offers is unshakeable. Complete. Lasting.

True victory occurs when we value what God values. When we look past the surface and refuse to let the opinions of others shape our concept of winners and losers. I'm sure the world viewed the early Christians as pretty big failures. They were mocked, scorned and persecuted for their faithfulness. But the fruit of their victory remains evident two thousand years later in the heart of every believer.

Don't be deceived. Consider whether your wins are consistent with God's wins. If not, reject that premature victory lap, re-lace your shoes, and get back in the race.

March 27th

In love a throne will be established; in faithfulness a man will sit on it—one from the house of David—one who in judging seeks justice and speeds the cause of righteousness. —Isaiah 16:5 NIV

Love Plus Judgment Equals Justice

Justice. The concept of justice resounds as a refrain in the human spirit. Most of us feel incensed when we see the "bad guys" getting away with wrongdoing and the innocent bearing the brunt of injustice. We were created to want the *right* thing to happen, and we feel everything from discomfort to downright outrage when justice is thwarted.

The Bible has a lot to say about justice. Isaiah tells us the God whose throne is established in love seeks justice in his judging. That tells me the combination of love and judgment equals justice. Judgment without love does not result in justice, nor does love without judgment. Therein lies the rub.

The challenge for Christians today comes in integrating both factors. We have to fight the cultural pressure to cave when accused of being "judgmental" every time we take a moral stand. But every stand we take must originate from a "throne of love." We judge because we care deeply, not just about the right prevailing, but because of the people involved.

Jesus presents the perfect illustration of judgment plus love in his confrontation with the rich young ruler (Mark 10:17–22). He judged accurately that the man was trapped by his wealth. So, he told him to go and give everything away to the poor. But before delivering such a dire directive, Scripture says Jesus looked at the young man and loved him. He took the time to see him—really see him. He recognized wealth had become a hindrance to the true treasure. With compassion, Jesus challenged him to let his money go. Love-motivated judgment—justice—met the young man that day.

The rich young ruler walked away. Justice doesn't always make people do the right thing. But it opens the door. As Christians, it's what we should be about.

Justice—love plus judgment = justice.

March 28th

"My food," said Jesus, "is to do the will of him who sent me and to finish his work."
                                                                    —John 4:34 NIV

Where's the Beef?

Nothing matters more than being in God's will. It sustains. It nourishes. It satisfies.

I had spent the last few days in solitude about seven hours from home. Drinking in God's Word as well as the surrounding beauty was a pleasant "assignment" to say the least. All other responsibilities faded as I focused on the tasks at hand—studying, praying and attempting to put my thoughts together like the pieces of a puzzle.

Into this near-idyllic state entered a call from my husband reporting he had taken my eighty-seven-year old mother to the emergency room. She was having trouble breathing, and it became apparent she needed intervention. He spent the entire day in the hospital with her as she underwent various tests, scans and x-rays. He had just returned home to call and tell me of the day's events.

I wish I could paint a clear picture for you. As my husband was reporting the details of Mom's situation, I sat on a bench next to the lake gazing at an incredibly beautiful sunset. My peaceful surroundings contrasted sharply with his hectic day. I began to feel more than a few qualms of guilt that I wasn't there.

I began to apologize profusely when my husband stopped me. He assured me he was doing exactly what God had planned for him that day. I didn't hear in his voice even a hint of frustration or weariness; I heard someone energized and satisfied, someone who sounded a lot like me. Both of us in very different situations, but both of us fulfilled as we embraced God's will.

Once when Jesus' disciples urged him to eat, he told them he had food they knew nothing about. They were perplexed. Had someone slipped him a fig bar? He explained the source of his nourishment: doing the will of the Father. He spent his whole time on the earth completing the work God assigned him to do. It provided all he needed.

It will for us as well. Whether we find ourselves in a place of solitude or in the noisiness of an ER, whether our plans go exactly as anticipated or are drastically altered, only one thing counts. Are we choosing the food of his will?

March 29th

Your love, LORD, reaches to the heavens,
your faithfulness to the skies.
Your righteousness is like the highest mountains,
your justice like the great deep.

— *Psalm 36:5–6 NIV*

What Is Your Default Mechanism?

I think as humans, we have our own default mechanisms. From the alcoholic who gravitates to a drink to the shopaholic looking for the next deal. From the liberal politician who instinctively leans left on every issue, to the conservative who tilts right. We all have them. They are the places where we almost seem "preset" to go. When we feel insecure, afraid, discouraged, worried—it's how we instinctively act in order to regain our footing. Two of the most common include fight or flight.

Fight. When life gets out of hand, the fight default uses anger to gain control and restore order. This mechanism tells us if we shout loudly enough or dictate strongly enough those responsible for the turmoil will somehow yield to our will. And although the fight default gives temporary relief, control tends to damage everyone it touches.

Flight. This default mechanism appears to provide a place of safety where the blows and bruises of life can't reach us. We withdraw because we feel like the ultimate loser. *What's the use?* It's easier to hide behind walls of isolation than risk further hurt. But the price of separation runs terribly high.

Those who look to God in challenging times have another option. In Psalm 36 David expresses his sense of being overwhelmed by the vast sinfulness surrounding him. Yet his automatic response was to neither fight nor flight. His place of default can be found in verses 5–6. David's default mechanism—the place where he instinctively turned in time of trouble—was the sovereign might and endless love of God.

So how about you? What do you turn to when life gets hard? Control? Anger? Withdrawal? Self-indulgence? Let God overhaul your system. He wants to lead you to a default mechanism that never fails.

March 30th

If anyone would come after me, let him deny himself and take up his cross daily and follow me.
                                                                    —*Luke 9:23 ESV*

Where Is Your Gethsemane?

Had there been no Gethsemane, there would have been no Calvary.

Gethsemane thrust Jesus into the once-and-for-all crucible of decision. Gethsemane—where sorrow pummeled him to the ground with the plea of whether there was another way. Gethsemane—where stark aloneness flooded him as his closest companions slept. Gethsemane—where anguished resolution released the most vital words ever spoken: "not my will, but yours be done" (Luke 22:42). The garden of Gethsemane prepared Jesus for the cross.

Those who want to follow Jesus face the same dilemma. The decision to die to our own wants and desires precedes the actual taking up of whatever cross we are to bear. Whether in big decisions or small, we first must wrestle with the challenge of self-denial. We have a real choice. And we have it, according to this passage in Luke, daily.

I think we sometimes overlook the importance of those daily opportunities to exercise self-denial. I'm not suggesting we dive into an aesthetic lifestyle of legalism. That's certainly not what Jesus modeled. No one denied himself more than Jesus and no one lived a fuller life. The heart of the matter lies less in outward actions and more in the soul's disposition. Taking up the cross without denying oneself is the mark of the Pharisee. That's why it is imperative to go first to the Garden.

It reminds me of a story I read about Billy Graham. At the dedication of his library, he was asked what he thought about it. He responded, "I've been here at the library once, and my one comment when I toured it was that it is too much Billy Graham." His words reflect a life-pattern of consistently denying the lure of self-focus in order to serve Christ.

So where is your Gethsemane? Are there places where you need to surrender your will? I pray you choose to deny yourself and take up the cross. Then, for the joy set before you, wholeheartedly, unconditionally, enthusiastically follow Jesus.

March 31st

Jesus turned and said to Peter, "Get behind me, Satan! You are a stumbling block to me; you do not have in mind the concerns of God, but merely human concerns." —Matthew 16:23 NIV

Unintended Consequences

From the war on terror to the war on poverty—good intentions can run amuck when we look at life solely from man's perspective, as in the situation with Peter cited above.

When Jesus told the disciples he was going to be killed at the hands of the high priests and elders, Peter bristled at such injustice, proclaiming it would never happen. Not on his watch! No doubt Peter's love for Jesus drove him. He wanted to help Jesus avoid any kind of suffering. But his protests were Satan's guise to tempt Jesus to circumvent the hard work of completing God's will and instead saving himself. Had Peter succeeded, the unintended consequences would have been astronomical.

Peter unwittingly played right into Satan's hands. Satan used natural "human concerns" to appeal to Peter's sense of right and wrong. Jesus didn't deserve to die. He shouldn't be the victim of an unjust religious system. Peter's indignation kept him from seeing the bigger picture: the wrong was necessary for the right.

When our perspective originates from "merely human concerns"—without God's—unintended consequences result. Scripture tells us all things work together for good for those who love God (Romans 8:28). We can bank on it. The problem comes when we misconstrue what the good looks like. That's when our thinking becomes a stumbling block.

We never have to worry about unintended consequences when we act from God's vantage. "For the wisdom of this world is foolishness in God's sight" (1 Corinthians 3:19). We can't let our zeal for justice, empathy for the hurting or even self-preservation cloud our perspective. The wisdom of the world never tells us we must lose our life to save it. The wisdom of God says we must. Our daily adherence to this carries intended consequences—the eternal kind.

So, don't be overwhelmed with human concerns. Trust God. Look for his perspective in your relationships and your work, in your triumphs and in your tragedies.

April 1st

Brothers and sisters, we do not want you to be uninformed about those who sleep in death, so that you do not grieve like the rest of mankind, who have no hope. —1 Thessalonians 4:13 NIV

Life, Death, and Incongruity

I woke up the first day of April to find a light dusting of snow covering the ground. This was not an expected occurrence in southeastern Pennsylvania. Birds chirping. Forsythia starting to bloom. Garden plowed and ready for planting. Not the time for winter's lingering coldness. I couldn't escape the overwhelming sense of incongruity. The night before I had watched as the undertaker took the body of my dear friend from the warmth of her home and family to be prepared for burial. She who was so filled with life and faith, now still and silent, beyond our reach. Not the time for death's coldness.

We were created for life. I think that's why we humans have such a fierce reaction to death. Even though Jesus knew he was going to be raising Lazarus from the grave, when he saw the weight of grief carried by Mary he was "deeply moved in spirit and troubled" (John 11:33). Death was an aberration, a deviation, an abnormality—the result of a fallen world. Its presence disturbed the Creator and Giver of life. No wonder it disturbs us as well, this uninvited guest, this intruder.

So, we grieve. We weep. We mourn.

Yet for believers, that's not where it ends. Paul tells us not to grieve as those who have no hope. Although we can't comprehend, on this side, what it is, we know enough from Scripture not to view death as final but as the next phase to something that never dies. Life does not conclude with a period, but an ellipsis, those three little dots (...) that tell the reader something is missing from the sentence. Those dots indicate there is more the writer is thinking than what is revealed. And so, it is with eternity.

I love to think of my friend, Barb, in heaven now. She's rejoicing in God's pleasure over her story. In perfect health and happiness, she's praising him, singing "All Things Are Possible" at the top of her lungs. For her, all the incongruities of life have vanished. And for us who remain a while longer ... we hope.

April 2nd

As Scripture says, "Anyone who believes in him will never be put to shame."

—Romans 10:11 NIV

Not Your Typical Messiah

John the Baptist. Elijah. A prophet come back to life. A lot of false notions about Jesus filled the Judean landscape. Peter knew the truth about who Jesus was—the Messiah of God. But he and the other disciples had their own misperceptions about what exactly that meant.

The Jewish community expected the Messiah would overthrow the Romans and establish himself as the king over Israel. They had no concept of the kind of kingdom he was advancing. The thought of a Messiah who would be rejected by the religious leaders and crucified by the Romans did not compute, even with the disciples. That's not what victory looked like! That is until Jesus came and turned everything upside down.

Jesus was not your typical Messiah. Neither was his message. Jesus recognized talk of carrying crosses and laying down lives would be hard for his disciples to hear, even harder to comprehend. He knew his words ran counter to all their preconceived ideas. But if they pursued victory/success as defined by the world, it would cause them to lose their souls (Luke 9:25).

How do we respond when Jesus doesn't act in the way we expect? When he doesn't answer our prayers like we thought he would? When the world doesn't stand up and applaud the righteous life he calls his followers to live? Are we tempted to be ashamed of him and his message? Jesus warns us of the severe consequences of misappropriated shame. If we are ashamed of him, he will be ashamed of us when he comes in his glory (Mark 8:38).

We will never be ashamed of Jesus if we understand he's not your typical Messiah. He's not confined by our assessments and expectations any more than he was by the empty tomb. Oswald Chamber writes in *My Utmost for His Highest*, "Our greatest fear is not that we will be damned, but that somehow Jesus Christ will be defeated." But we ought not fear.

Our not-your-typical-Messiah, Jesus Christ, will never be defeated! Do you believe that? I hope so, because those who believe in him will never be ashamed.

April 3rd

Who is a God like you, who pardons sin and forgives?
—*Micah 7:18 NIV*

Redemption: Nobody Does It Better Than God

"Easter is my favorite time of the year" echoes through my mind during Passion Week. My dad often spoke those endearing words the last few years of his life. It's no wonder. After sixty-five years of rebellion and regret, the power of Easter's claim broke through and Dad's life changed dramatically. He never tired of telling people about God's forgiveness for a sinner like him. Dad became Exhibit #1 of a redeemed life. He knew no one could have put the pieces of his life back together like God.

God has always been in the redeeming business. Always.

Even when Israel sunk to a new low. Years of spurning God's love and law resulted in complete misery. The prophet Micah lamented not one righteous man could be found in the land. He described those who remained as "skilled in doing evil" (Micah 7:3). They were blue ribbon winners when it came to murder, deceit and corruption. Treachery saturated the culture to such an extent people couldn't even trust the members of their own family.

If any nation lived beyond the borders of redemption, it would appear to be Israel. Yet into this quagmire of desperation rings the prophet's confident voice. "But as for me, I watch in hope for the LORD, I wait for God my Savior; my God will hear me" (Micah 7:7). Micah had reason to hope. He knew there was no one like the God of Israel who could and would forgive sin. Could and would pardon every iniquity. Could and would move them from defeat back to victory. Micah understood that God was in the redeeming business.

I don't know where your hope lies. Maybe you're facing circumstances that seem cast beyond redemption's reach. You think nothing—no one—can put the pieces back together. You might be right. Right, that is, if you remove God from the redeeming business.

This Easter season God wants to remind you no one does redemption better than him. As surely as Jesus rose from the grave, that's how sure you can be of God's incredible, supernatural ability to redeem the pieces of your life. Let the message of Easter resurrect your hope in this favorite time of the year.

April 4th

Being deeply grieved, they each one began to say to Him, "Surely not I, Lord?"
—Matthew 26:22 NASB

Surely Not I

Passover. The last Passover Jesus would celebrate with his disciples. It was the one he "eagerly desired" to share with them before his suffering. At this Passover, broken bread and poured out wine would leave an indelible mark. A common towel and basin of water would be used by the Master to reveal the Servant of love. And during this cherished, intimate meal Jesus would make the startling statement that one among them would betray him. *What?*

It must have sent shock waves through the gathering. Scripture describes their bewilderment. "It's not me, is it?" each one cried. They had been with Jesus long enough to be acquainted with their fallen nature. And they loved him enough to face the horror of the potential lying within their hearts. Although Judas did betray Jesus, all the others deserted him and Peter disowned him three times.

Fast forward a few centuries. I'm not seated at a table eating a Passover meal with Jesus. I don't have a crust of bread to dip into the wine. My feet aren't covered with Palestine dust and in need of being washed. But like the disciples, I've been around the Master long enough to recognize some pretty dark areas in my heart. And in the light of his love, I shudder at the thought I might be the one who would betray him, desert him or disown him. "Surely not I, Lord?" echoes through my own impoverished spirit.

Ah, but that's not the end of the story.

What began as an aching question concerning their loyalty to the Lord ended in a resounding affirmation. Emboldened by the power of the Holy Spirit, not one of those disciples ever deserted him again. History records that each man faced martyrdom for the sake of Christ, and although John did not die as a martyr, he lived as one, exiled from all human contact on the Island of Patmos. Their once wavering reaction of "Surely not I?" had been transformed into an unequivocal, "Surely not I."

You and I today can live with that same confidence. When tempted to betray our Lord, we can shout to the heavens, "Surely not I, Lord! Surely not I!"

April 5th

But Jesus answered, "No more of this!" And he touched the man's ear and healed him.

—Luke 22:51 NIV

Humanness

Sometimes our humanness just plain stinks—especially when we fail to recognize it. We think we are doing the "Lord's will," but our motivation is fueled more by our flesh than the Holy Spirit. It's comforting to know we serve a God who understands our fallen nature. A God who offers redemption.

Peter certainly ranks high as one with occasional outbursts of humanness. When the soldiers came to arrest Jesus, Peter sought to defend him. He pulled out his sword and sliced off the ear of Malchus, the chief priest's servant. Peter's misplaced zeal, however, was not overlooked. Jesus rebuked him. He then performed one last miracle before the cross. He touched the man's ear and healed him. He covered the mess Peter had made.

I hate to think of how many times my words or actions have reflected my human nature more than God's. How many times I've suffered outbreaks of humanness. How many "ears" I may have cut off in my defense of Christ. Yet no matter how misguided, how far I've missed the mark, the hope of redemption remains fixed. Rather than being weighed down with a barrel of guilt over my mistakes, I find forgiveness. And if that isn't remarkable enough, the Lord turns my messes into healing and restoration.

Although Scripture doesn't tell us what happened to Malchus, my guess is he was never the same after that touch from Jesus. I think the Lord wants us to know that whatever damage we have caused in our flesh, it is not the end of the story. Redemption is always at work. Oswald Chambers writes in *My Utmost for His Highest*, "Reality is not human goodness, nor holiness, nor heaven nor hell; but Redemption." Without that reality, I think many of us would throw in the towel.

Redemption. Oh, how I love that word. How I love the One who has brought it.

April 6th

When he came back, he again found them sleeping, because their eyes were heavy.
—Matthew 26:43 NIV

While They Were Sleeping

Jesus agonized in Gethsemane. The inconceivable awareness of the power of sin produced such anguish that his sweat took the form of blood (*hematidrosis*). For the first time, his will conflicted with his Father's, and it caused excruciating pain. His sorrow ran deeper than any human being will ever suffer. The most severe trial of his time on earth had arrived. And what were his closest companions doing? They were sleeping.

Jesus had told them to keep watch, to pray, to be on guard so as not to fall into sin's trap. But they slept. They slept until the betrayer came, leading a crowd armed with swords, clubs and a deadly kiss. When they finally awoke—the nightmare began.

It wasn't the first time Jesus warned his followers to keep watch. When he described the coming end of the age he cautioned them to remain alert. "Therefore keep watch because you do not know when the owner of the house will come back.... If he comes suddenly, do not let him find you sleeping. What I say to you I say to everyone: 'Watch!'" (Mark 13:35–37).

I guess that *everyone* includes us. We live in a world that appears to be plunging into destruction at an alarming speed. Are we ignoring the signs? Are we turning our heads over on our pillows because we think there's nothing we can do? There was nothing the disciples could have done to prevent Jesus' arrest. Yet he told them to watch and pray so that they wouldn't give in to temptation. One of the saddest verses in Scripture validates his caution: "Then all the disciples deserted him and fled" (Matthew 26:56).

There will be a time to rest. But that day has not yet come. Let's not to be lulled to sleep. Let's always be on guard and keep the severity of trials and the corruption of our surroundings from stunning our sensitivities. We have to stay in the arena, alert, attentive and ready to act.

You don't want to find yourself akin to those in Gethsemane—those friends of Jesus who fell asleep—do you?

April 7th

When he had received the drink, Jesus said, "It is finished." With that, he bowed his head and gave up his spirit.

—John 19:30 NIV

Last Words and the Beginning of Hope

A person's last words carry a hefty punch. I cared for my dad the final week of his life, and whenever he called my name, I was on it. I didn't want to miss a syllable. I experienced the same with my mother a few years later. I hung on every word she said, right up to her last breath.

So, what about the last words of the most important person who ever lived? Scripture tells us that although Jesus was fully God, he emptied himself of his divine nature to become man (Philippians 2:6–8). His last words—those uttered on the cross—reveal the extent of his humanity and offer us hope in our own humanness.

He experienced thirst, rejection, abandonment and excruciating pain. Every downside of the human condition fell on his head. Divine intervention was nowhere to be found. "My God, my God, why have you forsaken me?" (Matthew 27:46). Yet he refused to stay in that utter sense of abandonment.

Rather than letting his anguish dull his sensitivity to others, Jesus never stopped showing compassion. He assured the thief he would be with him in paradise that very day. He directed John to take care of his mother. He asked God to forgive those who tortured him.

This, my friend, should usher us into hope. Hope we don't have to remain stuck in our suffering. Jesus, as man, overcame, and because he did, so can we. He not only showed us the way, but has promised to give us the Holy Spirit to empower us to rise from our pain. And not only that, with his last declaration as he committed his spirit to God, he gave us hope we too can complete our assignment on the earth. Someday you and I can say with satisfaction, "It is finished."

So, let those last words of Jesus sink into your heart and renew your hope. They are too important to miss. Take heart!

April 8th

Early on the first day of the week, while it was still dark, Mary Magdalene went to the tomb and saw that the stone had been removed from the entrance. —John 20:1 NIV

Stones of Reproach

These acts shattered steel, but they can't dent the steel of American resolve." Those words of President George W. Bush sum up the mindset at the 9/11 Memorial where the World Trade Center once stood. After eleven years of nonstop clean-up and construction, three thousand workers, plus hundreds of security guards and policemen stationed throughout the site, the work reached completion.

When my husband and I visited the Memorial, it was impossible not to revisit the horrors of the attacks, but it also dawned on us that the reproach we felt as Americans that day was slowly being removed. The new tower stands taller than the others, like a witness to the country's determination not to let our enemies have the last word.

The natural tendency, whether attacked as a nation or an individual, is to do whatever we can to roll back the disgrace and humiliation of our circumstances. Who likes feeling vulnerable to even more attack? But human resolve, no matter how strong, can never erase the depth of shame that resides in the heart of man. It takes something supernatural to remove the reproach. Consider the stone sealing the tomb of Jesus.

It stood fixed as a stone of reproach. It declared that God—and all the hope of redemption he brought with him—was dead. Seemingly immovable, it wrapped him, as well as our shame, in a tomb of failure. But death's victory was short-lived. The stone could not hold back the Lord of life. When it was rolled away, the reproach it signified rolled right away with it.

Do you know the stone of reproach has been rolled away in your life? You no longer have to live under a cloud of shame or an ongoing sting of failure. No matter how many times failure tries to seal you in a grave of hopelessness, the supernatural power of God will roll the reproach away every time. And his is a resolve that can never be shattered.

April 9th

Peace I leave with you; my peace I give you. I do not give to you as the world gives. Do not let your hearts be troubled and do not be afraid.
—John 14:27 NIV

Loose Ends

Purseless. Phoneless. ID-less. That's how I suddenly found myself the Saturday of Easter weekend.

My family and I were in high spirits as we locked the car and started walking along a hiking trail not far from our home. The parking lot was filled with people coming and going, not the place you would expect someone to break into your car. But when we returned from our walk, the window on the driver's side had been smashed, my purse stolen. In less than forty-five minutes someone had brazenly grabbed the opportune time to wreak havoc on our pleasant day.

You can imagine the ensuing whirlwind of canceling credit cards, stopping cell phone service, changing passwords. I don't know about you, but loose ends have a way of dangling me over an uncomfortable sea of uncertainty. I want to get everything back in order as quickly as possible. But, of course, it never works that way.

When I went to get my stolen phone replaced, I discovered the AT&T store had also been robbed over the weekend! No new phone until the end of the week. It got worse. The Department of Motor Vehicles informed me (after a very long wait in the lobby) my Social Security number did not match their records.

So, I had to go to the Social Security office and have them issue me a new one before obtaining a new driver's license.

Loose ends interrupt our peace. We don't like undotted *i*'s and uncrossed *t*'s. The frenzy surrounding my ordeal posed as a huge distraction. It was the weekend I had wanted to focus on the cross. On the power of Redemption. I almost missed it.

Until I realized it was actually a quite fitting time to experience broken glass and a stolen identification. Wasn't this the season when we celebrate the One who repairs all our shattered windows and restores identities once lost to sin? Jesus meant it when he said he was leaving us with his peace. A peace that promises to put all things back in order.

A peace that sustains us through the loose ends of life.

April 10th

But God raised him from the dead, freeing him from the agony of death, because it was impossible for death to keep its hold on him.

—Acts 2:24 NIV

Death Could Not Hold Him

It was impossible for death to keep its hold on him.

What a profound truth! Sometimes I race past familiar Scripture with the mindset depicted in a Geico commercial— *Everybody knows that.* Well did you know it's easy to take well-known Bible passages for granted? To forget the Word of God is alive and active? That it continually has the power to penetrate our minds and bare our souls? (Hebrews 4:12) Sometimes we just have to stop and let the enduring words of truth soak in. Especially during holy seasons, like Easter, when we celebrate the great truth that death could not hold down the Author of Life.

J.R.R. Tolkien coined the word "eucatastrophe" to describe the sudden happy turn in a story which pierces you with so much joy that it brings you to tears. He says the resurrection was the greatest "eucatastrophe" possible. The agony of Jesus on the cross—led like a lamb to the slaughter, pierced, crushed, deprived of justice, punished by God for our sin—brought the most sadness the world has ever known. His crucifixion appeared to be the complete defeat of goodness, innocence and hope—the victory of evil, injustice and despair.

But death could not hold him down. And the sad news became the good news of the gospel. His resurrection produced, as Tolkien would say, the deepest intermingling of joy and sorrow, of catastrophe turning into euphoria. A universal sigh of relief encompassed all of heaven when he stepped out of that grave. Life did not and could not remain dead. It was impossible.

That impossibility changes everything. It lays the foundation for hope. No matter how ugly the world becomes, it assures us in the end all that is good and beautiful and holy will win. Death could not hold him down. And because of him, it cannot hold us down either.

I pray you don't let that truth slip past just because it's familiar. Pause and get drenched in its freedom once again. You might just experience a real "eucatastrophe."

April 11th

Where there is no revelation, people cast off restraint.
—Proverbs 29:18 NIV

Got Discipline?

Do you, like many, struggle with self-discipline?

When we have no vision or goal we aspire to, Scripture says we will "cast off restraint." Why go through the rigors of self-denial and self-discipline if there's no pay off? We need to have a clear picture of where we're going to exercise the discipline necessary to get there.

Defining our aspirations determines future success perhaps more than any other factor. Dave Ramsey has helped thousands of people find victory in finances because he instructs them how to form specific goals that require saving rather than spending their money. Successful weight loss programs help people obtain their desired weight by teaching them how to set precise objectives. They learn today's sacrifices will be rewarded tomorrow.

Those of you who run marathons know the importance of having a specific goal for a specified amount of time. Runners don't wake up on the day of the race and say, "I think I'll run a 10-mile marathon today." They make choices for weeks, possibly months, in advance to help them prepare in order to achieve the clear goal of making it across the finish line.

The importance of cultivating a lifestyle of discipline extends far beyond finances and physical fitness. As believers in Christ, we've been given a huge assignment. We carry something of God in us, something noble and holy, something the world needs. If we don't have a clear vision of that, we will not develop the necessary discipline to reach the goal. Remember Eve. She was tempted to forget the restraints given by a killjoy God, fling caution to the wind and be her own god. How did that work out? The world continues to reel from her lack of discipline.

Do you need to work on some areas of self-discipline in your life? Now's a good time to recast your vision and get rid of hindrances. God has a plan for you. It entails far more than you realize. Don't let your destiny be stolen.

April 12th

He who did not spare his own Son, but gave him up for us all—how will he not also, along with him, graciously give us all things?
—*Romans 8:32 NIV*

Our Extravagant God

God loves us extravagantly. Nothing proves it more than Calvary.

Our daughter received a stipend to be a fellow at the Witherspoon Institute in Washington, D.C., her senior year of college. I'll never forget the call we got two days after she was there. She talked a mile a minute about how much the instructors anticipated from their fourteen chosen students that semester. They expected their scholars to learn how to use godly principles to influence the culture. Their goal was that after the students received training, they would go on to be judges, congressmen/women, or be placed in other positions that would help shape our society.

The instructors believed in their students so much that every term they invested around $17,000 in each one. The effect of such extravagant investment and affirmation had a profound effect on our daughter, so profound that she decided to take her LSATS and apply to law school. She was convinced she could make a difference in the world.

What Witherspoon did for our daughter reminds me of what God desires for us. He wants us to discover new dimensions of who he has created us to be. And he has invested far more in each of us than $17,000. Scripture says he spared nothing on our behalf, giving us his Son to graciously make us the recipients of "all things." He's not a stingy God.

So, what is holding us back? Why do we settle for half-hearted aspirations? Why are we content to give conditional love when a vast supply of true love lies within our reach? Maybe the echoes of a fallen world have muted the voice that says, "Come up higher." Perhaps we've concluded our life is a tired cliché rather than a poem more sublime than the finest from Shakespeare's pen. Whatever the cause, it's not too late to let the extravagant love of our Father open our eyes, ears and hearts to the truth.

You and I are worth everything to him.

April 13th

He humbled you, causing you to hunger and then feeding you with manna, which neither you nor your ancestors had known, to teach you that man does not live on bread alone but on every word that comes from the mouth of the LORD. —Deuteronomy 8:3 NIV

On Bread Alone

I love bread. All kinds—bagels, croissants, multigrain, baguettes, Artesian, French, Italian. I've even eaten salads where my favorite ingredient was the croutons! Thankfully, I don't have a gluten allergy, but clearly the consumption of too much bread is neither healthy nor wise. We need more to sustain us than dough in its various forms.

Scripture warns us man "does not live on bread alone." We were created for more than mere subsistence. We were crafted to flourish, to "be fruitful and multiply," to experience life "in abundance." Any insistence on bread alone yields spiritual malnourishment and unfulfilled potential. Half-baked lives, so to speak.

The questions we must ask ourselves are, What does our *bread* consist of? What sustains us? Are we living on financial security? Affirming relationships? Pleasurable moments? All are fine aspirations, but in and of themselves, they fall dreadfully short of life's essence. If we consume such lesser goals to find fulfillment, such lesser goals will eventually consume us. We cannot thrive on them any more than we can thrive on Panera's finest.

When Satan tempted Jesus to turn stones into bread, Jesus quoted the passage from Deuteronomy that warns man's needs run much deeper than physical existence. The miracle of Israel's survival in the desert was not just the manna, but that God provided it. In the desert, they learned about a God whose word resulted not only in manna, quail and water, but in laws they could live by. God taught them how to depend on him alone, a dependence that would win them a land and an identity they could never have achieved on their own.

So how about you? Have you yet come to the place of recognizing fulfillment comes in God alone not bread alone? Don't settle for anything less than a relationship that stretches beyond your here-and-now needs. Be thankful for whatever kind of *bread* God has blessed you with, but even more that he alone knows and provides what you need.

What you truly need.

April 14th

See to it that no one takes you captive through hollow and deceptive philosophy, which depends on human tradition and the elemental spiritual forces of this world rather than on Christ.

—*Colossians 2:8 NIV*

Like a Dog in a Pickup Truck

I was on my two-mile walk the other morning when I witnessed something that caused a double take. A pickup truck sped past me when a dog literally rolled out of the back of the vehicle and landed on the road! Fortunately, the driver saw it too and immediately stopped the truck. A young boy rushed out of the passenger side to retrieve the dog. After a brief examination, the dog appeared to be unharmed and the boy led him into the safety of the cab. I couldn't tell how it happened, but my guess is the dog was enjoying the breeze and got too close to the edge.

The edge.

Whether in art, music, clothing, or just lifestyle, it's quite in vogue these days to be on the edge. It connotes excitement, danger, thrills. It's seeing how close you come to the match before getting burnt. How near to the boundaries without actually stepping over the line. How far the rules can be bent without breaking them. Those who deem coolness the measure of all things especially gravitate to the edge, because whatever else the edge might be, it's regarded as cool.

The draw to adventure resides in every human heart. None of us desire to live in a bland black and white world. Pop culture promises a kind of glory from living on the edge, but it's a promise it can't keep. Don't fall for a cheap substitute when you have access to the real thing.

Paul warns us not to fall for the lies of the world. Any philosophy that depends on human traditions and standards set by shifting cultural norms can't possibly sustain us. He cautions the church to remain steadfast in the boundaries defined by Christ. We must persist in being on guard. History is strewn with those who thought they were standing firm but ventured too close to the edge and were swept away—King Saul, Balaam, Ananias and Sapphira. Don't be one of them. Don't end up like that dog in the pickup truck.

April 15th

But where sin increased, grace increased all the more.

—Romans 5:20 NIV

When Sin Abounds

He was a great kid, always smiling ..." These words describe Martin Richard, the eight-year old boy who died a few years ago in the Boston Marathon bombing. His death captured for me, perhaps more than anything, the horrific nature of the tragedy. The innocence. The evil. The inexplicable. How can we not mourn?

Yet our national mourning—where we find some degree of comfort—was short-lived. Within twenty-four hours of the bombing, politicians resorted to blaming the other side of the aisle for the cause of the calamity. So, our disasters no longer serve to at least pull the country together. They are exploited for some political gain. The fabric of our nation continues to unravel before our eyes, and we mourn even more.

I have a feeling it's not going to get any better. Scripture warns us in the last days the increase of wickedness will cause the love of most to grow cold (Matthew 24:12). We need to know what we're facing. Sin will inevitably increase, but it cannot—*cannot*—grow greater than grace. We are assured in Paul's letter to the Romans, where sin increased, it was no match for the grace of God. Love overpowers hate every time, because God is love. Our job is to declare it.

You and I have been put on the earth at this particular time, in this particular country, through these particular circumstances. We mourn the effects of sin, but we must never lose sight of the truth. There is no evil Satan intends that God can't turn into good. We of all people ought to have this reality embedded into our hearts so we don't lose hope. When darkness falls, his people are to shine as beacons of grace illuminating the powerful words of the hymnist.

And though the wrong seems oft so strong, God is the ruler yet.

April 16th

*Give thanks in all circumstances, for this is God's will for you in Christ
Jesus.* —1 Thessalonians 5:18 NIV

Always an Option

Seventeenth century Bible scholar Matthew Henry is said to
have penned these words upon the theft of his wallet:

"I thank Thee first because I was never robbed before;
second, because although they took my purse they did not take
my life; third, because although they took my all, it was not
much; and fourth because it was I who was robbed, and not I
who robbed."

I love his mindset. Henry discovered the secret of finding
thanks in all things. When he encountered the unexpected, like
the robbing of his wallet, he instinctively turned toward
gratefulness for the good rather than bitterness for the
misfortune.

Gratitude is always an option. No matter what the
circumstance.

- Someone rejects me ... *Thank you, Lord, that I
  wasn't the rejecter.*
- Not many of my books sell at the conference
  ... *Thank you that I was able to write the book
  in the first place.*
- A relationship is not where I want it to be ...
  Thank you that there is something.
- I lose my job ... *Thank you there is still food on
  the table. And love.*
- My close friend dies ... *Thank you for the years
  we had.*
- Sin abounds ... *Thank you that grace abounds
  even more.*

I don't mean to sound glib. Hurts and disappointments come
with ruthless intensity. And with great frequency for some. But
I think at times we linger in sorrow too long. Complaining has a

way of draining our creativity. Of subduing our spirit. It causes us to lose sight of the bigger picture. It can make us forget that "our present sufferings are not worth comparing with the glory that will be revealed" (Romans 8:18). And be assured, God *does* intend to bring glory from all we experience.

So, start with the small issues. In whatever disappointment you face, search for the good that can be found and dwell on it. Give thanks for all those embedded blessings. As was the case with Matthew Henry, let gratitude instinctively take over. It's always an option.

April 17th

I entered the sanctuary of God; then I understood.

—Psalm 73:17 NIV

Caricature Culture

From drawings of Will Smith's enlarged ears to Bill Clinton's bulbous nose and Angelina Jolie's voluptuous lips ... we've all seen caricatures. A person's overall appearance is dwarfed in order to accentuate a particular feature. Jutting jaws become "juttier," toothy grins become "toothier," bulging eyes become "bulgier," as the artist attempts to highlight specific physical attributes. Caricatures are clever, creative and usually harmless.

But there exists another kind of caricature far from harmless. It's the sort we draw in our minds when we focus on the weaknesses of others. The longer we dwell on their flaws, the larger those flaws loom. Before we realize it, we come to identify the people more by the warped images in our thinking than by the totality of who they are as image bearers of their Creator.

Caricatures distort reality. Psalm 73 depicts the psalmist's inflated view of the arrogant and ungodly. "They have no struggles; their bodies are healthy and strong. They are free from common burdens; they are not plagued by human ills" (vv. 4–5). This caricature grew so strong in him that he concluded he had in vain kept his heart pure" (v. 13). His perception that the wicked live easy, painless lives of perfection fostered the image of yet another caricature—God is unfair. The lie took over.

That's the danger of caricatures. The single focus blinds us to "all" of the truth until our total outlook becomes distorted. And distorted it remains unless we allow the Lord to intervene. When the psalmist finally entered the presence of God he recognized his foolishness and repented. Truth was restored.

So, the next time someone's ego sticks out like a cell phone conversation in a library, or another's insensitive criticalness appears like exaggerated arched eyebrows, don't ignore it. But don't let it be the basis of your perception. Don't let the flaws become so disproportional to the entirety of the person that you mistakenly think it's who they are.

April 18th

For you died, and your life is now hidden with Christ in God.
—Colossians 3:3 NIV

New York's Finest

Every year at the college where I teach, a student is chosen to win the Public Bible Reading Award. From the moment I knew I had the opportunity to nominate someone, there was no question of my pick. Donavan.

Donavan had that gift of drawing people in whenever he spoke. Every time he got up to give a speech, we listened. His naturally timed pauses and accentuated phrases caught the attention of everyone in the class. But it was the authenticity that accompanied his words that made him so dynamic. Nothing was contrived. Oblivious to this God-given talent of communication, he fully underestimated his impact. But it's no wonder.

He was born and raised in Harlem. By the age of fourteen, he felt completely hopeless. His life was spiraling downward and he believed he would never escape his circumstances. Then, on his fifteenth birthday, his mother begged him to go to church with her. That night his life turned upside down. He discovered the love and power of Jesus Christ. A few years later he would be plucked from the streets of Harlem and planted at Lancaster Bible College where gifts he never knew he had would be nourished.

Although we rightly think of New York's police force as the "finest," to me, Donavan joins the ranks of "New York's finest." It takes a lot of guts to reject the ways of street life. To walk away from a culture that heralds drugs and violence as the road to survival and instead choose a path of humility and surrender to his Redeemer.

The morning of the awards ceremony, he read Colossians 3:1-17. His credibility of having a "life hidden with Christ" was etched in every word. As he echoed the passionate admonition of the apostle Paul to get rid of everything that leads to death and put on the "new self" we knew it was not a platitude. It emanated life.

So, will your words. So, will mine. Surrendered, grateful lives set on things above always do. Don't hold back. Become "Lancaster's finest" or "Nashville's finest" or "Portsmouth's finest" or "Boston's...." Wherever you are and in whatever you do, do it all in the name of the Lord Jesus. Someone will listen!

April 19th

If only for this life we have hope in Christ, we are of all people most to be pitied.
—1 Corinthians 15:19 NIV

How Do We Do Hope?

Everyone needs hope. Those scarred by life's hurts may try to resist it. But even the most hardened skeptic longs to have something to hope for. It's the way God made us. Hope is a gift from our Creator to warm our journey and comfort us in despair. It's something we are to do as Christians.

So how do we *do hope*? How do we keep the difficulties in life from smothering our hope? How does hope work in a world where headlines shout violent beheadings, Christian massacres and rampant injustice? When a parent's dream for his child is snuffed out? When medical bills swallow up life savings? When it looks like the "bad guys" are winning? How does hope lift us up?

Christian hope rests on the resurrection. The resurrection of Jesus Christ promises something good will rise from every grave of disappointment. We *do hope* when we embrace that promise and depend upon the unwavering character of God to fulfill it.

We *do hope* best when we turn our expectations from this world to the next. Paul says if our hope in Christ extends only for this present life, we should be pitied. Until we understand that all we experience in this life prepares us for the next, we will remain vulnerable to hopelessness. No one paints this perspective better than Lewis in the final page of the *The Last Battle* from the *Chronicles of Narnia* when the children are entering eternity:

> But for them it was only the beginning of the real story. All their life in this world and all their adventures in Narnia had only been the cover and the title page: now at last they were beginning Chapter One of the Great Story which no one on earth has read: which goes on for ever: in which every chapter is better than the one before.

If you are a Christian, you have access to unlimited hope. Hope that reaches beyond the circumstances of your past, present and future. Hope that releases you from the frustrations of life and tells you a day greater than you can imagine is on the way.

So, let's do it!

April 20th

I will extol the LORD at all times; his praise will always be on my lips.
—Psalm 34:1 NIV

It's Why I Sing

Your praise will ever be on my lips...." The refrain of Bethel Music's song by Kalley Heiligenthal ran through my mind as I recovered from the life-threatening illness of sepsis. Not strong enough to walk my daily two miles, I made a path between my kitchen and the living room. There, in my pj's and slippers, I walked that little path, prayed my concerns and sang those lyrics. Not the ideal situation, but I think sometimes the sweetest praise comes from those not-so-sweet moments.

The Lord had spared my life. Even though it would be a while before I was "back to normal," nothing could hinder my overwhelming gratitude. I wonder if that's what David was feeling when he wrote Psalm 34. He had escaped to Philistine territory due to Saul's relentless pursuit of him. When the Philistine king, Abimelek (named Lachish), realized who David was, the future king of Israel feigned insanity so as not to be killed at Abimelek's hand or be given over to Saul. His ruse worked. Abimelek drove him away. His life was spared (1 Samuel 21:11–15).

How can praise of God be always on our lips? Certainly not because of circumstances. Circumstances fluctuate as frequently as weight gain/loss.

Continual praise flows from our awareness of God's continual faithfulness. As David declares in the 34th psalm, the Lord always delivers us when we call (vv. 17, 19). He is good (v. 8). He is just (vv. 15–16). He is compassionate (v. 18). We praise God continually because of his unchanging, incomparable nature. There is never a moment—not one single moment—when God doesn't deserve our praise.

We don't always see God at work. But it shouldn't hinder our praise. We may hate our situation. But it shouldn't hinder our praise. We may think we'll never feel happy again. But it shouldn't hinder our praise. We have been blessed to be called God's child. And that's enough to keep us going through eternity! It's why I sing.

Won't you join me?

April 21st

Immediately the boy's father exclaimed, "I do believe; help me overcome my unbelief!"
—Mark 9:24 NIV

Faith Under Construction

I believe! Help my unbelief! I wish those words—those polar opposite words—weren't reflective of my own experience with faith. How can both be true? The footnote in my Bible says, "Since faith is never perfect, belief and unbelief are often mixed." I find that comforting.

When the father described in Mark 9 came to Jesus on behalf of his demon-possessed son, he asked him for the help Jesus' disciples had been unable to deliver. The disciples appeared to be as baffled as the father over their lack of power so they asked Jesus what went wrong. His answer was simple: "This kind can come out only by prayer" (Mark 9:29). Isn't that what they were doing?

Evidently, their faith needed some adjustment. Maybe they were taking faith for granted. It worked before, so it should work now. Maybe they forgot that the authority of God—not their prayers—constituted the source of their power. Maybe like the father, they were being forced to recognize unbelief tainted their belief.

All too often I think we succumb to discouragement when we feel our prayers ascend no further than the ceiling. The mountain didn't move so we're tempted to settle into a faith that if not attended to won't even move an anthill. This incident illustrates the importance of not letting that happen.

The key lies in not viewing our faith as a finished product. Jesus answered that father's plea to help him overcome his unbelief and his son was restored. The disciples also allowed their faith to be remodeled. History records they continued with a faith that changed the world.

Jesus said, "Everything is possible for one who believes" (Mark 9:23). If we hope to attain such confidence, let's ask God to keep working on us, to change, modify, alter and construct our beliefs into a living, vibrant faith. One that's not so double-minded.

April 22nd

The men were amazed and asked, "What kind of man is this? Even the winds and the waves obey him!"
—Mathew 8:27 NIV

Miracles in the Making

Lake Erie would never be mistaken for the Atlantic Ocean, but I might have thought I was at Acadia in Maine rather than Marblehead, Ohio. The usually calm body of water seemed infused with a furious mission. Its waves came crashing on the rocks, sending spray over the jutting pier and beyond. I have to say it's awe-inspiring when the ocean acts like the ocean— whether on the shores of San Diego or the Outer Banks—but when a lake acts like the ocean, it's downright breathtaking.

I'm sure Lake Erie finds contentment in being a lake, one of the Great ones, no less. The ocean-like display did not rise out of rebellion, just obedience to the One who commands the winds and waves. Only man, the highest form of God's creation, rebels. A rebellion that most profoundly manifests itself in trying to be what we're not. We're oceans who would rather be lazy streams or country creeks striving to be the Mississippi River.

When Jesus calmed the raging sea threatening to capsize their tiny fishing boat, his disciples' mouths dropped open. *How did he do that? Who is he?* He was just the Son of God being the Son of God. The sea yielded to him as he yielded to his Father. And it created a miracle.

We are miracles in the making when we yield to our Creator as well. The potential of a human soul surrendered to its Maker is limitless, beautiful and unbelievably fulfilling. It rips through our tendencies to compare ourselves with others. It assures us our value rests on who God says we are, not anyone else.

Do you realize we can bring him glory today by just being us? He calls some to be waterfalls tucked away in the forest ready to dazzle unsuspecting hikers with a cascade of his love. Others are roaring Lake Erie waves sounding warning where it might not be expected. Some of us are cups of cold water offered to the weary. If done in obedience to the Lord, no one act carries more significance than the other.

Psalm 93:3 declares, "The seas have lifted up their voice." How about we take our part in the chorus?

April 23rd

Praise the LORD.... Praise the LORD.   —*Psalm 150:1, 6 NIV*

The Power of Everyday Praise

It begins and ends with identical sentences. The word praise reoccurs in each of its six verses. In fact, praise is used thirteen times in this brief exhortation. Described as the "final great hallelujah," Psalm 150 is considered by many to be a manual on praise. It answers the questions:

- *where* to praise—in God's sanctuary and mighty heavens (v. 1)
- *why* to praise—for his acts of power and surpassing greatness (v. 2)
- *how* to praise—with trumpets, harps, lyres, timbre's, strings, pipes, cymbals and dancing (vv. 4–5)
- *who* is to praise—everything that has breath (v. 6)

But something I'd never thought of before struck me as I read this passage from my NIV Bible ... the absence of exclamation points. Wouldn't you think verses extolling the worthiness of praising the great and mighty God would be replete with punctuation that highlights excitement and command? But no, all we see is the lowly period. "Praise the Lord [period]." "Praise the Lord [period]." Perhaps the psalmist is sending us a subtle message.

Maybe praising God is not supposed to be an extraordinary happening. Maybe it should simply be matter of fact. Rather than being confined to Sunday morning hymnals, perhaps our souls—and voices—ought to be overflowing with praises for all kinds of reasons in all kinds of places.

The call to everyday praise abounds in the words of poets and songwriters. The Doxology, penned in 1674, exhorts us to recognize that since every good gift comes from the Father's hand we should praise him for everything. *Praise God from whom all blessings flow.* Contemporary artists like Matt Redman remind us the Lord is worthy of praise no matter our circumstances or the season of our soul. Chris Tomlin sings there are ten thousand reasons to bless the Lord.

Power is released when we praise God. It may even turn our circumstances around, but if it doesn't alter our situation, it will adjust our perspective. It will change us.

So, wherever you are right now, and in whatever condition, join in the reprise. Let your breath praise our wonderful, omniscient, faithful, loving God. He is worthy of your *Halleluiah Yah.*

April 24th

I consider my life worth nothing to me; my only aim is to finish the race and complete the task the Lord Jesus has given me.

—Acts 20:24 NIV

Who Are We Living For?

A group of Indians were walking by Mother Teresa when they saw her hugging a leper. One of the men commented, "I wouldn't do that for all the money in the world." Mother Teresa replied, "Neither would I. I am doing it for the love of Christ." Not because it made her feel good. Not because it made her rich and famous. Not because it paved the way for the Nobel Peace Prize. Completing the task the Lord had given her was the "only aim." Nothing in life trumped her love for Christ. She never forgot who she was living for.

Neither did Paul. In his farewell to the Ephesian elders he warned them difficult days lay ahead. Even some among the flock would distort the truth and draw others away (Acts 20:30). Despite the inevitable discouragement such betrayal would bring, he exhorted them to keep pressing on. He reminded them of Jesus' words—that a life of giving and investing in others exceeds a life marred with self-interest (Matthew 20:27–28). He exhorted them to follow his own example of completing the work Jesus had given him—an example that would encourage them not to forget who they were living for.

How about us? Have we slid from living for the love of Christ toward some lesser motivation? Have we exalted the good over the best? Have we allowed our faith to morph into "consumer-oriented spirituality?" Have we permitted the tentacles of self-centeredness to creep back into our hearts and drag us away from our first love?

Evidence abounds in Christendom of how we forget who we're living for. Let's not join the crowd. Let's purpose to live for Jesus in whatever we face.

- When we're discouraged, let's live for him in our surrender.
- When we're offended, let's live for him in our forgiveness.
- When we're confused, let's live for him in our trust.
- When we're happy, let's live for him in our dance.

My friend, let's not forget who we're living for.

April 25th

By this everyone will know that you are my disciples, if you love one another.　　　　　　　　　　　　　　　　　　　　　—John 13:35 NIV

Common Christianity

If love for one another is the way the world recognizes us as followers of Jesus, I'm afraid we have a way to go.

I recently read about a well-known pastor's response to a very public, unjust accusation hurled at him and his church. Rather than condemning his accusers, he encouraged his parishioners to show those who were slandering them the love of the Savior. Leaders throughout the body of Christ commended his reaction. I, too, was moved by his generous spirit. But I couldn't help thinking how sad it was that his behavior was viewed as "exceptional." Should it be front page news when followers of Christ chose forgiveness over self-justification?

We live in a gotcha culture. Everyone from politicians to protesters seems to have an angle that promotes self-interest. *What's in it for me* dominates the thinking of most. And it's not getting any better. I think that's why when Christians really act like "little Christs" it seems extraordinary. Those who take seriously the admonition to "do nothing out of selfish ambition or vain conceit" and instead "value others above [them]selves" are rare (Philippians 2:3).

But it doesn't have to be that way. Pastor Tim Keller writes in *The Freedom of Self-Forgetfulness* that when believers grasp the inestimable value God places on them through the cross, a "freedom of self-forgetfulness" emerges. Lives once suffocating in self-awareness breathe in the oxygen-rich awareness of being accepted. Such abundance provokes a longing to *give*, not *get* from others.

It causes us to pursue Jesus with reckless abandonment. And in so doing we forget ourselves. We forsake the need to defend ourselves, to justify our actions. We live for him, and in living for him we live like him. In living like him, we love.

I like how Billy Graham puts it in *The Secret of Happiness,* "The world can argue against Christianity as an institution, but there is no convincing argument against a person who, through the Spirit of God, has been made Christlike." I look forward to the day when we who follow Christ will so radiate his mark of selfless love that our behavior would not be a rarity, but common.

Common Christians living out common Christianity! It would change the world.

April 26th

In the beginning was the Word, and the Word was with God, and the Word was God.
—John 1:1 NIV

What's in a Word?

Never underestimate the power of words. I live in a world of words. I suppose it's an occupational hazard that comes with teaching composition. Equipped with my trusty red pen, I'm always on the lookout for incomplete sentences, dangling modifiers and redundant words that are unnecessary (like what I just wrote)! I love discovering well-crafted phrases that bring to life thoughts not yet spoken, thoughts searching for an avenue of expression.

But beyond the intricacies of the English language, words speak to me on another level about life. For example, columnist Peggy Noonan writes that the most powerful words are the simplest. *I love you. It's a girl. He died.* I think that's indicative of much in life. We over complicate our circumstances and rob ourselves of the power of peace and effortlessness of joy. Whatever happened to simplicity?

Even punctuation marks translate into metaphors. Commas remind me of the importance of pausing, of refusing to let life become one uninterrupted flow of accomplishing to-do lists. *Italics* highlight the presence of an Orchestrator in those rare instances when everything falls into place. And how about those days filled with exclamation marks!

But the most important usage of words comes in the gospel of John. Jesus is the Word of God. He communicates to the world what God looks like. Scripture says, in fact, that he is the "image of the invisible God" (Colossians 1:15), "the exact representation of his being" (Hebrews 1:3). Jesus' life silences all the distorted images of God's character. Words like and unrelatable don't fit. Words like compassionate, sacrificial and powerful do.

Jesus no longer walks on the earth. And we believers have the task, or a more apt word—privilege—of revealing who he is. How are we doing? Is our message clear or confused? Do we sometimes forget that the sentence is about him? That in fact every word, phrase and paragraph of our story is for him?

Be encouraged today to speak the message of Christ in all you do. The world needs to not only hear but see your words.

April 27th

But we had to celebrate and be glad, because this brother of yours was dead and is alive again; he was lost and is found.

—Luke 15:32 NIV

Redone or Redeemed?

If only I would have ... If only I wouldn't have ... Ever wish life included a replay button, one that would let you not just review what happened, but give you opportunity to redo it? Well, I know something better.

Everyone born bears the distinguishing mark of being a sinner (Romans 3:23). We cannot live without messing up. We mess up in our relationships, our work, our pleasures. We make lousy decisions. We lose our way. The past cements our mistakes.

Once sin entered the world, all of life became a story of redemption. Sometimes I think we forget that. We fail, but rather than simply repenting, we try to become our own fixer-upper. Our attempts to repair whatever went wrong become our version of the redo. When it doesn't work, we wallow in more guilt, drown in more regret. If not careful, we give up completely. We feel we've gone too far and beyond the reach of redemption. The addiction is too strong. The second chance came and went; there can't be a third, or fourth.

The story of the prodigal son exposes that lie (Luke 15:11-32). Jesus told the parable to let us know there is always room back at the table. Life can't be redone, but it can be redeemed. Redemption has the power to "buy back" what we lost and declare a new beginning.

So, don't waste your time wishing you could redo your mistakes. Or redo your life for that matter. Just as the prodigal laid it all before his father, so you can take your failures, fears and fiascoes to your Redeemer. He works in such a way that he can bring good out of the worst of your sins. You have a story to tell, and your mess-ups or others' mess-ups against you are an integral part of it.

It's time to shake off your chains of regret. You are not who you were. Live now in the freedom of redemption.

April 28th

Arise, shine, for your light has come.   —Isaiah 60:1 NIV

Time to Get Up

The fifth chapter of Mark describes three of the most hopeless situations recorded in the Gospels: a man whose sanity had been stripped away by not just one, but a legion of demons; a woman who, after twelve years, had exhausted every possible avenue looking for a cure to end her suffering; a dead little girl.

Overwhelming. Incurable. Ah, but not permanent.

Into each dark circumstance Jesus enters with the power of his light. The demon-possessed man may have been the first defined "cutter" we know of. He used the stones from the surrounding tombs as instruments of self-destruction, ripping open his flesh in a vain attempt to relieve his torment. But one word from Jesus and the demons charge out of his body, leaving him "dressed and in his right mind" (v. 15).

In her desperation, the woman had spent everything she had. But doctor after doctor, medicine after medicine, and treatment after treatment had resulted in her situation becoming worse, not better. The persistent bleeding robbed her not only of health but of all human comfort since she was deemed "unclean." One touch of Jesus' garment changed all that (v. 29).

Finally, the little girl. Mourners had already gathered to grieve her lifeless body. But Jesus entered the room where she lay and woke her from the sleep of death. *"Talitha koum!"* he commanded. "Little girl, I say to you, get up!" (v. 41). And so, she did.

I don't know about you, but these stories carry me to a place of hope. Hope for those who appear hell-bent on self-destruction. Hope for those whose suffering has isolated them for far too many years. Hope for those who need a Savior to take their hand and silence all the voices of doom as he speaks the ageless life-giving words. Words prophesied long ago by Isaiah: "Arise, shine, for your light has come!"

April 29th

"For I know the plans I have for you," declares the LORD, "plans to prosper you and not to harm you, plans to give you hope and a future."
—Jeremiah 29:11 NIV

Give In

Do you know the most popular Old Testament Scripture? Jeremiah 29:11 reigns as the most frequently requested single verse. When considering the whole Bible, it comes in second, right after John 3:16. I think there's a reason for this.

These words were spoken to the Jews when their destiny could hardly have seemed darker. Jerusalem had been annihilated and the people had been exiled to Babylon. Everything had perished, including their identity as a nation. Now captives in a foreign land, Jeremiah tells them to do something completely unorthodox, against all common sense and every fighting fiber of their being. He tells them to GIVE IN. To embrace their captivity and even go so far as to pray for the prosperity of their captors!

He assures them God still has a plan for their future. After seventy years of captivity, they would return to their homeland but arrive as a changed people. A purified nation who—because of those seventy years—would learn to call upon him and seek him with whole hearts, not with the half-hearted devotion they had become accustomed to.

Although today we often apply Jeremiah 29:11 to graduations, promotions and new beginnings, its significance as a beacon of trust in trying times should not be missed.

We all face those seasons in life where everything we hope for seems lost. Black holes of disappointment swallow our aspirations and at times drive us to the same kind of desperation the Israelites must have experienced as they sat by the rivers of Babylon and wept for their native soil (Psalm 137:1). Maybe God wants us, like Israel, to embrace our desolate state. Maybe it's a despair that will deepen our search for him. Maybe our anguish will cause us not to take our sins so lightly. Maybe the Lord wants us to give in.

To give in, not because our future holds nothing but so it can hold everything.

April 30th

So justice is driven back, and righteousness stands at a distance; truth has stumbled in the streets, honesty cannot enter.   —*Isaiah 59:14 NIV*

The Wild Truth

G.K. Chesterton writes, "The heavenly chariot flies thundering through the ages, the dull heresies sprawling and prostrate, the wild truth reeling but erect." Oh, how we underestimate the power of truth.

There's no question we live in a world where truth appears to have stumbled in the streets," where honest communication seems roadblocked. We question the government, news outlets, and about every opinion on social media we read. Who is telling the truth? I don't know about you, but at times I'm tempted to think the LIE is bigger than the TRUTH. But deceit, no matter how persistent, how ruthless, how successful in distorting reality, will eventually fall under the supremacy of truth. Our problem is we forget.

But Scripture resounds with reminders.

- Truth wins. Lies lose.
  "You destroy those who tell lies." (Psalm 5:6).
- Truth resurrects. Lies rot and decay.
  "Truthful lips endure forever, but a lying tongue lasts only a moment." (Proverbs 12:19).
- Truth clarifies. Lies distort.
  "But when he, the Spirit of truth, comes, he will guide you into all the truth. He will not speak on his own; he will speak only what he hears, and he will tell you what is yet to come." (John 16:13).

- Truth builds. Lies destroy.
  "You belong to your father, the devil, and you want to carry out your father's desires. He was a murderer from the beginning, not holding to the truth, for there is no truth in him. When he lies, he speaks his native language, for he is a liar and the father of lies." (John 8:44).
- Truth frees. Lies enslave.
  "Then you will know the truth, and the truth will set you free." (John 8:32).

So, if you're discouraged when truth appears to stagger and honesty seems barred from the arena, don't be deceived. Resist that old father of lies who wants you to be so disheartened that you give up. Truth will prevail in the end. As Chesterton penned, truth may reel from all kinds of heretical assaults, but in the end, nothing can stop the indomitable, unconquerable, invincible truth!

May 1st

Greater love has no one than this: to lay down one's life for one's friends.

—John 15:13 NIV

Relationships: Love Largely

One early Sunday morning at Lakeside I was walking when I spotted a small church on the corner. I decided to slip in for a minute. The wood paneled interior and stained glass windows were breathtaking. The single light shining on the altar gave the empty sanctuary a sense of, well, holiness. It moved me.

It moved me so much that I decided to attend the service later that morning. But as I entered "his gates with thanksgiving" my delight was short-lived. As people filed into the pews, the room that had earlier palpated with his presence didn't feel *holy* anymore. Instead, it resonated with fallen creatures just like me.

People. Human beings. We are the pinnacle of God's creation. We are its blemish. Francis Schaeffer once referred to man as a "glorious ruin." *Glorious* because we are created in his image; *ruined* because of the fall. We experience the heights of love and creativity as well as the depths of depravity. Our relationships with one another encompass the very sweetest of life's experiences but also the most bitter.

How do we keep relationships in proper perspective? How do we resist the temptation, on one hand, to elevate the dearest and nearest to idol status or on the other, let another's failures drive us behind walls of isolation? Jesus taught there was no greater love than to lay down one's life for a friend (John 15:13). Yet at the same time, he did not entrust himself to man because he knew what man's human nature was like (John 2:24). He was fully aware of our vacillating, ignoble ways, but his love for us never lessened—even to death.

That's the kind of love God wants us to nurture. It's large. It values the *glorious* and has grace for the *ruined*. It takes us through the ebb and flow of human interactions and provides borders of security—borders that broaden the more we love him.

God alone enables us to love largely with a passion so great that even *glorious ruins* can be transformed into a holy sanctuary.

May 2nd

Cheer up! On your feet! He's calling you. —Mark 10:49 NIV

Cheer Up!

Bartimaeus—a blind beggar on the side of the road. His affliction had stripped him of all dignity, leaving him, according to Jewish society, only a few steps above a leper. His self-sufficiency had been replaced with total dependency on human benevolence. Bartimaeus had nothing left to lose. Bystanders probably thought that's why he ignored their rebuke when he called out to Jesus. Rather than being swayed by their demands to be quiet, he shouted all the more. From the top of his lungs he cried, "Jesus, Son of David, have mercy on me!" (v. 47).

Unbeknown to the crowd, not all of Bartimaeus' resources had been depleted. His dismal existence had not extinguished everything. His eyes may have been blind, but he saw what the others did not. He called Jesus the "Son of David"—a term which designated the Messiah. When he heard Jesus was approaching, he knew who was really coming and his one precious commodity rose to the top. His faith.

It was a faith that refused to be silenced. A faith that carried the assurance Jesus would heal him. A faith that caused him to yank off the cloak which identified him as a blind beggar. A faith that propelled him to jump to his feet and place before the Son of David his need without qualifiers, without reasoning, without begging. Just a simple, eloquent request—*I want to see.* And light shattered the darkness. Bartimaeus was blind no more.

The crowd had wrongly assumed Jesus would have no time for Bartimaeus. Yet when Jesus instructed them to call him, they didn't hesitate. Their new directive drowned out their former mistaken advice: "Cheer up! On your feet! He's calling you!" Something about those words catch my attention.

When life gets hard, I don't want you or me to be so blinded by self-pity that we no longer see the precious commodity we've been given. Nor do I want us to be like the crowd and assume Jesus wouldn't have time for our needs. Let's choose to move from *begging* to *believing* when we hear those words of life.

Cheer up! He's calling you!

May 3rd

For what I received I passed on to you as of first importance: that Christ died for our sins according to the Scriptures, that he was buried, that he was raised on the third day. —1 Corinthians 15:3-4 NIV

First Things

First importance. What's of *first* importance in our lives?

When life starts spinning out of control, rather than getting sucked into the old familiar whirlpool of worry, I've been shifting gears. I've been going back to the foundation. I've been thanking

Jesus that he died for my sins and was buried and raised on the third day rather than launching into my woes. That simple re-focus has fortified my faith. It's caused me to remember exactly what I bank my whole life upon.

God warned Israel repeatedly not to forget what was of first importance. In Psalm 78, he described how they "turned back on the day of battle" (v. 9). Although they were equipped to take out the enemy, they wouldn't even engage! Why? Because they *forgot* what God had done—his wonders and miracles in delivering them from Egypt (vv. 11–12). The words "disloyal and faithless" (v. 57) reveal the sad consequence of their forgetfulness. They became a people devoid of loyalty. Devoid of faith.

Although I doubt that any true believer actually fails to remember the cross and resurrection, I can't help but wonder if we take what ought to be of *first* importance in our faith so casually it plays an increasingly minor role in our practical living. Do we, like Israel, tend to retreat from the spiritual battles we encounter? Do we forget the same God who raised Jesus from the dead is the One who lives in us? Beth Moore says faith rests its case on the resurrection. Wimpy faith fails to remember that most important truth.

There are many things in life we forget. Some we want to forget. Some we should. But if we hope to remain loyal to God and faithful to his promises, if we long to know victory instead of defeat, then let's remember this one thing:

> Christ died for our sins according to the Scriptures, was buried and resurrected on the third day.
> —1 Corinthians 15:3-4

That, my friends, is of *first* importance. Don't forget it!

May 4th

Be kind to one another.   *—Ephesians 4:32 NASB*

There's Nothing Random About Kindness

It is God's *modus operandi* and the thread running through redemption. It's the inevitable upshot of a selfless life and a fruit of the Spirit yielding an exponential harvest. Kindness.

Perhaps no other book in the Bible portrays it as clearly as the book of Ruth. Ruth exuded kindness to her bereft mother-in-law when she left her own country to care for her. Not thinking of her own desires, Ruth subjected herself to the backbreaking work of gleaning enough grain in the fields to sustain them. She was even willing to place herself in the awkward position of asking their kinsman, Boaz, to marry her to insure Naomi would be provided for. Such concern for another's interest was not lost on Boaz. He praised her, "This kindness is greater than that which you showed earlier: You have not run after the younger men, whether rich or poor" (Ruth 3:10).

Boaz recognized kindness because he was no stranger to it in his own life. When Ruth worked in his fields, Boaz instructed his workers to leave extra grain for her to gather. He was willing to jeopardize his own inheritance to redeem Naomi's property and marry Ruth. The ripple effect of their acts of kindness reached beyond their wildest dreams: they become ancestors of the kindest man who ever lived, the Savior of the world.

Illustrations of Jesus' kindness abound throughout Scripture. He didn't have to strike up a conversation with the Samaritan woman. Weary and thirsty, how easy it would have been to simply ignore her. But in kindness he extended himself to her (John 4). He could have sent the hungry crowds who had been following him for days home to fend for themselves. But his kindness toward them resulted in a miraculous provision of food (John 6). Even on the cross when he was suffering excruciating pain, he extended kindness to his mother by making sure John would care for her (John 19:26–27).

There's nothing random about kindness when "random" implies lack of direction or purpose. Acts of kindness are intentional decisions to go out of our way to help someone else. It packs a powerful punch. Just the kind of punch our world so desperately needs. Just the kind you have to offer.

May 5th

Is it not written: "My house will be called a house of prayer for all nations"? But you have made it "a den of robbers."   —Mark 11:17 NIV

Habitats of Hypocrisy

When Jesus entered the temple area and drove out the money changers, he wasn't playing around. Their offense outraged him. The religious leaders of the day had allowed the temple to become a "den of robbers." But the theft stretched much further than the buying and selling of sacrifices. Something much dearer to God was being stolen. The place he intended to house his holiness and provide the means of communicating with his people had become a habitat of hypocrisy. The Pharisees' misrepresentations robbed the people from seeing who God really was—not unlike the fig tree Jesus had just cursed (Mark 11:14).

Jesus had spotted it right before arriving in Jerusalem. The presence of branches covered with leaves indicated a tree that should have been loaded with figs. But when Jesus approached the tree, he found it was barren of any fruit. The tree had "misrepresented" itself, claiming to have something it didn't. To be something it wasn't. Just like those Pharisees. By the next day the fig tree had withered. Soon the Pharisees would as well.

It's a warning to be heeded.

I think hypocrisy reigns as one of the worst of sins. It's a common reason unbelievers give for not coming to the faith. But I doubt many people have as their life aspiration to become a hypocrite. How does it start?

It begins with a lack of honesty. We shade the truth ... a little here to keep us from looking bad ... a little there because we don't want to hurt someone's feelings. No doubt driven by insecurities, we justify our sins. We let our consciences fall asleep. But God doesn't approve of deception, even a little bit. When we deceive, we communicate disrespect for both God and man. We rob others from seeing God's faithfulness and cheat them out of tasting the authenticity everyone longs to see.

So, if dishonesty is spoiling your fruit, let the Holy Spirit prune you. If your life has become more image than reality, stop pretending. It's not worth the consequences. You don't have to wither like that fig tree. Just repent and produce fruit in keeping with your repentance.

May 6th

If you, then, though you are evil, know how to give good gifts to your children, how much more will your Father in heaven give good gifts to those who ask him!
—Matthew 7:11 NIV

I Hope You Dance

Do you know we have a Father who longs to give us good, good gifts?

I was chased today by a mother robin. She sat dutifully on her nest until my approach when she flew off to the nearest tree branch. I couldn't help but peek above the menagerie of straw and twigs to see two little bare heads snuggled into their new home. I knew better than to linger, so after seeing them, I quickly moved on. Apparently not soon enough for the mother. She followed me down the sidewalk yelling at the top of her little bird lungs. "Stay away from my babies!" Have you ever been chastised by a bird?

I didn't blame her. What mama doesn't want the best for her offspring? When my son asked me what song I would like for the mother/son dance at his wedding reception, only one came to mind: Lee Ann Womack's "I Hope You Dance." It expresses a mother's desire for her child to always engage life. To never lose that sense of adventure, to be full of gratitude and faith. And when given the choice "to sit it out or dance," she hopes her boy (or girl) will dance.

As fiercely as a mother hopes the best for her children, it's but a reflection of our heavenly Father's hopes and desires for us. He not only hopes, but gives—freely, lavishly, tenderly. He's not a stingy God. More than any parents could give to their children, God gives to those who ask him. His profound love reaches far beyond what we can imagine.

So, I hope my son chooses always to dance. I hope you do too. I hope you never choose to sit out even one song. I hope when God extends his hand to you, you'll take it and let him lead you in the greatest dance of all time.

Yes, I hope you dance.

May 7th

Blessed is the one whose delight is in the law of the LORD,
and who meditates on his law day and night.
That person is like a tree planted by streams of water,
which yields its fruit in season and whose leaf does not wither—
whatever they do prospers.

—Psalm 1:1-3

From "I Have To" to "I Have To"

The other day I was discussing the importance of having a daily devotional life with some students when one girl remarked how she went from "I have to do devotions each day" (in an obligatory way) to "I have to do devotions each day" (in a desperate way). I knew what she meant.

Most believers consider spending time each day with God in prayer and reading the Bible essential for spiritual growth. Yet making it a priority doesn't come easily. I've known pastors who look to the Bible primarily as a resource for sermons, not as a means of developing intimacy with God. Students at the Bible college where I teach have confessed how it's sometimes easier to neglect devotions when they are taking Bible classes all the time. The Word of God becomes more like a textbook to them than the source of life. Their relationship with the Lord weakens and they don't know why.

Scripture says those who meditate "on his law day and night" are blessed. They aren't quick to get dehydrated in the race of life because they are watered by streams that flow from God's Word. They bear fruit in every season of the soul because they receive daily nourishment. Their witness doesn't wither like a leaf. It flourishes. And if that's not enough, "whatever they do prospers." Sounds like a pretty good deal to me.

There was a time in my life when reading God's Word did not hold the importance that it does today. But somewhere along the way, I got hungry for more. I became desperate and like my student, I flipped from daily devotions being something I had to do, to something I can't live without. It will happen to you too. If you're struggling with a daily devotional life, don't stop pursuing it. Even if it feels obligatory right now, as you continue to seek God, one day it will turn around.

And life will never be the same.

May 8th

Very truly I tell you, unless a kernel of wheat falls to the ground and dies, it remains only a single seed. But if it dies, it produces many seeds. Anyone who loves their life will lose it, while anyone who hates their life in this world will keep it for eternal life.   —*John 12:24–25 NIV*

A Kernel of Wheat

A pint of pure nard in an alabaster jar. A widow's mite. Abandoned fishing nets. Offerings that appeared small by the world's standards but ones which proved to be of inestimable worth to God. These simple acts of love-laced obedience have had lasting power—over two thousand years of lasting power.

Most of us don't realize the fruit of our sacrifices any more than Mary of Bethany did when she poured out the costly perfume on Jesus' feet. The poor widow didn't even know Jesus was watching when she dropped all she had into the offering plate. The disciples left their nets to *follow* without any assurance of what that *following* might entail. Neither they nor we experience the luxury of knowing our acts of devotion will pay off in the end.

The disease of the Pharisees in Jesus' day was that they *did* care about the results. They not only wanted to see the fruit of their work—they hoped everyone else would too! Theirs were lives fueled by the praises of men. Their obedience was love-motivated all right, but love of self, not God. So, whatever fruit in life they would have borne was buried with them in the grave.

How different for those who simply choose to give it all. Since my husband and I studied with Francis Schaeffer at L'Abri, I've often thought of how he described his call to the ministry: a "kernel of wheat that falls to the ground and dies." Unbeknown to him, that one kernel would end up producing a truckload of seeds. Just as Jesus said it would. And so, for each of us.

Whether God calls us to offer something seemingly small or reach for a sacrifice deep within, let's not get stuck in looking at results. Let's not catch the disease of the Pharisees and focus on short-lived gains. Be assured our obedience to God will result in seeds infused with lasting power.

Lasting power—as in eternity.

May 9th

Look at the birds of the air; they do not sow or reap or store away in barns, and yet your heavenly Father feeds them. Are you not much more valuable than they? —Matthew 6:26 NIV

What's Really Valuable?

The words, "Becky, I don't know where my purse is!" stopped me in my tracks. The look of horror on my eighty-seven-year-old mother's face spoke even louder than what she was saying. We had been shopping at the mall all morning, and she was just getting ready to make her last purchase of the day when she made the startling discovery. I immediately ran to the store's customer service, but no one had turned in a lost handbag. Our hearts sank.

I found a seat where Mom could rest while I attempted to figure out what to do. "Stay here and pray. Let's try not to panic," I assured her. However, as I thought of her losing not only her money, but driver's license, credit cards, etc., I felt my own panic start to set in.

I located a saleswoman who offered to contact mall security. When no one answered, she gave me directions to the security office; but as I started out the store, I happened to spot a mall cop. After hearing my dilemma, he made a call and learned that in fact someone had turned in a purse. It was being held in a store next to the bench where Mom had been sitting earlier. I was sure it was hers. But I believe the Lord wanted us to know it was neither luck nor coincidence that got Mom's purse back. As I looked at the badge on the mall cop, engraved was the name *J. Christ.*

It's easy for us to forget how much God cares about the details of our lives. He encourages us not to worry about those details ... what we eat, drink or wear. If he watches over the birds, can't we trust him to watch over us as well? My goodness, even the hairs of our head are numbered! (Matthew 10:30). Such is the love of our heavenly Father. It's a truth we would do well to remember.

Never forget what Jesus assesses as "much more valuable." You!

May 10th

So then, each of us will give an account of ourselves to God.
—Romans 14:12 NIV

Excuses

"But Mom, everyone else is doing it! My printer broke [modern version of the dog ate my homework]. I couldn't help it!"

Nothing will hinder our growth as a Christian more than making excuses for our sins and weaknesses. We live in a world of self-justification. We breathe it in the air. There's always someone or something else to blame. But there is never a justified excuse to disobey the commands of God.

Consider the Rekabites, a tribe in Israel who obeyed the instructions of their forefather, Jehonadab, in two things: to always live as nomads (outside the cities) and to abstain from wine (Jeremiah 35:6–10).

Around 600 BC the Babylonians are bearing down on Israel. The Rekabites have temporarily relocated in Jerusalem to escape the ruthless Babylonian armies. While there, the Lord sends Jeremiah to offer them safety in one of the side rooms of the temple. There, he offers them cups of wine. Compounded by the threat of foreign invasion, excuses to disobey God are saturating the culture. It would have been "understandable" if the Rekabites had taken Jeremiah up on his offer. I mean, what's wrong with a drink of wine?

But they did not renege on their commitment. They stayed true to the commands they had been given. Despite precarious circumstances. Despite rampant compromise. Despite that a prophet of God himself was proposing the toast! They kept the command. And because of such stellar faithfulness, God used them as an example to the whole nation (Jeremiah 35:16).

The Rekabites' fidelity serve as a model for us as well. They remind a generation characterized by broken promises and unprecedented faithlessness that disobedience has no excuse. Paul warns we will all be held accountable before God. We will never find good enough reasons to harbor resentment toward those who hurt us—no matter how justified our complaints. We'll not discover new grounds to cheat on our taxes—no matter how bad the economy. And even if all our friends and family members compromise, make no mistake, "But God, everyone else was doing it" isn't going to fly on judgment day.

May 11th

Praise the LORD, my soul, and forget not all his benefits.
—Psalm 103:2 NIV

Nourish Your Soul

I'm looking over the labels on my daily vitamin supplements: calcium reduces the risk of osteoporosis; vitamin E promotes heart health; B Complex energizes metabolism and strengthens the nervous system. All are important components for maintaining a healthy body. But what about my spiritual body? What keeps my walk with Christ from becoming as rigid and inflexible as calcified bones? What prevents the beat of irregular moods from setting off an emotional heart attack? How do I "keep going" like a spiritual Energizer Bunny™ when circumstances have sapped my last ounce of faith?

Brother Lawrence offers some nutritional advice to help us avoid spiritual deficiency. He says, "We must nourish our souls with a lofty idea of God." Yet how do we intentionally do that? It seems a lot easier to cram our lives with the empty calories of mindless pleasure and busyness than to consume spirit-healthy nutrients. A look at Psalm 103 may help us put Brother Lawrence's encouragement into practice.

The psalmist begins by telling his soul to "Praise the LORD...and forget not all his benefits"—benefits like forgiveness, health and redemption (vv. 2-4); love and compassion, satisfaction of his desires, and even reinvigoration of his youth (vv. 3-5). Acknowledging God's *specific* benefits offers us a new menu, one that is rich in the life-giving forces of gratitude and humility.

But the psalmist doesn't stop there. His personal experience of God's goodness serves as a springboard of praise for who he is to all mankind. God's righteousness and justice extends to all who are oppressed. He treats none of us as our sins deserve. His love for those who fear him reaches as "high as the heavens." And in contrast to man's quickly fading span on earth, the Lord—and his covenant—lasts forever (vv. 6-18).

Lofty ideas of God? Indeed. Exhaustive? Not even a little bit. But it's a fine place to start if we want to prioritize the nourishment of our souls. So, the next time you're tempted to indulge in "junk food" that robs you of spiritual vitality, resist! You have the choice to opt for a better diet, a choice to taste and see that the Lord is good!

May 12th

Everything is possible for one who believes. —Mark 9:23 NIV

A Mountaintop Miracle

God is in the business of making the impossible possible.

It was early Saturday morning in Boulder, Colorado. I went to the gas station to fill up my Renault. The overcast skies looked threatening, but when the station attendant commented it looked like we were in for a shower, I confidently replied, "Nope. It's not going to rain today. I'm getting married this morning on top of that mountain in Boulder Canyon." I had learned a lot about faith that week.

Since I was a little girl, my grandpa and I had plotted that when the day came, he would perform my wedding. But it almost didn't happen. Chip and I had decided to have a somewhat unconventional wedding ... just him, me and Grandpa on the mountaintop. No one would be at the ceremony besides the three of us and God.

Grandpa was to fly to Denver on the Thursday before the wedding and stay until after the reception when he would fly back to Ohio. That Sunday I received the distressing call he might not be able to come. He was experiencing severe back pains and was unsure as to whether he could make the trip. Worry flooded me. I couldn't imagine getting married without Grandpa.

The next few days were a roller coaster of emotions. He thought he could come. Then a day of spasms screamed "it's impossible." My hope started to dim. In desperation, I sought God for a miracle. It was then I landed on the passage from Mark 9:23: "Everything is possible for one who believes." I don't consider myself a name-it-and-claim-it type Christian, but I *knew* the Lord was speaking to me. Faith comes by hearing the word of God and that day, I heard it. I began believing God was going to make it possible for Grandpa to come. Later that night, I got the last call. "Pick me up tomorrow afternoon!"

Grandpa, Chip and I walked up that mountainside on what had turned into a brilliant sun-filled morning. My childhood dreams had been fulfilled—and more. I had tasted for the first time the power of prayer. And I experienced firsthand the personal I-know-who-you-are kind of love that streams from a heavenly Father.

Do you know this Father with whom all things are possible?

May 13th

"Where is your faith?" he asked his disciples. —Luke 8:25 NIV

Where Is Your Faith?

I'm sure you've experienced it. You're reading the Scripture when suddenly regular print jumps out at you as if it's in big bold letters. Something transpires that causes you to move from simple reading to listening. The Word of God is speaking to you, muting every other sound. You sit up and take notice. Like the other day when I was reading the eighth chapter of Luke.

Jesus and his disciples had set sail on the Sea of Galilee when a violent squall rose. The threat of being capsized created more than a little panic in the disciples. They cried out to Jesus, fearful they were all going to drown. After rebuking the wind and sea, Jesus rebuked the storm residing within the men with the question that bared their souls, "Where is your faith?"

The Lord spoke those same words to me that morning. Was my faith at the same place it had been a year ago? Was it growing? Or just subsisting? Had it weathered the brutal storms I'd encountered? Or was it holding on for dear life?

I don't think I'm alone. I've had some recent conversations with people who are also assessing their faith. People who don't understand why ... why their house hasn't sold, releasing much needed funds ... why their teenager is turning away from God ... why another year has passed with no job, no husband or no change in a broken relationship.

We will not be able to prevail through such "squalls" if we base our faith on anything other than the character and Word of God. The answer to where is your faith ultimately rests on what we believe about God. Do we believe each gut-wrenching circumstance we face grants us the opportunity to say, "I trust you. I don't have to understand. I trust you"?

Jesus asked whether he would find faith on the earth when he returned. I want to be among those whose faith has not been thrown overboard. I want it to be obvious, observable and obedient to his every Word. How about you?

Where is your faith?

May 14th

On the third day a wedding took place at Cana in Galilee.... What Jesus did here in Cana of Galilee was the first of the signs through which he revealed his glory.

—John 2:1, 11 NIV

When the Natural Becomes Supernatural

On the third day a wedding took place at Cana in Galilee.... What Jesus did here in Cana of Galilee was the first of the signs through which he revealed his glory.

Even the start of the day hinted toward something supernatural.

It began while I was sitting by the pool in the early morning having my daily time with God before the day's festivities. My Scripture reading just happened to be the second chapter of John. I didn't plan it that way. But I know who did. You see, it just happened to be my son's wedding day. God—in a way only he could do—was reminding me a miracle would be taking place that afternoon.

John 2 records Jesus' first miracle. It took place at a wedding in Galilee. There he rearranged the elements in H_2O and transformed them into CH_3CH_2OH (wine). He converted natural everyday water into wine. In doing so, he "revealed his glory." Inexplicable.

But not more so than the other miracle occurring that day: Two people, an individual man and an individual woman were also being rearranged—realigned to make them one. "For this reason a man will leave his father and mother and be united to his wife, and the two will become one flesh" (Ephesians 5:31). Paul describes this uniting as a "profound mystery" that reflects Christ and the church (v. 32). We can't understand how two becoming one can happen any more than we can understand how water became wine. Or how Christ could call the very imperfect church his bride. We can't comprehend the supernatural through natural eyes.

Marriage is a miracle. Always has been. Always will be, no matter how hard society attempts to deny its sacredness or redefine its meaning. Some see weddings as ordinary water, but in reality, every time we observe a wedding we witness a supernatural miracle of wine.

Jesus was as present at my son's wedding in Rougemont, North Carolina, as he was at Cana in Galilee. Even at the reception when the wind blew in a brief rain shower and upended everything in the outdoor tent, God was there. As if not wanting anyone to miss the message, he painted a rainbow across the sky and once again "revealed his glory."

That's what happens when the natural becomes supernatural.

May 15th

He has made us competent as ministers of a new covenant—not of the letter but of the Spirit; for the letter kills, but the Spirit gives life.
—*2 Corinthians 3:6 NIV*

A Manual or Immanuel?

As my husband and I were praying the other morning, he said, "Thank you, God, for not giving us '*a* manual,' but '*Imm*anuel.'" The profundity of how one simple syllable could separate the Christian faith from every other belief excited me.

When we think of a manual, we picture a handbook or instructional guide. It consists of detailed information on how to accomplish a task or put something together. If we just follow the directions, we'll acquire the desired result. Even *dummies* can supposedly achieve success if the rules are adhered to. Therein lies the problem when we're talking about life. We are human. We mess up. In fact, we mess up so badly, that it is impossible for any of us to follow a manual on life. Muslims, Buddhists, Humanists—they all try. But fallen man can never meet even his own standard of right and wrong.

Enter Immanuel. God knew our human nature would always miss the mark. He proved it by giving the nation of Israel the Law. No matter how strictly the Law was followed, it could not take away the stain of rebellion and the heart's penchant to sin. So, he sent us a Savior. One who would not only be "with us," but whose Spirit would live "with*in* us." Immanuel changes us from the inside. He writes laws on our hearts, not ledgers. Loved-laced laws that transform us into new creatures.

When "manual" is used as an adjective, it refers to work accomplished by human effort, skill or energy as in "manual labor." Mechanisms like "manual gearshifts" are operated by the hands in contrast to an electrical or electronic device. Polar opposite from Immanuel. The work of Immanuel flows from God, is sustained by God and completed by God. His finished work causes all man-centered endeavors to pale.

I've often heard the Bible referred to as the *Manufacturer's Handbook*. Some would look at it as a manual of sorts, but it is so much more than a how-to book. It leads us to true truth. To true love. To true life.

It leads us to Immanuel.

May 16th

For all have sinned and fall short of the glory of God.
—Romans 3:23 NIV

My Bad

Ever hear the expression, "My bad?" It's a phrase used to apologize for making a mistake without really apologizing. Someone spills coffee on a friend's shirt or turns up late for a meeting and exclaims, "My bad." No real responsibility is taken to right the wrong. *It just happened and hopefully won't happen again* seems to be the general thinking behind the term. An apt phrase for a society light on taking personal responsibility. A society that thinks if we believe there's no such thing as sin, then we can't be sinners.

It's one of many delusions infiltrating our culture. Dr. Keith Ablow writes about how a combination of technology and media is producing a "generation of deluded narcissists." He explains how Facebook, Twitter, computer games and reality TV are turning young people into "faux celebrities—the equivalent of lead actors in their own fictionalized life stories." Ablow observes that because false pride cannot be sustained, the bubble of narcissism will inevitably burst, generating an epidemic of depression, suicide and unprecedented hatred toward self and others.

Although I agree with Ablow's assessment of how technological advances have accelerated the problem, love of self and avoidance of responsibility has been alive and well on the planet since Cain slew Abel. The solution lies not in avoiding twenty-first century innovation but in acknowledging the timeless truth: man doesn't just *do* bad; we *are* bad. Until we understand that, it's impossible to find the *good.*

We will never be able to compensate for our "bad." No amount of charitable works, successes or followers on social media can substitute for true repentance. It takes something radical to wake us up from the stupor of our self-justifications. Something which penetrates the heart of our sinful nature. Something so powerful that it both drives us to our knees and lifts us to the highest place.

Jesus said we had to be "born again." There's no other way to get rid of "our bad."

May 17th

Therefore what God has joined together, let no one separate.
—Mark 10:9 NIV

It's a Marathon Not a Sprint

My Grandpa Creech was a great storyteller. The story he most often loved to tell revealed his deep affection for Grandma. Their life together taught me a lot about marriage.

After Grandpa returned home from the army, he spotted a woman in a shining red dress working in his uncle's chipyard. He liked to describe how his heart started beating fast and his breath shortened as he heard the voice of the Lord say, "This is the one." They married not long after.

They were an unlikely match, personality wise. Grandpa enjoyed being around people. Grandma tended to be shy and reserved. But they both took the Word of God seriously. When Jesus said, "what God has joined together, let no one separate," they believed it. The bond between them proved far stronger than their differences.

It carried them through over seventy years of marriage. They walked together through all the ups and downs of his being a country preacher while maintaining a full-time job as a telephone lineman. They walked together when their son rejected everything they'd instilled in him to pursue a path marked with divorce and heartache. They walked together in joy when years later at age sixty-five, he returned to the faith. They walked together in grief when their daughter died unexpectedly in her late forties. They walked together when Grandma began experiencing Alzheimer's and had to go to a nursing home. They walked together when Grandpa refused to leave her side and moved into the facility to be next to her.

Grandma and Grandpa knew marriage was a marathon, not a sprint. They never once considered their commitment to be for anything less than the long haul. They learned through the joys and sorrows of life that they were better together because God had joined them.

How do you view marriage? Do you see it as an inseparable sacred bond between a man, a woman and God? Worthy of persevering through the rough patches? If you are married, keep running—even when everything in you is screaming, "Stop." Press on to the finish line. Be a marathon couple.

May 18th

For the word of God is alive and active. Sharper than any double-edged sword, it penetrates even to dividing soul and spirit, joints and marrow; it judges the thoughts and attitudes of the heart.
—Hebrews 4:12 NIV

The B-I-B-L-E

The B-I-B-L-E, yes that's the book for me. I stand alone on the Word of God, the B-I-B-L-E!

If ever a song could make the "Sunday School Top Hits List," it would have to include "The B-I-B-L-E." After all these years, it remains a staple in children's gospel music. The downside of those familiar songs (and truths) we learned in Sunday school, however, is our tendency to relegate them to the past as we become more sophisticated.

Well, I'm happy to say after all these years, the B-I-B-L-E is still the book for me. I have a library of books ... old friends I cherish. They ignite my imagination and broaden my thinking. They stimulate, entertain and educate me. They've taken me to pre-revolution France, to the streets of London, to Narnia, to Middle Earth. They serve as my dessert at the end of a long day. But no book, even the most beautifully crafted, contains the power of the Bible.

The Bible lives. Its words actively connect with our souls to bring conviction, encouragement and counsel, judging "the thoughts and attitudes of the heart." It reveals the extravagance of God's love for us and teaches us how to respond. It explains what *is* and why.

We have no other means of developing our faith than through the Bible. Researchers Greg Hawkins and Cally Parkins studied people in one thousand churches. Their findings: "Nothing has a greater impact on spiritual growth than reflection on Scripture. If churches could do only one thing to help people at all levels of spiritual maturity grow in their relationship with Christ, they would inspire, encourage and equip their people to read the Bible." Our faith does not grow through the good works of *busy-ness but through Scripture-ness*.

I hope the B-I-B-L-E is the book for you. I hope its easy accessibility isn't causing you to take it for granted. I hope you feast on it every day. I hope you let it transform you. If you don't have a regular pattern of reading this ever-timely, victory-enabling, soul-sustaining, living Word of God, I can't think of a better time to start than now.

May 19th

"As surely as the LORD lives," he said, "the LORD himself will strike him, or his time will come and he will die, or he will go into battle and perish."

—1 Samuel 26:10 NIV

Knowing God Knows

Don't we all at times have trouble holding situations in life loosely? Speaking as someone who has a track record of holding on too tight, take heart. I'm changing. And if I can move from self-reliance to God-reliance, so can you. It requires one unwavering conviction: Knowing God knows.

David knew it. When King Saul relentlessly pursued him, he fled for his life. Fear and jealousy that David would usurp his throne drove Saul beyond reason. He had no justification for his actions. David's loyalty to God's anointed king stood unshakeable. Even when his life was at stake, David refused to undermine Saul and take the situation into his own hands.

Like the night he discovered Saul's army camping in the wilderness. David and one of his men, Abishai, crept into the camp and found Saul and his bodyguards sound asleep. Abishai urged David to make the most of this fortunate moment. Let him kill Saul! But David responded, "Don't destroy him!... The LORD himself will strike him, or his time will come and he will die, or he will go into battle and perish" (1 Samuel 26:9–10).

David wasn't naive. He knew Saul was treating him unjustly. He could have easily rationalized whatever means it took to grab control of the situation, but he refused to take the bait. His confidence did not rest on himself, but on *knowing God knew* his predicament. He placed his future completely in the hand of the God who knows.

What a profound revelation: God knows more than we do! So, if I'm forced to drastically alter my class schedule for the semester, I don't have to stay stuck in the past, even if the change is inconvenient. Because the Sovereign God knows.

When I'm facing a deadline crunch and my neighbor tells me he might be bringing ten dozen ears of corn to freeze—the day before we're leaving town—I don't have to cling to my plan. Maybe God has a better one. Because the Sovereign God knows. You might think *knowing God knows* promotes passivity. But letting go and entrusting to God requires a lot of work and, dare I say, practice.

But you can do it, friend.

May 20th

"You have done a foolish thing," Samuel said. "You have not kept the command the LORD your God gave you; if you had, he would have established your kingdom over Israel for all time. But now your kingdom will not endure."
—1 Samuel 13:13–14 NIV

Lost Legacies

Are we "all in" doing life God's way or do we have a Plan B in reserve in case he doesn't come through? The first king of Israel shifted to Plan B when waiting stretched his limits. It cost him a legacy.

Samuel instructed King Saul to wait for him seven days before engaging in battle against the Philistines. It turned out to be a long seven days. The Philistines assembled "three thousand chariots, six thousand charioteers, and soldiers as numerous as the sand on the seashore" (1 Samuel 13:5). Overwhelmed with fear, Saul's troops began abandoning him. By the seventh day with no sign of Samuel, the pressure on Saul to do something, *anything*, tightened.

So, he caved. Rather than obeying Samuel's instructions, he took the situation in his own hands. He offered a burnt offering—something only the priests were authorized to do—in order to garner the Lord's favor before battle. Soon, Samuel arrived with a harsh rebuke. Because Saul failed to obey the Lord, he would have no heir to sit on the throne. Like the old Frank Sinatra song, he did it "his way." And a legacy was lost.

Legacies that last are legacies sustained by faith. Whether building a family, a business or a ministry, we don't stop trusting God when it gets hard. And we certainly don't circumvent God's plan to get the results we want. Saul's legacy lasted about as long as the monument he built to himself (1 Samuel 15:12). When I impatiently revert to my own efforts, I must ask whether I'm trying to build a monument for my glory or God's.

In choosing to believe God, we become part of a never-ending legacy. We let faith determine our actions, not outside pressure or half-hearted convictions. We're "all in" with God's ways. No

Plan B. Unlike Saul, we can wait on God's timing, even if the troops around us are quaking in their boots. You don't want to abort your legacy, do you? A legacy of blessing awaits everyone who believes in God. Don't be enslaved to doing things "your way."

May 21st

"Not by might nor by power, but by my Spirit," says the LORD Almighty.
—Zechariah 4:6 NIV

I Can't But He Can

I've been noticing a lot of heads hitting brick walls lately. Mountains not moving. Circumstances refusing to change. Issues once conquered creeping back to life. Situations that remind me of our vast limitations ...

When Atlanta Pastor Louie Giglio attended college, he walked sixteen blocks to classes. As he walked, he repeated one phrase, *I can't but He can.* From home to school, *I can't but He can. I can't but He can.* Although a simple mantra, it produced in him a passionate abandonment to God. He must have taken Zechariah 4:6 seriously. "Not by might nor by power, but by my Spirit."

Obviously, a mindless repetition of *I can't but He can* won't deepen our dependency on God any more than willing ourselves to be thinner transforms us to a size 5. But three factors contributing to a strong reliance on the Holy Spirit include desperation, dissatisfaction with the "norm" and a healthy dose of humility.

It's probably easiest to say *I can't but He can* when we're so desperate we know if God doesn't come through, it's over. Someone has said, "God's office is at the end of our rope." He sometimes lets us get to the end of ourselves until there's no place else to go but to him.

I can't but He can thinking acknowledges our best efforts pale in comparison to what Christ can do through us. It invites the Holy Spirit to transform our everyday circumstances into something extraordinary. It's praying the classes I teach would go beyond my *I can;* loving relationships would soar above my *I can;* unsolvable problems would find resolve because *He can.*

But without a healthy dose of humility, the words *I can't but He can* remain little more than a vain repetition. Many view humility as feeling bad about ourselves. However, there's a huge difference between low self-esteem and humility. Humility consists of more than a realization of *I can't.* True humbleness lies, as many have noted, in not thinking of ourselves at all. It moves us from introspection to God-spection, from the *I can't* to the *He can.*

So, let's not get caught up in "might and power" to do life. Let's join in Pastor Giglio's mantra and rely on the Holy Spirit for everything.

May 22nd

God, I have heard you say two things. One is that you, God, are strong. The other is that you, Lord, are loving.

—*Psalm 62:11–12 NIRV*

It's All About the Who

A friend posed an interesting question the other day. How can I keep legitimate concerns from tuning into worry? Faced with an onslaught of physical as well as financial difficulties, it wasn't hard to see where she was coming from. She didn't want to be irresponsible, yet she faced the dilemma of how she could keep anxious thoughts from consuming her. Have you ever been there?

Paul says the road from anxiety to peace lies in bringing our concerns to God. But if we have not learned how to ask, I'm afraid it's a road less taken. We may pray and petition, and do it all with thanksgiving, but ultimately, the how reflects our perception of who we're asking. It's all about the who....

Do we believe we're petitioning a God who loves us and encourages us to lay every single one of our burdens on him? Or do we view him as a distant Sovereign unconcerned about our daily griefs? Do we envision God as ultimate authority, able to do whatever he wants, even go beyond nature's boundaries on our behalf? Peace of mind comes with the assurance he is able to help. Peace of heart comes in knowing he is willing.

For believers, God's compassion and power are not exactly a news flash. But many of us seem to lapse into a kind of spiritual amnesia when the struggles of life bear down. *Are you really there God? Are you going to come through this time? Are you still the God of miracles?* Haunting questions. Questions that only find resolve when we remember who we're entreating. Scripture puts it succinctly: God is strong; God is loving. This strong, loving God offers us a great exchange:

- transcending peace for anxiousness
- rest for sleeplessness
- rhythmic calm for racing heartbeats
- strength to do all things for weary worries.

Don't miss that exchange. Remember who it is that's listening and get on that road to peace.

May 23rd

If it is possible, as far as it depends on you, live at peace with everyone.
—Romans 12:18 NIV

Divide and Conquer

Divide and conquer. It's one of the enemy's most successful strategies against the human race. It's intensifying.

I can't remember a time when the fissures have run so deep. In families, husbands and wives are pitted against each other or children against parents. Division abounds within local churches as well as the body of Christ worldwide. Our country is being pulled apart at the seams by political factions who feed on disunity. Race divides us. Social issues divide us. Income divides us. The educated versus the uneducated. The secularist versus the religious.

Every line drawn weakens the whole. Although diverse opinions can strengthen the structure, division destroys it. I'm afraid that's what we now face. Satan has cunningly woven into the fabric strands of such intense discord that almost every sphere of unity faces unraveling. Such disconnectedness makes us easy prey for destruction. How are we to respond?

Romans 12 offers a counter-strategy.

Cultivate genuine love as we vigorously safeguard the truth. Bless those who persecute us. Refuse to return evil for evil and let humility direct us to harmony. Trust God to avenge wrongs as we show compassion to our enemies. Overcome Satan's strategy of divide and conquer by overcoming evil with good (vv. 9–21).

It's the mindset displayed in the 2015 shooting at the Charleston AME Church when the white gunman killed nine of their members as they gathered for a Bible study. Those who lost loved ones neither made excuses for the killer nor hurled condemnation. They fully acknowledged his wrong, yet fully offered him the same forgiveness they received when they came to know Christ. Satan's strategy to divide blacks against whites failed. The whole city—and nation—stood united with these brave believers. They loved when tempted to hate. Forgave when tempted to curse. They lived out Romans 12 through the power of God. And so can we.

Let's be aware of Satan's divide and conquer strategy on whatever level it surfaces. We have opportunity always to overcome his evil with God's good.

May 24th

Then Peter said, "Silver or gold I do not have, but what I do have I give you. In the name of Jesus Christ of Nazareth, walk."

—Acts 3:6 NIV

Beyond Survival

He had been a cripple for over forty years. He depended on others to literally carry him every day to his begging spot at the temple gate. He had no other option. His full-time employment consisted of unemployment. He was forced to rely on the pity of man, which has always been at best—shaky. When Peter and

John came by he asked them for a coin. What he received was an overflowing bank vault! This crippled-from-birth man was instantly transformed into an athlete "walking and jumping, and praising God" (v. 8).

Chronic conditions have a way of crippling our expectations, don't they? Whether physical illness or emotional distress, after a while our hope reduces to nothing more than mere survival. But for this man on this day, meager expectations exploded into a miracle. He received healing, and Peter made sure everyone knew why. It was not because of any power or godliness he or John possessed. The man was healed "by faith in the name of Jesus" (v. 16).

God intends our seasons of waiting to produce something more than a survival mindset. They become opportune times for our faith to develop. Times where we learn not to limit God. Not to shortchange his love. Not to second guess his plans. No matter what the source of delay, the choice to keep relying on God in our circumstances provides the architectural integrity we need to expand our house of trust.

John and Peter's daring faith landed them in prison. But rather than weakening their confidence, they were emboldened even more. As a result, the "bank vault" offered to the crippled man became accessible to about five thousand new believers! (Acts 4:4). We'll never know how great our faith can grow unless we give it the opportunity.

If you are living in survival mode, be assured that God wants to use your situation—its difficulty as well as its duration—to construct something better than silver. Better than gold. Something that comes from Jesus of Nazareth.

But God chose the foolish things of the world to shame the wise; God chose the weak things of the world to shame the strong.
—1 Corinthians 1:27 NIV

Weak Things

Never underestimate God's ability to use less than perfect vessels.

He was far from the best speaker in my speech class. Poor eye contact, monotone voice, nervous fidgeting. He worked hard, though, and by the end of the semester he had gained ground. The turning point came when he gave his persuasive speech, arguing against abortion. Although the class consisted of Bible college students, rather than using Scripture to support his points, he took a clear, logical, fact-based approach. It turned out to be a solid speech.

I had forgotten about it. That, however, was about to change.

The last day of class another student gave her final speech on what she had learned over the semester. She explained she had always been personally opposed to abortion, but considered it to be a woman's choice—until she heard her classmate's speech. She said the most significant factor of the semester was the impact that one speech made on her. It caused her to move from being "pro-choice" to "100 percent pro-life."

My student didn't let his marginal skills at public speaking deter him from addressing such a huge, controversial issue. He somehow realized the message was greater than the messenger. Because he went for it, despite his *weakness*, a life was changed. And who knows how many other lives?

How often do we sit on our gifts and abilities because we think they don't measure up to those who are far more gifted? I sometimes wish I could craft words like Max Lucado. Present the gospel like Beth Moore. Teach as skillfully as some of my professor friends. But just because we're not as gifted as others, it doesn't mean we have nothing to offer.

Scripture says God chose the foolish and weak to shame the wise and strong. Isn't that interesting? He asks us to use whatever we have no matter what our self-assessment. He is choosing you and me to advance his kingdom in some unique capacity even if we regard ourselves as weak.

May 26th

Now this is what the LORD Almighty says: "Give careful thought to your ways. You have planted much, but harvested little. You eat, but never have enough. You drink, but never have your fill. You put on clothes, but are not warm. You earn wages, only to put them in a purse with holes in it."

—Haggai 1:5–6 NIV

Purses with Holes

Their work was fruitless. Their expectations unmet. Even their best efforts fizzled into frustration. What in the world was going on?

That's the question Israel must have been pondering when the prophet Haggai brought the answer. The people didn't understand why God wasn't blessing their labors. He had delivered them from Babylon after years in exile. Now they could go on with their lives. Right? Not exactly. Although they arrived in Jerusalem, they hadn't *arrived*. They failed to see their return was not the end but the beginning.

Sound familiar? Do we, like Israel, suffer from the disease of chronic misplaced priorities? We start well, but how easy it is for us to revert to building our own houses while neglecting the house of God. Or in other words, prioritizing self-interests over the Lord's. Like Israel, we make all kinds of lame excuses to rationalize doing what *we* want to do, all the while neglecting what God deems more important.

What do we prioritize over Christ? Our family? Church? Work? Success? The Bible has a name for misplaced priorities—idols. Idolatry comes in all shapes and sizes, but it most often revolves around what gives us pleasure or comfort or validation. For most of us idolatry takes the form of good things gone bad— bad because we elevate them to heights that are unsustainable with Christ-centered lives. If God isn't first, no amount of justification can compensate for worshipping other gods, no matter how good.

But it's a disease which can be cured. God told Israel, "Give careful thought to your ways." In his mercy, he let them experience the results of self-focused lives: inadequacy, insufficiency and unfulfillment.

So how about you? Do your purses have holes? If so, maybe it's time to consider your priorities. Israel repented when they realized their shortsightedness. Thankfully, we can too.

May 27th

The LORD was with Joseph and gave him success in whatever he did.
—Genesis 39:23 NIV

Blueprint for Integrity

They're dropping like flies—politicians, sports figures, businessmen, church leaders. It seems anyone who experiences any modicum of success faces the integrity issue at some point. Why does it appear that fewer and fewer are passing the test? Not many have articulated the problem more clearly than C. S. Lewis in *The Abolition of Man:* "We make men without chests and expect from them virtue and enterprise. We laugh at honor and are shocked to find traitors in our midst." We are a *dis-integrated* people. We have failed to build our house on the bedrock of integrity.

But we do have a blueprint.

It's found in Genesis 39. You're familiar with Joseph ... sold by his brothers to slave owners who took him to Egypt. Although a slave, he so impressed his master, Potiphar, that he was soon elevated to the highest position in his household. Then came the test.

Potiphar's wife wanted him, and she tried again and again to lure him to her bed. His resistance to her seduction models integrity. First, Joseph realized that all sin was sin against God. "How then could I do such a wicked thing and sin against God?" (v. 9). Second, to the extent he could, he removed himself from even being in the presence of the temptation. "And though she spoke to Joseph day after day, he refused to go to bed with her or even be with her" (v. 10). Next, when all else failed, he got out of Dodge "he ran out of the house" (v. 12).

But perhaps the greatest test of integrity came to Joseph when standing firm in his convictions landed him in jail. Rather than letting the bitterness of injustice push God aside, he kept his heart open and "the LORD was with him" (v. 21). Joseph maintained his integrity by refusing to view his circumstances in a way that would have been disloyal to the God he knew.

We can reflect the same kind of integrity in our seasons of temptation. We can be those whose words and deeds are in sync. We can reclaim our heritage of being men and women with virtue—no matter the cost. Because we know how.

We have a blueprint to follow.

May 28th

Let us hold unswervingly to the hope we profess, for he who promised is faithful. —Hebrews 10:23 NIV

When We Don't Get It

There are times when I just don't get what God is doing. To paraphrase Shakespeare, my prayers seem to be "filled with sound and fury, signifying nothing." I feel helpless in the face of injustices and frustrated that God doesn't just fix it! When that happens, doubt creeps in like a fog—it obscures my faith and dampens my spirit. The finish line blurs, tempting me to stop short.

If that sometimes describes you, take heart! We are not alone. The writer to the Hebrew Christians exhorted his fellow believers to "hold unswervingly" to their hope. He challenged them to recall earlier days when they stood their ground in the face of suffering, when they didn't give in to insults, when they joyfully accepted the confiscation of their property (Hebrews 10:32–34). These were *seasoned* believers. Yet they were in danger of not just losing their confidence in God but of throwing it away! They were being urged to persevere, to believe, to trust in his faithfulness.

If we hope to endure in Christ when life doesn't make sense, we can't be restricted by our lack of understanding. Our loyalty to God rests on our faith in who he is. No other attribute of

God's character takes center stage in both the Old and New Testaments more than his love. From "Your love, LORD, reaches to the heavens" (Psalm 36:5) to "God demonstrates his own love for us in this: While we were still sinners, Christ died for us" (Romans 5:8).

When we don't understand *what* God is doing, if we remember *who* he is, the question of *why* will dissipate. Nothing he allows in our lives falls outside the context of his love. No matter how perplexing your circumstances are right now, don't chuck your confidence in the character of God. Grab hold of his unchanging love and don't let go.

Eventually the fog will clear, and you'll see the finish line. You'll get it.

May 29th

Woe to you when everyone speaks well of you, for that is how their ancestors treated the false prophets. —Luke 6:26 NIV

All You Need is Like, Uh, Love

Everyone wants to be liked. My goodness, Mark Zuckerberg has built a billion-dollar business on "likes." We feel wonderful when we're liked, somewhat devastated when we're not. There's nothing wrong with desiring to be liked. Even in evangelistic terms, who listens to someone they don't like? The problem comes when "like" takes precedent over love.

Jesus warned us of the lurking danger in being liked, or rich, or well-fed. He didn't want us to get so caught up in the creature comforts of life that we miss the true blessings. He points out how some pretty despicable people were well-liked. No one wants to end up like them.

How do you react when you feel someone doesn't like you? One natural human tendency is to withdraw. We then interpret everything through the lens of negativity. Someone doesn't wave back at church. Someone else doesn't respond to an email. Another disagrees with something we believe. They all become evidences that we're not liked. So, we wallow in rejection.

A second danger for like-addicts is failure to confront someone with the truth for fear they won't, well, like us anymore. But no matter how much we try to justify it, there is nothing loving about letting people believe lies. That's using cheap grace to hide our selfish tendencies.

So, what about love? Love is not "live and let live." It's "die to let live." Love doesn't mull over rejection; it chooses a higher road. When we soak our minds with the truth of God's unconditional love for us, our need to gobble up man's affirmation like a starving waif starts to die. We're full. So full, that even if our perceptions are true and someone *is* rejecting us, what difference does it make? We respond out of the love God has given us, not out of a desperate need for man's approval.

Blessed are those who seek to love more than be liked. The Beatles aside, it's all we really need.

May 30th

These stones are to be a memorial to the people of Israel forever.
—Joshua 4:7 NIV

Make a Memorial

It was Memorial Day weekend. I was conducting a public speaking workshop for the Boston YWAM staff. For their final assignment, I asked students to prepare a speech that described a "memorial" in their lives. Their presentations confirmed my suspicions—how God so often uses "memorials" to remind us of his faithfulness.

When Israel entered the Promised Land, Joshua instructed the tribes to build a stone memorial at the Jordon River. The purpose of these twelve stones was clear. When children of later generations asked, "What's with the stones?" they would be told of how God miraculously stopped the flow of the Jordan to enable the nation to cross to the other side. It would be "a memorial to the people of Israel forever."

Although most of us don't have tangible memorials standing in our front yards, I believe we all have those moments when we experience the providence of God in unique, exceptional ways. We think we will always remember them, but the truth is we forget. Maybe it's time we intentionally build some memorials in our minds.

Recently I was speaking with a woman overwhelmed with potential financial needs in the future. What ifs flooded her mind. Immediately I thought of how faithful God had been to her and her family in the past. In fact, I remembered one specific situation where they needed about $25,000 and God supplied it all at just the right time in a way not expected. As I reminded her of God's faithfulness, I told her to "build a memorial" of that event in her mind. Recall it. Rehearse it. Let it renew her confidence that the same God who showed himself faithful in the past would remain faithful in the future.

That's what memorials do. They redirect our thinking from the anxieties of the moment to the peace of the past. Peace when God came through. So, if you're struggling with an issue right now, has the Lord provided you with a "memorial" in the past from which you can draw strength? He wants you to remember. In remembering you will infuse your faith. And when faith is infused, you find yourself on the other side of the Jordan.

May 31st

You will keep in perfect peace those whose minds are steadfast, because they trust in you. —Isaiah 26:3 NIV

Toe-Dippin' Serenity

It seems like an old-fashioned word. It's a bit out of sync in our fast-lane, high-stress society. Maybe its rarity in our vocabulary reflects its scarcity in our living. Yet as elusive as peace of mind might be, more than ever we need ...

Serenity

Serenity is the child of gratitude. Thankfulness has a way of pushing out our fears and overshadowing our anxieties. It lifts us above our troubling circumstances, weary problems and fragile faith. Paul tells the Philippians not to be anxious about anything, but to present their requests to God "with thanksgiving." As they do, he promises they will have "the peace of God, which transcends all understanding" (Philippians 4:6–7). Yet we live in a world where the mentality of thankfulness is being usurped by a mindset of "I deserve." Life clamors for my rights, my wants, my lusts. More than ever we need hearts of ...

Gratitude

Gratitude births serenity because in our quietness we find time to connect the dots between what we've been given and who gives it. It ultimately moves us to a deeper confidence because it helps us see the Giver—the One who knows what we need even better than we know ourselves. Therefore, he can be trusted. Isaiah proclaims "perfect peace" the result of trusting God. Trust in God is the antidote to troubled hearts (John 14:1). Trust exponentially grows when it's nurtured with gratitude found in the pools of serenity. But trust in the midst of our frenzied society has been shattered on oh so many fronts. People don't know who or what to trust. More than ever we need direction to the right source of ...

Trust

Serenity. Gratitude. Trust. This life-giving triad enables us to enjoy life, not just frantically move through it. So, go ahead, take time to dip your toes in the sweet waves of serenity. Let your mind dwell on the many things you have to be grateful for. And let that spirit of gratitude fill your heart with trust in the One who gives all good things.

Ahhhhhh.

June 1st

Blessed is the one who trusts in the LORD, whose confidence is in him.
—Jeremiah 17:7 NIV

A Fixed Landmark

When we encounter situations requiring us to wait on God's timing, we often see no outward movement. We've prayed, yielded, maybe even cried and begged, still it appears nothing is happening. It makes me think of the transfer of the Cape Hatteras lighthouse.

In 1999 our family vacationed on the Outer Banks in North Carolina. It happened to be the year he famed Cape Hatteras Lighthouse was being moved. The tallest brick lighthouse in the United States at 200 feet, beach erosion over its almost 130 years of existence was threatening its future survival. Its relocation was a monumental task, to say the least.

Each day hydraulic jacks slowly lifted and carried the lighthouse 25 to 100 feet until it would be newly situated about 3,000 feet inland. *Slowly* is the operative word. We would go to the site, and no matter how much we stared at that lighthouse, we couldn't see it move an inch! Only when we returned later in the day or the next morning and viewed it relative to a fixed landmark, could we tell it had moved.

Waiting is the incubator of trust. Jeremiah says the Lord blesses those who wait and trust him. The prophet witnessed Israel refusing to wait for the Lord and instead putting their trust in man. For this, Jeremiah declares them cursed. The prosperity they longed for would wither away. But not so for those whose confidence in God isn't dependent on understanding what he's doing. They see the fixed landmark of God's faithfulness and it develops in them a trust that cannot be shaken.

Trusting necessitates that we "stop gazing at the lighthouse" and quit demanding to *see* action. Trust says *see* the "fixed landmark." A landmark that is the same yesterday, today and forever. As we continue to wait and pray, we don't lose heart because our focus rests not on outward circumstances but on the immoveable, unshakeable, eternal character of God. The more we understand who he is, the more we learn to trust.

Remember the Cape Hatteras Lighthouse in your times of waiting. Be assured God is moving even when you don't see him. Be among those who are blessed. Look to God and trust!

June 2nd

During the days of Jesus' life on earth, he offered up prayers and petitions with fervent cries and tears to the one who could save him from death, and he was heard because of his reverent submission.

—Hebrews 5:7 NIV

Reverent Submission

Jesus lived a perfect life. But his prayers weren't heard because he was perfect. If all his accomplishments were written down, John tells us the whole world would not have room for the books written. But his prayers were not heard because of his works. Crowds followed him everywhere he went. But his prayers were not heard because of his popularity.

He was heard because of his reverent submission. "Not my will but yours be done."

Even if we could achieve perfection in this life, even if we could fill a library with books of all we've accomplished, even if we could accrue a following of thousands—none of those factors would cause us to gain the ear of God.

If Jesus was heard because of his reverent submission, might not that also be true for us? Scripture tells us the Lord's eyes go to and fro throughout the earth searching for hearts fully committed to him (2 Chronicles 16:9).

God loves it when we earnestly seek him in prayer. He loves the blistered-knees-wear-the-carpet-out kind of prayer. He also loves those brief "Son of God have mercy on me" kind of prayers whenever and wherever a problem arises. It's not the length of the prayer that counts, but the depth.

God doesn't care what we look like when we pray. We can sit, stand, fall on our face or bend our knees. Reverent submission consists of inward kneeling. Inward kneeling acknowledges our total dependence on him. It humbles us; it relinquishes any idea of vying for what we think we "deserve." The desire for God's will dwarfs all others.

If you're looking for God to hear your prayers and petitions, your loud cries and tears, come to him with reverent submission. Follow the example of the author and finisher of our faith.

June 3rd

For God so loved the world that he gave his one and only Son, that whoever believes in him shall not perish but have eternal life.
—John 3:16 NIV

Mind the Gap

Mind the gap, please! We heard that warning every time we prepared to disembark the London Underground on our trip to England. The words echoing from the public-address system cautioned passengers to be aware of the opening between the subway door and the station platform. The unique British term captured my attention.

Gaps. Splits. Divisions. We experience a lot of them in life, don't we? But no gap bears greater significance than the one between God and man.

When the Jewish tabernacle was constructed, God gave very specific instructions as to how it was to be built (Exodus 26). Curtains of heavy, tightly woven linen separated the Holy Place from the Most Holy Place where God's presence dwelt. That linen cloth might as well have been an iron curtain. The separation between a holy God and sin-filled man stood impenetrable. But God *minded the gap.* He sent One who would bridge the great divide. The only One who could ... His One and only Son.

When Jesus died, that tightly woven curtain of separation was literally torn in two. His sacrifice atoned for every sin ever committed and provided a way for us—through him—to step safely onto the platform. No longer do we have to fear slipping into the cracks and being crushed by a subway loaded with our sin and shame. His grace carries us into the very presence of God that heretofore had been inaccessible.

Yet God grants us free will. He doesn't force anyone across the platform. We can choose to ignore the gap he minded, even though he speaks to us as regularly as that heard on the London subway. *Mind the gap. Mind the gap.*

Have you heard his voice? Are you mindful of any gaps between you and God today? There doesn't have to be. Jesus paid a tremendous price to bridge the gap and bring us back to our Father—a Father so filled with love for his children that there's not a moment when he doesn't *mind the gap.*

June 4th

But small is the gate and narrow the road that leads to life, and only a few find it.   —Matthew 7:14 NIV

Anything Goes

I have a right to be unlimited!

Wow! That tagline from a popular iPhone ad proudly voices what is becoming a predominant cry in our culture. Stop a moment and think about where that kind of thinking takes us. Do we really have a right to live without limits? Although the creators of the ad may not have had broader implications in mind, they probably knew they were tapping into a perspective that *sells*.

Although most people agree that for society to function, we need certain restrictions, human nature is quick to dismiss the idea of limits when it comes to morality. (We are told what size sodas we can drink and how many hydrocarbons we may extract for fuel, but woe to those who call any kind of sexual license sin). Limits define right and wrong. You may go so far, but not over *that* line. A world without limitations is a world where anything goes. And when anything goes, eventually everything goes. Absent are apps for self-control, restraint, or denial of any pleasure. Limitlessness offers a cheap and unsustainable imitation of freedom.

We don't have to guess where lifestyles of unlimited freedom take us. The 60s gospel of "if it feels good, do it," brought the world unprecedented increases in drug addiction, sexual disease, and family breakdown. The consequences of believing we have the right to anything we want wreaks insatiable appetites; the more we get, the more we want. We ought to know better.

Jesus said the road leading to life is narrow. Getting through the gate requires leaving behind things that don't fit through its small portal. Things like what our anything goes mindset has accrued over time.

So, no matter how appealing those iPhone advertisements may be—buy the product if you want, but don't buy the message behind it. The creator God, in his mercy, has given us limits. Limits that save us from inevitable chaos. Limits that enable us to live in real liberty.

June 5th

At that time Moses was born, and he was no ordinary child.
—Acts 7:20 NIV

No Ordinary People

Do you see yourself as ordinary?

You're probably familiar with the account in Exodus 2 where the infant Moses was delivered from the edict of death issued to all Hebrew boys living in Egypt. With the desperate hope of sparing her baby's life, Moses' mother carefully laid him in a basket and placed him in the Nile River. There, Pharaoh's daughter found him and took him as her son, thus securing his future. The footnote in my Bible states his rescue foreshadows Israel's future deliverance from Egyptian bondage. And, of course, Israel's deliverance foreshadows the escape of all believers from the slavery of sin and death through the blood of Christ.

Just as the Scripture states that Moses was no ordinary child, so Israel was no ordinary nation, and believers today are no ordinary people. It made me think of a movie I saw in the 80s, *Ordinary People.* The movie portrayed how tragedy affected a so-called ordinary middle class American family, exposing the depth of its dysfunction.

Without the blood of Christ, we remain ordinary people. We are bound to our flaws and failures. We may look good on the outside, but the arrival of adversity all too often reveals our dysfunction. We find no more hope for our deliverance than what existed for Moses or Israel. But just as something extraordinary happened to them, so something extraordinary has happened to all of us who believe. An extraordinary God has made it possible for us to be delivered from sin and its devastation.

When we look at ourselves and at others in Christ, we ought

not to think in terms of *ordinary*. We are no longer stuck in sin. There is always hope for redemption, for restoration. We find freedom from the ordinary for ourselves and liberty to view others in the same life-giving light.

So, how do you see yourself? Do you realize God purposes your life to be extraordinary? Don't settle for anything less than viewing yourself as he does. You as his child are no ordinary person.

June 6th

I will give you hidden treasures, riches stored in secret places, so that you may know that I am the LORD, the God of Israel, who summons you by name.

—Isaiah 45:3 NIV

Got a Diamond In Your Pocket?

It was Sunday morning and I had just finished the last talk of five I had given at a weekend retreat for pastors' wives. We were breaking into groups for discussion when one of the ladies realized she had lost her diamond. Her wedding ring was still on her finger, but the diamond setting was gone. We were all sympathetic to her situation. No woman wants to lose her wedding ring! So, everyone began the search. Just as the near panic-stricken lady started to run back to her room to hunt, I felt a nudge from the Lord. *Ask them to stop and pray.*

Even though I felt a bit awkward (I was not the retreat leader, only the speaker), I blurted out, "Could we pray?" They all looked a little surprised, but of course agreed. So, I asked God to help us. While I was praying, the woman put her hand in her pocket. When I finished, she pulled her hand out saying, "I think I feel something." It was her lost diamond.

It was a clear sign to me God wanted us to know he was with us. She could have easily not put her hand in her pocket and thrown her jeans in the wash, never finding the diamond. But in response to prayer, I believe a miracle took place. It reflected what had happened that weekend. Healing was occurring in the ladies' lives. A deep work—not a quick fix—that would continue long after the retreat was over. It's as if the Lord wanted to assure the women they were returning home with a diamond of healing in their pockets not to be overlooked.

Isaiah declared the Lord's promise to give us hidden treasure, treasure stored in secret places. He does this to show us he is the Lord. That Sunday morning the Lord led us to the diamond, but the hidden treasure of knowing he heard our cry proved a far richer treasure.

How about you? If you're wondering whether God hears your prayers, even whether he is with you, don't abandon your hope. Don't throw your jeans in the wash and lose the diamond.

June 7th

With our tongues we bless God our Father; with the same tongues we curse the very men and women he made in his image. Curses and blessings out of the same mouth! My friends, this can't go on. A spring doesn't gush fresh water one day and brackish the next, does it?

—James 3:9-11 MSG

Diamonds and Toads

Ouch! This Scripture makes a clear—and convicting—case for the importance of controlling what we say. But the decision that allows the "brackish" water to flow from our lips is made long before we open our mouth. We have a choice, you know, to direct what we think about. We don't have to let negativity about others pollute our thoughts. We can turn off the spigot as soon as we sense the first drip.

Pure water and bitter water cannot flow from the same spring. A little bit of poison contaminates it all. It's easy to overlook this. We're inclined to think *what happens in thoughtville stays in thoughtville.* Don't bet on it! "Out of the abundance of the heart the mouth speaks" (Matthew 12:34 ESV). Eventually, the toxins we put in our system will surface.

It reminds me of a fairy tale, *Diamonds and Toads,* I used to read to my children. It was about two daughters, one kind and virtuous, the other rude and altogether nasty. One day a fairy blessed the virtuous daughter by decreeing every time she spoke diamonds and flowers would flow from her mouth. When the ill-mannered daughter saw what happened to her sister, she wanted to get in on the action. So, she sought out the fairy but maintained her despicable disposition. As a result, the fairy proclaimed that every time she spoke not diamonds—but toads—would complement her foul talk. In both cases, the sisters' words reflected the attitude of their hearts.

Thankfully, frogs don't fall from my mouth every time I speak (or think) critically about someone. The ugliness, however, may not be that much different. When I fail, I have a choice to ask God to help me replace that distasteful croaking of toads with the shimmering grace of diamonds.

How about you? Do you struggle with judgmental thinking? Are you allowing your fresh water to be polluted with the brackish? Try turning off the spigot in your thought life. Don't let the toads out!

June 8th

In these last days he has spoken to us by his Son, whom he appointed heir of all things, and through whom also he made the universe.
—Hebrews 1:2 NIV

Everything Jesus

When my cousin gave birth to her first child, her photography bent kicked in. Throughout her pregnancy and the birth, she compiled her many, many photos into an album entitled "Everything Baby." All who have expected and experienced a newborn know those words aptly describe the lives of novice parents. Those newly born little ones have a way of consuming our minds, hearts and activities 24/7.

Her album made me think of another "everything." Lately I've been repeating the phrase "everything Jesus ... everything Jesus." Fifteen letters, five syllables, two words that I want to permeate the sentences, paragraphs and chapters of my life. When I enter a room, rather than sucking the air out of it with self-consciousness, I want to bring a God-consciousness. I'm tired of working on my agenda; I want to herald his.

The book of Hebrews offers a litany of "everything Jesus." He is the maker, sustainer and heir of all things, the exact representation of God (1:2–3). He suffered death to atone for the sins of all mankind to make us his brothers and sisters (2:10). He is able to sympathize with us in our weaknesses and help us find grace in our time of need (4:16). He lives to intercede on our behalf (7:25). His blood cleanses our consciences (9:14). The list goes on.... No wonder Scripture tells us to fix our thoughts on Jesus (3:1).

Sometimes I think we consign Jesus to the part of our lives entitled Spirituality. Look for him in the Intellectual, Social, or Professional sections and he's nowhere to be found. Yet the true joy of living comes when he infuses every slice of life. Oswald Chambers puts it this way: "I am here not to realize myself, but to know Jesus." So, whether I'm counseling a friend or cleaning my house, watching a movie with my husband or teaching a class, writing at a secluded cottage by Lake Erie or surrounded by fans at a football game, I want it all to be about Jesus. A photo album of "Everything Jesus."

How about you?

June 9th

I will stand at my watch and station myself on the ramparts; I will look to see what he will say to me, and what answer I am to give to this complaint.

—Habakkuk 2:1 NIV

The Devil's 3 D's: Distract, Discourage, Defeat

Picture a man positioning himself on a rugged jutting ledge, peering over the tumultuous waters below. Undeterred by the elements, he is determined to station himself on the ramparts until he hears from the Lord. He waits. Nothing deters him from standing, watching, listening.

This is one of my favorite images in all of Scripture. At this point in Israel's history the winds of cultural corruption and spiritual apostasy were howling; the rains of God's wrath were pouring down on the nation. The prophet of God wants to know why. So, Habakkuk says he will stay at his post and listen for the Lord.

I believe the lure to leave our post is one of the first lines of strategy Satan uses against believers. He distracts us in oh so many subtle ways: *You're really too tired to read the Word tonight. Take a break from church this week. God knows you deserve it! Your prayers don't matter so why bother.* A little distraction goes a long way. Our mindset begins to shift and without even realizing why, discouragement moves in. Over my years in ministry, "weak" or "non-existent" has been the most common response when I've asked a discouraged Christian about his or her devotional life. Distractions in whatever form eventually lead to discouragement and discouragement leads to Satan's ultimate goal: defeat. It's the working of his 3-Ds.

But we don't have to be ignorant of his schemes. Throughout the New Testament we are admonished to "watch out," to "stay alert," to "be on our guard." Of course, this doesn't mean looking for Satan under every rock. But it does mean as long as we live on the earth, we will be targets he wants to destroy.

Let's be ever watchful lest we get trapped by the devil's 3-Ds. Let's remain at our post, adhering to God's trifecta of 3-Ds: let's be discerning, devoted and diligent to the end.

June 10ᵗʰ

Here comes my betrayer!

—Matthew 26:46 NIV

Where's Your Identity?

We become what we do. It can cement our identity, for better or worse.

How awful to be identified as a "betrayer." This is how Jesus referred to Judas on the night of his arrest. On the other hand, Peter denied Jesus not once but three times, yet the next time Jesus encountered Peter, he didn't refer to him as the "denier." Why the difference?

Judas had allowed his sin to literally take over his identity. Although he showed remorse for what he had done, Scripture gives no indication that he repented of his sin. Peter, however, repented. He separated who he was from what he did. That's what repentance does. It slices through our will and ushers us into freedom—freedom to become unidentified with our sin.

We all sin (Romans 3:23) but we don't have to become so identified with our sinful behavior that the totality of who we are gets sucked into a label that sticks like *Gorilla Glue®*. Are you an alcoholic or one who struggles with alcohol? An addict? Homosexual? Adulterer? A thief? An abuser? Whether or not we take on the identity of our sin rests on whether we truly repent of our behavior. Otherwise, we will become what we do.

But there is a positive side.

Jesus became his actions:

- *Savior of the world*— *"She [Mary] will bear a Son; and you shall call His name Jesus, for He will save his people from their sins."* (Matthew 1:21 NASB).
- *Faithful and True*— *"I saw heaven standing open and there before me was a white horse, whose rider is called Faithful and True."* (Revelation 19:11).
- *The Resurrection and the Life*— *"Christ died for our sins according to the Scriptures … he was buried … was raised on the third day."* (1 Corinthians 15:3–4).

So, how about you? Where do you find your identity? Have you over identified with your sin and let it define you? Or have you been able to live out your true identity as a redeemed child of God?

June 11th

And God is able to bless you abundantly, so that in all things at all times, having all that you need, you will abound in every good work.
—2 Corinthians 9:8 NIV

The Fuel of Love

An interesting thing happened on my way to class the other day.

For a limited time, McDonald's offered free coffee during breakfast hours. I'm a pushover for free stuff, so I thought I would buzz through the drive-thru and pick up a cup. I asked for a *free* decaf, but when I got to the pick-up window, awaiting me were *three* cups of coffee—*three free coffees!* Clearly misunderstood, I didn't want to further the confusion by trying to explain, so I thankfully took the tray and headed for school, praying I could find someone to give them to before they got cold. (I'm also a pushover for not letting anything go to waste.)

As I got out of my car, somewhat loaded down with one very large bag, my purse and a tray of three coffees, one of my former students spotted me. He hopped out of his truck and asked if he could help me. Immediately, I said, "Yes, would you like some coffee?" Not only did he welcome my offer, but a friend riding with him took the other cup. They stopped to bless me, but in turn they were blessed with the coffee and I was blessed in being able to give.

Kingdom Economics 101: The greatest blessings come in being a blessing. The fuel of love is giving. Every time we pour out God's love to another, he fills our tank right back up. Only when we buy into the false thinking we have nothing to give does our fuel supply start to wane.

When Paul encouraged the Corinthians to be more generous, he revealed how this works. God gives to us abundantly (more than we could think or imagine). We, in turn, having all things at all times, and all we need, abound in giving to others. He enriches us in every way so we can be generous in every way. The result: thanksgiving all around.

So, don't ever think you have nothing to give. God made you to be a giver. Fuel up!

June 12th

I tell you, among those born of women there is no one greater than John.
—*Luke 7:28 NIV*

What Do You Do With Doubt?

Ever doubted God? Then feel guilty for doubting God? We should know better than to doubt, but circumstances we were unprepared for have a way of short-circuiting the memory of God's faithfulness. I would guess most of us have questioned either God's love or sovereignty at some point in our Christian walk.

John the Baptist certainly did. Languishing in prison, he who was once so filled with certainty now found himself perplexed as to whether Jesus really was the Messiah. His growing doubts culminated in sending his disciples to ask Jesus the most pointed of questions: "Are you the one who is to come, or should we expect someone else?" (Luke 7:19). The "voice in the desert," the "preparer of the way," the "baptizer of the One on whom he had witnessed the Holy Spirit descend" was having second thoughts. Whoa!

How did Jesus respond to John's all too human apprehension? Did he condemn John for his lack of faith? Did he chastise him for being a poor witness? Did he whip out a law that declared, *"Thou shall not doubt"*? None of the above.

Jesus told John's disciples to report what he was doing ... healing the sick, raising the dead, preaching the good news. All were prophetic signs of the Messiah, and John knew the Scriptures. The *Word of God* was affirming God's Word. Although John's response is not recorded, I think it's safe to say his doubts vanished.

The larger lesson for me in this story lies in how Jesus viewed John in the midst of his doubts. He neither dismissed his questions nor disregarded his discouragement. Instead, he reaffirmed John's call and lauded him to the people: "I tell you, among those born of women there is no one greater than John." I find that remarkable. It's so unlike how my short-sighted vision expects Jesus to react to my doubts.

Doubt will dog us as long as we live on the earth. But let's try not to linger in its shadows. Let the grace of Jesus remind us of all that is true and lead us back to certainty.

June 13th

At once they left their nets and followed him.

—Matthew 4:20 NIV

Adventure or Fear?

I'm definitely a stick-to-your-plans type of person. Once I set my goal, I hold on to it like a dog with a bone. That's why when I had the thought to remain an extra day in Ohio to write before heading home, I surprised myself by even considering it. The pros and cons of what to do resembled a tennis match in my mind ... back and forth ... back and forth. But you know what took me off guard? I recognized a part of me that was simply afraid to alter my plans.

Following the plan makes me feel secure. I'm comfortable with patterns. Without plans and patterns a lot in life would fall to the wayside. But when we get so locked into a particular blueprint that we're afraid something bad might happen if we don't follow it, we've misplaced our security. We've also killed any hope of spontaneity and adventure.

When Jesus called his first disciples, they were fishing. Peter, Andrew, James and John no doubt had their plans set for the day. But when Jesus told them to leave their nets and follow him, they did. And without hesitation. They had no idea their yes was going to turn the world upside down, but they knew enough to shift their plans and go. What if they had refused to shift gears?

As Christians, we know the importance of walking in God's will. The only time we ought to worry over our decision-making comes when we treat God's will recklessly. If our desire is to please him in all we do, we can trust him to show us if we're manipulating our plans to please ourselves more than him.

This is not about failing to keep commitments or reneging on our promises. Dependability is a tremendous virtue. It's about opening ourselves up to the unexpected when the unexpected calls. It's about being ready if someday he tells us to stop what we're doing, leave our nets and follow.

So, let's not be afraid to embark on the adventure God lays before us. Let's not depend on our plans for security but on the One who says, "Come, follow me."

June 14th

He came to a broom bush, sat down under it and prayed that he might die. "I have had enough, LORD," he said. "Take my life; I am no better than my ancestors."
—1 Kings 19:4 NIV

An "Un-Day"

Ever have one of those "un-days?" You feel un-loved, un-productive, un-inspired, un-necessary. Every good you hope for—negated by a two-letter prefix. Before you know it, you find yourself wading into the gloomy swamp of dejection. That seems to be what happened to Elijah.

He had just triumphed over the prophets of Baal. The brilliant display of God's power working through him had demonstrated to the wavering nation that God possessed more power than anything the servants of Baal could muster. Elijah's faithful obedience had brought results. The people "fell prostrate and cried, 'The LORD—he is God! The LORD—he is God'" (1 Kings 18:39). Yet his apparent "success" vanished with the setting sun. Queen Jezebel vowed to kill him, and he ran for his life. It wasn't a victory lap!

Despondency distorts the truth. Elijah complained to the Lord that in spite of his zealousness, his life's work had essentially been a bust. Although he had just witnessed the people's repentance, he allowed Jezebel's threat to negate the very answer to his prayers. He believed that of all the prophets in Israel, he was the only one left who remained true to God. But he was wrong. Seven thousand other Israelites refused to worship Baal.

We all face discouragement. If we want to avoid a free fall into despair, it is essential not to feed our weary souls with the bread of lies. When you are down, listen to what you tell yourself. Are your thoughts inconsistent with what you have known about God's faithfulness in the past? Do they fail to line up with the truth revealed in Scripture? Is your mindset like Elijah's: "I've had enough ... take my life?" If your thinking is leading you down such paths, turn around. You still live and breathe. God is not finished with you or the work in you he plans to complete.

Why not un-leash the truth and let God turn that un-day into an un-expected blessing?

June 15th

Jesus said, "Let the little children come to me, and do not hinder them, for the kingdom of heaven belongs to such as these."
—Matthew 19:14 NIV

Stolen Children

Satan is stealing our children.

In 2014, he came in the form of Islamic militants to a remote Nigerian secondary school comprised of young girls, most of whom were Christian. Almost three hundred children were abducted. They waited in horror for the Boko Haram leader to make good on his threat to sell them as slaves all because they dared to seek an education and perhaps chose to follow a faith other than Islam. The anguish of grieving mothers was carried across the globe. Pleas requesting prayer for each stolen girl wrenched our hearts, even as we realized those were not the only ones. I prayed for them until the day most were released.

Satan is stealing our children.

He comes in the form of a sex-saturated society to lure them away from innocence. The celebrity artists who serve as role models for these little ones have abdicated the good and embraced the obscene. In their competition to see who can be the most outrageous, they tell little girls coolness is measured in how well they can twerk. They tell little boys moral absolutes are passé.

Satan is stealing our children.

He comes in the form of mothers and fathers who don't love each other anymore. They find the sacrifices needed to make a family work are too much of a long haul. The resultant instability forces these little innocents into dealing with mixed signals about loyalty and commitment much too soon. They become foundationless, ripe for picking.

Satan hates God. And he takes revenge on God's children. He is relentless in bringing destruction and devastation. He hopes we'll get so used to it that we throw our hands in the air and with a resigned sigh conclude that it's so pervasive there's nothing we can do. Don't buy it. Don't you become the next victim of his lies. We may not be able to go to other countries and physically rescue even one abducted little girl. We probably will never convince one pop star to put on more clothes or single-handedly convince a mom and dad to give their children the most important gift of all.

But we can pray for the children. And prayer is a powerful weapon.

June 16th

And Elisha prayed, "Open his eyes, LORD, so that he may see." Then the LORD opened the servant's eyes, and he looked and saw the hills full of horses and chariots of fire all around Elisha.

—2 Kings 6:17 NIV

Night Vision Goggles...Day by Day

Have you ever needed night vision goggles?

You're familiar with them. They are used primarily by the military, law enforcement, hunters and, of course, many high-suspense TV shows. They take the small amount of light available at night and intensify it, allowing the viewer's eyes to perceive images in the dark they wouldn't normally see. But do you know about spiritual night vision goggles?

Elisha's servant certainly needed night vision goggles. The army from Aram surrounded the city where Elisha and his servant were lodging. This powerful militia had orders to capture Elisha. When his servant saw the great force, he cried, "Oh no! What shall we do?" Elisha calmly explained to him not to fear. There were more on their side than the enemy's. Then he asked the Lord to open his servant's eyes to reveal what before was invisible. The hills overflowed with the celestial army of the Lord. The enemy had no chance.

Some of my greatest joys in life occur when I see God working behind the scenes. When he opens my eyes to recognize the spiritual reality of his hand working for my good, I'm doubly blessed. Blessed because something worked out; blessed because I perceive he did it. Like the time I came home after my week-long stay in the hospital. Wondering if I would ever be useful again, I received a call out of nowhere to speak at a ladies' retreat. I knew the Lord wanted to assure me I still had something to give.

Lyrics from *Godspell* come to mind. When I put on those night goggles, I see the Lord more clearly, and that moves me to love him more dearly, which compels me to follow him more nearly. I hope you, too, put on those night goggles and pray for those three things. Every day. Every single day.

June 17th

For we know in part and we prophesy in part, but when completeness comes, what is in part disappears. —1 Corinthians 13:9–10 NIV

Foggy Mountain High

It was one of the most anticipated moments of our vacation at Acadia National Park: viewing the sunset from Cadillac Mountain. There's nothing quite like it. But we almost missed it.

Fog was rolling into the valley. As we drove toward the summit, we had almost concluded our venture was fruitless. We could hardly see ten feet in front of us, so how could we possibly observe the distant sun making its evening descent? But a funny thing happened on the way to the top. The further we climbed, the clearer the sky became. It's as if the sun was playing hide-and-seek behind the clouds and the fog—diffusing its rays—was lending a hand. It created one of the most breathtaking scenes I've ever witnessed.

Paul warns we don't always see things clearly. We will encounter foggy days when we can't see where we're going. God's plan appears about as clear as the pea-soupers of London.

Foggy times present a different challenge than those when darkness engulfs us. Despair often drives us straight to the heart of God because we have no other alternative. Songs about trusting God in pitch-black storms abound. But uncertainty? Not too many lyrics about the splendor found in ambiguity. Since foggy situations fall short of full-blown crises, we're tempted to look at our confusion as something to either figure *out* or sit *out*—with*out* God. We bypass a level of trust and depth of beauty that can only be discovered in the fog.

When we choose to trust God in those haze-laden times, a great foghorn resounds in the heavens that delights the Lord. In time, the mist will lift and one day we will see God clearly. Foggy times offer us the chance to enact our faith until that promise finds fulfillment.

So, if fog is occluding your path right now, seize it as an opportunity, not a hindrance, to trust. Don't drive back down the mountain and miss the beauty.

June 18th

Walk with the wise and become wise, for a companion of fools suffers harm.

—*Proverbs 13:20 NIV*

Frugal Friends

Who surrounds you? Do your closest friends spur you on in your spiritual journey or distract you? In the words of author Liz Weisman, do your associates multiply you or diminish you?

Since we are affected far more by people than we probably realize, it's important to consider the influencers in our lives.

For example, my daughter recently relayed a story about someone who suggested ways to live within a budget. One of the top recommendations included choosing frugal friends. It's hard to resist lavish lifestyles when surrounded by people who think nothing of spending hundreds of dollars for a night of entertainment. It's tempting to compromise when our values make us the odd man out. On the other hand, hanging out with folks who share our ideals reinforces our goals. This proves true whether found in Weight Watchers, Alcoholics Anonymous, or the local church.

Proverbs encourages us to see that walking with the wise makes us wise. Their habits rub off on us. When I'm around people who possess a zeal for God, who fight the good fight of faith, who pursue righteousness and endure hardship, I want to be more zealous, faithful and persevering. When I have friends who would rather die than forsake the Lord, my devotion to him is increased.

But what if we find ourselves in a season where we are somewhat isolated from multipliers? What if we're living in the last homely house on the edge of darkness? How do we keep shining? Do the next best thing. Let books be your friends. Study the lives and teachings of beloved followers of Christ. For me, *Mere Christianity, Ruthless Trust, Prodigal God* and *How Should We Then Live?* are just a few trusted companions. Devotionals like *My Utmost for His Highest* and *Streams in the Desert* have carried me through valleys and propelled me beyond myself. Podcasts and blogs can serve as great multipliers. Of course, our greatest friend and influencer remains Jesus. The greatest book—his book.

In our brief moment on the earth, let's not align ourselves with "fools" who diminish us, but choose friends who along with us multiply God's presence and advance his kingdom.

June 19th

Save me, O God, for the waters have come up to my neck.
—Psalm 69:1 NIV

His Hold

Have you ever wandered into situations that were clearly "over your head"? You thought you could handle whatever it was, but as time went on, you realized you were drowning in your efforts. Maybe you never thought you would lose your grip on God, but you found his grasp on you to be the only force that kept you from sinking.

It reminds me of a scene in *The Fellowship of the Ring*. Frodo has slipped away from the others in the company to continue his journey alone. The ring has caused increasing turmoil, and he doesn't want to subject his friends any longer to his burden—taking the ring to the Mountain of Doom for destruction.

When faithful friend Sam realizes Frodo is nowhere to be found, he rushes to the bank of the river. There he spots Frodo rowing a canoe downstream. No way would he let Frodo go it alone. Devoted companion that he is, he plunges into the water to pursue him. But there is a problem ... Sam can't swim. The scene shows him sinking deeper and deeper, until he's no longer able to rise to the surface. Then suddenly an arm reaches down in the water and seizes Sam's hand, pulling him up to safety. It's Frodo. Seeing his friend's struggle, he rescues him from danger and the two continue their venture down the river together. The moment when Frodo's hand grasps Sam's paints an indelible picture to me of how God stretches his hand—his loving, capable hand—to rescue us.

Scripture depicts similar imagery when David experienced the "hold" of God. His enemies hated him, his family rejected him, and his own guilt and shame flooded his mind. He was drowning. His only hope of rescue came from the only source of salvation he'd ever known. He cried out to God. And just like Frodo's arm extended down to reach Sam, so God pulled David from the neck-deep waters threatening to overwhelm him (Psalm 69).

Do you know there's no water too deep to keep God's hand from rescuing you? Just as God rescued David when he cried out, so he will bring you and me from overwhelming floods. His hold will never slip. Of that you can count on.

June 20th

You have rejected the LORD, who is among you, and have wailed before him, saying, "Why did we ever leave Egypt?"

—Numbers 11:20 NIV

The Mark of Disloyalty

They complained about their enemies. They complained about their lack of water. They complained about their food. The nation of Israel could be characterized as one big complaining machine. All the good they had experienced—including more than a few mighty miracles—was overshadowed by clouds of grumbling and ungratefulness.

Their complaining expressed dissatisfaction with God's provision and reinforced the idea he wasn't looking out for them. In the midst of their moaning, they chucked his sovereignty and allowed their perceptions to become distorted. To think they "wailed" to go back to the slave pits of Egypt! Their vision of the past took on a false luster of contentment that simply never was. Complaining tends to do that.

Israel's grumbling was so pervasive even Moses said he would rather die than continue to listen to them! (Numbers 11:10–15). No wonder their complaints aroused God's anger. Their rejection of him was like a slap in the face—the ultimate mark of disloyalty.

In my book, *Virgin Snow,* I describe fourteen "marks" that reflect the character of God, attributes he wants to engrave in our nature. Just as significantly, we can develop patterns of behavior that *mar* rather than *mark* God's likeness in our lives. Patterns like complaining.

If complaining arouses God's anger, how pleasing our gratitude must be to him. Those times of frustration when we don't get what we want but continue to press on, serving him in faithfulness, nourish both our love and loyalty. It must especially delight him when we declare our devotion in those dark times when our manna has grown stale and the things we thirst for lie hidden in the desert of his higher purposes. "Godliness with contentment is great gain" (1 Timothy 6:6).

There will always be situations to complain about. But there are many more we can find to praise him. It's up to us as to what fills our souls—whether we will be true to his likeness or bear the mark of disloyalty. Let's meditate on some of those reasons and silence the grumbles.

June 21st

On this rock I will build my church, and the gates of Hades will not overcome it.
—Matthew 16:18 NIV

The Invincible Church

At least five times ... the Faith has to all appearance gone to the dogs. In each of these five cases it was the dog that died." Not only do I like those words of G. K. Chesterton, I believe they remain pertinent today.

There's been a lot of recent speculation about the church's relevancy—or lack thereof—in the world. Some predict if the church doesn't start accommodating the culture and adapting new "normals," her demise is imminent. Don't buy it.

Like the early church fathers who were imprisoned, stoned and crucified upside down didn't buy it. Like those brave Christians who stood firm in the face of gladiators and were lit as human torches at Nero's palace didn't buy it. Like those in this century who are being electrocuted, beaten and tortured in ways unimaginable because they dare to call themselves followers of Christ aren't buying it. It takes a kind of arrogance and self-absorption to think the challenges faced by the church today can only be met by shifting its foundation. It's a failure to recognize the immovable rock on which the church is built.

Oh, it's not that the church hasn't blown it. Ours is a sad commentary of bitter divisiveness, corruption and good intentions gone bad. But we remain the bride of Christ and he said in spite of all our human failings, and the schemes plotted by our enemies, hell itself would not prevail against us. Jesus declared he would build his church on a rock, and he did! Nothing in the last two thousand years has succeeded in moving it.

The church is here to stay no matter what twenty-first century pundits think. And as long as the church exists, we who are a part of it are called to be salt and light to the culture. I consider it a privilege. And what a privilege it is to be part of the eternal, indomitable, invincible church!

June 22nd

Where there is no revelation, people cast off restraint.
—Proverbs 29:18 NIV

The Highest Goal

Do you, like many, struggle with self-discipline?

When we have no vision or goal we aspire to, Scripture says we will "cast off restraint." Why go through the rigors of self-denial and discipline if there's no pay off? We need to have a clear picture of where we're going in order to exercise the discipline necessary to get there.

Defining our aspirations determines future success perhaps more than any other factor. Dave Ramsey has helped thousands of people find victory in finances because he instructs them how to form specific goals that require saving rather than spending their money. Successful weight loss programs help people obtain their desired weight by teaching them how to set precise objectives. They learn today's sacrifices will be rewarded tomorrow.

Those of you who run marathons know the importance of having a specific goal for a specified amount of time. Runners don't wake up on the day of the race and say, "I think I'll run 26.2 miles today." They make choices for weeks, possibly months, in advance to help them prepare to achieve the clear goal of making it across the finish line.

The importance of cultivating a lifestyle of discipline extends far beyond finances and physical fitness. As believers, Christ in us is the hope of glory. We have been given the assignment of sharing that hope with everyone in our world. If we don't have a clear vision of this noble, holy goal, we will not develop the discipline necessary to carry it out. We'll be less likely to practice self-denial for another's sake, more inclined to resist conviction of the Holy Spirit, and we might refuse to get uncomfortable—even if that's what it takes—to advance his kingdom.

Are there areas of self-discipline in your life that need some attention? Are you forgetting the highest goal? Now's a good time to recast your vision and get rid of hindrances. God has a plan for you. It entails far more than you realize. Don't let your destiny be stolen.

June 23rd

Trust in the LORD with all your heart and lean not on your own understanding. —Proverbs 3:5 NIV

Borderless Trust

Wouldn't you like to develop the kind of trust that stretches beyond the borders of your thinking?

The call to trust God remains a constant cry. I've trusted the Lord for a husband, for the well-being of my children, for sicknesses to be healed, for friends and family members to be saved, for fruitful work. You name it. I've trusted for it. And God has always proven to be faithful. Not that he's worked all things together according to my desires. Instead, he has done something far greater. He has worked all things together for my good.

One would think after all these years my trust would be well expanded to that place without borders. But there's always something new. Nothing blocks my trust in God more than me. Rather than trusting him with all my heart, I still tend to lean on my own understanding. In other words, I prefer to trust myself: a flawed, mistake-ridden human being rather than the invisible, sovereign creator of the universe who loves me more than I can imagine. Doesn't make a lot of sense, does it?

Borderless trust depends on a borderless God. It's like the woman described in the Song of Songs who comes up from the desert "leaning on her lover" (Song of Songs 8:5). The vast wasteland of trial in the wilderness must have stripped her of all illusions of self-sufficiency. As she reached the limits of her own ability to figure things out, she found something—someone—stronger and more reliable to trust.

The lover of our souls desires we learn to lean on him as well. He wants to lead us through those sandstorms that blindside us. He longs to quench our thirst of needing to know why by giving us the assurance that whatever the why, he is enough. I wonder if Elisha A. Hoffman had in mind the woman described in the Song of Songs when he penned these famous lyrics.

> *What have I to dread, what have I to fear,*
> *Leaning on the everlasting arms?*
> *I have blessed peace with my Lord so near,*
> *Leaning on the everlasting arms.*
> "What a Fellowship, What a Joy Divine"

Want to develop borderless trust? Let's lean on him today instead of our own understanding.

June 24th

Because you have seen me, you have believed; blessed are those who have not seen and yet have believed. —John 20:29 NIV

Not Seeing is Believing

Seeing is believing. Seems like a harmless expression. An idiom that describes the necessity of physical, concrete evidence to accept something as real. It's how most people live the greater part of their lives. It's also the exact opposite of faith.

The concept of faith as depicted in Hebrews 11—the great faith chapter—revolves around the *unseen*. In fact, the writer defines faith as being "certain of what we do not see" (v. 1 NIRV).

- God formed the universe itself by what was not visible (v. 3).
- Both Cain and Abel offered visible sacrifices, but Abel's was accepted because it was accompanied by the invisible quality of faith that reflected a thankful heart (v. 4).
- Enoch pleased God so much by his faith he was "taken" rather than experience death. He believed that the unseen God "exists and rewards those who earnestly seek him" (vv. 5–6).
- Noah believed what God said about the impending—yet unseen—flood, so he built the ark in holy fear (v. 7).
- Abraham believed he would inherit a land he had not yet seen and have descendants through a child who was not yet born (vv. 8–12).
- Moses denied himself the treasures and pleasures of Egypt because he was looking ahead to an unseen reward. He persevered because he saw him "who is invisible" (vv. 24–27).
- Rahab hid the spies and was spared because she believed she could have a new life, one yet to be seen (v. 31).

The chapter lists many other heroes of faith. They refused the worldly perspective of demanding concrete evidence before believing. They exchanged the natural for the super-natural by first believing then seeing. As a result, they share the distinguishing mark that "the world was not worthy of them" (v. 38).

Jesus said those who believe in him—although they don't see him—are blessed. That applies to us. Today. I don't know about you, but I often have more *seeing is believing* in me than *not seeing is believing*. If the whole universe is founded on faith, it's time to get onboard ... fully onboard. Let's join the faithful so it can also be said of us, "the world is not worthy of them."

June 25th

Then their eyes were opened and they recognized him.

—Luke 24:31 NIV

Hidden Beauty

Early one January morning a scrubby looking young man arrived at a D.C. metro and pulled out his violin. With his case open to receive donations from busy passersby, he played a repertoire of classical pieces. Hardly anyone even noticed him. At the end of forty-five minutes, the musician had received a whopping $32.17.

But this was no ordinary performer and no run of the mill instrument. The subway player turned out to be renowned violinist Joshua Bell, who plays for sellout concerts, garnering as much as $1,000 a minute. His violin—a Stradivarius worth over three million dollars. Hidden beauty.

I think life is filled with hidden beauty. But like the hurried crowd at the D.C. metro, we rarely slow down long enough to discover it. We take pride in our busyness. It makes us feel important. *Today I did three loads of wash, cleaned the whole house, took the kids to soccer practice, had a friend over for lunch, answered ten e-mails, updated my status on Facebook, squeezed in a rigorous Bible study, and made a caramel macchiato cheesecake!*

Not a lot of time to recognize hidden beauty.

The "beauty" of beauty lies in its power to help us escape our self-absorbed lives. Not an easy feat, by the way. Francis Chan writes in *Crazy Love* that it's time we get over ourselves. We're like an extra, 2/5 of a second long in a movie that's not even about us. It's about him, and we are to use every 2/5 of the second to point to him. Beauty helps us refocus our "movie."

The disciples on the road to Emmaus didn't recognize the resurrected Jesus when he joined them on the road. They were so absorbed with grief over his crucifixion they couldn't see who stood in front of them. They were blinded to the hidden beauty that longed to comfort them. We often miss hidden beauty because we're not looking for it.

Friend, let God open your eyes to the hidden beauty in life. Let it draw you away from the frantic pace—if even for a moment—and redirect you to the place where true meaning lies. You might discover a Stradivarius, or better yet, like the disciples on the road to Emmaus, you might get a glimpse of the Savior.

June 26th

But while they were on their way to buy the oil, the bridegroom arrived. The virgins who were ready went in with him to the wedding banquet. And the door was shut. —Matthew 25:10 NIV

Just Enough?

Half-hearted lives. Lives created for greatness, but somewhere along the road, our budding potential gets snuffed out and we become satisfied to just get by. In the report cards of life, we'll be content, or so we think, with a C. Leave full-fledged commitment to the radicals. Perhaps that's what happened in the parable of the ten virgins Jesus told us about in Matthew 25.

These women were bridesmaids. Their sole responsibility consisted of meeting the bridegroom. They all carried lamps, but only five of them took enough oil to keep their lamps lit. When the bridegroom finally arrived at midnight, he summoned them to meet him. But in horror, the five without oil realized their lamps were going out.

Now why would someone take a lamp with no fuel supply? More than likely they thought they had "just enough" to get by. Why bother carrying more than needed? Their miscalculation resulted in severe consequences. They were shut out of the wedding banquet. The one thing they were given to do is the one thing they failed to accomplish.

A "just enough" mentality causes us to miss our purpose. It entices us to settle for less than what God plans for our lives. It makes us function on the assumption we have "just enough" faith, so we don't press into the Word of God—where faith gets built. Or it makes us think we've offered "just enough" forgiveness, so we justify carrying small grudges. Or we've made "just enough" sacrifice so we stop at the extra mile when God may be asking us to go three more. But whatever the "just enough" oil in our lives might be, it won't be sufficient to carry us through any more than it was for the bridesmaids.

So, if you have been operating under the illusion of "just enough," it's not too late to change. God spared nothing to make you great. He provides "more than enough" to help you move from the mediocre to the extraordinary. Be ready.

Don't let that precious oil run out.

June 27th

In the midst of a very severe trial, their overflowing joy and their extreme poverty welled up in rich generosity.
—2 Corinthians 8:2 NIV

Being Squeezed

An unpleasant part of life involves the experience of being squeezed. Pressure forces something on the inside to end up on the outside. Anything from trying to fit into skinny jeans to being forced out of a job. So, what happens when you get squeezed? What comes out of you when you feel the pressure?

For some, being squeezed brings out rebellion, exponential self-centeredness, bitterness or depression. This was not the case, however, for the Macedonian church. Their extreme poverty squeezed out "rich generosity." Their severe trial squeezed out love and grace. Rather than letting their difficulties press them into despair, their trials released the exact opposite. When they felt the squeeze, the presence of Christ within sprang into action. Paul describes them as an example for believers to emulate.

The joy overflowing in the Macedonian church was the result of their uncompromising abandonment to God. The core of their lives belonged to him (2 Corinthians 8:5). No wonder only goodness surfaced when they were squeezed! Christ was living in them fully and abundantly.

We have more of a choice of what comes out of us when we're under pressure than we think. When we're being squeezed by finances, we can choose to let stinginess come out, rationalizing we can't afford to give. Or we can choose to intentionally ask Christ within to help us be even more generous. When we're squeezed with life-shattering disappointment, we can choose to ask Christ within to help us find hope. When we feel the pressure of someone's rejection, we can choose to ask Christ within to enable us to forgive.

Many times, when I get squeezed, insecurity pops out. As a result, I tend to withdraw and maybe entertain a little self-pity. But I'm learning the best way to face down insecurity lies in activating the security I already have in Christ. "His divine power has given us everything we need for a godly life" (2 Peter 1:3). It's a matter of letting God's grace squeeze it out.

I want to live more like the Macedonians. How about you? Do you want to be so filled with the Lord that when you're squeezed, you'll choose to let the good stuff surface?

June 28th

For God did not send his Son into the world to condemn the world, but to save the world through him. —John 3:17 NIV

It's a Bad, Bad, Bad, Bad World

The classic 1963 movie, *It's a Mad, Mad, Mad, Mad World,* featured more iconic comedians than any film that's ever been produced. It also contained more adjectives in its title than most productions. It's those four adjectives (the mads) that keep echoing in my mind.

As I watch the nightly news, I can't help but think the world is not only mad but bad. Plain down bad. How can we see people being beheaded and innocents being slaughtered for the purpose of advancing a political agenda and not be convinced evil exists? Corruption runs rampant. Life is becoming a whirlpool of exploitation and sorrow for many.

So, the world is not only a bad world, but a sad one. People, especially in western cultures, strive for happiness perhaps more than at any time in history, yet turn up empty. It's a sad world because it's a world forgetful that true joy comes in self-sacrifice. It's a sad world because it thinks accommodation of the bad will result in peace. It's a sad world because the beauty found in truth is being eclipsed by the shadow of ugliness.

And yet, whether the world is mad, bad or sad, it's a world God loves. He loved the world so much that he gave what he cherished the most—his only Son—to save us from the madness, badness and sadness we created with our free will. So, no matter if three thousand mads, bads and sads describe the world ... nothing can cause him to stop loving his creation. And because he loves deeply, he redeems profoundly.

God alone can turn the worst of circumstances into something positive. There is no madness he can't restore to sanity, no badness he can't use for good, no sadness he can't transform into quiet contentment.

I don't know about you, but the state of the world discourages me until I am brought back to the eternal truth of a God who loves. A God who spared nothing so we would find hope in the midst of a world gone bad. Take heart.

June 29th

Jesus reached out his hand and touched the man. "I am willing," he said. "Be clean!" Immediately he was cleansed of his leprosy.
—Matthew 8:3 NIV

I Am Willing

I am willing. What words of power! Of healing. Of love. Words every single person needs to hear.

The man who came to Jesus was a leper. The only thing he had going for him was his desperation. But although he believed Jesus had enough power to heal him, he wasn't sure about the love. It's no wonder. His whole miserable existence consisted of rejection. When people saw him, they shouted "Unclean!" and ran in the opposite direction. He had learned to anticipate looks of disgust and repulsion, not compassion. So, he asked Jesus whether he was willing to make him clean.

Jesus' willingness continues to be chronicled throughout the eighth chapter of Matthew. He heals a soldier's servant, even though a Gentile (vv. 5–13). He calls people to follow him, although they struggle with the cost (vv. 19–22). He calms a life-threatening storm despite the lack of faith displayed by his disciples (vv. 23–26). He delivers two men so steeped in evil spirits that the demons he cast out fill a whole herd of pigs (v. 28–32).

Something about those words—I am willing—strike a deep chord in me. The same Jesus who was willing then, remains willing today, offering a love undaunted by

- leprous cynicism
- judgmental disassociation
- self-centered "I'll-follow-you-but-let-me-do-this-first" please
- unbelief in the midst of storms
- demon-inspired thoughts fit only for pigs.

Despite the condition of our hearts, Jesus says, I am willing to touch you.

It draws such a sharp contrast with my unwillingness. All too often, I find my willingness framed by emotion. Like Peter, in a moment of passion I proclaim, "Lord, I am ready to go with you to prison and to death" (Luke 22:33). Then he asks me to trust, or forgive, or simply let go, and the rooster crows. Yet even then, he is willing to swallow up my unwillingness and help me find rest in his will.

I don't know your circumstances, but I do know those life-altering words of Jesus—I am willing—extend to you. Nothing you have done or can do alters his love. He *wills* that you be whole. His life proves it.

June 30th

O Lord, you have searched me and known me!

—*Psalm 139:1 ESV*

Language of Love

Our daughter sought to learn Mandarin when she was dating her husband who is Chinese-American. My friend wants to learn Spanish so she can better help Spanish-speaking people who apply for mortgage loans at her work. My husband leaves flowers for me to enjoy on every occasion imaginable. What do all these have in common?

The desire to speak love in a language each recipient can understand.

Since Gary Chapman's book *The Five Love Languages* came on the scene over twenty years ago, we've become more aware of how different people experience love, well, differently. Speaking someone's *love language* means caring enough about them to get into their world.

No one has done this more profoundly, more powerfully, than Jesus. Listen to how it's described in *The Message*:

> When the time came, he set aside the privileges of deity and took on the status of a slave, became *human!* Having become human, he stayed human. It was an incredibly humbling process. He didn't claim special privileges.
> —Philippians 2:7–8

Talk about learning a love language! Jesus paid an inestimable price to get into our world. He knows more about you than you know yourself. He understands what ticks you off and what makes you tick. He remembers the worst day of your life as well as your sweetest memory. He smiles at your quirks and cheers at your successes. It may be hard to believe, but he actually likes you (as they say) warts and all.

He speaks your love language because he loves you. And because he knows you, he can speak to you up close and personal. This comes not only as good news, but as "knowledge too wonderful" (Psalm 139:6 ESV). It moves the psalmist to respond with unrestrained vulnerability. "Search me, O God, and know my heart! Try me and know my thoughts!" (Psalm 139:23).

The God who knows all about us yet loves us enough to speak our language should provoke in us great trust. But don't take my word for it. Go ahead and tear down your defenses, open your heart, say with abandon, Search me, Lord, and speak, for I'm listening!

July 1st

All they asked was that we should continue to remember the poor, the very thing I had been eager to do all along.

—Galatians 2:10 NIV

Remember the Poor

"*They're here!*" It had come together at lightning speed. The time between our first meeting with Bethany Christian Services to the night the Congolese family of four arrived at the airport happened in a way only God could orchestrate. Our church was adopting a refugee family.

In a matter of two weeks, we had secured an apartment and furnished it with all the essentials and more. Everything from bunk beds for the two young children to a beautiful picture one of our ladies had painted with the words "as for me and my house, we will serve the Lord" in Swahili. As we gathered at the airport to greet them with flags, signs and boisterous cheers, many of us found tears hard to suppress.

We soon learned the father had been in a refugee camp for over twenty years. Twenty years is a long time to be without a place to call home. He came to America in hopes of finding stability and a future for his family. To think the Lord was asking our small church body to participate in that hope was both an honor and challenge. In a very tangible way, we were given an opportunity to remember the poor.

The one thing James, Peter and John asked Paul and Barnabas to do as they sent them on their mission to the Gentiles was to "remember the poor." Interestingly, Paul responded it was the very thing he was eager to do! We can't dismiss the high priority the early church placed on reaching out to the less fortunate and disadvantaged. It mirrors the love of Christ.

Lately, I've been asking God each day to show me a way I can remember the poor. Helping the refugee family has provided ample opportunity, but I don't want to stop there. Maybe it manifests in something as simple as putting more change in a tip jar or gathering clothes for the rescue mission. In being more intentional in my prayers. Maybe it begins with living a life of gratitude. Of resisting the entrapment of materialism in my own life.

Whatever form remembering the poor might take, I believe it's a mindset we should, like Paul, be eager to embrace. How about you?

July 2nd

If your right eye causes you to stumble, gouge it out and throw it away. It is better for you to lose one part of your body than for your whole body to be thrown into hell. —Matthew 5:29 NIV

Hell—Thy Fruit

Unlike those in days past, I think it is hard for us moderns and postmoderns to comprehend the reality of hell. Some of that, I think, stems from wrong or distorted images we've come to associate with hell. Demons in red tights with pitchforks are hard to take seriously. The scriptural images of hell, however, are horrible. The word Jesus used for hell was *Gehenna,* the valley outside of Jerusalem used for the perpetual burning of garbage. Like smoldering ashes, hell constitutes an eternal dying that severs all ties with life.

- Hell separates us from God and so from the source of everything that comes from him— love, joy, peace, kindness, wisdom, mercy, goodness.

- Hell separates us from people. Because of the absence of love, all that remains is hatred, anger, vileness. Mark Twain's quip that he would take heaven for climate but hell for sociability is sadly mistaken. There will be no "camaraderie" in hell.

- Hell separates us from ourselves. Remember the demon-possessed man who said his name was Legion? His name means many. Even the integration of self is dissolved in hell.

Jesus warns if our eye causes us to lust or our hand causes us to sin, it's better to get rid of them than let them lead us on a projectory to hell. He wants us to understand every time we decide to sin, we are choosing hell over heaven in a very real sense because hell is sin coming to full fruition. C. S. Lewis says that in each of us there is something growing up which will of itself be hell unless it is nipped in the bud. While that something remains, there can be no heaven. Or as George McDonald put it, "Out Satan must go, every hair and feather."

Let's deal drastically with sin today. No one put it in stronger words than Jesus.

July 3rd

But I tell you, do not resist an evil person. If anyone slaps you on the right cheek, turn to them the other cheek also.

—*Matthew 5:39 NIV*

Woolly Bully

Bullying: the use of superior strength or influence to intimidate someone, typically to force him or her to do what one wants.

As a culture, we are more informed about bullying than ever before. What causes it. How to prevent it. Symptoms. Statistics. There's even a government website about bullying. We've learned that bullies can be found in every segment of society. On playgrounds, on sports teams, online. They do not respect one political party over another. They surface in kindergarten classes as well as the world stage. They take the form of Islamic extremists who want to kill everyone who differs with their faith and social activists who try to shut down anyone who not only disagrees with their agenda but doesn't support it wholeheartedly. With all the awareness directed toward bullying, you would think it might be diminishing. I believe the opposite is happening. And clearly, Christians are being targeted.

If an onslaught is on its way, how do we prepare? One response might be to whine about it. Take on a victim mentality and retreat into isolation. Another reaction is to fight back; seek revenge by bullying the bullies. Become like them. A third course of action is to compromise our beliefs enough to get the bullies off our back. We think if we give in a little, maybe they'll go away. I do not find comfort in any of these approaches. But there is another possibility. A biblical one. Love them.

This approach requires confidence in our identity as a Christ-follower. Unless we know Jesus and possess his inner strength—strength that's not dependent on what others say about us—we will gravitate toward one of the other reactions. Underlying every bully lurks a cavern of insecurity. That's why bullies feel such compulsion to force others to think like them. As authentic Christians, we can let the love of Jesus shine no matter how hard the slap might be.

So, don't be afraid of the bullies. Draw on the Lord of love to deal with them. Show them a better way.

July 4th

It is for freedom that Christ has set us free.

—Galatians 5:1 NIV

Freedom Fighters

"FREEDOM," shouts William Wallace with his last breath as his undaunted fervor to free Scotland from British tyranny reaches its final climax. In what is arguably one of the most powerful scenes in film history, *Braveheart* stands as a testimony to man's longing for freedom.

As Christians, we possess a freedom that surpasses all other forms. But we are in danger of losing it from unexpected forces—forces within the church of either license or legalism. Both extremes fight against believers' freedom. If the church hopes to retain the liberty for which Christ died, it must guard against these freedom-threatening forces.

Lining up on the side of license are those who see freedom as a pass to engage in whatever they feel is okay. This increasingly manifests itself in moral behavior—or lack thereof. A recent study by a Christian online dating service reported that 63 percent of its respondents said they would engage in sex before marriage. *I'll take one Christ with forgiveness; hold the moral absolutes please.* Feelings, sans biblical standards, become the arbiter of right and wrong. Forgotten is the warning given in Galatians 5:13, "You, my brothers and sisters, were called to be free. But do not use your freedom to indulge the flesh."

On the other end of the freedom-dismantling spectrum live the legalists. Although they may appear righteous on the outside, they use the Word of God as a cudgel against those who differ. Colossians 2:21, 23 describes them well. "'Do not handle! Do not taste! Do not touch!' Such regulations indeed have an appearance of wisdom ... but they lack any value in restraining sensual indulgence." Both sides judge the other and justify their positions by dissecting Scripture that reinforces their own perspective.

"It is for freedom Christ has set us free." The kind of freedom Christ died for is infused with holiness. This freedom looks different from any other kind known to man. God paid an extremely high price to make his people both holy and free. So, let's not blow it. Let's show it! Let's shout it from the rooftop— *FREEEEEDOM!*

July 5th

Do not be surprised at the fiery ordeal that has come on you to test you, as though something strange were happening to you.

—1 Peter 4:12 NIV

When Easy Doesn't Work

Life is supposed to be easy. Right? Times get tough, and we look for the proverbial *easy button* to push. At least that's what the advertisements tell us to do. So, what happens when easy doesn't work?

We all too often rationalize ways to avoid suffering of any kind. I once counseled a woman who was trying to lose weight. I remember how she considered her suffering near-martyr status because she ate only six donuts instead of the whole bag!

Reality check: life isn't easy. It hurts to resist temptation, to say no to our wants and desires, to inflict pain on our self-indulgence. As Pope Benedict noted in one of his final addresses, "It is not easy to be faithful to Christian marriage, to practice mercy in our everyday lives, or to leave space for prayer and inner silence. It is not easy to publicly oppose the decisions that many consider to be obvious." We shouldn't expect ease-filled living.

What we should expect is life's hard turns. If we haven't yet experienced the fiery ordeal Peter warned us about, we most likely will in the days ahead. And let's be honest, standing up for one's beliefs poses a real challenge. Our job of speaking the truth in love takes more and more courage, less and less self-preservation.

Another reality check: those fiery ordeals—in the end—make us more like Christ. "I consider that our present sufferings are not worth comparing with the glory that will be revealed in us" (Romans 8:18). Our pain is heaven's gain, just as it was for the Lord.

So, until the day of our completion, we ought to expect life in a fallen world to be hard. And although there's no easy button, we have access to something far more powerful. I call it the surrender button. As we give our hard places to the Lord, he promises to sustain us. No quick fixes, just peace that passes understanding. Peace that enables us to do life, no matter how demanding. Peace which assures us of the oft quoted truth—

Although life is hard—God is good.

July 6th

The Mighty One, God, the LORD!
The Mighty One, God, the LORD!
He knows!

—Joshua 22:22 NIV

Misconnecting the Dots

Did you ever work any of those dot-to-dot pages when you were a child? You move your pencil from one dot to another and by the time you're finished—*voila!*—a picture appears. Unless of course, you misconnect the dots. Then a misshapen figure emerges with little semblance to the real thing.

I think that happens a lot in relationships. We assume from others' behavior what they are thinking or feeling. Then we react according to our assumption and before we know it, anything from a funny anecdote to an unnecessary separation takes place. So, how do we manage assumptions?

I like what the Reubenites, Gadites and half tribe of Manasseh did when the rest of Israel made a near fatal assumption about them. These tribes had returned to their land on the east side of the Jordan. There they built an altar that would stand as a witness to future generations that although they lived on the other side of the river, they remained a part of the nation. The other tribes mistakenly thought they were building an altar on which to worship the Lord. This would have violated their covenant with God because the only altar sanctioned for worship was at the tabernacle. Israel's misconnection of the dots caused them to prepare for war against their brothers. They were ready to wipe them out.

Incredibly, before the two and a half tribes even declared their innocence, they cried, "The Mighty One, God the LORD! The Mighty One, God, the LORD! He knows! And let Israel know! If this has been in rebellion or disobedience to the LORD, do not spare us this day. If we have built our own altar to turn away from the LORD ... may the Lord himself call us to account" (Joshua 22:22-23). They sought God first and made themselves completely dependent upon him. It resulted in communication, understanding and restored fellowship.

How many assumptions do we make about others, especially in the body of Christ? We get bits and pieces of information and conclude something we shouldn't. So, the next time you feel like rushing to judgment concerning someone's conduct, think about that altar of witness and cry out to the Mighty One. Let him be the one to connect the dots.

July 7th

The gatekeepers had been assigned to their positions of trust.
—1 Chronicles 9:22 NIV

Positions of Trust

I love reading the Word of God, but I have to admit, I tend to rush through the long lists of genealogies. However, nine and a half chapters into 1 Chronicles, my eyes were drawn to this gem: *positions of trust.* It refers to the gatekeepers given the task of guarding the doors of the tent where all the treasures of Israel were housed. The idea of having a position defined by trust struck me as something invaluable.

You—as God's child—have been given a position of trust. Maybe others haven't trusted you. Maybe you barely trust yourself. Perhaps for good reason. Yet, there is One who still believes in you. He calls you to carry out assignments designed to bring him glory. Consider it an honor and privilege to be given a position of trust.

God entrusts each of us with free will. Not only do our personal decisions determine our eternal destiny, our Creator has chosen to let us partner with him in writing history. By placing us in a position of trust, he allows us to influence the world in a real, tangible way.

God has also entrusted us with blessings innumerable. The husband (or wife) we thought would never come, the baby we prayed for year after year, landing the job of our dreams, success—all potential rivals that could steal our hearts from worshiping him alone. He risks we will not come to love the gifts more than the Giver, again placing us in a position of trust.

Positions of trust arrive also in the form of suffering. When the shadow of the fall looms over our path and pain shreds our hearts, the opportunity arises to grow beyond ourselves. Armed only with the promise of his Word and the testimony of his faithfulness, we—like those gatekeepers of old—have the option to stand true and guard the treasure he has deposited in our hearts or walk away. God trusts we will stay.

May you and I be worthy of this position of trust. May the quiet confidence the Lord has in us propel us into a deeper life of integrity in all our choices. Of gratitude in our blessings. Of faithfulness in our trials.

July 8th

You call on a Father who judges each person's work without favoring one over another. So live your lives as outsiders during your time here. Live with the highest respect for God. —*1 Peter 1:17 NIRV*

Stranger on the Shore

Are you a stranger?

In Peter's first letter to the church, believers are referred to as aliens, the exiled, foreigners, outsiders, strangers. The terms may differ according to which version of the Bible is used, but the message is consistent: Christians don't fit in the world. Is that our experience? Do we, especially in America, feel like strangers in our culture, or have we adjusted quite comfortably? And what exactly does it mean to be a stranger?

According to Peter, strangers face difficulties differently. "In all this you greatly rejoice, though now for a little while you may have had to suffer grief in all kinds of trials. These have come so that the proven genuineness of your faith...may result in praise, glory and honor when Jesus Christ is revealed" (1 Peter

1:6–7). Christians live with the assurance that God intends to use even the darkest moments of their lives for something good. Unlike the world, they have reason to hope the suffering they experience is not for naught.

Strangers abound in holiness. They have been "redeemed from the empty way of life" (1 Peter 1:18). Lives like empty cargo trains going nowhere are now loaded with the fruit of "love, joy, peace, patience, kindness, goodness, faithfulness, gentleness, self-control" (Galatians 5:22–23 NASB) because they are filled with the Holy Spirit.

Strangers love in a much different way than the world. "Now that ... you have sincere love for each other, love one another deeply, from the heart" (1 Peter 1:22). Believers discover freedom from love inhibitors like self-centeredness, competition and control. They find access to a love the culture can't imitate because it flows from the very source of love itself.

When I think of being a stranger in the world as consisting of a life full of hope, holiness and whole-hearted love, it no longer bothers me that I don't fit in. What does bother me—and should—is how much I do fit in.

God is calling you and me to be strangers on the shore of this poor world. We can't let our insecurities drive us to conformity with lifestyles that fail to connect with the Creator. It's okay not to "fit in." In fact, for the kingdom of God to advance, it's a necessity.

July 9th

"You will not certainly die," the serpent said to the woman. "For God knows that when you eat from it your eyes will be opened, and you will be like God, knowing good and evil." —Genesis 3:4–5 NIV

No, We Can't

Beware of deception.

No, we can't spend our money with reckless abandon and find financial security.

No, we can't consume a diet of unhealthy media and not have weakened consciences.

No, we can't make God in our own image and expect adequate help in a crisis.

No, we can't ignore our weaknesses and expect them not to affect our future.

Despite political slogans and Hollywood fantasies, we can't have it all. No more than Adam and Eve could. They were the first to be tricked into replacing "No, we can't" with "Yes, we can." The serpent promised if they just listened to him and ate the forbidden fruit, they could do anything—even be "like God." But it was a lie.

We still fall prey to the same ruse. Then when reality smacks us in the face and reveals what we can't do, our dissatisfaction quadruples. "We can't get no satisfaction" in the words of Mick Jagger. No wonder! The bar looms too high. Or not high enough. Lasting satisfaction will never be found in this life; it was never meant to. Restrictions are a beautiful thing.

Jesus teaches there are consequences for our behavior— whether good, bad or ugly. When his Word instructs us to avoid certain activities and put checks on our thought life, it serves a purpose. It protects us. It teaches us how to live in a real world. Author Eric Metaxas writes that the only thing distinguishing us from lab rats is our ability to say no to things we want to do but shouldn't.

So, perhaps it's a good time to question the source of our dissatisfactions. Are we being set-up by a culture high on promises but low on actual fulfillment? Let's not be frustrated when the Holy Spirit closes a door. The lie of *Yes, we can* is appealing because it's what our fallen nature craves. But true contentment lies within the borders of truth—truth that recognizes there will be times we must say *No, we can't!*

July 10th

So you also, when you have done everything you were told to do, should say, "We are unworthy servants; we have only done our duty."

—Luke 17:10 NIV

Forgiveness: Mission Impossible?

Not a suggestion. Not an option. Not even an inch of wiggle room. Jesus makes it quite clear one of the duties of his followers is to forgive.

Jesus told the disciples even if someone sins against them seven times in one day but comes back and repents, they must forgive. Recognizing the difficulty of such a command, they cried, "Increase our faith!" (Luke 17:5). They knew without faith they were facing "mission impossible." Jesus responds by helping them see forgiveness as part of their job description. He parallels the call to forgive with a servant who would not expect to sit down and relax with his boss before completing his work. The servant simply fulfills his responsibility. That's the perspective they were to have with forgiveness. No heroics. No medal of commendation. Simple duty.

Duties aren't always convenient or fun. Most nurses aren't thrilled about all the paperwork that accompanies their job. Teachers probably don't gravitate toward cafeteria supervision. One of my favorite examples of doing one's duty is the NyQuil™ commercial. A coughing man opens a door and says, "Dave, I hate to interrupt, but I gotta take a sick day tomorrow." The camera spans and reveals Dave to be a toddler standing in his crib. The tagline: "Dads don't take sick days."

Duties comprise a huge part of life. And some, like forgiveness, seem as impossible to fulfill as lifting a ten-ton weight. That's why we need faith to accomplish the task. We don't even need a lot of faith. Mustard-seed size will do just fine.

You're probably familiar with the movie series *Mission Impossible.* Agents receive a recording with instructions to complete a difficult task. After accepting the assignment, the recording self-destructs.

I think forgiveness may be a bit like that. Once we accept it as a part of our mission in life and call upon God to help us activate the faith needed to complete it, a kind of self-destruction takes place. We die and Jesus lives.

Mission accomplished.

July 11th

What, then, shall we say in response to these things? If God is for us, who can be against us?

—*Romans 8:31 NIV*

Everything Is Against Me

Have you ever had any of those "I'm gonna eat some worms" days? Or worse? Self-pity engulfs you and the darkness of unbelief threatens to suck the memory of every blessing, every provision, every answered prayer you've known into a black hole. Maybe you relate to Jacob.

"Everything is against me!" That was Jacob's lament when told by his sons that to get more grain from Egypt he would have to send Benjamin along with them (Genesis 42:36). He had already lost Joseph. The thought of also losing his youngest son seemed more than he could bear.

Jacob's claim that everything was against him could not have been further from the truth. In fact, everything was for him because God was for him. Jacob had resigned himself to let Benjamin go to Egypt because he had no other choice. It was not an act of faith. His faith had long ago vanished, probably with the supposed death of his beloved son Joseph. But the harsh and bleak *everything* was about to change into colors more alive than those of Joseph's childhood cloak.

I can't imagine the reunion between Jacob and the son he had lost. All those years of sorrow and grief were swallowed up in their tearful embrace. Jacob's satisfaction resounds in his exclamation, "Now I am ready to die, since I have seen for myself that you are still alive" (Genesis 46:30). But the God "who is able to do immeasurably more than all we ask or imagine" (Ephesians 3:20) didn't let him die. He blessed Jacob with seventeen more years—years to reconnect with Joseph and even establish a relationship with his grandsons.

Paul assures us in the book of Romans nothing can stand between us and God. He is for you. And he's for me. He intends to turn our devastations and disappointments into unimaginable good. I blush when I think of my short-sighted excuses for self-pity. What else must God do to convince me of his love? He has already spared nothing.

So, don't be deceived. Don't underestimate the love and power of God. Spit out those worms of discontentment.

July 12th

As a result, Jesus could no longer enter a town openly but stayed outside in lonely places. Yet the people still came to him from everywhere.
—Mark 1:45 NIV

End Runs

Satan is the master messer-upper. He fans the flames of separation and hatred, incites violence and does anything within the power he's been granted to inflict pain and suffering on the world. But we serve a God who is bigger. A God whose name resounds with redemption. A God who takes the evil Satan intends and turns it into good. God knows how to do end runs.

When Jesus healed the man with leprosy, he cautioned him not to tell anyone, but to go to the priest and offer the required sacrifices (Mark 1:43–44). The former leper, however, functioned at internet speed, and before long everyone in Galilee heard the news. It's hard to keep quiet about life-altering miracles. And I suspect there may have been a crafty demon whispering in his ear to disregard Jesus' warning. The man's loose lips resulted in Jesus no longer moving freely, but being confined to "lonely places" outside the towns. If Satan couldn't stop the healing and hope, he would try to isolate its bringer. But it didn't work out the way Satan planned. Scripture tells us "the people still came to [Jesus] from everywhere." His scheme backfired.

Jesus continues to do end runs. I recently read the story of two Iranian women unjustly forced into prison because of their faith in Christ. Despite the deplorable conditions, their fellow prisoners—prostitutes, drug addicts, wives who simply failed to please their abusive husbands—women who would never otherwise have heard the gospel, found Jesus through them.

The most notorious, dehumanizing prison in Iran was transformed into a sanctuary of hope because of the witness of these two brave Christians. Satan meant their imprisonment for harm; God used it for good.

Do you know there is nothing that comes our way that God cannot use for good? Satan tries to steal our health, wealth and security; Jesus ushers us to our knees and reveals true health, true wealth and true security. There is no hurt, no wound, no failure we face that Jesus can't move from the negative to the positive column.

Although Satan may indeed be the master messer-upper, he stands as no match for the master end runner.

July 13th

But as for me, I am poor and needy;
may the Lord think of me.
You are my help and my deliverer;
you are my God, do not delay.

—Psalm 40:17 NIV

Selfie-holics

The need for deliverance runs deep in the human soul.

Deliver me, Jesus. Those words were scribbled on the carton of a half-empty case of beer I discovered behind our church at the foot of the cross. Whether the abandoned Coors Light was left in an alcoholic's drunken stupor or in quiet desperation, the profoundly personal cry for help touched a deep chord.

We all need to be delivered. Whether our symptoms are glaringly obvious or more subtle, without a Deliverer we pursue a path of self-destruction. We may try to hide it with alcohol, with success, with a variety of pleasures—even religion—but until we come face-to-face with our spiritual poverty, we find no escape.

Jesus succinctly defined the nature of our need. He prayed, "Deliver us from evil" (Matthew 6:13 ESV). We encounter evil on a daily basis. We read about it in our newspapers. We view it on our TV screens. But most unexpectedly, we battle it within our hearts. Few of us recognize the bastion of evil living in our fallen self-seeking nature. Tim Keller writes in *Walking with God through Pain and Suffering*, "We are so instinctively and profoundly self-centered that we don't believe we are."

Self-centeredness lies at the root of most of our addictions. That's bad news for a society documented by many social scientists as having a strong "turn toward self." Do you know Oxford's 2013 word of the year? Selfie. We're becoming selfie-holics. As long as we're addicted to our own self-interests, we will be in need of a Deliverer.

I don't think I'm a lot different from that unknown seeker who left the carton of beer at the cross. Nor was David when he cried out in Psalm 40: "I am poor and needy; may the Lord think of me." How about you? Are you tired of being addicted to your self-centeredness? If you are, join me in asking Jesus to deliver us from the self-centered bent of our souls. From our selfie selves.

July 14th

Until we all reach unity in the faith and in the knowledge of the Son of God and become mature, attaining to the whole measure of the fullness of Christ. Then we will no longer be infants, tossed back and forth by the waves, and blown here and there by every wind of teaching.
—*Ephesians 4:13–14 NIV*

Riding the Waves

Un·du·la·tion: a regular rising and falling movement.

Although most commonly associated with the back and forth movement of waves, I'm struck with how much of life consists of undulations. One day we soar to the heights; the next we plummet to the pit. *Up. Down. Up. Down.*

It reminds me of a time we took our son back to school in Nashville. We started the 750-mile trek in great spirits. Then, right after crossing the Tennessee border, we decided to find a motel for the night. After seeing a billboard that read LOW RATES—we were *Up.*

But unknown to us, the NASCAR races were in town and all motels were booked—we were *Down.* However, the clerk at the Best Western gave us a number to call when we got further down the road. So, we started off again—relatively *Up* until we realized we were leaving a trail of brake fluid behind us— definitely *Down*.

We coasted into a Hardees parking lot where the manager offered to drive my husband to an auto shop. Such kindness helped us rise back *Up*. Unfortunately, no one at AutoZone could fix the car until Monday. In addition, there were no car rentals open so we had to find a motel for the night (in the town where all rooms were booked)—*Very Down*.

We made it back to the Best Western and the sympathetic clerk found a handicapped room for us to stay in and charged us half-price. When we walked into the room I couldn't believe what I saw. On the desk was a Bible opened to the Psalms. Under it a note read: "We hope God will grant you peace and rest while you are under our roof"—more *Up* than you can imagine.

Seasons come and go in life. Paul warns us about being caught in the undulations. He says the mature are those who learn to ride the waves. So, let's not be infants tossed back and forth by either circumstances or "every wind of teaching." Let's be steady in our faith so we can ride those waves for his glory.

Surf's up!

July 15th

And the people of Israel went up and wept before the LORD until the evening. And they inquired of the LORD, "Shall we again draw near to fight against our brothers, the people of Benjamin?" And the LORD said, "Go up against them."
—Judges 20:23 ESV

It's Only a Battle, Not the War

It's just a battle, not the war." Those were the words I spoke to a friend who had just lost a big job his company was bidding on. He had prayed, hoped and believed God was going to give him the work. Now he would be forced to lay off employees and continue the search for new work. The disappointment overwhelmed him, thrusting him into an onslaught of questions concerning his company's future.

I imagine his feelings ran parallel to what the Israelites must have felt when God directed them to go to war against the tribe of Benjamin. Some of the Benjamites raped and murdered a young woman. But when asked to hand over the "worthless fellows" for punishment, the tribe refused to give them up (Judges 20:13). Their sin stunk so bad God commissioned the whole army of Israel to take arms against this small, very outnumbered clan.

But victory did not come as expected. In fact, Israel lost! Not only did they lose twenty-two thousand men in the first battle, they lost eighteen thousand in the second. This tiny tribe of Benjamin—the ones who had defied God—decisively cut down the mighty army of Israel. Stunned beyond imagination, Israel wept, fasted and prayed. They were obeying God, fighting for his honor, yet they were losing. To their credit, they did not turn away from God. When he told them to engage a third time, they courageously returned to battle. This time they completely defeated the Benjamites.

Can you relate to this? Have you walked in the will of God, yet found yourself on the losing end? Just because we are doing the Lord's will, there is no guarantee we will win every skirmish. Sometimes our enemy will gain the upper hand. In those dark times, the most important battle of all is won or lost.

Keep your eyes on the Lord. Stay faithful to his call—even if you lose a battle. Do that, and you will win the war. As to my friend—he now can barely keep up with all the work coming his way!

July 16th

When she recognized Peter's voice, she was so overjoyed she ran back without opening it and exclaimed, "Peter is at the door!"
"You're out of your mind," they told her.

—Acts 12:14–15 NIV

You Must Be Out of Your Mind

Are you out of your mind?

Peter had just been arrested for preaching the gospel. A small band of believers had gathered to pray for him. Their prayers weren't mere lip service either. Scripture says they were "earnestly praying" (Acts 12:5). Yet after an angel miraculously led Peter to freedom and he arrived at the house where they were interceding, he was met with an unexpected response. The servant girl, Rhoda, was so excited when she recognized Peter's voice that she ran to tell the others without even opening the door! And how did they respond to the miracle? Did they exclaim, "Praise God who has answered our prayer"?

Afraid not. Their words were far from a resounding affirmation of faith. They said to the servant girl, "You're out of your mind." And when they finally opened the door and Peter stood there in front of them, these earnest pray-ers were "astonished" (v. 16).

Sometimes my reaction to answered prayer runs along the same line. I'm surprised when the Lord comes through, oh me of little faith. Other times I ask, but I don't even recognize the answer when it comes. If I'm not careful, my prayers can turn into a matter of form. I rattle off my concerns without really considering my prayers could be making a difference. I seem to forget "the prayer of a righteous person is powerful and effective" (James 5:16).

How about you? Do you ever let your thinking interfere with the limitless possibilities of God? Or do you let his supernatural ways and thoughts prevail over your logical pragmatism? Don't let your faith lag behind your hope. Maybe those disciples' assessment of Rhoda wasn't so bad after all. Maybe it's okay to be "out of our minds."

Maybe getting out of our minds is the only way to get into the mind of Christ and pray like we mean it.

July 17th

Fight the battle well, holding on to faith and a good conscience, which some have rejected and so have suffered shipwreck with regard to the faith.
—1 Timothy 1:18-19 NIV

Don't Lose Your Conscience

A clear conscience. It's a terrible thing to lose.

Once we start ignoring that inner voice when it dictates a direction other than what we want, everything we think about moral truth begins to get fuzzy. Oh, it rarely seems that way at first. Rationalization for any behavior we want to justify is readily provided by the enemy of our souls. But conscience-rejecting always results in unmitigated disaster.

The more we entertain thoughts that violate our conscience, the greater the risk of losing our capacity to distinguish right from wrong. Before we know it, as Paul warns, our faith becomes completely shipwrecked. How does this happen?

Those baptized into Christianity are those who pledge a clear conscience before God (1 Peter 3:21). They make a promise they will let the Holy Spirit remove the dirt they accumulate while doing life. It's not a once-and-done thing. It often happens for me during morning devotions. I recall something hurtful someone has done and start to build an attitude. But my conscience whispers, "You're judging that person." Sometimes I think I can't do anything about it, so I'm tempted to ignore the whisper. Yet if God is speaking through my conscience, I know he wouldn't convict me of something and let it hang there. So, I repent. I repent and ask him to help me do what I can't do without his help. My conscience begins to clear. I realize if I don't maintain a clear conscience when confronted with relatively small challenges, I won't be ready for the big ones.

Let's do everything we can to keep our pledge of a clear conscience before God. When tempted to compromise the right and justify the wrong—even in small increments—let's drink the pure milk of the Word and strengthen our faith. If what the good God calls us to do involves some inconvenience, let's not use lame excuses to resist. And when we do fail, let's not turn away from the opportunity to repent. Let's hold on to the gift God gives to make us holy.

Is your conscience clear? I hope so. Nothing is worth shipwrecking our faith.

July 18th

They perish because they refused to love the truth and so be saved.
—2 Thessalonians 2:10 NIV

Resist the Drift

"Having allowed oneself to drift, unresisting, unpraying, accepting every half-conscious solicitation from our desires, we reached a point where we no longer believed the Faith," says one of C. S. Lewis' characters in his book *The Great Divorce.*

The process of "allowing ourselves to drift" springs into action whenever we want to believe self-serving lies. It is a natural progression that can only be stopped when we intentionally refuse to yield.

A battle resides within the soul of each of us. Our fallen nature bends toward justification of our actions, including the bad ones. We have to resist the currents of rationalization or we'll eventually be swept so far off course that we will come to believe the lie. But no matter how strong our belief, a lie remains a lie, and we will not be spared from the consequences of false thinking.

I remember a woman we met years ago when we were living in Florida. She and her husband were evangelists who traveled throughout the south. One day she said God told her she was going to marry a doctor. She allowed this thought to take such a strong hold on her, that in spite of its glaring contradiction to Scripture, she divorced her husband and married a doctor who, by the way, had been traveling with the couple.

As preposterous as this situation sounds, I believe if we don't anchor ourselves in truth, the waves of a fallen world will eventually capsize us. Paul described the outcome of those who refuse to love the truth: they perish! They reach the point where they no longer even recognize the truth (2 Thessalonians 2:11).

So, are you resisting the drift?

- the drift toward believing the worst about people who have hurt you?
- the drift toward softening biblical standards so you don't come across as irrelevant?
- the drift toward compromising sin in your own life?

Don't let yourself be deceived. You have a choice—a choice carrying eternal consequences. A choice that begins with studying the truth found in the Word of God and praying for courage. Courage to resist the drift.

July 19th

His mother said to the servants, "Do whatever he tells you."
—John 2:5 NIV

The Best Advice

It was the third day. The wine at the wedding feast was depleted, but the party wasn't over. Mary recognized what was happening, but she had neither the power nor the resources to fill the need. She had an inkling, however, that her son did.

When she informed Jesus about the impending social faux pas, it appeared he might not intervene. Bad timing for the Son of God to be revealed. Yet, Mary instructed the servants in charge of the wine, "Do whatever he tells you." As a result, the first faith-evoking miracle of Jesus' ministry made its way to the lips of the feast master and the hearts of his disciples. Mary's instruction proved to be great advice.

"Do whatever he tells you" continues to hold the number one position of Best Advise Ever Given. Whether our wine has run out or our bank account emptied, whether our patience has run dry or our forgiveness drained, when the need demands more than we have to offer, be assured Jesus has an answer.

In fact, it's the exact advice Jesus himself lived by. He did whatever he saw his Father doing (John 5:19). The results could not be more breathtaking. From choosing his disciples, to feeding the five thousand, to raising Lazarus from the dead—every decision, every crisis, every impossibility was met as he did whatever the Father told him.

Only if we take Mary's advice for ourselves can we offer it to others. And offer it with full confidence. We are not called to fix everyone's problems, but we are commissioned to lead others to the one who can. "Do whatever he tells you" surpasses any other counsel we could possibly take or give.

So, the next time you find yourself wrestling with a dilemma, or someone comes to you with a problem, as they say, above your pay grade, don't sweat it. You are connected to the smartest problem-solver who has ever lived. The Lord does not expect you to have every answer, but he does expect you to seek him ... then do whatever he tells you.

And that's the best advice. Ever.

July 20th

The tongue has the power of life and death, and those who love it will eat its fruit.

—*Proverbs 18:21 NIV*

Words Can Kill

Words matter. The writer of Proverbs says the power of life and death reside in the tongue. Words have a way of exposing our identity. Sometimes in lethal ways.

The book of Judges describes when the tribes of Gilead and Ephraim went to war. In this conflict, forty-two thousand men from Ephraim died due to the misarticulation of a word.

> And the Gileadites captured the fords of the Jordan against the Ephraimites. And when any of the fugitives of Ephraim said, "Let me go over," the men of Gilead said to him, "Are you an Ephraimite?" When he said, "NO," they said to him, "Then say Shibboleth," and he said, "Sibboleth," for he could not pronounce it right. Then they seized him and slaughtered him at the fords of the Jordan.
>
> —Judges 12:5–6

Wow! Life and death dependent upon the ability to say "*sh*."

The ancients notwithstanding, today reigns supreme as the communication age. It seems like every word uttered, especially by a celebrity, gets repeated and retweeted. Everyone voices an opinion on everything. All the while, word Nazis lurk behind the corner eager to pull out the gotcha gun for any word not correctly spoken. If ever there was a time to be cautious in what we say—welcome to the twenty-first century!

Words are like tattoos. Once spoken, they create a sense of indelibility. They both shape and solidify our persona, negatively or positively. In a sense, we are what we say. The more we whine, the more dissatisfied we become. The more we speak positively about people, the more love defines us.

How are your words? What do they disclose about you? Do they reflect honor toward the One who gave you the ability to speak in the first place? God hears your every word. He is listening not to "catch" you, but because he loves you. Be assured: your words matter. Choose them wisely.

July 21st

For to me, to live is Christ and to die is gain.

—Philippians 1:21 NIV

Who's Got This?

John showed me the right way to die." That was the sentiment one of my friends expressed upon the death of a dear brother in our church.

John's battle with cancer lasted only a few months, ending far too soon for his forty-five years. But interestingly, as his fight intensified, his faith grew stronger. Every time the doctor came with new bad news, John immediately assured his wife, *"Don't worry, God's got this."* In spite of ongoing pain and revolving door stays between the hospital and home, he managed to be an encouragement to everyone who came to visit. Even to the end.

John was moved to a hospice facility the day before he died. That evening a few people from our church gathered around him to pray and sing hymns. By this time his breathing was so labored he could hardly catch his breath, even with the oxygen mask. But after every song he managed to give a two thumbs up in a show of resounding approval. After they finished, he tried to say something, but no one could quite make out his words. So, in one valiant attempt to communicate, he ripped off his mask and with every ounce of remaining strength he shouted, "Hallelujah!" It served as his final testimony. Although John's body was dying, his faith pulsated with life. No fear. No sting. Just victory. *God's got this.*

The apostle Paul had no fear of death. He knew his destination, so he could proclaim, "to live is Christ and to die is gain." God would take care of him no matter what, in life as well as death. He didn't want believers to be concerned for him. He said to them, and to us today, *God's got this.*

John's brave words echo in my mind. God grants us dying grace as well as living grace. He remains with us in the valley of the shadow of death but also in the trenches of everyday living. I don't want to forget that. I don't want to forget my brother's words ... *God's got this.*

I pray you, too, would apply them to whatever challenge you're facing today.

July 22nd

As it is, we are in danger of being charged with rioting because of what happened today. In that case we would not be able to account for this commotion, since there is no reason for it.

—Acts 19:40 NIV

Causing a Commotion

Those early Christians had no fear of rocking the boat. They simply spoke the truth—and riots followed. The gospel has a way of causing a commotion, both externally and internally. We have to face some disrupting bad news before getting to the good news.

When Paul appeared before Governor Felix to defend himself against his Jewish accusers, an inward commotion erupted in Felix's heart (Acts 24). Although at first Felix listened to Paul explain his faith, when Paul began talking about "righteousness, self-control and the judgment to come" (v. 25), Felix dismissed him. Apparently, listening to Paul proved too convicting.

Wherever the Word of God is revealed, accountability to the truth surfaces. Those who reject the truth will go to any means to stifle the commotion. Scripture says Felix hoped Paul would offer him a bribe (v. 26). I have a feeling more than greed motivated him. Maybe if he could just get Paul to compromise, he himself would be off the hook. If Paul hedged on righteousness, perhaps he would have justification for his own indulgent lifestyle.

When confronted with the truth, human nature will either bow to it or try to find ways to circumvent it. Maybe that's why Christians continue to undergo such microscopic inspection. When we bear witness to the gospel and a commotion takes place in the hearts of those who hear, some will seek to quiet the disturbance by discrediting the messenger. Discredit the messenger; invalidate the message.

This looms as a stark reality for those of us who are in the process of becoming like Christ. We will never reach perfection in this life, but we must not let the fear of scrutiny hinder us from causing a commotion. So, with a clear conscience let's step up to the plate and give those who have gone before us something to cheer about. Let's resist the pull toward being either spineless or graceless in ways that offer nonbelievers an excuse to say no thanks.

Go ahead. Present the gospel. Cause a commotion!

July 23rd

I tell you, I have not found such great faith even in Israel.
—Luke 7:9 NIV

What Do We Deserve?

What does faith have to do with humility? A story from Luke 7 sheds some light.

A Roman soldier's beloved servant was deathly sick. When the soldier heard Jesus had entered his town, he sent some of the Jewish leaders to ask Jesus if he would come to his home and heal him. They implored Jesus on the basis that the man, although a Roman, "deserved" to have his servant healed. He was a good man.

Yet, as Jesus approached the house, the soldier sent friends to stop Jesus with the remarkable comment that he didn't deserve to have him even come under his roof. Recognizing the authority Jesus carried, he asked if he would just say the word and his servant would be healed. The soldier's request rested on who Jesus was, not his own deservedness. This soldier knew—in the light of pure goodness—he was not a good man.

And how did Jesus respond? He was "amazed" at "such great faith." Not the man's good deeds and reputation, not his love for God's people, not the compassion he displayed for his servant. What stopped the King of Kings and Lord of Lords in his tracks was the man's faith.

Humility makes room for faith. It empties us of thinking we deserve to have certain things or be treated in certain ways because of our moral goodness or our accomplishments. It helps us see that every good thing we encounter is a gift from heaven. Even the paychecks we earn are the result of a Father who provides us with the ability and opportunity to work.

I'm afraid we're losing that concept. I'm afraid even in the Christian culture, faith is being divorced from humility. Like the citizens in Capernaum, we judge others and ourselves as being deserving or not deserving of God's grace with shallow eyes. We resist humbling ourselves and instead strive to do it ourselves. That way we don't have to wrestle with our lack of faith.

We can't please God without it. We can't walk in the power of God without it. Ultimately, it is the victory we have over the world. But faith can't grow without this humble realization—

We deserve nothing.

July 24th

On hearing the Philistine's words, Saul and all the Israelites were dismayed and terrified. —1 Samuel 17:11 NIV

Two Steps Ahead of Depression

Ever have any of those days when you feel you're about two steps ahead of depression? Even though it hasn't caught up with you, it's in hearing range. It shouts, "Loser!" "Failure!" If you're not careful it will suck you into a full-blown defeatist attitude. A depressing thought.

How can we live in a way where defeatist and Christian don't occupy the same space? Where the giants in our lives don't cause us to respond in the same way Israel's army did in the face of Goliath's taunts? They were "dismayed and terrified." They saw no way out. Their vision was limited to what they alone could do in the face of such an overwhelming enemy. No one could imagine standing up to Goliath.

That is, no one but David. To him, Goliath displayed no greater a threat than the lion or bear who attacked his flock. The Lord had delivered him from their claws, and he was confident God would rescue him from Goliath's sword. He remembered what the army evidently had forgotten: God was on their side. David fearlessly cried out, "Who is this uncircumcised Philistine that he should defy the armies of the living God?" (1 Samuel 17:26). His trust in God—not his own skill—never wavered. He knew the battle belonged to the Lord (v. 47). So, did the victory.

When I face circumstances where that defeatist attitude seems to be barking at my heels, nothing helps me resist it more than recounting the faithfulness of the Lord. I remember how he brought our church through difficult changes. How he's empowered me to stare down my own Goliaths of rejection and fear of failure. It's then I sense that indomitable spirit of trust displayed in David beginning to rise. I move from relying on my scrawny, frail resources to faith in the living God.

If depression is threatening to overtake you, shift the battle from how you can control the outcome to how the Lord can. That despondency will start to evaporate and before you know it, depression will lie far behind, squirming in the dust.

July 25th

"The days are coming," declares the LORD, "when I will raise up for David a righteous Branch, a King who will reign wisely and do what is just and right in the land. In his days Judah will be saved and Israel will live in safety. This is the name by which he will be called: The LORD Our Righteous Savior."

—Jeremiah 23:5–6 NIV

The Last Idol

George Whitfield, the famous eighteenth-century preacher, referred to self-righteousness as the last idol to be rooted out of our heart. What a profound connection! Righteousness indicates the source of our standard for virtue, morality and decency. When that standard rests upon anyone other than God, we run the risk of compromising our worship. I think that's why Whitfield could so clearly call self-righteousness out as idolatry.

One of the names for God in the Old Testament is Jehovah Tsidkenu (Jeremiah 23:6). It means "the Lord our righteousness." God revealed this name to Jeremiah when the source of Israel's standard had slipped from God to themselves. Evidently, they were replacing Jehovah with their own names. It resulted in chaos as well as apostasy because the standard just wasn't big enough. With the name Jehovah Tsidkenu, God promised to send One who would restore a righteousness based on his name alone. A "Righteous Savior" who could rescue his people from the folly of self-adulation.

Jesus addressed the same issue when he told the parable of the wedding feast (Matthew 22). Although the invitation to the banquet extended to everyone, this was no free-for-all. The one who showed up without the wedding garment was thrown out because he refused to yield his estimation of what was right. His insistence on "my way or the highway" landed him on the highway all right—the highway to hell!

If we don't understand the Lord is our righteousness, we're going to be swept away with the rest of the world. Unless God himself is our standard, we have no foundation. So, it's time to abandon all notions of self-righteousness. Stop calling upon Becky (insert your own name) Tsidkenu to determine the right way. Don't pollute your worship of God with idols of self. Rest on the only standard big enough, wise enough, complete enough to bear the weight of every decision you make.

Jehovah Tsidkenu.

July 26th

Anyone who loves their brother and sister lives in the light, and there is nothing in them to make them stumble. But anyone who hates a brother or sister is in the darkness and walks around in the darkness. They do not know where they are going, because the darkness has blinded them.

—1 John 2:10–11 NIV

Hate Blinds

Love is blind. We've all heard that expression, right? Well I think hate blinds far more than love. Love blinds the lover to the flaws of its beloved. It "covers a multitude of sins." John says hatred plunges us into darkness, making us blind. It keeps us from seeing anything redeemable in its object of hate. Quite a sharp distinction. Love blocks the bad; hate blocks the good.

No one can deny the toxic atmosphere of today's trash-talk culture. It seems whole industries thrive on anger. Anger that leads to hatred. It's a sad state of affairs when men and women feel validated most when they're offended. Especially when they channel those offenses into malice.

Demonizing people who look differently, think differently and act differently to justify our own cause can only happen if we let the darkness overcome the light. If we refuse to see the "fellow" in our fellowman, the "brother" in our brotherhood. If we would rather nurture our grievances than do the hard work of looking beyond the surface.

As devastating as hatred can be, it often arrives subtly. It doesn't come pounding on our door in full-blown ugliness. It's usually disguised in a variety of rationalizations. Knock-knock: *Look how he took advantage of you.* Knock-knock: *You idiot, get off the road if you can't drive!* Knock-knock: *If they're elected, I'm leaving the country.* Beware of entertaining even the small shadows of hatred.

So why am I telling you to watch out for hate? You already know this. But Jesus warned in the last days sin would run so rampant that the love of most will grow cold (Matthew 24:12). I don't want you or me to be in that majority. When sin increases, we're not to abound in righteous indignation, but we're to let the grace of Christ flourish even more. Let's be in the glorious minority. Let's refuse to be blinded by hate. Let's choose light.

Let's overcome the world through the unfailing, inextinguishable, everlasting love of God.

July 27th

I have come that they may have life, and have it to the full.
—John 10:10 NIV

Viva La France

I guess I've always been a die-hard romantic. When I was in graduate school, my grandpa took me on a tour of the Holy Land. I'll never forget our layover in Paris. It was my first time out of the country, and the idea that we were actually in Europe awakened every dreamy notion I ever had. While the rest of the tour group was having lunch, I slipped away to find a French bakery. Before long, I spotted a little café and proceeded to ask the proprietor for a loaf of French bread—in English. He smiled as he gave me the bread and I proceeded to pay for it in American dollars.

In my confusion, an older French gentleman stepped up and purchased my bread in francs. Although I tried to reimburse him, he insisted on paying for it. "You give to me your smile and I give to you the bread," he persisted in the most wonderful French accent. Well, that did it. I floated back to the tour group, bread in hand.

So, what does all this have to do with God? I think all too often we box God into parameters of pragmatism and efficiency. We think he only rewards us when we "toe the line" or perform certain "acts of righteousness." But I suspect his arms reach much broader than we realize. I think he delights in giving his children gifts—all kinds of gifts like extravagant sunsets, cool breezes on stifling hot days, crackling fireplaces in winter, French bread.

He didn't have to give me that experience in Paris. But here I am, almost fifty years later, writing about it. The recollection directs my attention to a Father who was smiling on his daughter in spite of her silly sentiments and self-focused world. I didn't recognize him then, and that makes me wonder how many times I miss him today.

How about you? Are you aware of how God has come to give you abundant life? Jesus said he came not only to give us life, but "life to the full." Let's not miss his many blessings.

Viva à vie!

July 28th

It is written that "no eye has seen, no ear has heard, and no human mind has known." God has prepared these things for those who love him.
—1 Corinthians 2:9 NIRV

Heaven's for Real Alright

It is written that "no eye has seen, no ear has heard, and no human mind has known." God has prepared these things for those who love him. 1 Corinthians 2:9 NIRV

I believe Heaven is real, not because I've had a life-after-death experience or seen the movie describing a child's venture to the other side. There was never a time when I didn't believe in Heaven. I grew up singing "I'll Fly Away" and "I've Got a Mansion Just over the Hilltop." But in all honesty, I've taken Heaven for granted. I'm apt to set my mind on the "earthly things" of today.

Heaven gives us the needed perspective on how to live in a fallen world. It keeps us from putting all our eggs in one basket. It lets us know around the bend lies more than *that* relationship, *that* position, that failure, that success. As C. S. Lewis writes in *Mere Christianity*, "Aim at heaven and you will get earth thrown in. Aim at earth and you get neither."

So, what about Heaven? Although no eye has seen, no ear has heard, and no mind has conceived what God has prepared for those who love him, we can wonder. Heaven assures us death is not the end, but the beginning. It's not, as one poet has described, "hitting the period and closing the book." It's discovering the book for the first time. It's not the final destination of the train; it's getting *on* the train—a train headed for the greatest adventure we've ever known.

Nothing impure or deceitful will find its way into heaven (Revelation 21:27). Much of what has been esteemed on earth will be exposed like the emperor who had no clothes. Celebrities will no longer be worshipped. Ruthless dictators, sex traffickers and all who despise human dignity will be nowhere in sight. Heaven will be devoid of hate, jealousy, selfishness and pride (Revelation 21:8).

God's love permeates Heaven like light streaming from the sun. His love will embrace us until every tear is dried and every lingering doubt about our significance has been answered. If there was a *Heaven Daily Times* it would have our arrival splashed in big bold letters ... front page ... above the fold ... announcing to all of Heaven's residents we made it.

Heaven. Go ahead. Wonder a bit.

July 29th

In those days there was no king in Israel. Everyone did what was right in his own eyes.
—Judges 17:6 ESV

In Your Own Eyes

Jewish society during the time of the Judges was characterized by cultural compromise, underlying uncertainty, increased immorality and fickle faithfulness.

No less than three times, the author of Judges states, "in those days Israel had no king" (Judges 17:6; 18:1; 19:1). The connection between the lack of strong moral authority and the ensuing apostasy could not be clearer. When various judges rose to lead the country, Israel conquered their enemies. When there was no one to rule, a sordid mix of cultural influences, religious tradition and each one "doing as he saw fit" filled the void of leadership, resulting in oppression and subjugation by surrounding nations.

Israel fell to such a state of compromise that one woman thought she was doing a good thing by consecrating her silver to the Lord before casting it into an idol (Judges 17)! Samson's intoxication with Philistine women proved so overwhelming he didn't even realize the Lord had left him after Delilah shaved his head (Judges 16:20).

Jesus never did what was "right in his own eyes." In fact, he said, "I do nothing on my own authority, but speak just as the Father taught me" (John 8:28 ESV). He always went back to the moral authority and refused to veer from it. He never compromised the truth. Or justified sin. Nor should we.

Beware of that fatal tendency to make up your own rules to justify your actions. Proverbs 14:12 (ESV)says, "There is a way that seems right to a man, but its end is the way to death." We must resist the temptation to twist the Word of God to make it more relevant. One tablespoon of arsenic kills a human being within minutes. If you think a small compromise won't hurt, just read about the wretched results when everyone in Israel did what was right in their own eyes.

Let's never substitute the authority of God for doing what is right in our own eyes.

July 30th

You have come to God, the Judge of all, to the spirits of the righteous made perfect, to Jesus the mediator of a new covenant, and to the sprinkled blood that speaks a better word than the blood of Abel.
—Hebrews 12:23–24 NIV

Listening to the Better Word

Jesus' blood or Abel's? That's the question the author of Hebrews poses to us. Will we choose the blood of Christ that offers redemption and restoration or the blood of Abel that cries out for retribution and revenge? The options could not be more distinct. Or relevant.

Some of you may be like me. You cringe at injustice, you can't bear to see the innocent treated unfairly, the wrong trumping the right. I think God cringes at injustice, too, so we're in good company. But the rub comes when we feel it's our job to right the wrongs, our responsibility to serve the consequences.

Sometimes, our call does entail righting wrongs. Parents discipline their unruly children, employers fire unproductive employees, judges pronounce sentences on law breakers. We warn a wayward brother or sister in sin. Those aren't the situations that usually get us in trouble. It's the circumstances we take upon ourselves to fix that move us toward Abel's word.

Rather than facing our need for the blood of Christ, we persist in thinking that somehow we can compensate for our weaknesses. Someone hurts us and rather than drawing on the grace of God to forgive, we harden our hearts, rationalizing it as the just way to act. Our lips drip with criticism toward others' faults, flaws and failings. Our judgments grow resistant to the seasonings of mercy, even toward ourselves. Such actions do not speak the *better* word.

Francis Schaeffer once remarked we should always confront injustice with a tear in our eye. We should be sad, not vengeful, about the weaknesses in others. Remember how the blood of Jesus has freed us from the worst of consequences—eternal damnation. His word of redemption has spoken louder than the word of judgment over our hearts.

Now it's our time to speak it.

July 31st

The only thing that counts is faith expressing itself through love.
—Galatians 5:6 NIV

All That Matters

Two things. Just two things.

Some of us have a penchant for making life complicated. We parse every word, speculate on every motive. We assess ourselves, our spouses, our friends. Our finances, our failures, our futures. I teach at a Bible college where theological debates abound around every jot and tittle of Scripture. Although I enjoy a hearty discussion as much as anyone, the big questions and answers can usually be reduced to a few. The most profound truth often lies in simplicity.

Paul reminded the Galatians the only thing that mattered was not circumcision or uncircumcision, but faith expressing itself through love. To the Thessalonians, he expressed thankfulness for two things: they were growing in faith and increasing in love (2 Thessalonians 1:3). These two virtues were so apparent in the Thessalonians Paul concluded it evidenced they were worthy of God's kingdom (v. 5). Faith and love matter. Expanding faith and love matter even more.

I can't help but wonder if a lot of what we face in life pivots on learning to walk in growing faith and increasing love. Maybe God wants to shrink our complex situations down to size, to lead us to the bottom line, to use all our convoluted situations to simply teach us how to move from meager faith to much, from paltry love to profuse. Getting a handle on the significance of these two things could change our perspective of everything.

When we encounter either real or imagined rejection, does God want to use this situation to increase our faith and love? When our beliefs are misunderstood, is this purposed to increase our faith and love? When we experience difficulty with a co-worker, does a bigger issue lie at the root that is intended to increase our faith and love? And what about those days when all goes well? Could the blessings also be the means to move us toward greater faith and love?

Such questions give us a peek into what's important to God and what ought to be important to us. They direct us to look beneath the surface and discover deeper threads. May you and I be kin to the Thessalonians, commended for what really matters.

Two things. Just two things.

August 1st

Yet I hold this against you: You have forsaken the love you had at first.
—Revelation 2:4 NIV

Pull-Quote Love

Good works—*Check.* Perseverance—*Check.* Purity of doctrine—*Check.* Endurance for the sake of Jesus' name—*Check.* Maintaining love for God—*Whoops.* The believers at Ephesus boasted a pretty impressive résumé, but a résumé that fell short because they were missing one vital element: love. Love not nurtured intentionally is love that will not last.

So how is your intimacy with Jesus? Is it the same as when you first met him? Does he still hold first place in your affection? Do you communicate with him not just in morning or evening prayers but throughout the day? Are you relying more on your résumé of good works than communion with him?

It makes me think of pull quotes in books or blogs. Pull quotes take excerpts from the text and highlight something particularly interesting or insightful the author said. They stand out because the publisher uses a different font, color or typeset to make sure the reader notices. Our communication with God can devolve into pull quotes. We limit our conversation to the highlights of our day or week. Or maybe the only time we communicate is reserved for crises, so all our words consist of emergency pull quotes. We fail to discuss the whole chapter. And when we don't discuss the whole chapter with God, we eventually lose intimacy.

It may be hard to recognize what's happening because the pull quotes give us a false sense of being caught up. This can happen in communication with spouses, children or friends as well as with God. But when it happens with God, the results are as devastating for us as it was for the church at Ephesus. We run the danger of losing our light.

Cultivating our love for God takes time and effort, but its importance cannot be overstated. Don't let the fire of your love for him go out. Fuel that fire. Talk to him daily, regularly. He wants you to tell him about more than the highlights, more than the emergencies. Start right now. Tell him all your thoughts. Let him hear the whole chapter. Refuse a love consisting only of pull quotes.

Our offenses and sins weigh us down, and we are wasting away because of them. How then can we live? —Ezekiel 33:10 NIV

Bullet Points on How to Live

In 1976 Francis Schaeffer published his classic work, *How Should We Then Live?* Twenty-eight years later Charles Colson wrote what he considered to be his most important book, *How Now Shall We Live?* Both men echo Ezekiel's cry to God when the nation of Israel appeared to be rotting away due to moral and spiritual decay. The relevancy of their question has not faded.

Paul's words in 1 Corinthians 16 strike me as bullet points on how we should live in any age, in any culture (vv. 13–14).

- **Be on guard.** It is easy to forget we live in a spiritual combat zone. Paul warns us to keep our eyes open so we don't give Satan opportunity to distort the way God wants us to live. Our enemy tries to afflict all of us with Attention Deficit Disorder. Don't let the distractions he throws at you pull you away from the battle.

- **Stand firm in the faith.** Faith that stands firm is faith that comes from hearing the Word of God. If we hope to live in victory over the world, we cannot afford to neglect a daily, steady nourishing of our faith through Scripture.

- **Be courageous and strong.** This reminds me of the instruction given to Joshua as he led Israel into the Promised Land. It would be impossible for them to take the risks needed to go forward in his call without courage. It's the same for us. Cowering in a fear-filled corner of doom and gloom is not the way God desires us to live.

- **Do everything in love.** If love does not envelop all we do, our words, talents and deeds will reflect nothing more than empty chatter. Love for God should motivate every aspect of our lives if we hope to live in his purposes.

So how are you living? Do any of these bullet points need strengthening? As the world grows increasingly dark, we don't have to wring our hands in despair. We are called for such a time as this to shine. Although the "offenses and sins" of the world threaten to "weigh us down," let's not waste away. Let's live!

August 3rd

I will repay you for the years the locusts have eaten.

—Joel 2:25 NIV

The Hard Work of Dying

Dying is hard work," a friend said to me as I stayed with my dad during his final days on earth. "It's like childbirth, with its accompanying labor and transitory pain into a new world." I saw this firsthand—this mysterious cycle of life—in the few days surrounding Dad's final journey.

Dad was taken to the hospital on a Wednesday morning. By Thursday afternoon he returned to his home under hospice care and was given less than two weeks to live. But Dad was ready to go. As I've written in my book, *Virgin Snow*, he didn't accept Christ as Savior until he was sixty-five years old. But what happened upon his conversion was one of the most radical transformations I've ever witnessed. His last years were characterized by a daily prayer life that covered hundreds of people and visitations to the sick and dying encompassing over a thousand hours a year.

Dad was a natural evangelist. He told people the truth about what God could do every chance he got. His testimony rang with compassion and authenticity. And people listened. From his old drinking buddies, to his doctors, to his barber, to family members. He never stopped witnessing, even on his deathbed.

Dad's brother-in-law had been on his prayer list for years. A few days before Dad died, he came to see him. As I went into Dad's room, his brother-in-law sat in a chair next to the bed, tears streaming down his face. But Dad was smiling. In his now weak, raspy voice he whispered, "This is the happiest day in my life. I got to talk to Bobby about his soul." If ever a man kept the focus of his call to the end, it was my dad.

Dad was far from a perfect man. But he was a redeemed one. Although it was difficult to watch Dad's life ebb away in this "hard work of dying," it was a sacred time. I witnessed the fulfillment of God's promise that he "would restore the years the locusts had eaten." He had brought Dad full circle and prepared him for what has been described as the beginning of the real story.

If Dad were still alive, he would ask you, "Are you ready to start the real story?"

August 4th

There is a time for everything ... a time to be born and a time to die.
—*Ecclesiastes 3:1-2 NIV*

Timing is Everything

I don't always understand God's timing, but sometimes I get a glimpse.

If I hoped to see my dad alive, I needed to get to Ohio as soon as possible. My flight from Lancaster, PA to Columbus, OH, should have been smooth. It was anything but. One of my connecting flights was cancelled without notice, and the airlines took the liberty of booking me another flight that would not arrive in Columbus until midnight. Consequently, I would be stranded at the Philly airport for eight hours. Through a flood of tears, I begged the airline to bump me up on the standby list for the next available flight. I ended up fifth in line, taking the *last* seat and putting me in Columbus by late afternoon.

When I finally reached my dad's apartment, I was told he might not make it through the night, yet he lived another eight days. With the support of daily hospice visits, my brother and I were able to care for him all week. Every hour proved to be precious, sacred.

The day Dad died, he was more alert than he had been since I arrived. I left the house to get a pizza for supper and returned to Dad's room where I joined him and my brother. I joked with

Dad, asking him if he wanted some pizza. (He hadn't eaten all week.) He smiled and said, "I don't think so ..." The next moment, his chest jerked and his head thrust back. He was gone. Just like that.

All week I had been praying for the Lord not to take him *a minute before or a minute after* his appointed time. It would have been so easy for either my brother or me to be out of the room. Only a few minutes before, I was picking up pizza. But we were both there, with Dad, at the exact moment he left this world and entered eternity.

The writer of Ecclesiastes says God has appointed for each one a time to be born and a time to die. God got me to Dad at the right time despite my flight ordeal. And he purposed for me to be with him until he took his last breath. God's timing was perfect. Do you know it always is?

August 5th

I know what it is to be in need, and I know what it is to have plenty. I have learned the secret of being content in any and every situation, whether well fed or hungry, whether living in plenty or in want.
—*Philippians 4:12 NIV*

Never Enough

Fruitless. Insignificant. Just a "medium" in a super-sized setting. Ever feel like that? Like you're not measuring up? It's a mindset that undermines our sense of significance ... the very thing we were created for.

Author Brene Brown has researched this societal characteristic extensively. She concluded in her book *Daring Greatly* that ours is the "scarcity culture." It shouts we're not good enough, thin enough, extraordinary enough. So, no matter how hard we try or how much we succeed, we think we're falling short of some imagined standard. It keeps us trudging on the treadmill, striving for some sense of satisfaction but always missing the mark.

Nothing robs us of contentment more than feeling we don't have enough—enough money, enough success, enough affirmation, enough insight, enough time... As long as our perspective rises from a baseline of insufficiency, we set ourselves up for a life marked with discontentment.

Paul reveals the "secret" of being content in Philippians 4:13: "I can do all this through him who gives me strength." He understood true contentment comes from God alone. Scripture says God's "divine power has given us everything we need for a godly life" (2 Peter 1:3). So, the "scarcity culture" is a hoax. Its steady drumbeat of *not enough* succeeds only when we believe it—when we focus on what we don't have more than what we do have.

You and I will someday stand before God and be judged for what we have done with what we've been given, not for what we've not been given. You have enough to do exactly what he has called you to do. And you can do it through him who gives you strength. Be content in that knowledge, my friend. And go for it.

August 6th

Ask, and it will be given to you; seek, and you will find; knock, and it will be opened to you. —Matthew 7:7 NASB

Keep Knocking

We're not a very persevering people, are we? We usually want what we want, and we want it now. We're a *Carpe Diem* culture, afraid we'll miss out on life if we don't grab what we can when the opportunity rises. Our world doesn't exactly extol waiting as a virtue. But God does.

Remember the story of the persistent widow? She kept going to the judge again and again until she received the justice she was seeking. Although the judge was both unjust and uncaring, the woman finally wore him down because of her relentless asking. Jesus relayed this parable to his disciples to encourage them not to give up when praying (Luke 18:1–8). He wanted them to learn how to persevere. He wants us to learn it as well.

We cannot live in a hurry-up mindset and develop perseverance. When we face situations that require more time and effort than we originally expected, we must resist the tendency to give up. Especially in prayer. D. L. Moody tells the story of a woman who decided to pray every day for one year that her unbelieving husband would find Christ. After that time period, with no signs of change, she purposed to pray daily for another six months. With still no evidence of conviction after eighteen months, she committed herself to continue her daily pursuit of God on behalf of her husband until she took her last breath on earth. Not long after that renewed commitment, she found her husband on his knees crying out to God for salvation. Like the persistent widow, this woman did not stop asking or seeking. Instead, she kept knocking.

So, should we. If the Lord has placed burdens on your heart, don't be tricked into thinking your persevering prayer doesn't matter. Don't think you could be doing something more productive with your time. Keep knocking, my friend. Keep knocking until your fist turns raw. Keep knocking until you have no more tears to shed. Keep knocking and waiting, waiting and knocking. One day, perhaps when you least expect, the door will open.

August 7th

I will not fear though tens of thousands assail me on every side.
—Psalm 3:6 NIV

From Fear to Security

It's easy to say, "I will not fear," when the lights are on and our enemies gone. When the wedding ring is placed on the girl once terrified she would never find a husband. When the son has safely returned from Afghanistan. When the test results show no cancer. Funny how fear vanishes once the danger has passed.

So, can we learn to live without fear when the threat still looms? Jesus thinks so. Do you know he urges us to not be afraid twenty-one times in the gospels? That's thirteen more times than he instructs us to love! And he never gives us commands we can't keep.

On numerous occasions the Old Testament admonishes us not to be afraid. "I will not fear" David proclaims when he is smack dab in the middle of danger. "Tens of thousands" are pursuing him. To make matters worse, his own son is leading the assault. It must have felt as if the whole world was crashing in. But rather than giving into the fear nipping at his heels, he fights it.

He does not, however, fight it alone. He boldly asserts his trust in God to deliver him. He refuses to focus on the fear-provoking circumstance. Instead he fixes his eyes on the only One capable of rescuing him—the Lord, who stands as his shield, his glory, the lifter of his head. That's what I call s-e-c-u-r-i-t-y! (Psalm 3:3).

I don't mean to make light of our fears. I can get struck with a lightning bolt of panic as much as anyone. And clearly some situations warrant a healthy dose of fear. Yet we must not let it control us.

I once had a friend who suffered from agoraphobia. Anxiety squeezed her so tightly that some days she had to literally leave her shopping cart in the middle of the grocery aisle and rush home. She reached the point, however, where she learned how to fight back. She began to devour God's Word. And her fears began to shrink. In the end, she became one of the most fearless persons I've ever known.

No matter what kind of frightening circumstance you may be facing right now, listen to the words of Jesus and fear not. He's got your back. And that's a promise!

August 8th

Then Jesus said to him, "Get up! Pick up your mat and walk."
—John 5:8 NIV

Creativity: It's Not Just for Artists

Art? It was my freshman year of college, and my schedule included an Art Class. This did not make me a happy camper.

The first night of class the instructor had each of us draw whatever came to mind. As my fellow students crafted beautifully shaded apples and intricate portraits, all I could think of was a house, tree and sun! Not quite college-level drawing. But such was my concept of "art" and along with it "creativity."

My thoughts on creativity have expanded since that time. I now realize that because we are made in the image of our Creator we all have a measure of creativity that reflects him whenever we put it to use. It may not be expressed in lines and shapes and colors, but appears in the way we combine words, or musical notes, or spices, or flowers or in how we plan a party or design a room.

We shouldn't overlook this aspect of our lives. God has given us innumerable unique ways in which to express creativity. If we never act on the gifts we've been given, we most likely will lose them.

When Jesus told the invalid at the Pool of Bethesda to pick up his mat and walk, he was calling him to leave behind thirty-eight years of paralysis. Jesus even asked the man if he *wanted* to be made well (John 5:6). There were some internal obstacles that had to be overcome before he could be healed. I think the same is true for many of us in our approach to creativity. Maybe we need to tear down some roadblocks of laziness, complacency or fear of failure that lull us into the sleep of immobility.

So, recognize the call of your Creator. Don't wait any longer. Pick up your "mat," whether it be your pen, or guitar, or spatula or hammer. Walk into a world that needs what you have and give it. Be assured your creativity brings both glory and pleasure to God.

The second is this: "Love your neighbor as yourself." There is no commandment greater than these. —Mark 12:31 NIV

Unselfish Ambition

Do you ever have a hard time getting out of your bubble? Reaching out to others? Loving them as you love yourself?

How can we break through our tiny world? Maybe it begins with realizing we share more commonalities with other people than meets the eye. Who would have thought the guy sitting at the table next to me in the coffee shop would be having a conversation about God with the young man across from him? Yeah, that guy. The one whose skull-bone headband holds back his green hair and whose number of piercings on his eyebrow alone make me wonder how he keeps his eye open. Who knew? He likes to talk about God. So, do I.

It's easy to be so engrossed in our own perspectives we miss the common bond of people-ness. Hard to love someone as our self if we don't take the time to connect with them.

The other day my husband and I were traveling when we stopped at a McDonald's for coffee. As we headed back to our car, a family pulled in next to us. The teenage daughter wore a T-shirt with the word SENIOR emblazoned across the front. That's all my husband needed. Without hesitation, he asked, "So you're just about through school?" A big smile covered her face as her mom acknowledged they were on their way to Tennessee to check out her new college. "Where in Tennessee?"

"Nashville."

"Our son went to school in Nashville at Belmont."

"Belmont!" Mom, Dad and daughter all laughed. "That's our destination!" It was a small moment, but one of those connecting kind. People to people. Our day, and I'm sure theirs, was richer because of it.

Scripture says the second greatest command is to love your neighbor as yourself. When we take the time to get into someone else's world—even for a minute—we reflect the attitude of Christ. He always took the time to connect with people, and he wants us to relate to others like that.

I want to be more engaging with people. To love like Jesus did. To think more about the person in front of me than myself. It's my unselfish ambition. Care to join me?

August 10th

We do not know what to do, but our eyes are on you.
—2 Chronicles 20:12 NIV

Where Do Your Eyes Go?

Where do your eyes go in times of trouble? Do they frantically dart from one potential source of help to another? Do they gaze inward, pummeling yourself with blame? Maybe you simply close them, pretending there's really nothing wrong.

When a vast coalition of enemies advanced against King Jehoshaphat, Scripture says he was "alarmed" (2 Chronicles 20:3). No wonder! He knew he was outnumbered, out resourced, and outsmarted. But he didn't let his panic take control. Instead, he fixed his eyes on the Lord. "For we are powerless against this great horde that is coming against us. We do not know what to do, but our eyes are on you" (2 Chronicles 20:12 ESV). That fixation on God resulted in a rout so big that it took Jehoshaphat and his army three full days to collect the spoils!

Eyes fixed on God always win. They never lose focus on what's important. On where the real battle lies. They perceive not knowing what to do is their greatest asset.

Last winter heavy snows took a toll on our roof. We knew it would have to be replaced, but we were completely stumped in how to resolve the problem. In our relatively small dilemma, like Jehoshaphat, we cried out to God, "We do not know what to do, but our eyes are on you." One morning while we were praying, my husband heard a steady *tap, tap, drill* from our neighbor's yard. When he went to inspect the sound, he found an Amish roofing team replacing our neighbor's roof! We knew immediately they embodied the answer to our prayer.

Not only did the roofers put up a solid roof at a reasonable price, but more importantly, the whole situation deepened our trust in God. We had set our eyes on the Lord, and he showed us with great specificity what to do. So, whether you are facing a vast coalition of problems right now, or a small impasse, don't let your eyes shift from one place to the next. Fix them on the Sovereign Lord. You may not know what to do, but he does.

August 11th

Show proper respect to everyone. Love the community of believers. Have respect for God. Honor the king. —1 Peter 2:17 NIV

Question Authority

I realize somewhere along the line I threw the proverbial baby out with the bathwater. It probably happened in the turmoil of the 60s when the mantra of peace and love also included a charge to "question authority." Once Pandora's Box was opened, legitimate questions surrounding the establishment progressed into an ongoing state of rebellion toward anyone and everything connected to it. Consequently, at times I still find myself dishonoring positions when I disagree with the behavior of the people holding them. This is not only unhealthy, but unbiblical.

David certainly got it right. In spite of Saul's determination to kill him, time and time again David refused to take Saul's life when he had opportunity. Even when his men encouraged him to take Saul out, David responded, "The Lord forbid that I should ... lay my hand on him; for he is the anointed of the Lord" (1 Samuel 24:6). "Who can lay a hand on the LORD's anointed and be guiltless?" (1 Samuel 26:9).

Although Saul's behavior was reprehensible, David knew the position of King demanded honor. I believe it was David's honoring of the position that made him the great ruler he eventually became.

Observers note more than anything, Americans value freedom. The formation of our country was rooted in resistance to monarchy of any sorts. We want presidents, not kings. But Scripture warns us not to use our freedom as a cover-up for evil. Because we disagree with authorities, be it emperors, governors or presidents, we are not licensed to dishonor God by dishonoring their position (1 Peter 2:13–14).

When we treat others—including authorities—with the same disrespect others do, we look a little less like Jesus and a lot more like the world. There is nothing wrong with questioning authority. Blind obedience never produces good fruit. But no matter how much we differ from those over us, our questioning must not lead to dishonoring.

Respecting others, loving fellow believers, fearing God, and honoring positions of authority causes us to live up to *our* position as children of the Most High.

August 12th

He causes his sun to rise on the evil and the good, and sends rain on the righteous and the unrighteous. —*Matthew 5:45 NIV*

Put Down the Umbrella

Put down the umbrella! The words could not have been clearer. We were singing about God's mercies being poured out, his blessings being "showered down." Interrupting this sweet reverie came the realization we can't experience a drop of God's favor if our umbrellas are up. He may be sending a torrent of grace our way, but we'll never know it if we have installed permanent fixtures of protection.

Umbrellas in the natural are useful. They shelter us from either getting drenched by the rain or roasted by the sun. Umbrellas in the spirit present another story. They block us from the blessings of God and shield us from soaking in his love. Why in the world would we want to guard ourselves from that? What do we deem more important than letting God rain down on our parched souls?

It makes me ask myself what my umbrella consists of. What have I constructed that keeps me from receiving God's poured out mercies? Shame? Self-sufficiency? Pride? Distractions? How about unbelief? Unbelief makes a pretty hefty umbrella. It does a great job in protecting me from disappointment. If I expect nothing, when nothing comes, at least I won't be devastated. Better to play it safe. But in shielding myself from potential pain, I also shield myself from love, joy, peace—all the things that make life worth living.

Umbrellas of any kind obstruct the truth: God wants to bless all of his children—the just as well as the unjust. Thinking his outpouring of mercy is conditioned on our behavior creates blind spots that make us want to cling to our "protection." Until we recognize God desires to pour down his favor just because *he* is good—not because *we* are—I'm afraid we'll never close our umbrellas.

So, go ahead. Put that umbrella down. Get sopping wet in the beauty of his goodness and the favor of his love.

August 13th

We wait eagerly for our adoption to sonship, the redemption of our bodies.
—Romans 8:23 NIV

Gotcha Day

Maybe you've heard of it—the day when adoptive parents finally get to receive the child they've so long awaited. For my brother and his wife, the wait lasted over six years before they could bring their little girl home from China. But to them Gotcha Day was worth the wait.

The joy of childbirth didn't last long for one of the most famous mothers in the Bible. Moses' mother realized if she kept her baby boy, he would be murdered by Pharaoh. For three months she poured into her little one every ounce of love she had. Then, to spare his life, she gave him up and Pharaoh's daughter experienced her own *Gotcha Day*. Moses grew from a "fine child" into one of the greatest leaders in history.

Not every child is literally plucked from death as was Moses. Not every child is rescued from abandonment like my niece. But the love, potential and security that adopted children discover reminds me of the adoption experience of every believer.

It makes me think of another parent—a father, a heavenly Father. One who also poured every ounce of love into his Son, his firstborn, and then, to spare the lives of his other children, gave him up. "For God so loved the world that he gave his one and only Son, that whoever believes in him shall not perish but have eternal life" (John 3:16). He relinquished his Son to rescue us from a life of unwantedness, and abandonment. No matter who we are or where we come from, we can know for certain that a day is coming when we will find loving arms waiting to hold us and to welcome us home. On that day we will hear the words of pure love saying, *Gotcha.*

August 14th

Therefore, as God's chosen people, holy and dearly loved, clothe yourselves with compassion, kindness, humility, gentleness and patience.
—Colossians 3:12 NIV

What Are You Wearing?

I just wore that. Those pants don't fit. Wrong color. Out of style. You don't have to be a Fashionista to find yourself staring in the closet wondering what in the world you are going to wear for the day. But how about your spiritual wardrobe? Do you ever consider what you're wearing on the inside? Or that maybe it's time for some new spiritual clothes?

I happen to know the greatest Fashion Designer in the world. In fact, he wears splendor and majesty and even wraps himself in a garment of light (Psalm 104:1-2). He's able to see exactly what looks good on us. He wants us to try on some compassion and kindness, get fitted with some humility, gentleness and patience. But to make room for our new attire, we'll have to get rid of some of the old clothes. Maybe we've worn those shabby grudges long enough anyway. And what about that ugly coat of self-righteousness? It never looked as good as we thought it did. Those dark glasses of criticalness will have to go too. They keep us from seeing others in the same way we want to be seen. No place, either, for those gaudy beads of gossip and harshness.

The new clothes designed by our Maker are woven in love. Every stitch! Love binds everything together in a way that makes us as resplendent as a bride on her wedding day. With our new clothes comes a new confidence. The longer we wear them, the better they fit. Constant wearing doesn't make them ragged, but more beautiful.

Make no mistake. People see our inward apparel more than we realize. They recognize whether we're holding on to the tattered hand-me-downs of our fallen nature or putting on new attire. More importantly, God knows. He has gone to great lengths to provide us with Designer clothing that far exceeds any fashioned by Yves Saint Laurent or Christian Dior.

Is it time for a wardrobe check in your life? Time to put on some new clothes? I pray what you *wear* reflects the Lord's handiwork. Who knows. Maybe some of the people around you might even want in on your secret.

August 15th

I intend, therefore, to build a temple for the Name of the LORD my God, as the LORD told my father David, when he said, "Your son whom I will put on the throne in your place will build the temple for my Name."
—1 Kings 5:5 NIV

Live Up to the Name

All hail the power of Jesus' name ... What a beautiful name it is ... Your name is a strong and mighty tower ... We sing about the name of God. We pray and baptize in the name of the Father, Son and Holy Spirit. We're commanded not to take the Lord's name in vain. Solomon built the temple for the Lord's name. Clearly, the name of the Lord carries great significance.

Scripturally, name denotes more than a tag or label. It signifies God's revealed character. Jesus came in the name of the Father to illuminate what the invisible God would look like in human form (Colossians 1:15). After Jesus ascended back to Heaven, his followers were to reveal the *name.* That's why those in the early church were designated by the term "Christians." Christian literally means "little Christ." Now that's a name to live up to!

We undoubtedly misrepresent his name. We are imperfect people seeking to portray a perfect God. Our doubts, insecurities and wounds can paint a picture of the name that doesn't run true. At times, we veer so far off course that our image completely overshadows his. It's no wonder some today have an aversion to even calling themselves Christian.

In spite of our mess-ups, however, God entrusts us with this privilege. He calls us his children and gives us his name for the exact purpose of empowering us to live up to it. "You may not feel like God's child, but you are," shouts heaven. "So act like it!"

Don't dismiss this great call because of all the weaknesses you see staring back at you in the mirror. As a Christian, let his name be seen in all you do. Even when you inevitably fall, remember who you are. Repent, get back up and go about the business of once again reflecting his name.

You and I are now the temple where he has chosen to put his name. Let's live up to it!

August 16th

Let your light shine before others, that they may see your good deeds and glorify your Father in heaven. —*Matthew 5:16 NIV*

A Call for All Seasons

Tony Campolo tells the story of a bedraggled bag lady who managed to duck security and stroll into the top floor of Nordstrom's, the high-end fashion retailer. The top floor housed their most luxurious dresses. As she got off the elevator, a saleswoman came right up to her and offered her assistance. When the lady said she wanted a party dress, the saleswoman enthusiastically replied she had come to the right place. She then led her to the fitting room where she tried on two dresses. Upon deciding she didn't want a dress after all, the saleswoman graciously responded, "That's quite all right, madam. But I'd like you to take my card. Should you come back to Nordstrom, I would consider it both a privilege and a pleasure to wait on you again."

This salesclerk knew her work in life went far beyond selling expensive clothing. Her *call* was to shine the light of Christ no matter what the situation. And so is ours.

We each have different assignments in life. We fulfill roles as students. As singles. As spouses. As parents and grandparents. We have different jobs throughout life. My first employment consisted of washing people's dirty clothes as a laundromat attendant. I've been a waitress, a librarian, a speech therapist, a teacher. Some jobs don't entail a paycheck. We care for elderly parents or sick neighbors. We volunteer at a food pantry or go on mission trips to minister to the needy.

No matter what our circumstances, Jesus says the light of our deeds brings praise and glory to our Father in heaven. It's a call shared by all believers. When we treat our fellow human beings with dignity, like the Nordstrom saleswoman, it's one clear way we shine the light of Christ.

And that's a call for all seasons!

August 17th

But the high places were not taken out of Israel.
—2 Chronicles 15:17 NASB

High-Placed Influence

They did not remove the high places. This is a frequent commentary about the kings of Israel and Judah. It was important. Failure to remove these Canaanite places of worship became the standard on which the kings were evaluated.

Out of the forty kings who succeeded David—twenty in Israel and twenty in Judah—only two receive full commendations: Hezekiah (2 Kings 18:3–4) and Josiah (2 Kings 23:4–15). Both destroyed the high places. Both consequently orchestrated major revivals in the nation. Two other kings, Asa and Jehoshaphat, are referred to as good kings with qualification. They were able to get rid of the high places at one point in their reign only to have them resurface in later years, resulting in the nation's detriment. So even the good these kings accomplished was tainted by the high places' stubborn refusal to stay down. Why was getting rid of high places so significant?

God hated them. Not taking them seriously set the people on a trajectory that led to idolatry and rebellion against him. High places became the proverbial inch that takes a mile.

I can't help but think we have our own high places today. We may be more susceptible to them than we realize. One writer suggests the high places of American culture can be found in the media, academia and the courts. Not negative forces in and of themselves, they become high places when their influence beckons us to trust in them more than we trust in God.

So, does that make them evil forces that need to be destroyed? Of course not. No more than the hills in Israel where pagan worship occurred were to be leveled. What may need to be torn down, however, is the influence we let them exert over us. Do we consider the wisdom of academia higher than God's wisdom? Do we believe the standards of right and wrong heralded by media are more sophisticated than those presented in the Bible? Does government have more say in our decision-making, than the Holy Spirit's leading?

Beware of the influence of high places. Don't let them trap you into a place where they sabotage your trust in God. There's room for only one at the top.

August 18th

I pour out before him my complaint; before him I tell my trouble.
—Psalm 142:2

The Sweetest Hour

Sweet hour of prayer! Sweet hour of prayer! That calls me from a world of care ...

How incredible to know we have someone who always makes time to hear us. Someone who doesn't pull out a smartphone and start texting while we're pouring out our heart. Who never says, "I'll get back to you" before we've even finished our sentence.

When we cry out to God, we are not calling up an imaginary friend, an icon or someone who wields no authority to help us. We are not spilling out our guts to someone who lacks compassion for our plight. We are praying to a God who listens.

He listens, when unbelief seeps through our desperation. He listens, when confusion overrides peace. He listens, when we're holding on by a fingernail. He listens, when no one else will.

David's prayer in Psalm 142 makes it clear he was well acquainted with God's listening ear. He who had been the delight of Israel is now forced to hide in a cave to avoid Saul's insane pursuit of his life. In great distress, abandoned by friends, the rejection and betrayal overwhelm him. But rather than blame God for his predicament, he turns to him. Fully.

He tells him all about his trouble. Isn't that interesting? He knows God perceives every detail, but he finds it necessary to lay it all out before him. David bares his soul and discovers a new dimension of intimacy. His exposure before God leads him to a sense of safety and security, as well as a place of faith. He vows to tell everyone about God's goodness in delivering him. His sweet hour of prayer cemented his trust in the Lord.

What an example for us to emulate. When life gets hard, we should not hesitate to tell God all about it. We ought not hold back. Although he already knows what we're going through, we need to tell him. Our transparency before him will increase our trust. And trust in the God who listens sets us on a sweet road.

And since He bids me seek His face,
believe His Word and trust His grace,
I'll cast on Him my every care,
And wait for thee, sweet hour of prayer!

August 19th

Do not judge, and you will not be judged. Do not condemn, and you will not be condemned. Forgive, and you will be forgiven. Give, and it will be given to you. A good measure, pressed down, shaken together and running over, will be poured into your lap. —Luke 6:37–38 NIV

Hoarding Hearts

Money, resources, time. Generosity comes in different shapes and sizes. Scripture provides clear examples of generous givers from the widow's mite (Mark 12:42) to the churches in Macedonia (2 Corinthians 8:2). It connotes *largesse*, bigness, liberality, giving without expectation of return. But Jesus takes it further.

In Luke 6, he admonishes us to be generous in the way we view other people. When we see others in their weaknesses, he calls us not to hoard judgments against them. Not to stockpile reasons to condemn. When someone hurts us, we are not to fondle our grievances like a miser poring over his gold. A judgmental heart is a stingy heart. It refuses to release love. It penny-pinches kindness.

You've probably heard of people afflicted with hoarding. They can't let go of anything. The thought of discarding newspapers, old clothing, food, even plastic bags and cardboard boxes throws them into an anxiety attack. A common reason hoarders keep accumulating lies in their perception of the future. They're afraid if they let something go—even something insignificant—they may end up needing it in the future. Eventually their environment becomes so cluttered with piles upon piles of stuff, they barely have room to move. Their world shrinks.

I think that can happen to us spiritually when we hoard the love God has lavished on us—love he wants us to share with others. The "good measure, pressed down, shaken together and running over" that returns to those who give can't be poured into our lap. There's no room! And when we hold on to judgments because we think if we let go of them we will somehow be diminished in the future, our world actually does shrivel up. Hoarding hearts eventually suffocate and wither.

So, how's your heart? Are you holding on to things you should be discarding? Things constricting your growth? Now's a good time to let go. Don't put up with a hoarding heart. Go for an extravagant one!

August 20th

For you have been born again, not of perishable seed, but of imperishable, through the living and enduring word of God.

—1 Peter 1:23 NIV

Just Live With It...Not!

I can never change. It's just who I am.

Have you ever heard people say those words? My friends thought their relationship could never change until they found a new perspective at a marriage retreat they attended. The speaker asked everyone to write their signature with their dominant hand. Then he told them to do the same with their non-dominant hand. He explained although it is harder to use your less dominant hand, you can do it if you're willing to work at it. If you want your marriage to work, you must first believe change is possible.

The possibility of change extends beyond our handwriting skills and beyond marriage. We are not bound to our habits. Change is not only possible but plausible for those who have been born again. Peter says a new seed—an imperishable one—is planted in believers at conversion. Before, there existed little hope of transformation, but now we have the capability of ridding ourselves of malice, deceit, hypocrisy, envy and slander, to name a few areas of darkness. The old seed produces sin. But once we come to Christ, that seedbed of corruption no longer has to bear fruit in our lives. We don't have to just live with it!

Sometimes I forget about the powerhouse that exists in the new seed. When the familiar voices of insecurity and doubt pepper my mind, I surrender, and soon defeat is the only sound I hear. The early church forgot too. Peter had to "remind" them that God's divine power had already given them everything they needed to live a godly life (2 Peter 1:3). He encouraged them to utilize that power by making "every effort" (v. 5) to put into practice the virtues Christ had planted in them.

Believing we can be different is not a mystical type of mind-over-matter training. We rely on the Holy Spirit to aid us. He empowers us to exercise love over selfishness, self-control over indulgence, kindness over cruel intentions.

Friend, we will never be perfect in this fallen world. But rather than giving in to that perishable seed, let's keep on rejecting it, repenting and calling on the Holy Spirit for help. Let's not *just live with it.*

August 21st

The words of the mouth are deep waters, but the fountain of wisdom is a rushing stream.

—Proverbs 18:4 NIV

Cowardly Conversations

None of us like to think of ourselves as cowards, do we?

Although we typically think of cowardice on the battlefield, it can extend to almost every aspect of life. Even conversations. Have you ever been in a situation where you wanted to say something to another person, but lacked the courage to say it? Maybe you didn't want to hurt the person's feelings. Maybe you didn't want to swallow your pride. Maybe you didn't want to risk rejection. Whatever the motivation, you discovered a massive roadblock between your mind and your mouth.

The bestselling book, *Crucial Conversations,* explains how honest, respectful conversations from the family room to the boardroom impact our relationships perhaps more than any other factor. The authors' research of over one hundred thousand people reveals the key skill of effective leaders, teammates, parents and loved ones is the capacity to skillfully address emotionally and politically risky issues.

For many of us, it only takes a few crucial conversation attempts gone bad to transform us into cowardly communicators. We become experts in avoidance. Specialists in self-preservation. Our conversations become safe, saltless and unsatisfying. Why risk potential unpleasantness? Maybe we should be asking "why not?"

Do we really want to get to the end of our life and regret not having had crucial conversations that should have taken place? Do we want to be wishing we would have gently confronted a fellow believer for not living up to his call? That we would have challenged an out-of-line boss? That we would have been more vulnerable and told someone how much we cared?

Cowardly conversations, in the end, turn out to be non-conversations. And when there is no conversation, relationships deteriorate. Why not embrace a little unpleasantness for the hope of something better? None of us have to be locked into cowardly communication. Proverbs 18:4 assures us that the words of the mouth are deep waters. Take courage my friend to draw from those streams of honesty, of truth, of love.

It may be more crucial than you think.

August 22nd

And this is eternal life, that they know you the only true God, and Jesus Christ whom you have sent.   —John 17:3 ESV

Getting to Know You

Getting to know you, getting to know more about you.

I woke up with slightly altered lyrics from *The King and I* echoing through my mind. They were an apt reflection of thoughts surrounding my time of semi-solitude at the little cottage on Lake Erie. I was there to write, to discover more about the Lord. To receive more of him.

When Jesus came to earth, he broke open the opportunity for us not only to know about God with our mind, but to know God personally with our heart. That's why he said the least in the kingdom of heaven is superior to the greatest of men—men like John the Baptist and prophets like Elijah, Jeremiah, Ezekiel, Daniel (Matthew 11:11). They could only know God from a distance. Their righteous adherence to the Law demonstrated what they knew about God, but a relationship of intimacy remained out of reach.

Until Jesus.

Jesus likens all of us repentant sinners who seek to do the will of the Father to his natural family (Matthew 12:50). And families know each other. He invites us to get to know him through the course of our day-to-day living. As writer Dean Nelson explains in *God Hides in Plain Sight: How to See the Sacred in a Chaotic World*, God is always sending us signals indicating his presence, but we simply miss them because we aren't tuned into looking for him in everyday life. We should be paying more attention.

Drawn to watch Deborah Kerr singing in *The King and I* was one of those signals for me. Through a simple clip on YouTube of a Rodgers and Hammerstein musical, Jesus let me know he was there, with me, right then. And his presence ushered me into "getting to know him more."

Let's not miss eternal life, life that begins with knowing the only true God and Jesus Christ. Let's look for those signals of his presence.

August 23rd

In all this, Job did not sin by charging God with wrongdoing.
—Job 1:22 NIV

Staying Steady in the "All This"

Satan hurled everything he could to throw Job off track and derail his relationship with God. He will try the same strategies with us.

First, Satan sends invaders to kill Job's servants and steal his livestock. In an instant, his only means of income vanishes. No bank account. No 401(k). No government assistance to tide him over. All of his considerable wealth—gone.

Satan's next ploy gets close and personal. A wind sweeps in from the desert and causes the house where his sons and daughters are gathered to collapse. They all die. It's hard enough to think about losing one child, but all your children? No more family dinners. No more family anything. His legacy—gone.

Satan is sure he can get Job to turn on God if he experiences physical suffering. He afflicts him with pain from the top of his head to the soles of his feet. Job endures so much agony he wishes he'd never been born. Even his wife incites him to "Curse God and die!" (Job 2:9). His health and vitality—gone.

Finally, Job undergoes perhaps the greatest test of all when his three friends offer him a twisted form of religion. They misrepresent God's character (Job 42:7). But Job rejected their misguided theology. And although Job's perception of God was incomplete, when he eventually saw the truth, he repented. All that had been lost—restored.

Make no mistake. Satan continues to use our crises to distort our perception of God. He tries to make us believe a God of love would never let us suffer. Pain, physical or emotional, has a way of distorting the truth, and our enemy takes full advantage of our vulnerability in hard times. We must not let him do that.

Whether you are facing financial difficulties, deep emotional loss, ongoing illness or a false theology that makes you think God's grace depends on your own righteousness, don't let anything weaken your relationship with God. More lies behind those circumstances than you or I can see. Stay steady, my friend, in "all this" no matter what your "all this" might include.

August 24th

This is how we know what love is: Jesus Christ laid down his life for us. And we ought to lay down our lives for our brothers and sisters.
—1 John 3:16 NIV

Sacrifice...What's Love Got To Do With It?

Love without sacrifice is like food without nutrition. No sustenance. No life. Christianity is planted on the foundation of sacrificial love. John reminds us we know what authentic love is because of Jesus' sacrifice for our sake. A sacrifice we're inspired to emulate.

Sacrificing for the sake of someone else does not come easy for most of us. All too often our definition of love does not include sacrifice. We like the warm feelings, the sense of satisfaction that accompanies love—but how often do we actually put someone else's interests ahead of our own? I can't help but wonder if love without sacrifice is love at all. Scripture's definition of love could not be less ambiguous.

I've long held a mother's fierce bond with her children develops because of her countless hours of sacrifice on their behalf. For example, sleep. When my kids were young, I was convinced they had a secret "mommy alarm" that automatically sounded when I tried to take a nap. No laziness on their watch! Moms forego everything from careers to the last cookie on the plate to benefit their little ones. They even accept the premise they may never think in full sentences again! They freely lay down their lives for their sons and daughters—and in doing so, they discover a profound secret.

Sacrifice teaches us to love. Even if it begins as a responsibility, every time we deny ourselves to meet another's need, we grow in love. No wonder Scripture makes such a strong case about sacrifice. From the very beginning Christianity has been about loving. The whole purpose of becoming a Christian is to become like the one who laid down his life for another's sake. Yours. Mine.

Don't let yourself be deceived by cheap imitations. Be willing to sacrifice. It has everything to do with love.

August 25th

If we are faithless, he remains faithful—for he cannot deny himself.
—2 Timothy 2:13 ESV

God's DNA

I recently told someone who worried about being irresponsible, "You couldn't be irresponsible if you tried. It's not in your DNA." I think the same way about God's faithfulness. The limitless, unfathomable creator of the universe could not be unfaithful if he tried. Our trust in him ultimately hinges on whether we believe that irrevocable fact: God is faithful.

Author Mark Buchanan notes in *The Holy Wild* how much we take faithfulness for granted. Its very nature is unwavering, sturdy, routine—so much so that we almost grow blind to it. In fact, Buchanan writes faithfulness can sometimes appear almost "boring."

Yet without the faithfulness of God we wouldn't last an hour. His favor toward us does not depend on our actions. Even when we are faithless, Scripture says he remains faithful. He can't help himself. It's who he is. He can't love us one day and spite us the next because of our failures. No matter what, God remains true to himself. Count on it. Especially when situations don't turn out the way we expect.

It's easy to confuse faithfulness with predictability. God is faithful, but he is not predictable. Those who love him don't know how he will work circumstances out for good, but they know with certainty he will (Romans 8:28). We must refuse the temptation to reduce God to our own experience when our circumstances seem to contradict his nature.

As God's children, he wants us to share his DNA. He has designed us in such a way that every time we faithfully carry out our assignments—even the small ones—more of his faithfulness takes hold in our lives. The thread running through what we do becomes the fabric of who we are (Luke 16:10).

So be faithful in those major responsibilities in your life, but don't overlook the small, seemingly insignificant tasks you are called to do. In a world where faithfulness has become a rare commodity, be different. Wouldn't you like for God's DNA to be so engraved in your character that you couldn't be unfaithful, even if you tried?

August 26th

So God created mankind in his own image, in the image of God he created them; male and female he created them. —Genesis 1:27 NIV

Spiritual Cataracts

"Say something you like about the speech, then offer one suggestion for improvement." Those are the instructions I give my public speaking students when I ask them to critique each other's presentations. The feedback not only helps the speakers improve, but it also forces us listeners to intentionally look for the good. That's something I need to practice more outside the classroom.

I can't remember when I didn't believe every person's dignity stems from the fact he or she is created in the image of God. All persons—no matter who we are or where we come from—bear the distinct mark of our Creator. Even though I know this, I don't always look at others through that lens. I develop spiritual cataracts.

Physical cataracts cloud the normally clear lens of a person's eye. People with cataracts feel like they're looking through foggy windows. As the cataracts grow, their environment becomes more and more blurred until they require surgery to keep them from losing their vision altogether. Spiritual cataracts block us from seeing the intrinsic worth of others. We focus on the sin that *mars* the image of God rather than the image that *marks* them as his child.

Jesus had neither physical nor spiritual cataracts. Nothing marred his vision from seeing the Father's thumbprint on each person and calling it out. Within the volatile Peter, Jesus identified a "rock" (Matthew 16:18). In the prejudiced *can-anything-good-come-out-of-Nazareth* Nathaniel, Jesus perceived "an Israelite in whom there is no deceit" (John 1:46–47). Beneath the proudly labeled Pharisees of Pharisees, Jesus knew there hid a man who would eventually refer to himself as the "very least of all saints" (Ephesians 3:8 NASB). Jesus refused to let people's flaws and weaknesses cloud his vision of them.

I believe he wants us to view others as he did. To intentionally look for the good, for the image of God they bear no matter how hidden it might be. We may need to undergo some spiritual cataract surgery to make this happen, but interestingly, as our cataracts are removed, fuzzy thoughts about our own worth begin to clear up as well.

The image of God marks you and marks me. That's a critique we can live with.

August 27th

So even though I wrote to you, it was neither on account of the one who did the wrong nor on account of the injured party, but rather that before God you could see for yourselves how devoted to us you are.

—2 Corinthians 7:12 NIV

Test Result: A+

I get Paul's concern. He had confronted the Corinthian church over a moral issue and didn't know how they would handle his letter. Confronting is not for the faint of heart. He anxiously awaited Titus' arrival to report on their response. Would they reject his authority? Would all the trust he had built with them come crashing down? Would they return to their old way of living?

What overflowing, joyous relief when Titus relayed the church's reaction. Yes, the letter had caused sorrow, but it was godly sorrow that resulted in heartfelt repentance. It evoked in them a new earnestness, a longing to clear themselves and readiness to see justice done (2 Corinthians 7:10–11). Paul says it helped them recognize their depth of devotion to him and to God (v. 12). They passed the test, not to prove their faithfulness to God. He already knew what they were made of. The test revealed what they were made of to themselves.

Have you ever wondered whether you would be able to stand firm in the tests of life? Imagine after coming through a trial you see at the top of your paper the mark of A+ in blazing red ink. How would that make you feel? Wouldn't it spur you on even more? Peter says trials prove the genuineness of our faith (1 Peter 1:7). It reminds me of couples who have come to us for pre-marital counseling over the years. They believe they love each other, but until they face a brick wall in their relationship and come through it, they don't have confidence in their future together. Their love passed the test.

So, we will inevitably face tests in life. Not because God is a hard, demanding teacher. But because he wants us to see ourselves the way he does when we pass—A+ students!

August 28th

If only we had been content to stay on the other side of the Jordan!
—Joshua 7:7 NIV

Are You Stuck?

Beyond our victories. Beyond our defeats. Beyond our somewhere-in-the-middles. If we hope to fulfill God's destiny in our lives, we must refuse to settle for anything less than God's plan. But sometimes it's easy to get stuck.

Israel got stuck after the victory at Jericho. It had been a magnificent feat. You know the story. The people marched around the city seven days, then on the seventh day, with a blast of the trumpet and a shout from the army, the walls of Jericho disintegrated. The city fell, giving Israel their first triumph on the road to the Promised Land. But it was almost their last. They got stuck in their success. Unknown to them, the waves of winning had left a deposit of sin. They forgot to seek the Lord before the next battle at Ai, and the consequences proved devastating (Joshua 7:11-12).

They got stuck again—this time after defeat. They became so mired in the loss at Ai Joshua even questioned God as to why he had brought them from Egypt only to be defeated by the Canaanites. "If only we had been content to stay on the other side of the Jordan!" They couldn't go back. Couldn't go forward. Only after they sought the Lord and dealt with the sin, could they move on to victory. To the Promised Land.

I have a friend who freely admits how he can get "stuck" when all is going well. Success tends to lessen his pursuit of God. Like Israel, his natural tendency shifts from reliance on God to himself, especially if the next project is one he thinks he can handle on his own. He settles for what he can do rather than pushing on toward something higher, something exceedingly better. I know others who get stuck after defeat. Rather than trusting God to bring redemption, they focus on their failure, echoing Israel's complaint, "Why did you bring us this far to let us fall?"

Do you fall into either of these camps? You don't have to. Neither do I. The Holy Spirit will always help us get unstuck. Ask him. Don't settle for anything less than the Promised Land.

August 29th

Oh, that Job might be tested to the utmost.   —Job 34:36 NIV

Circumstantial Evidence

Guilty until proven innocent. That's not the way it's supposed to work, is it? I'd like to say the rush to judge people simply accused of wrongdoing is a sign of the times, but viewing others through the prism of "circumstantial evidence" has been in play for centuries.

Circumstantial evidence draws conclusions based not on direct verification, but on information that infers guilt. Take Job. Job's friends condemned him based solely on what they observed. They figured the tragic turn of events in his life must be the result of some great hidden sin. They had no direct evidence to prove this, but they believed all hardship in life was a form of punishment from God. Since Job was suffering, he must be guilty of something.

The more Job maintained his innocence throughout his ordeal, the more his friends heaped on the accusations. At one point, his friend Elihu, cries, "Oh, that Job might be tested to the utmost!" Uh, no one in all of history had ever endured the kind of test Job faced.

But Job's friends weren't the only ones operating on circumstantial evidence. Satan boasted to God he could make Job fall if he took everything away from him; he could destroy Job's integrity if he afflicted him with enough suffering. God, however, said, "not a chance." He *knew* Job. He *knew* Job from the inside out. All Satan knew was Job's external cushy lifestyle. His judgment of Job was based totally on circumstantial evidence. Just like Job's friends. They were all wrong.

Thankfully, God never relies on circumstantial evidence to judge us. He doesn't let circumstances define the truth. He lets truth define the circumstances. He sees us as we are. He knows our motives. And although he doesn't expect us to see other people (or even ourselves) to the same depth as him, he wants us to be charitable in our judgments—innocent until proven guilty at the very least.

False accusations leave ruthless scars. Let's not be like Job's friends and add to others' pain by jumping on the bandwagon of circumstantial evidence. Go for the truth.

August 30th

Jesus returned to Galilee in the power of the Spirit.   *—Luke 4:14 NIV*

The Magnificent Duel

The temptation Jesus encounters after his baptism sounds like a sword fight—a duel more profound than any graphic arts designer could capture, even with the finest visual effects possible.

Satan begins by wielding his blade of doubt—*If you are the Son of God.* Its sting misses Jesus completely because the Son of God suffered no confusion as to his identity. Jesus counters with a thrust of the most powerful sword in the universe. *It is written ...*

Satan advances again. This time he attempts to distract Jesus. He displays before him all the authority and splendor of the world. He lunges forward with the promise to give it all to Jesus if he worships him. Jesus, diligently on guard, deflects the enemy's weapon. *It is written ...*

Satan is sly. Seeing how well Jesus' sword is working, he makes one last desperate attempt to strike a final blow by turning Jesus' sword on himself—*For it is written.* Somehow his use of the Word of God doesn't brandish the same power. In fact, one imagines the sword burning right through his spiny fingers as Jesus declares, "It is said: 'Do not put the Lord your God to the test'" (v. 12).

The contest ends. Satan retreats, slinking away in the darkness. He will return, of course, but for now the old serpent is subdued. And what of Jesus? How did this great conflict affect him? Scripture tells us he returned from this magnificent duel in the power of the Spirit. The Holy Spirit who had led him into this wilderness of temptation, now floods him with his power. Jesus goes forward to fulfill his call (vv. 18–19).

And how does this apply to us? Could it be that, like Jesus, each time we say no to temptation we grow in the power of the Spirit? Could it be that every time we use the Word of God to resist Satan's attempts to thrust us into doubt, defeat and destruction something transpires to further God's call in our lives?

I pray we will not forget the tremendous weapon God has entrusted to us. This sword of the Spirit which is the Word of God, proves to be living, active, sharp and penetrating. It leads us to victory every time.

En garde!

August 31st

Let perseverance finish its work so that you may be mature and complete, not lacking anything. —James 1:4 NIV

Per-se-ver-ance

Shingles. All I knew about the notorious infection spawned from chicken pox was that it triggered pain. Lots of pain. Now I was experiencing it firsthand. Initially the pain came as intermittent spurts, but as the days and weeks continued, those little spurts started to feel like mini electrical shots pulsating my elbow, upper arm and chest. The pain medication offered temporary relief, but the aching intruder kept returning. It was wearing me down. By the fourth week self-pity made a valiant attempt to attach itself to my misery.

But rather than giving in to the woe-is-me syndrome, I began focusing on things I could be grateful for. *Thank you, Lord, that I could sleep last night. Thank you for helping me be alert for my classes. Thank you that even though I'm hurting right now, you are still God and are deserving of my praise.* Gratitude stimulates perseverance.

Scripture tells us the perseverance developed when we endure suffering generates more than momentary strength. It matures us and completes us (James 1:4). Romans 5:3–4 says perseverance that comes from suffering produces the kind of character that leads to hope. So, although we cannot escape pain in a fallen world, we can be assured that when we persevere, God makes our suffering count.

Perseverance isn't easy. Our enemy seeks to wear us down by attrition. The source of our suffering makes no difference.

Chronic physical pain, chronic temptation, chronic disappointment—such ongoing challenges make us vulnerable. Thoughts of throwing in the towel intensify. We lose sight of the bigger picture that God wants to use our afflictions to make us more like the man or woman he designed us to be.

So whatever challenge you may be facing right now—don't give up. Ask God to help you press on. Let your pain work for you, not against you. Let perseverance "finish its work" according to God's timetable, not yours. You will never regret having held firm through your affliction.

Per·se·ver·ance: it's worth it.

September 1st

Diligent hands will rule, but laziness ends in forced labor.
—Proverbs 12:24 NIV

The Dignity of Work

We complain about it. We resist it. We blame the fall for it—even though Adam and Eve relished in it before they tried to expand their résumé to include being like God. *Work.*

God created us in his likeness, and a part of his likeness consists of work. Whether we realize it or not, work provides us with a sense of dignity. We were made to accomplish and to feel good about our accomplishments. The sense of a "job well done" can occur in great achievements or in the most menial of tasks. It all depends on our perspective.

I remember the Saturday morning my husband and I spent volunteering at a homeless shelter. Our job assignment consisted of washing the windows. I was into it. I wanted to make every smear and smudge disappear. No streaks on my watch! Since no one there even knew me, my reputation was not at stake. So why the inward push to give it all I had? It's how God made me. And how he made you.

Scripture says, "diligent hands will rule." Work instills in us something greater than a paycheck. It lifts us above the lazy chains of apathy and creates a sense of satisfaction and purpose. God uses our labor to shape us into who he wants us to be.

As the Protestant work ethic declines in our society, the dignity of man suffers. Stagnant unemployment steals not only jobs but motivation. We've shifted from a mindset of work then play, to play then work, and finally to play, play, play. As one writer has suggested, our culture is "amusing itself to death." Consequently, our sense of well-being as individuals and as a country is eroding.

As believers, we should reclaim the dignity found in work. Jesus brought glory to God by completing his labor (John 17:4). So, can we. Let's not underestimate the light that shines from those who do their work, and do it well. Without complaint. As God's "workmanship" you can bring him glory through your work. In whatever kind of task or assignment you've been given—let those diligent hands rule!

September 2nd

"Meaningless! Meaningless!" says the Teacher. "Utterly Meaningless! Everything is meaningless."

—Ecclesiastes 1:2 NIV

From Here to Eternity

Meaningless! Quite the assessment on life coming from a man who had it all. Solomon lacked for nothing. Wealth, position, wives (lots of them), legacy. The mention of his name was synonymous with wisdom. But in the end, none of it mattered. No one knew the emptiness of life without God more than Solomon.

Contrast this with his father, David. Although David had likewise known the good life, he'd also experienced some pretty dark pits of despair. And David arrived at a completely different conclusion about man's existence. "Therefore, my heart is glad and my tongue rejoices; my body also will rest secure, because you will not abandon me to the realm of the dead, nor will you let your faithful one see decay" (Psalm 16:9-10). David remained positive because he knew this present life—whether saturated with pleasure or pain—held meaning because of something beyond it. He understood this life was not "all there is."

In a culture where the hunt for significance rests on the acquisition of knowledge, wealth, status and every creature comfort imaginable, the thought of meaning coming from something beyond the tangible here and now seems almost profane. But if we hope to find contentment in life it is necessary to aim beyond the present of what we see. To put our focus on the only goal that makes sense out of everything else. Eternity.

The light of eternity shines into everything that happens on the earth and places it in the big picture. It helps us hold our failures as well as our successes loosely. It assures us we are being prepared for something far greater. Eternity teaches us how to handle the accolades of some, the rejection of others. It fills the mundane with purpose. It keeps us humble. It protects us from the bankruptcy of overspent souls. It counters the cry of Meaningless with Meaningful.

You and I were made to live forever. We're in training for it this very day. Whatever we are going through right now—is it meaningless? Not by a long shot. A very long shot.

September 3rd

Each person is tempted when they are dragged away by their own evil desire and enticed. Then, after desire has conceived, it gives birth to sin; and sin, when it is full-grown, gives birth to death.

—James 1:14–15 NIV

Nuts in the Light Bulb

When our son was young, he and his sister got into an argument. He said something verboten in our house. When I asked what it was, he put his hand over her mouth in an attempt to silence her. Not wanting to rat him out, she wisely left him with the responsibility to confess. Turns out confession was the last thing on his mind. Even when I sent him to his room. Even when his dad threatened him with a spanking. Even when dinnertime came and went. Finally, he said he was ready to confess. Yes! Victory! "Ok, what did you say?"

"Nuts in the light bulb."

"Nuts in the light bulb?"

"Yep."

"That doesn't make sense. Why would we discipline you for saying nuts in the light bulb?"

In a desperate attempt to escape his lonely prison and fill his empty stomach, he came up with the only thing that came to mind. Lying on his bed, gazing at the ceiling, his six-year-old eyes were engrossed on the light fixture. He figured admitting what he really said would definitely land him in trouble, so why not try a complete, total fabrication?

All his efforts to escape the inevitable only dug him in deeper. The consequences for uttering those forbidden fateful words—*shut up*—to his sister would have been far less grim had he just confessed and repented in the first place.

Such is human nature.

James warns if we don't nip temptation in the bud, it will conceive into desire—desire that leads to sin. Once we choose to ignore the do not enter sign, the path back to the highway runs through an awful lot of detours. I guess we think, like our son, we can find a less painful route. Instead we find ourselves slogging from one pothole to the next. Rationalization for sin may initially appear harmless, but it strangles the truth and any hope of redemption. Best to fess up before we start calling on "nuts in the light bulb" to save us.

September 4th

When Jesus landed and saw a large crowd, he had compassion on them and healed their sick.

—*Matthew 14:14 NIV*

Do Something

He did something!

Jesus healed those in the crowd who were sick. He taught them about the kingdom of God. And he fed them bread and fish until they were satisfied. His compassion made him do it. That's what compassion looks like. It compels us, in the words of songwriter Matthew West, to "do something."

True compassion goes beyond sentiment, always directing to some action. I have a friend who has so much compassion for kids that she uses her modest salary to sponsor thirteen third-world children. I have other friends who have such a heart for the lost they've spent their whole lives—time, money, resources, privacy—to train young people with the same passion to spread the gospel. Compassion leads others to send money to victims of natural (and unnatural) disasters. Those who love the church are driven by compassion to forsake an easier lifestyle in order to feed and nourish its sheep.

Compassion motivates people in almost every arena of life. Those who grieve over injustices, may seek work in law or politics as a way to bring relief. Compassion for one's country leads some to the battleground. Compassion for the sick creates doctors, nurses and EMT's. Soup kitchens and half-way houses exist because compassion stirred someone to care for the needy. As my friend Carol Cool writes, we don't have to be a Mother Theresa to have compassion.

Compassion is not something we possess because we happen to be kind people. It is a gift from God. He gives compassion freely, even if we misuse it. We can misappropriate the gift by taking credit for it ourselves (See what a caring person I am) or we can be satisfied with the feeling of compassion (It's the thought that counts). Let's not fall into either of those camps. Instead, let's fall on our knees and ask the Father of lights from whom we've received this gift how he wants us to use it. Then....Let's do something!

September 5th

They triumphed over him   by the blood of the Lamb   and by the word of their testimony; they did not love their lives so much   as to shrink from death. —Revelation 12:11 NIV

Martyred Christians

Persecution of Christ followers is nothing new. Since the stoning of the first martyr, Stephen, believers have been targeted throughout the centuries. The U.S. Department of State reports that today Christians in over sixty countries face persecution because of their faith. For years organizations like Voice of the Martyrs, Open Doors and others have ministered to the persecuted church. Although I've been aware of the atrocities, the now iconic picture of those twenty-one Coptic Christians kneeling on the beach in orange jumpsuits a few years ago brought it home. As they awaited their beheading from the swords of the Islamic State, reports say most of them died with the name of Jesus Christ on their lips.

Almost every day, new information surfaces about more slaughtered Christians. It seems like the bad guys are winning. But no matter how it may look to their genocidal persecutors, or to the world, these martyrs are the true victors "for they did not love their lives so much as to shrink from death."

So, what about us? What once seemed remote no longer feels as distant. What if one day it's my head or yours? Would we be whispering the name of Jesus Christ with our final breath? It reminds me of a story told by Corrie ten Boom in her book, *The Hiding Place*. As the Nazi presence grew in Holland, Jews and all those harboring them were being rounded up and sent to prison camps. One day, Corrie expressed her fear of martyrdom to her father.

> "Corrie, he began gently, when you and I go to Amsterdam—when do I give you your ticket?"
>
> Why, just before we get on the train."
>
> "Exactly. And our wise Father in heaven knows when we're going to need things, too. Don't run out ahead of him, Corrie. When the time comes that some of us will have to die, you will look into your heart and find the strength you need—just in time."

How important to remember God will always supply us with enough grace at the right time to face whatever lies in front of us. Even martyrdom.

September 6th

You turned my wailing into dancing;
you removed my sackcloth and clothed me with joy.
—Psalm 30:11

Rising from the Ruins

Bad things happen in a fallen world. Hope rises from the ruins in a redeemed one.

A friend of mine lost her husband after his long battle with a chronic illness. She and her two teenage girls plummeted into a whirlwind of grief and sorrow at his passing. The healing from their loss progressed painstakingly slow, but progressed it did. Six years later my friend has remarried, she and her girls have relocated, and a whole universe of new opportunities has opened up before them. A God of redemption caused them to rise from the ruins.

Scripture abounds with stories of people who overcame devastating loss and found a joy that at one time seemed unreachable. Joseph languished in the loneliness of a dank prison cell before he was elevated as the king's right-hand man and reunited with his family (Genesis 40–42). Naomi was so demoralized at the death of her husband and two sons she told people to change her name to "Mara" which meant "bitter" (Ruth 1:20). She didn't know God would use her daughter-in-law to bring about redemption beyond her wildest dreams—a son who would be in the lineage of Christ. A God of redemption caused both Joseph and Naomi to rise from the ruins.

During Jesus' ministry, lepers escaped lives of isolation and once again felt the touch of another human being. Demoniacs dropped their chains of torment and found sanity. The blind, deaf and crippled exited debilitating worlds of confinement and entered ones of freedom. Dead children experienced the breath of life coursing through their limp bodies once again. A God of redemption caused them to rise from the ruins.

Because that's what God does. He turns bad into good. Certainly not because we deserve it. If this were a *quid pro quo* universe we would all be goners. God redeems our situations because he loves us. He desires to turn our wailing into dancing, our mourning into joy. The God who transformed the darkest of nights into the brightest of mornings at Calvary knows how to cause us—no matter what our situation—to rise from the ruins.

Always take hope, friend. Hope because of redemption.

September 7th

I have been crucified with Christ and I no longer live, but Christ lives in me. The life I now live in the body, I live by faith in the Son of God, who loved me and gave himself for me. —Galatians 2:20 NIV

Condemn, Condone, or Compromise

Condemn. Condone. Compromise. These seem to be the most prevalent alternatives for the church in how to deal with the culture.

Condemn. There's certainly enough Scripture people use to justify a condemning outlook. And it's the one of which we're most likely to be accused. Believers can come across as quick to judge, harsh and righteously indignant.

The *Condoners* don't want to judge anyone. They like to quote the Scripture where Jesus says to the woman in adultery, "Neither do I condemn you" but don't quote the rest of it— "Go now and leave your life of sin" (John 8:11).

Those who opt for the *Compromise* position want the best of both worlds—not too hard, not too soft. Kind of like Goldilocks. Solomon casts it in stronger language: "Like a muddied spring or a polluted well are the righteous who give way to the wicked" (Proverbs 25:26).

So, what do we do? Must we put shades over our light for fear the glare will drive people away? Do we have to prove to the alcoholic we love him by buying him a drink? Do we have to sell our birthright in order not to be viewed as legalists or bigots? I don't think so. I believe there's another way.

Be crucified with Christ. When we die to ourselves and let Christ live within us, we discover options other than condemning, condoning or compromising. In being crucified with Christ we let him "love us to death" by sending all our agendas, biases and defensiveness to the grave. He replaces the "plank" in our eye with vision to see the "speck" in others through the lens of a love refined (Matthew 7:5). That is the good news of the gospel of which we ought never be ashamed.

So, are you being squeezed into one of the caricatures of the church? Will you instead, by faith in the Son of God, be the real thing? Will you be crucified with Christ? Will you then speak the truth from a heart of love?

September 8th

If I were still trying to please people, I would not be a servant of Christ.
—Galatians 1:10 NIV

Stop Trying

Ever get tired of try, try, trying? Wish someone would say you don't have to try so hard? Don't get me wrong. I think putting forth our best effort—no matter what the task—brings both success and satisfaction. But sometimes our trying gets tainted. We become harried waitresses attempting to serve too many entrees at too many tables. It starts to wear thin.

Our longing for God's approval can be even more damaging. It can thrust us on a treadmill of thinking we have to do more and more to maintain his favor. Our pursuit of the acceptance we already have distorts God's image. It moves him from a loving Father whose directives are for our good, to a difficult-to-satisfy Master. It causes us to miss the point: he values who we are over what we do.

When I was a new grandma, I remember thinking how my grandson didn't have to try one single thing to make me love him more. Whether he was sleeping, fussing or nursing—it didn't matter—he had my full approval. An approval based not on what he did, but on who he is. He's my daughter's son. My grandson. How sad if somewhere in his little baby-mind he started thinking *Maybe if I didn't cry,* or *if I slept through the night,* or *if I didn't have to eat so much they would love me more.* Ridiculous, right?

About as ridiculous as our futile attempts to earn God's approval. It's funny how the more intimate our relationship with God, the less we care about proving ourselves to others. That's why Paul could say if he were still trying to please people, he wouldn't be a servant of Christ. He had discovered the only approval that matters.

The truth is you don't have to try so hard. Never compromise who God created you to be to win the approval of anyone. Trust in the wisdom of a Father who created you for his unique purpose. Don't run yourself ragged.

Stop try, try, trying ... and start trust, trust, trusting.

September 9th

Jesus Christ is the same yesterday and today and forever.
—Hebrews 13:8 NIV

A God for All Seasons

Decades of faithfulness and constancy have a way of building trust, at least in my life.

In those teenage years when my half-hearted devotion to him should have disqualified me from any hope of a deeper life, God remained fully devoted to me. My twenty-something years thrust me in a search for identity that took me to the edge—an edge that solidified rather than destroyed who I was becoming—because of his protection. The next decades of living life as a "responsible adult" brought inevitable pain as well as unexpected pleasures. Through every crashing wave of failure and lofty crest of happiness, God's love remained immoveable.

The last few years have been marked with significant shifts. Of saying goodbye to some loved ones, of saying hello to others. Of expanding and shrinking spheres. Of more caution, probably too much caution. Yet the God who never changes has carried me through every transition.

God is a God for all seasons. He remains faithful when we are not (2 Timothy 2:13). He brings stability in our confusion (Philippians 4:7). He is Someone to thank when our cup overflows (James 1:17). Someone to seek when we're running on empty (Psalm 16:11). Not one moment of our existence lies beyond his reach. "If I go up to the heavens, you are there; if I make my bed in the depths, you are there" (Psalm 139:8).

How could we not trust such a God? The One who formed us in our mother's womb and crowned us with the dignity of life has a track record of remaining when all else fades. God is a God for all seasons. But he also goes beyond seasons. Someday when our seasons cease to exist, God will bring us through the valley of death. The Everlasting God, without beginning or end, will be with us even when life on earth ceases.

No matter what season of life you're experiencing right now, you can trust in the God who never changes. The stability you long for can be found in no other place. The God who is the same yesterday, today and forever remains with you, before you, behind you. Let him walk you through each day, each year, each decade—to eternity.

September 10th

After that whole generation had been gathered to their ancestors, another generation grew up who knew neither the LORD nor what he had done for Israel. Then the Israelites did evil in the eyes of the LORD.
—Judges 2:10-11 NIV

In One Generation

One generation. That's all it took to lose everything.

The Lord promised not to break his covenant with Israel and warned them not to break their covenant with him. He commissioned them to drive out *all* the Canaanites living in the land. He said failure to do so would result in a disastrous compromise with the pagan nations. So, what did they do? They compromised.

They lost their zeal. Just as the Lord said would happen, they adapted to the surrounding culture, worshiping their gods, oblivious of the impending danger of losing their identity as God's people. As a result, God removed his protection over them, causing them to face plunder and defeat time and time again.

The key to understanding how they let this happen lies in Judges 2:10-11. The generation of Joshua and Caleb, who led Israel into the Promised Land, had died out. The next generation grew up knowing "neither the LORD nor what he had done." Had no one relayed to them how God drove out nations more powerful than them? Of how one routed a thousand because God was on their side? What about the drying up of the Jordan? What about Jericho? Ai? In one generation, the knowledge of everything the Lord had done to establish Israel vanished. They dropped the baton.

Scripture admonishes us to tell our children about the great and mighty deeds of the Lord (Psalm 145:4). If we don't tell them, they certainly won't get it by osmosis. My grandpa's faithful witness of the Lord's work continues to affect my own life. For the last few years I've slowly been reading his diaries. Every week, entries reveal his devotion to God: *Jennie and I to church to pray for the boys* [Korean War]. *To Bible Study tonight. Revival continuing another week. Good liberty tonight, many to the altar.* Grandpa's sold-out dedication to the Lord inspires me. It reminds me where I've come from. Where I'm going. It helps me remember what's of utmost importance.

Let's be intentional in passing on the good news. We don't want all we have found to get lost in one generation.

September 11th

And let us consider how we may spur one another on toward love and good deeds, not giving up meeting together, as some are in the habit of doing, but encouraging one another—and all the more as you see the Day approaching.

—Hebrews 10:24–25 NIV

Flight 93 and the Big Picture

9/11. A date that reminds me of the importance of knowing we're part of something bigger.

Thoughts of "Let's roll," Todd Beamer's indelible words, spun through my mind as we approached the Flight 93 Memorial near Shanksville, PA. Certain facts struck me. Did you know the plane was delayed twenty-five minutes in taking off due to weather? The hijackers attempted to control the passengers by telling them to remain seated—that there was a bomb on board and they were heading back to the airport to have their demands met. However, as the passengers began calling home on their cell phones, they soon learned the true story: The World Trade Center and Pentagon had been attacked; theirs was no "ordinary hijack." Flight 93 was to be the next instrument of destruction against the United States if they did nothing to stop it. Their decision to take over the cockpit stands as one of the greatest acts of civilian bravery in American history.

But what if their plane hadn't been delayed those twenty-five minutes? The holdup gave time for reports of the other bombings to be broadcast. The passengers discovered they were part of something bigger than themselves. Something so big it motivated them to lay down their lives for the sake of their fellow Americans.

As followers of Christ, it's vital to realize we're a part of something bigger than ourselves. It's an awareness that motivates us to lay down our lives on behalf of others. God designed us to have a part to play in the lives of fellow believers. We are not to forsake meeting together. Similar to the hijackers, Satan wants to isolate us so we can be more easily deceived. Scripture admonishes us to encourage each other and to spur one another on to love and good deeds. Our job is to help each other's faith not get hijacked. So, let's do it.

Let's roll.

September 12th

Day after day, in the temple courts and from house to house, they never stopped teaching and proclaiming the good news that Jesus is the Messiah.
—Acts 5:42 NIV

Maintaining Momentum

What kept those first followers of Christ going? Scripture says they "never stopped." Even as the opposition against them grew, the fire in their belly only burned brighter.

As I read the book of Acts, it's clear the early believers kept their momentum because they relied more and more on the Holy Spirit, not less. They never got to the point where they said, "Ok, God, we'll take it from here." Not for a minute. They knew their enemy.

Oh, Satan tried. He pulled out all the tricks in his book to slow down the momentum. Remember how he played on Ananias and Sapphira's greed and hypocrisy? After selling some land, the couple conspired to keep some of the profit for themselves and present the rest to the apostles as if it was the total amount. "How is it that Satan has so filled your heart that you have lied to the Holy Spirit?" Peter questioned Ananias (Acts 5:3). Satan tried to infuse the church with a little deceit, knowing it would eventually pollute the whole body. But his scheme backfired. Both Ananias and Sapphira fell dead when the Holy Spirit exposed them and the church catapulted into a new realm of reverence for God (vv. 1–11).

If Satan could not corrupt the church from within, maybe external pressure would halt the progress. This time he played on the jealousy of the Jewish leaders. The high priest had the apostles arrested, but during the night the Holy Spirit sent an angel to release them. So rather than slowing them down, their imprisonment and supernatural delivery drove them even more "day after day" (vv. 17–42).

If we hope to maintain the momentum in our personal lives, in our churches and in our witness to the world, our need for the Holy Spirit can't be overstated. We have an enemy who continues to play upon our weaknesses—and the weaknesses of others—to stop us. Only through the Spirit of God can we keep him from succeeding.

Are you struggling to keep the fire burning? Ask the Holy Spirit to stoke up the coals of intimacy with God. Rely on him for everything. Then keep going, my friend.

September 13th

We love because he first loved us.   —*1 John 4:19 NIV*

Jesus Loves Me This I Know

Brennan Manning says on judgment day the Lord Jesus will ask only one question: *"Did you believe that I loved you?"* Kind of turns the table around, doesn't it? Not, *"Did you love me?"* Not, *"How many souls did you save?"* Not, *"Were you successful?"* Not, *"Did everyone speak well of you?"* I could list pages of questions I think he might ask. But none would reveal my time on the earth more than the haunting one Manning proposes. How we view God determines everything we do and how we do it.

I have to let that sink in.

Knowing God loves me supersedes my roles, my jobs and my relationships. It silences all those inner voices that tell me I'm not a good enough wife, a good enough mother, a good enough daughter, friend, teacher, reflector of Christ. As Brennan Manning points out, "God loves us as we are, not as we should be, because none of us are as we should be." So, knowing God loves me upends all my inclinations to base my value on what others say.

Knowing God loves me determines how I love others. It opens my eyes to see all love originates from him. John says the reason we love God—or anyone—is because he first loved us. Only as we receive love from its Source do we have anything to give others, and to give it freely.

When my daughter was young and I would tell her I loved her, she would sometimes remark, "Well of course you do. You have to, you're my mother." What she couldn't possibly have known at that time was the profound bond a mother feels with her child, a love that extends far beyond responsibility. I could not *not* have loved her even if I tried. But I'm afraid I can view God's love in a similar abstract kind of way. He loves me because he has to, or because I do something good. The amazing blows-my-mind truth, however, is that God loves me because he wants to, and it's not dependent on my behavior.

It's who he is. It's what he does. Jesus loves me, this I know. Do you know he loves you?

September 14th

The heart of man plans his way, but the LORD establishes his steps.
—Proverbs 16:9 ESV

Coincidence? Nah!

If I ever questioned whether God could or would involve himself in my life, it was put to rest when I got my first "real" job.

I was finishing my graduate work at the University of Colorado when I decided to look for a job and stay in the area. I, along with a few thousand other people, had fallen in love with Boulder/Denver. I didn't want to leave, even though I knew of PhDs relegated to pumping gas. The employment opportunities were slim. When I heard of an opening for a speech therapist in the Denver school district, I sent in my application and set up an interview. What did I have to lose?

I regularly attended a little church in Boulder, but occasionally visited a large church in Denver on Sunday nights. Knowing how the sanctuary always filled to capacity, I arrived early to secure a seat. I finally found a spot. It wasn't long before I was engaged in a conversation with the couple sitting next to me. "So, how long have you been a believer? Do you attend this church? Where do you work? You're a superintendent for the Denver school district? I think you're the person I have an interview with tomorrow!" I basically walked into his office the next day and signed the contract.

Was it a coincidence that I happened to go to Calvary Temple that night? A coincidence that out of every seat in the large sanctuary I happened to sit next to the man who would be interviewing me the next day? A coincidence that in a job market tighter than a lid on a pickle jar I would secure a position in my field? Nah, I don't think so.

Scripture tells us that although we make our plans, the Lord establishes our steps. That's how much he cares for his children. We may not recognize it at the time, but when we do, far more than our steps are established. No amount of my planning could have accomplished what God did in that Sunday night service. He planted seeds of confidence in *his* plan that continue to bear fruit.

Friend, never confuse the "coincidences" in your life with luck. It just may be God!

September 15th

Meanwhile, the Midianites sold Joseph in Egypt to Potiphar, one of Pharaoh's officials, the captain of the guard. —Genesis 37:36 NIV

Meanwhile

Sometimes situations hit us like an ominous storm. We're thrust into a tornado of despair and whirling grief. Hopelessness suffocates our faith. The aftermath leaves us with little more than the debris of brokenness. But *meanwhile,* a God who cares about every hair on our head is working not only to bring us through the storm but to help us land in a better place. Like Jacob.

Jacob had just heard the news that his son, Joseph, was killed and devoured by a wild animal. His other sons had presented him with Joseph's distinctive robe, deceptively dipped in goat's blood, to cover their dastardly deed of selling him to a traveling band of Midianites. Overcome with sorrow, Jacob put on sackcloth and grieved deeply, refusing "to be comforted," declaring he would go to his grave in mourning.

Then comes the meanwhile.

Unknown to Jacob, his son was alive, serving in Pharaoh's household. Unknown to Jacob, the foundation of a nation was being laid. Unknown to Jacob, before he took his last breath he would once again embrace his beloved son. Behind the scene, a force greater than the "seen" was at work to transform what was intended for harm into good. All of that in the meanwhile.

Do you know there are meanwhiles in your life? When the "seen" threatens to encroach on the "unseen" reality of faith, remember God always works a meanwhile to turn the tide. Often, the most painful parts of life lie surprisingly close to the most sublime. Our vision is limited and often distorted by the pain we experience. Whatever difficulty you may be facing today, resist the natural tendency to think that what you "see" is all there is.

Be assured, although presently unknown to you, there is a meanwhile.

September 16th

But if I say, "I will not mention his word or speak anymore in his name," his word is in my heart like a fire, a fire shut up in my bones. I am weary of holding it in; indeed, I cannot. —Jeremiah 20:9 NIV

Souls on Fire

They're headquartered in an abandoned monastery that overlooks the Pittsburgh skyline. They live within walking distance from a street notoriously known for its abundance of bars. They help kids in afterschool programs. They reach out to refugee communities. They play basketball, run cosmetology clinics and teach Bible stories. They are Youth With A Mission. And did I say they love God? They love God fiercely.

This group of mostly twenty-somethings comes from Columbia, St Croix, Australia, Canada, Germany and Texas. Some have lived in Pittsburgh all their lives. No matter where their country of origin, they each possess a deep passion to show people all over the world what the love of Jesus looks like. Even in places like Saudi Arabia where sharing the gospel could land them in prison, or worse. Their love for God compels them to go where he wants them to go and do what he tells them to do.

They don't consider themselves more righteous than others. His love instills them with courage not only to live in places below the poverty line, but to deal with their own spiritual poverty. They cultivate humble hearts at this former convent.

They want to learn how to do life well from the inside out. So, they pray. They repent. They forgive. They grow. They give the label of *Christian* a good name.

In the words of song writer Mac Powell, they are running for the heart of God till they are souls on fire. Being around them reminds me God wants all of us believers to be souls on fire. Souls who know his love in such a personal way that the blaze keeps burning brighter. Souls like Jeremiah who experienced God's presence like a fire in his bones that could not be contained.

How is the fire in your bones? Are you burning with the love of God? Whether a youth or an octogenarian, it's never too late to stoke the coals. To make your mission one of running for the heart of God. Running ... till you are a soul on fire.

September 17th

How long, LORD? Will you forget me forever? How long will you hide your face from me? But I trust in your unfailing love.

—*Psalm 13:1, 5 NIV*

The Other Side of the Ledger

Unanswered prayer is draining. It saps my energy. It confuses me. Especially when I'm praying for things that appear to be in God's will—for a marriage not to end in divorce, for a hard heart to repent, for an unjust decision to be reversed. Sometimes I feel like my requests end up being the victim of some celestial delete button. I wrestle over my ledger of defeat, and like the psalmist I cry out, "How long, Lord?"

That's when I have to stop and remember there's another side to the ledger. A whole stockpile of answered prayers exists to counter the ones I deem "unanswered." This side of the ledger reminds me I always have something to be thankful for. The power of gratitude leads me back to the truth. When I can't see what God is doing, I can still count on who he is.

For the psalmist, one simple statement canceled out his litany of despair. He voided his ledger of unanswered prayers as he recalled the character of God: "But I trust in your unfailing love." He didn't experience a revelation as to why there was no answer. Nothing indicated how much longer he would have to wait or whether he would even receive an answer at all. He simply remembered God's unfailing love could be trusted. And that was enough.

Knowing why some prayers are answered and some are not will most likely remain a mystery while we live on the earth. It's how we deal with the mystery that affects us so deeply. When we feel forsaken, but still choose to pray, to trust, to obey, we grow into the sort of man or woman God purposes us to be.

So, the next you're relegating all your prayers to the "unanswered" column, pull out your ledger and start making a new list on the other side.

September 18th

He will wipe away every tear from their eyes, and death shall be no more, neither shall there be mourning, nor crying, nor pain anymore, for the former things have passed away. —Revelation 21:4 NIV

The Sad Bank

Ka ching. Ka ching. Ka ching. I found myself depositing a lot of coins in my sad bank. News about the death of a former classmate moved from shock to heartbroken grief. I became aware of how the passing of his life diminished something in my own.

Grief at all levels extracts from our emotional account. A son or daughter leaves home. *Ka ching.* A job ends. *Ka ching.* A relationship doesn't survive the ebb and flow of change. *Ka ching.* Anyone hate to see the final pages of the last chapter of a good book? *Ka ching.* Grief, like a shroud, separates us from the land of the living. It forces us to bid bon voyage to what was. It kills our hope. Yet it's part of our human experience, our fallen human experience.

God never intended for us to walk through its shadows. To be overcome with the *Ka chings* of sadness. He authors life, not death. Scripture says Jesus "was deeply moved in his spirit and greatly troubled" when he saw the grief caused by the death of his friend, Lazarus (John 11:33). He hated the fallout of the fall.

And he came to do something about it. He stared down death, and in the wake of his victory assured mankind that all our griefs on earth would someday turn to joy. Jesus promises to dry our every tear. He assures his followers that someday the sad banks will be emptied for good. In fact, they will go into full foreclosure! That's a pretty powerful expectation.

So, how's your emotional bank account these days? Are you filling it with more sadness than hope? Take heart, friend. A day is coming with no more *ka chings* of sadness. Every unfulfilled desire, every numbing disappointment, every depleting loss will be replaced with the pure, reverberating sound of gladness.

September 19th

When Simon Peter saw this, he fell at Jesus' knees and said, "Go away from me, Lord; I am a sinful man!" Then Jesus said to Simon, "Don't be afraid; from now on you will fish for people."   —Luke 5:8, 10 NIV

The Truth About Repentance

It takes both truth and love to complete repentance. Truth exposes our sin; God's love consumes it. We're forgiven. We're free. I love how the intersection of truth and love played out when Jesus first called his disciples (Luke 5).

Jesus directed Peter to sail back out to sea and cast his nets again. The disciples had fished all night and come up empty. It seemed a futile task, but Peter obeyed. Although he respected Jesus enough to do what he said, he did not yet realize the immensity of who he was. That was about to change. The haul of fish proved so heavy the nets began to tear. And fishing nets weren't the only thing being torn apart. The miracle revealed Jesus' holiness and in its light, Peter was undone. His self-sufficiency began to unravel. Any illusion he was a good man, maybe even better than most, began to crack. All he could do was fall on his knees and ask Jesus to leave. He wasn't worthy of being in his presence. That was the truth part.

In the light of this earth-shattering revelation, how did Jesus respond? He told Peter not to be afraid. Even though Peter now realized Jesus knew everything about him—every dark corner—Jesus said I want you. I want to take your natural gifts and transform them into something for God. Don't worry about cleaning yourself up to make yourself suitable. I'll take care of it. That was the love part.

It was so powerful Peter, as well as the others, "left everything and followed him" (v. 11). Truth and love working together qualified the first followers of Christ to lay the pattern for the rest of us. To help us not be afraid to repent. To see that when truth exposes our sins, his love will be there to complete the process.

And that's the truth about repentance. Let's not miss it.

September 20th

You have heard that it was said, "You shall love your neighbor and hate your enemy." But I say to you, Love your enemies and pray for those who persecute you. —Matthew 5:43–44 ESV

Bop It on the Head

*Little bunny Foo Foo
Hopping through the forest
Scooping up the field mice,
And boppin' them on the head!*

If you've heard the children's song about Little Bunny Foo Foo, you most likely haven't forgotten it. It's one of those tunes that sticks, especially when your young daughter plays it incessantly on her little recorder. To describe it as annoying would be an understatement. But Little Bunny Foo Foo possesses one redeeming characteristic. It reminds me of how to deal with my reoccurring sin. I gotta keep boppin' it on the head. Take resentment.

C. S. Lewis writes in *Mere Christianity* to love our enemies in the way God calls us, we have to kill the feeling of resentment whenever it occurs, "day after day, year after year, all our lives long, we must hit it on the head." Otherwise it will eventually consume us. Lewis concedes it's not an easy task and suggests we begin with something easier than the Gestapo. Start with a spouse or parent or our misbehaving children.

When Jesus said we must love our enemies, he offers no room for holding grudges. We must pray for those who persecute us. A radical way to respond to hatred, but radical is what he meant. Thankfully he also promises to help us do what we can't do ourselves. So, we have no excuse for feeding resentment.

Sometimes I just don't want to "bop it." I can enjoy the thought of someone getting his just deserts. Resentment can pollute my sense of justice to the point I like the idea of my enemy suffering the consequences of bad actions more than I desire his change. That's a problem. That's when I need to fall on my knees and ask God to forgive me. To help me love my enemy.

As long as I'm in this mortal body, I have to keep boppin' those sightings of my sinful nature on the head. It's the only way to keep those pesky field mice from taking over. How about you? Need to do some head-bopping today?

September 21st

She did what she could. She poured perfume on my body beforehand to prepare for my burial.
—Mark 14:8 NIV

She Did What She Could

I've recently been re-reading Charles Sheldon's classic, *In His Steps*. He describes one incident where two sisters are getting into their carriage when the younger one notices a shabbily dressed little boy, shivering in the cold. Before getting into her carriage, she unpins the bouquet of violets she's wearing and gives them to the child. He takes them, buries his nose in their fragrance, and with a big smile, thanks her. Her sister chides her, saying what he really needs is a hot meal, not a bunch of flowers. But violets were all she had to offer, so that's what she gave. She did what she could.

I wonder how many times we stifle the instinct to give simply because it won't meet the larger need. But what if God isn't calling us to meet the whole need? What if he's calling us to simply do what we can with our limited resources? Jesus always received acts done in kindness, whether large or small.

Once when he was at a dinner with his disciples, a woman came and poured an alabaster jar of perfume on his head. It was expensive, and some of those present rebuked her, saying she should have used the money from the perfume to help the poor. Rather than agreeing with their indignation at her extravagant gift, Jesus praised her. Although unknown to her, and beyond the imagination of the disciples, she was using what she had to prepare Jesus for his upcoming burial. He lauded her, proclaiming her act of kindness would be remembered wherever the gospel was preached. Jesus said, "she did what she could." Such was the impact of Mary of Bethany.

Whether offering a small bouquet of flowers or perfume worth a "year's wages," the Lord wants us to be an active part of his plan. I can't meet all the needs of a refugee family, but I know the father likes watermelon, so I can take him a watermelon when I visit. I may not have all the answers for my grief-stricken friend, but I can give her my ear. I would rather have "she did what she could" written on my tombstone than "she kept what she had."

How about you? Don't miss your opportunities.

September 22nd

"Lord, if it's you," Peter replied, "tell me to come to you on the water." "Come," he said. Then Peter got down out of the boat, walked on the water and came toward Jesus. —Matthew 14:28–29 NIV

Risk

"What keeps pushing you to grow closer to the Lord?" questioned my student as we sat across from each other at the college café. One word summed up my response: RISK.

Risks I've taken have fostered the deepest spiritual growth—even when the risk resulted in pain. Every risk brings with it the opportunity to fail, and fail greatly. But every risk also brings the chance to experience fulfillment we would otherwise never have known. I've had my share of both.

My husband and I took a risk over forty years ago when we felt the Lord direct us to store all our possessions, board a stand-by flight to Luxemburg, and find our way to a Christian community in the Swiss Alps called L'Abri. We took another risk when he accepted the call to pastor a small group of people. Risk was involved when we had children, when I decided to write and publish a book, when we opened our home to others. Despite the many ups and downs, I have no regrets about the risks. God has used them to stretch, shape and fit me into his plan.

I recently heard a man refer to the "wild purposeful life God wants us to live." To that I say, "Count me in." That doesn't mean we're to throw all caution to the wind for the sake of adventure. Nothing spiritual about that. The kind of risk-taking that results in a closer walk with the Lord comes through responding to his voice.

When Peter saw Jesus walking on water, he thought it worth the risk to ask if he could come. Even though he soon got distracted and fell into the water, I bet he never regretted his courageous attempt. He actually walked on water, even if for a few moments!

When God calls you to walk on some water, go for it. Keep walking every time Jesus says, "Come." And if your faith is too weak to walk, swim. If you can't swim, doggie-paddle. Don't be afraid to risk getting closer.

September 23rd

Therefore everyone who confesses Me before men, I will also confess him before My Father who is in heaven. But whoever denies Me before men, I will also deny him before My Father who is in heaven.

—Matthew 10:32–33 NASB

Full Disclosure: Child of God

In the interest of full disclosure ...

We sometimes hear that disclaimer in news reporting. Failure to reveal connections—whether with political candidates lobbyists or others who may influence reporting—tarnishes the credibility of journalists who purport to be fair and unbiased.

So, in the interest of full disclosure, let me say—I am a child of God. When it comes to reporting about him, there's not an impartial bone in my body. I'm not objective. Because he is truth, he influences the way I think. Because he is love, he shows me how to relate to people. In fact, no area of my life lies untouched by him.

Although he certainly doesn't need me to defend him, when folks distort the facts about him, my bias shows. Statements like these frustrate me. "A God of love would not have let this happen. He must not care about me. He doesn't hear my prayers. He's just a myth in the minds of weak people." Such misreporting about his character grieves me. Why? Because I know him.

In a culture where political correctness increasingly crowds out integrity, the need to unabashedly speak the truth about God could not be more important. This doesn't mean we thump Bibles over people's heads. We don't have to. We simply, boldly, disclose his nature through our words as well as our actions.

Jesus states it clearly: if we confess him before others, he will confess us before God; if we deny him before others, he will deny us before God. Let's not be afraid or reserved or ashamed about who and whose we are. No relationship in life carries significance like the one we have with our Father. Those we live with, work with, pray with, in fact everyone in our sphere, needs to know about it. Someone's eternal destiny, including our own, may rest on our full disclosure.

September 24th

Ebed-Melek the Cushite said to Jeremiah, "Put these old rags and worn-out clothes under your arms to pad the ropes." Jeremiah did so, and they pulled him up with the ropes and lifted him out of the cistern.

—Jeremiah 38:12–13 NIV

Kinder than Necessary

"Be kinder than necessary because everyone you meet is fighting some kind of battle." Maybe you're familiar with this quote.

When I think of kindness, words like gentleness, affection and warmth come to mind. Rarely do I consider acts of kindness as possessing an element of danger, or even boldness. What's not to like about friendly concern? Yet many acts of kindness would never take place without someone's willingness to take a risk. Someone like Ebed-Melek.

Ebed served in King Zedekiah's palace. When he heard the king had given his officials authority to throw the prophet Jeremiah and his inconvenient message into a mud-filled pit, he refused to be silent. He boldly confronted the king and asked if he could rescue Jeremiah. He risked his own position to secure Jeremiah's release. Ebed even provided rags for Jeremiah to place under his arms so the ropes wouldn't cut through his skin as they lifted him up from the cistern. He proved to be kinder than necessary.

Risks taken in acts of kindness don't have to be life-threatening. Once when our church was experiencing a devastating crisis, a friend wanting to encourage us appeared on our doorstep with a turkey. He didn't give us sage advice on how to deal with the matter. He didn't even offer to pray with us. He simply extended kindness to us in an unusual way—perhaps the only way he could think of—but it communicated he cared. That was about forty years ago. I still remember it. Kindnesses offered in crises always seem kinder than necessary no matter how small the gesture.

We live in a world where refugees flood more stable nations. Where children are exploited as slaves. Where people are targeted because of the uniforms they wear or the color of their skin. We live in a world in need of people willing to be kinder than necessary. Will you be one of them?

September 25th

Why is the LORD bringing us to this land only to let us fall by the sword? Our wives and children will be taken as plunder. Wouldn't it be better for us to go back to Egypt? —Numbers 14:3 NIV

Assumptions

"I'm thirty years old and not married. God must want me to be single." "If I lose this job, I'll never get another one." "If that person gets elected, our country will never survive."

Assumptions run the gamut from the totally illogical to simple second-guessing. They range in scope from the personal to wide scale. They can take us down roads we were never meant to travel. In Israel's case, quite literally.

When the twelve spies returned from checking out the Promised Land, all but two, Joshua and Caleb, made a dismal assessment. Although the land looked good, they reported the giants living there would be impossible to defeat. They assumed because the Amalekites and Canaanites were bigger and stronger, Israel didn't stand a chance. The spies' fear ran so rampant in the camp that the whole nation was ready to turn tail and run before there was even a skirmish! They *assumed* God had brought them out of Egypt to let them die in the desert. Forget God's promises; forget his miracles; forget his looming presence on Mt. Sinai. Fear-fed assumptions overtook faith.

In the end, their assumptions determined their fate. They wandered in the desert forty years until that generation did, in fact, die. That's what makes assumptions so dangerous. If we're not careful, they will undermine our faith and sabotage our destiny.

I don't know about you, but I must fight against making assumptions. It takes effort for me not to fall into pessimistic worry. The only antidote I've found lies tucked away in Psalm 37:3: "Trust in the LORD and do good." Trusting and fretting can't inhabit the same space. Nor can faith and fear. So, join me in releasing those troubling circumstances and voice a new assumption—the God who loves us is in control!

It's the only assumption that takes us to the right place.

September 26th

Be still, and know that I am God. —Psalm 46:10 NIV

Present in the Present

Do you have trouble being present in the present?

I appreciate multitasking. Although a recently added word to our lexicon, the feat of being able to do several things at one time didn't begin with this generation. From millennials who text, type and talk at the same time to the mother who balances a baby on her hip, puts in a load of wash, and instructs her three-year-old not to run on the just-mopped floor, all while consuming a half-eaten sandwich, multitasking is here to stay.

Although efficiency comprises a necessary part of life, I'm afraid all the multitasking is making it harder to appreciate the beauty found in a singular moment. The other morning, I found myself behind a very slow-moving truck. Instantly, I felt the Lord checking my frustration. *Enjoy the ride.* Not long after that, I was preparing to go out of town for a week-long teaching seminar. I began thinking about how I could best use my free time when I wasn't teaching. I could work on this project, on that upcoming class. The Lord interrupted my thoughts again. *Don't plan on accomplishing anything else.*

How often does our flurry of activity lock us into the shallow lands of life? I wonder what might happen if we took the time to dig a little deeper, examine a little closer. Not just hear what someone says, but pause to listen. Not methodically check items off our to-do list, but engage them. Not rush through obligatory morning devotions, but *wait* upon the Lord.

No one accomplished more in his brief span on earth than Jesus. And no one was more fully present. Jesus said he did nothing but what he saw his Father doing (John 5:19). Constant communication with God taught him how to value every single moment. He experienced no conflict between the stillness of knowing God and the efficiency of working his plan. If we hope to be more present in the present, it begins with letting God's presence infuse our present. Of heeding the words found in Psalm 46.

Pause. Be still. Know he is God. Savor it.

September 27th

Jesus replied. "There is only One who is good." —Matthew 19:17 NIV

I'm Good

"Want some more coffee?"

"No thanks, I'm good."

"Can I get you anything else?"

"Nope, I'm good."

I'm good. It's a common idiom we use these days. It's not intended to say we possess a certain character virtue, but that we're satisfied and content with what we have We don't need anymore.

The rich young ruler who came to Jesus asking him what good thing he needed to do to get eternal life could say he was "good" in a lot of areas. He had money, position and was even morally upright. He possessed so much he had to ask Jesus what he lacked! (Matthew 19:16–20).

The blessings of life can do that, can't they? Blind us to our real needs? If we're not careful, we interpret the good things we experience as an assessment of ourselves. We've been given good stuff because we must *be* "good stuff." But even Jesus said the only one good is God.

Jesus told the rich young ruler that entering the kingdom required him to let go of all the trappings which propped him up—all the things telling him he was good. He would have to come with a blank résumé, like a trusting unpretentious child. He needed a just as I am without one plea moment. Only then would he discover goodness.

God is always good to us. As the late Rich Mullins penned, sometimes he is "doubly good" even though he doesn't have to be singularly so. Our response to his goodness ought never be to turn it back on ourselves as if we're getting something we deserve. On the contrary, we should thank him. Simply, profoundly, thank him. The more we thank him, the more we see how good he is.

When we soak in his goodness, it becomes a part of us. The impossibility of ever becoming good on our own becomes a reality with God. We find complete satisfaction, good in every sense of the word. Some have put it quite succinctly: I am not saved because I am good. I am good because I am saved. And you know what? I'm good with that!

September 28th

Many waters cannot quench love;
rivers cannot sweep it away.
If one were to give
all the wealth of one's house for love,
it would be utterly scorned.

—Song of Songs 8:7 NIV

Are You an Earthmover?

The Song of Solomon describes the unstoppable nature of love. Waters can't quench it. Rivers can't sweep it. Money can't buy it. Even death cannot rival its strength. It's a power to be reckoned with.

Take Rick, a teenager from Michigan. Forced by his parents to attend church, he had little use for religion. Especially the kind that comes in the form of a visiting evangelist from the South. He didn't like the preacher's looks, his southern drawl, his style. But a funny thing happened on his road to dismissal—love.

The preacher invited Rick to play basketball the next day. And the next. And the next. And the next. Basketball was Rick's game; clearly not the preacher's. It didn't matter. His willingness to get into Rick's world cracked all misperceptions and prejudices. The love of God broke through and Rick embraced it. He's still embracing it after thirty years, and as a pastor at that.

Take the Jewish reporter who was assigned to investigate a NYC megachurch. Turns out in spite of all her skepticism and ideological opposition to the congregation's position on moral issues, she couldn't help but be touched by the authenticity of the pastor's love. His concern for her soul awakened her own dormant longing for purpose, meaning and truth. Love does that.

I forget sometimes—maybe you do too—that we don't have to have some kind of super-spiritual skill to lead a person to Christ. We don't have to earn a theology degree. Don't have to be called to the "mission field." Don't have to have an amazing testimony. We just have to love.

That's where we start. When we let the love of Jesus move through us, through our habits, quirks, passions, gifts, flaws, we become bulldozers, earthmovers in every sense of the word. His love incarnate shakes the earth in people's hearts and makes room for heaven. It breaks down barriers like nothing else.

So, do you want to be an earthmover? Try love.

September 29th

Then you will know that I am the LORD.   —*Ezekiel 36:11 NIV*

Then They Will Know

Tragedy and triumph. God reveals himself through both if we're looking. When we're thrown to our knees by sudden job insecurity or a relationship gone sour. When a loved one dies. When prayers become miracles. No matter what circumstance in life we face, God uses both the depths and heights to help us know him.

The book of Ezekiel demonstrates this clearly. The dire consequences of Israel's idolatry and rebellion against God resulted in the unthinkable. As a nation, they were exiled to Babylon, stripped of both their homeland and their identity. Yet, Ezekiel declares, God's judgment is not without purpose. The refrain of *then they will know that I am the Lord* runs throughout the book of Ezekiel. Again and again the prophet proclaims their punishment has happened to lead them to repentance and acknowledgement of the one true God. The road to truth is sometimes a rough one.

Yet God reveals himself no less through victories. In Ezekiel 37 the prophet received the vision of dry bones. The "bones" of Israel lay scattered, devoid of all hope. God instructed Ezekiel to breathe life into them as a sign Israel would indeed return to their homeland. The restoration would be so powerful that not only Israel, but the nations would know the Lord is God (vv. 14, 28).

When God hears our prayers and breathes life into the dry bones of our faith, we know he is the Lord. When he restores our hope and enables us to look beyond our pain, we know he is the Lord. When he empowers us to love others, not only we, but the world knows he is the Lord (John 13:35).

God has always intended to reveal himself through his people. We possess the incredible, amazing task of helping the world see who he is and what he's like. As we look for him in our tragedies and triumphs, we find him. And when we find him, we can't help but let the world know he is the Lord.

September 30th

Let the redeemed of the LORD tell their story—those he redeemed from the hand of the foe. —Psalm 107:2 NIV

Redeemed Storytellers

They know God's goodness and love will never end because they've been to the end.

Psalm 107 lists them as wilderness wanderers. Rebel prisoners. Foolhardy sufferers. Imperiled adventurers. They have a story of redemption to tell. Maybe you can you relate.

Have you ever been a wilderness wanderer? You escaped the bondage of Egypt but somehow lost your way en route to the Promised Land. You no longer feel at "home" in the world, but instead of setting up shop in Canaan, you're going around in circles. You're thirsty for righteousness, but no matter how hard you try, living a life worthy of God seems unreachable. Maybe you could do what those wilderness wanderers in Psalm 107 did. They stopped trying and started trusting. "Then they cried out to the LORD in their trouble, and he delivered them from their distress" (v. 6).

Can you identify with the rebel prisoners? Your insurgence against God landed you in a prison darker than any you could have imagined. You think no one can break your chains, and you're convinced no one would want to. Ah, but you're wrong. No matter how sin-stained your life, there lives a Redeemer whose love "breaks down gates of bronze and cuts through bars of iron" (v. 16).

Maybe you're one of those foolhardy sufferers. Your lust to be free of all restraints shows in your body. Some may even think you deserve the pain. You've made your bed, now sleep in it. Thankfully, God's not part of that crowd. The same One who spared the Psalm107ers can deliver you. "He sent out his word and healed them; he rescued them from the grave" (v. 20).

Finally, how about those imperiled adventurers? Life was good. You were riding high on the waves. The thrill of the wild called your name and you answered with a hardy yes. That is until the storm came. And suddenly, your courage collapsed like locked legs. A hand is reaching out through the tempest. A hand that stills the storm and leads you home (vv. 29–30).

Like those described in Psalm 107, we who know Christ have a story of redemption. A story needing to be told. A story someone is waiting to hear. Won't you tell yours?

October 1st

Let the one who walks in the dark, who has no light, trust in the name of the LORD and rely on his God. But now, all you who light fires and provide yourselves with flaming torches, go, walk in the light of your fires and of the torches you have set ablaze. This is what you shall receive from my hand: You will lie down in torment. —Isaiah 50:10–11 NIV

When It's Dark

Confusion. Unresolved differences. Problems with no apparent solutions. Don't we all, at one time or another, feel like we're in a dark room with no light switch? Such times tempt us to move our reliance from the unseen God to what we can see—ourselves.

One time when our son was younger, I had planned to serve a special dessert at halftime while we were watching the Super Bowl. His excitement had him running back and forth from the TV into the kitchen to see if it was ready, even though I assured him it wouldn't be served until the half. Finally, in exasperation I asked, "Don't you trust me?" His response was telling. "I can't trust you when I don't see you."

Sometimes I'm not much different when it comes to waiting on God's timing. I may not be running back and forth from the family room to the kitchen, but my thoughts dart in all kinds of directions. It's because I refuse to wait, to trust in a God I can't see. So, I try to "light my own fire." I frantically strive to stir up the embers of my understanding, hoping to provide myself with the "flaming torch" of insight. I end up as the one Isaiah described. "I lie down in torment" (or at least sleepless nights of tossing and turning).

The search for understanding is not wrong. Scripture says it's the glory of kings to search out a matter (Psalm 25:2). But if we replace trusting God with striking our own matches to deliver us, we cross a line. Comfort in the darkness of insecurity comes when we trust God whether we see him or not. I will continue to seek understanding when I'm in the dark, but not as a prerequisite to trust. I've decided I would rather be with God in the darkness than without him in the light. How about you?

October 2nd

Who dares despise the day of small things? —*Zechariah 4:10 NIV*

It's the Small Things

Tiny becomes titanic when offered to God.

As powerful as small things can be, it's amazing how we tend to take them for granted. We sometimes forget them as soon as they happen. I was recently reading one of my journal entries where I'd recorded my thankfulness for an unexpected conversation with my son, kind words spoken by a former student and the opportunity to take a friend out for dinner. The recollection of those small occurrences not only put a smile on my face, they reminded me in a tangible way of God's practical, personal goodness.

From the trenches of war, upon receiving a supply of provisions, C. S. Lewis wrote: "such little attentions are infinitely cheering when one is dull, lonely and disappointed." In an environment with few pleasures Lewis appreciated the slightest acts of kindness. Small things can sometimes move mountains of dullness, loneliness and disappointment, can't they?

They also empower us to accomplish more than we think possible. As governor of Jerusalem, Zerubbabel was given the daunting task of rebuilding the once resplendent temple. Nothing went right. He faced growing opposition from Israel's enemies, lethargy from his people, and numerous inconveniences. But before giving up completely, God sent Zechariah with the encouraging words for him to not despise the small beginnings of the project. Yes, the task was formidable, but God's own Spirit would help him complete the job. Zerubbabel learned not to get frustrated with the slow beginning but embrace it as a source of encouragement, not discouragement.

If we hope to overcome life's challenges, an appreciation of the small things is a good place to start. If I don't take the time to be grateful for my morning coffee, the beauty of my little grandson's smile, and the warmth of my fireplace on a cold evening, I forfeit the foundation needed to experience life as God intended.

So, whatever you might be facing right now, can I echo the words of Zechariah? Don't despise the small things in your life. Recall them. Renew your gratitude for them. Then go and live a *big* life!

October 3rd

Praise the LORD, my soul, and forget not all his benefits.
—*Psalm 103:2 NIV*

When Life Happens

Sometimes life gets in the way of *life*.

Have you ever experienced this? You're moving along, full of faith, then you hit a pothole of disappointment. Your prayers get punctured by betrayal and loss, your joy runs headlong into a detour sign. You remain on the road, but what once filled your heart with hope and wonder has evolved into a foggy kind of skepticism. What happened?

Life. Fallen-world life.

When fallen life interrupts our journey and intrudes our space, we get tempted to lock into human answers and explanations. We stop fixing our eyes on the Fixer and instead stare at our circumstances until they loom like giants. Like Israel in the wilderness, we walk in circles toward a Promised Land which seems out of reach. Why? Maybe because unlike the psalmist, we don't command our souls to praise the Lord and remember his benefits.

Benefits like:

- "His divine power has given us everything we need for a godly life" (2 Peter 1:3).
- "No temptation has seized you except what is common to mankind. And God is faithful; he will not let you be tempted beyond what you can bear. But when you are tempted, he will also provide a way out so that you can endure it" (1 Corinthians 10:13).
- "If God is for us, who can be against us? He who did not spare his own Son, but gave him up for us all—how will he not also, along with him, graciously give us all things?" (Romans 8:31–32).

The greatest threat to having our victory stolen is forgetting we have it. Forgetting that our inability to turn the other cheek, to go the extra mile, to show grace, to release expectations, is just that—our inability—not God's. He makes victory possible in every area we face, but we must choose to access it.

The truth is, we don't have to live like Jews wandering in the wilderness. We can invite God into every aspect of our lives and let him use even the potholes to move us forward. Because that's the kind of God we serve. Let's not forget his benefits. Let's remind one another of those benefits and help each other refocus back on him when life gets in the way of *life*.

October 4th

Not that the troubles should come as any surprise to you. You've always known that we're in for this kind of thing. It's part of our calling.
—1 Thessalonians 3:3 MSG

Trouble with a Capital "T"

The college where I teach presented Meredith Wilson's *The Music Man*. One of the songs, "Ya Got Trouble" and the cast's splendid performance of it keeps going through my mind. Fast-talking, snake-oil salesman Harold Hill warns the townsfolk trouble is heading their way and the mayor's pool hall stands as proof. They are in for "Trouble with a capital T." Of course, Hill presents himself as the answer to the town's impending catastrophe.

Although the trouble Hill predicted never materialized in River City, trouble in a fallen world will. Despite its inevitability, trouble—no matter the size, shape or extent—can shake the strongest heart. Many believers feel the culture is crumbling. They see the world as Isaiah described: "Justice is driven back, and righteousness stands at a distance; truth has stumbled in the streets, honesty cannot enter" (Isaiah 59:14). Trouble indeed.

So, trouble poses as nothing new. Especially for Christians. Paul warned the Thessalonians about his approaching trials (1 Thessalonians 3:3-4). James told the church trouble was not only unavoidable but necessary for spiritual growth (James 1:2-4). Peter sought to comfort believers by helping them see their faith would be proved genuine through the fire of suffering (1 Peter 1:6-7).

Christians can't expect a pass when it comes to trouble. What we can and should expect, however, is to find a God who promises to be "our refuge and strength, an ever-present help in trouble" (Psalm 46:1). A God who will not only walk with us through the struggle, but will use the pain to make us better, purer, stronger.

Let's not be "unsettled" by the trials we or fellow believers face. Let's be like those who have gone before us and remain firm in our faith and love. It won't be easy. To counter the kind of Trouble that starts with a capital "T," we need Courage. It starts with "C" and that rhymes with "T." Folks, we need Courage.

October 5th

They consecrated themselves to that shameful idol and became as vile as the thing they loved. —Hosea 9:10 NIV

Oh Be Careful Little Heart What You Love

Be careful what you love.

I remember a song we sang in Sunday School. "Oh, be careful little eyes what you see.... Oh, be careful little ears what you hear.... Oh, be careful little hands what you do...." It served as a warning for us rambunctious grade schoolers not to sin.

Too bad the nation of Israel didn't embrace those lyrics. In their desire to be like other nations, they threw all caution to the wind. They imitated the evil practices of those surrounding them. They worshiped their idols. They exchanged God's standard for Assyria's and Egypt's. Oh, they continued to give God lip service. They mistakenly thought their morning mist love would somehow appease him (Hosea 6:4). They were wrong. He gave them what they wanted. And the consequences were devastating. No fruit. No children. No homeland. Their sins had found them out. They became what they loved.

The psalmist also warns that we become like what we worship. If we trust in idols that cannot speak, our voices of influence will be silenced. If our idols have no eyes or ears, we eventually will be blinded and deafened to the truth. Bowing down to idols without hands or feet ultimately immobilizes our dreams, our hopes, our purpose in life (Psalm 115).

Let's not forget, "There's a Savior up above, And He's looking down in love." That's how the rest of the Sunday school song goes. God created us to be his people. He entrusts us with the incredible opportunity of showing the world what he looks like. He is watching to see himself in you, in me. He is looking at our hearts. Looking to see what we love. Because what we love determines everything we see, everything we hear, everything we do, everything we say.

So, my friend, let's be careful. Let's seek to replace our idols with the love and worship of the God who comes after us in our prostitution and idolatry, the God who wants to give us life and purpose, the God who wants us to love what he loves and so become like him.

October 6th

And the peace of God, which transcends all understanding, will guard your hearts and your minds in Christ Jesus.   *—Philippians 4:7 NIV*

Occupy All Streets

Does peace occupy the streets of your mind?

The iconic protest against financial inequality a few years ago made "Occupy Wall Street" a household term. But how about your Wall Street? Do you realize a Wall Street exists in each of our minds? It's where we think about money. If we've been blessed with a lot of it, we're prone to worry about how to keep it, use it, or invest it. If our bills outweigh our paychecks we worry how to spend what we don't have. Our Wall Streets provide ample opportunity for anxiety occupation.

Another street in our minds revolves around relationships. We might call it People Place. Some of life's richest treasures inhabit that address. Also, some of the greatest distractions. Relationships, I must admit, occupy a pretty big space in my thoughts. It's easy for me to be consumed with concerns about my family, friends, students. Those concerns sometimes occupy my "people place" more than trust in God.

Avenues of worry about the direction of our country, religious liberty, injustices and corruption can easily merge into a major interstate of interrupted peace. Legitimate questions detour into a road of fruitless speculation and dead ends.

Alleys of pre-occupation with the details of living gnaw around the edges of my thought-life. I let my mind be filled with all kinds of unnecessary vanities and fears. *Does this dress make me look fat? Did I prepare enough for that class? Am I doing a good job?*

The apostle Paul tells us what God desires to occupy the streets of our mind—his peace. A peace not based on understanding. A peace that surrounds us when we place all our worries in his hands. We do an about-face, or better put— an about-thought. We intentionally de-occupy anxieties by choosing to replace them with things more worthy—like whatever is true, noble, right, pure, lovely, and admirable (Philippians 4:8).

So, what's occupying the streets of your mind? If your thoughts are robbing you of God's peace and presence, maybe it's time to re-think. Time to occupy all your streets with something far better.

October 7th

Do not be anxious about anything, but in every situation, by prayer and petition, with thanksgiving, present your requests to God.

—*Philippians 4:6 NIV*

Talking Points

Talking points. We hear them on the news all the time. Surrogates of politicians saturate the media with carefully crafted statements to sway people to their point of view. They hope by repeating the exact same words ad nauseam people will be convinced their information rings true. Talking points rarely detour from the script, and although they may give the appearance of dialogue, they are about as far from true communication as polar bears in the Philippines.

Sometimes my prayers sound a lot like talking points. "Please bless this day, Lord. Watch over my kids. Touch John's body. Help Joanne get a job. Let the right officials be elected. Protect Christians who are being persecuted." Now there's nothing wrong with presenting our lists before God, but if that's the extent of our communication with him, we end up forfeiting both the intimacy and peace he offers.

The apostle Paul's exhortation to the Philippians about prayer bears little resemblance to talking points. He says we should bring any and every concern to God by prayer and petition with thanksgiving. I've been working on it.

A woman recently told me how overwhelmed she felt due to her heavy responsibilities. She didn't know how she could make it much longer. I asked if I could pray for her, but rather than plunging into my request, I began thanking God for this dear woman. I thanked him for his faithfulness to her through the years, for specific incidents of answered prayer, for promises given in his Word, for her devotion to him. The overflow of thankfulness evoked something else. Something I wasn't quite expecting—faith.

By the time I got to the asking part of my prayer, faith once overshadowed by concern began to surface. Thankfulness had stimulated faith. It peeled my eyes off the problem and focused them on the Solver. A solid assurance God would take care of the situation filled my Amen.

So how is your prayer life? Are you limiting your communication with God to mere talking points? I pray thanksgiving accompanies your petitions ... thanksgiving that leads to faith ... faith that leads to intimacy ... intimacy that leads to the real thing.

October 8th

But Daniel resolved not to defile himself with the royal food and wine.
—Daniel 1:8 NIV

Healthy or Deadly?

To compromise or not to compromise?

It's a question faced continually by politicians, parents and just about anyone facing a tough decision. To what length do we go in standing up for our principles? When is it okay to entertain ideas contrary to our own? What marks going too far? Not all compromise is wrong. I can't imagine a successful marriage without compromise. Unwillingness to compromise creates stalled government and fosters broken friendships. No one has the full picture—well, maybe Daniel did. Daniel knew the difference between healthy compromise and the deadly kind.

Daniel, along with other Israelites, had been exiled from Jerusalem to Babylon. Chosen to undergo training for an elite position with the Babylonian king, he faced one caveat. His training included a diet requiring him to violate standards God set for his people. It posed a compromise he was unwilling to make. Daniel "resolved not to defile himself with the royal food and wine."

Years later when Daniel had to choose whether to bow to Babylonian gods or be thrown in the lions' den, his resolve surfaced again. This time, he faced a potential life or death situation. Nonetheless, he refused to compromise. Better to be eaten by lions than dishonor God. You know the story. God rescued him and entrusted him with visions of the future we still study today.

Daniel possessed a keen awareness of when compromise required him to violate his identity in God. Eating the king's food may sound like a small thing to our modern ears, but Daniel knew it might as well be poison. He didn't play around with it. He confidently said no.

We've all had experiences where God calls us to refuse "royal food." I remember a TV show I enjoyed watching. Although I liked the clever story line, I began feeling uncomfortable watching its increasing normalization of sin. It became clear the Lord was telling me to stop consuming it. A small decision, but for me, an important one.

How about you? How's your diet? Does it include "food" enticing you to compromise your standards? Be encouraged by Daniel's example. It's far better to ruin your menu than your mission.

October 9th

Keep your lives free from the love of money and be content with what you have, because God has said, "Never will I leave you; never will I forsake you." —Hebrews 13:5 NIV

Isn't Money Everything?

You would think, especially in these days of partisanship and polarization, the Right and Left have nothing in common. But I believe extreme opposites share a number of commonalities. For example, the idea *money is everything* seems to be the underlying force behind both ends of the political spectrum. Their approaches differ, of course, but each side tends to view wealth as the key to happiness. No wonder we're missing it.

Although no one would deny the misery caused by poverty, it's well documented big bank accounts do not ensure happiness. We're looking for contentment in the wrong places. Contentment rests more upon our choices than our circumstances. The writer of Hebrews puts contentment based on anything other than God right next to sexual immorality (13:4–5). Both reflect a choice to sin.

Yet we live in a culture that runs on the premise *money is everything*. It's a notion we need to reject. We can't let our security rest on 401(k)s and pension plans. On promises of job advancement and gold investments. We live in a world of fragile economies and bleak financial forecasts. But we don't have to let it control us. We are made for more.

When Scripture warns us to live free from the love of money, it reveals God's promise to never leave us or forsake us as the source of our contentment—not wealth. Knowing he's with us to the end gives us the peace we need in both plenty and want.

Whether the stock market crashes or banks default, whether the rich get richer and the poor poorer, we have access to what really matters. And that is a treasure we can bank on.

It's the *true* everything.

October 10th

Do not leave Jerusalem, but wait for the gift my Father promised, which you have heard me speak about. —Acts 1:4 NIV

The Weight of Waiting

Most of us hate to wait. We don't like wasting time and feeling irritated, impatient and helpless. And our fast-paced culture doesn't help matters. It reinforces the idea we should have what we want and have it now. Waiting bears a hefty weight.

Yet from a scriptural view, waiting is good. Waiting on God—essential. It makes us stronger (Isaiah 40:31). It protects us from shame (Psalm 25:3-5). It brings us great blessing (Isaiah 30:18). In fact, we can't even conceive what God has in store for those who wait on him (Isaiah 64:4).

All the patriarchs of our faith endured waiting periods before God used them. Noah. Abraham. Joseph. Moses. David. The times of waiting purified them and taught them to trust in God more than themselves. It prepared them when they didn't even know they needed to be prepared.

Waiting releases power. One of the last commands Jesus gave his disciples was to wait. So, they gathered in that upper room and waited. As they did, the Holy Spirit came on them with power. Enough power to change the course of human history (Acts 1-2).

Recently, I was confronted with being stuck in a long line of slowly moving traffic, a tardy doctor whose lateness caused my appointment to be extended far more than it should have been, and a post office worker who couldn't figure out how to send my package media mail. Small incidents in a day where I was already concerned I wouldn't accomplish everything I'd hoped to.

But rather than giving into my typical frustration, I started looking at each of the incidents as "practice times." God gave me opportunity to live out his perspective on waiting in these small ordinary instances. As I shifted from the urgency of my agenda to the freedom of his, the burden of waiting started to shift.

Maybe the Lord has been giving you some practice times too. Don't miss the opportunity to work those "weights of waiting." Let the waiting—whether for a single incidence or a season—build up muscles of trust that prepare you for more than you can conceive.

October 11th

However, I consider my life worth nothing to me; my only aim is to finish the race and complete the task the Lord Jesus has given me—the task of testifying to the good news of God's grace. —Acts 20:24 NIV

Unlikely Lessons from Speech Class

"Your speeches are not about you." That's one of the first things I tell students in my public speaking classes. I want them to realize their speeches are about the audience. The more students focus on how they sound and look when speaking, the greater their self-consciousness, the shakier their nerves and less effective their delivery. "There is in that act of preparing the moment you start caring," says Churchill. When the audience senses you care more about them than your performance, they will listen and your speech will flow. I can't help but see application beyond the classroom.

Your life is not about you.

When we make ourselves rather than our Audience of One the focal point of life, we don't flow any better than faltering speeches. Questions like "Am I godly enough? Successful enough? Happy enough?" consume us. Ironically, the more we absorb ourselves in ourselves, the less godly, successful and happy we become. Because God didn't create us that way.

God created each of us to tell his story. His story depicted through uniquely crafted jars of clay which contain an immeasurable treasure. When we dare lay down our lives for his sake, we find the only life that matters. And, oh, does it matter!

Paul encourages us through his example. Like a laser beam, Paul kept his focus on finishing the task God gave him to testify about the good news of God's grace. Nothing else in life held such importance. He learned the secret to a successful life was to remember it wasn't about him.

This understanding isn't the only life application I've learned from speech class. I encourage my students to be grateful for the opportunity to speak, to pepper their speeches with timely pauses, to maintain eye contact with their audience. And shouldn't we be filled with gratitude for being given the opportunity to even have a shot at life? Shouldn't we insert pauses in our nonstop busyness? And shouldn't we always keep our eyes focused on Jesus?

How about you? Ready for speech class?

October 12th

Go, eat your food with gladness, and drink your wine with a joyful heart, for God has already approved what you do. Always be clothed in white, and always anoint your head with oil. —Ecclesiastes 9:7-8 NIV

Don't Give Power to the Negatives

I don't like to admit it, but I think I'm more of a see the glass "half-empty" person than a see it "half-full" optimist. I give disappointment and unmet expectations far too much power in my life. I want to change that.

Not long ago I invited a few people for dinner. On the morning of the event, half of those coming bailed out. Yep. Half. At first, I was so disappointed I almost cancelled the whole thing. But rather than stewing on it, and empowering the negatives, I found myself adjusting both the menu and my attitude. I decided to discard my original expectations for the night and let God set a new agenda. Guess what? We had a great evening! Actually, a far better one than I had even hoped for originally. It never would have happened had I continued to fuel my disappointment.

The problem with allowing negatives to overshadow the positives is that it drains us of joy. And God wants us to be joyful people (Galatians 5:22). No doubt life in a fallen world can be hard, but much in life exists for our enjoyment. As a friend recently noted, "Joy is a matter of how you focus." Will I let the fact the cashier shortchanged me for the pastry I purchased eclipse its tastiness? When I evaluate my class, will I let the one student who fumbled through his speech override those students who worked hard? Will I let the rejection of one friend cancel out the faithfulness of three others?

One of the wisest persons who ever lived encouraged us to celebrate life. Enjoy our food and drink. Enjoy our relationships. Enjoy our hard work. He recognized our tendencies to let worry and regret sabotage our happiness. God gives us opportunities each day to discover hidden pockets of pleasure. The more energy we exert in looking for the good, the weaker our disappointments become.

So, don't let the little foxes in life spoil your vine (Song of Songs 2:15). Express your gratitude for the half-full glasses and before you know it, overflowing joy just might fill you to the brim.

October 13th

He moved on from there and dug another well, and no one quarreled over it. He named it Rehoboth, saying, "Now the LORD has given us room and we will flourish in the land." —Genesis 26:22 NIV

Dig Deeper Wells

Rehoboth Mission. That's the name of my childhood church in Southern Ohio. Grandpa always told me it meant "room for all." The small band of dedicated believers who started the church faced opposition in the community. They were a shoutin' church, and their display of passion made some folks uncomfortable. But they knew God had called them so they worked, prayed and believed until the foundation was laid and Rehoboth Mission became a reality—a place welcoming all who thirsted for God.

The name referenced the biblical account of Isaac's search for water in the desert. Every time Isaac's tribe dug a new well the locals argued the water belonged to them; Isaac had no right to it. So, his tribe moved to another spot, then another, until he landed at a place where no one bickered over water rights. He called the well Rehoboth proclaiming it to be a place with enough water for everyone, room for all to flourish.

When I'm not flourishing, I realize it's time to start digging. Not necessarily another well, like Isaac or the patriarchs of Rehoboth Mission, just a deeper one. I have to silence the voices arguing in my mind—voices trying to convince me the world's water rights to my withering soul are stronger than God's.

God is the One who says, "Though the mountains be shaken and the hills be removed, yet my unfailing love for you will not be shaken" (Isaiah 54:10). He is the One who remains close to the brokenhearted and crushed in spirit (Psalm 34:18). When I dig deeper into the unchanging character of God, praise begins to flow. Praise that carries me to the underground waters of trust. Without trust, our relationship with God remains shallow. But the circumstances that deplete us can drive us to the source that replenishes us.

How's your well these days? Feel like you're coming up dry? You don't have to. There is room for all at God's well. Even you. Even me. So, dig deeper. Drink heartily!

October 14th

Sing to the LORD a new song; sing to the LORD, all the earth.
—Psalm 96:1 NIV

What's On Your Playlist?

What's on your playlist?

Oh, I don't mean the sequence of songs on your iPod or MP3 player. I'm talking about the tunes running through your mind.

Refrains that shuffle to the front of your thoughts again and again like a broken record. (Sorry, I couldn't help myself.) We all have playlists to some extent. They either inspire us or immobilize us, depending on our circumstances.

When I feel like I'm falling short—or maybe even apart—songs that echo my inadequacies shift to the top of the list. Unfortunately, I have a full library encompassing every possible area of failure. Pessimism about the future surfaces a playlist of pretty dark tunes. Harmonies of worry, worry, worry loop endlessly over many matters—even those of which I have no control over.

Jesus addressed people's playlists when he was on the earth. He told them not to be consumed with what they would eat or drink, with their bodies, with what they would wear. He encouraged them to focus on songs of a different sort, the kind that seeks God's kingdom first (Matthew 6:25–34). He directed them to choose a playlist that would lead them to something bigger than themselves.

The psalmist directs us to "sing to the LORD a new song" and he knew a thing or two about music. We don't have to choose the same tired melodies that keep us stuck in the past. Each day we have opportunity to belt out something brand new. It may take examining our playlists and deleting some selections that keep us tied more to earth than heaven. We might have to get rid of lyrics that focus on our performance more than his presence.

So, what's on your playlist?

God has some pretty cool songs on his playlist. Songs booming with life. Songs chock full of his love. Of grace. Of second chances. He compiled his playlist before time, but it remains as current as the next minute. Don't miss out. He's inviting you to be part of his mighty symphony.

October 15th

What is man that you are mindful of him, and the son of man that you care for him? —Psalm 8:4 ESV

Why Me?

The exact same words. The exact opposite meaning.

The question, "Why me?" can be asked in one of two ways. The two ways stand miles apart. In fact, you might say the two "why me's?" are polar opposites. One mindset speaks of depletion; the other of fullness. One reflects self-pity; the other self-effacement. The darkness of despair shrouds one; the light of gratitude beams through the other. I've known both.

The first "why me?" is the woe-is-me kind. We ask it when we feel we're the brunt of some injustice. Who can't relate to feelings of being treated unfairly? We cry out to God, probing him for answers. Why have I been singled out? Why did I lose my job? Why can't I get pregnant? Although a natural human response to pain, this "why me?" will lead to bitterness if we linger too long in its shadow.

The second "why me?" is the whoa-why-me kind. We ask this when we become aware of God's unmerited blessings toward us. It echoes the psalmist when he asks God, "What is man that you are mindful of him ... that you care for him?" Why should I have any comforts in life at all? Why should I know what it's like to be loved? Why should I get to work in a job I relish? I could fill a page. In fact, the more "why me's" I think of, the more my cup overflows. This kind of "why me?" leads us on a path toward unmitigated joy.

We are human. Each of us experience both kinds of "why." I believe the more we saturate ourselves in the second kind, the more equipped we'll be to withstand the first.

Someone close to me was recently diagnosed with multiple sclerosis. Although she may have initially experienced the first "why me?" she certainly didn't wallow in it. She had already matured in the ways of gratitude so when the test results came, she was prepared. As the Holy Spirit reminded her of all the good things in her life, she became more aware of God's care for her, not less.

How about you? Are you letting the shadows of woe be replaced with the radiance of whoa? I hope so, but if not, why not begin now?

October 16th

But when you ask, you must believe and not doubt, because the one who doubts is like a wave of the sea, blown and tossed by the wind.
—*James 1:6 NIV*

COPD Christians

We all wrestle with doubt at points in our Christian walk. The healthy kind of doubt, as some have noted, leads to certainty. It directs us to wrestle through issues and in the end makes us stronger. But the kind of doubt James refers to is not healthy. It can suffocate us.

My mother suffered from chronic obstructive pulmonary disease (COPD). The airways traveling to her lungs were damaged, making it difficult to breathe. Eventually, she had to be on oxygen 24/7. In similar fashion, we as Christians sometimes suffer from a kind of spiritual COPD when we are co-opted by doubt.

Doubt clogs the airways that breathe life into our faith. Sometimes we inhale doubt when what we've prayed for hasn't happened. Days, weeks, even years go by, and our faith weakens. The other day I was walking down the street questioning God as to whether I should continue to pray for answers to situations that have, in my estimation, been long overdue. Right at that moment I glanced over at a house. In its window hung a huge sign that read DON'T GIVE UP THE SHIP. That seemingly insignificant sign offered me a fresh breath of encouragement that dispelled the mounting doubt. Doubt always tells us to give up, to stop praying, to stop hoping, to stop believing.

Doubt hinders our journey from faithfulness to faith. It entices us to settle for all things natural without the possibility of divine intervention. Doubt feels quite comfortable when we lean on our own understanding and refuse to move beyond. But if we reach no further than our intellect can take us, how far can we go? We will end up with compromised airways. Limited. Confined. Just like a person tied to an oxygen tank.

Whatever you are facing today, don't be co-opted by doubt. James says we are to believe when we ask God and not let doubt sabotage our requests. Does it take effort? Yes. But our resolution to trust the Lord will keep the winds of uncertainty from whipping us around.

Do you believe that? Breathe in the faith that will keep you from becoming a COPD Christian.

October 17th

As the heavens are higher than the earth, so are my ways higher than your ways and my thoughts than your thoughts.

—Isaiah 55:9 NIV

When the Pieces Don't Fit

Enjoying my morning walk by the lake, I basked in the sun shining on the water. I even belted out some John Denver "Sunshine on my shoulders makes me happy." The simple beauty of manicured lawns and the wind's gentle nudging of waves over the rocky shore created a picturesque scene of peacefulness. Into my idyllic reverie I happened to notice the name of the road where I was walking. You might be guessing something like Serenity Street or maybe even Leisure Lane. But no, I discovered my jaunt had put me on Harsh Road. Harsh Road? How could this slice of tranquility be labeled *harsh*? Next, I noticed a window box filled with artificial flowers. Artificial flowers! They looked as out of place as tofu at a meat-eaters convention.

Much in life doesn't fit our expectations, does it? Sometimes the pieces just don't come together, and no matter how hard we try, like Cinderella's stepsisters, we can't squeeze a 9-sized foot into a size 5 shoe. Hmmm ... I still don't understand why my daughter's wedding reception fell on the very same day my son had to leave for college over seven hundred miles away. These two major life events were not supposed to overlap. But they did.

We don't expect projects we pour our heart and soul into to flounder. But they do. We think surely God will speak to us when we seem to need him most. But he doesn't. How do we deal with these incongruities in life?

We might keep insisting on knowing why until the strain causes a hairline fracture in our faith. We might try to spiritualize the situation by conjuring up explanations to justify God's allowances. Or we might accept the truth found in Isaiah: God is infinite; we are finite. Although he sometimes grants us access, his thoughts and ways remain far above our understanding.

So, if you find yourself on Harsh Road and in the midst of artificial flowers, remember there's a God who fits the pieces together perfectly. In time. Trust Him.

October 18th

If it is possible, as far as it depends on you, live at peace with everyone.
—Romans 12:18 NIV

Everyday Redemption

A small, but poignant experience, made me aware of the beauty found in everyday redemption. I had just paid for getting my hair done at the beauty salon, when I realized I was short on what would have been an appropriate amount for the tip. I gave her what I had, but I knew it was insufficient. All the way home, my thoughts wrestled with what I should do. Convicted by my lack of generosity, I could hardly wait to call the salon and verify the beautician's name. I sent her a brief note with the additional tip money. And I was relieved.

I was relieved that God's grace allowed me to participate in the redemption process. He gave me the opportunity to make up my lack. What if I hadn't been able to find her name? What if circumstances would have prevented me from giving? Often, we are not offered the chance to make it up. We try to compensate for our failures, but those we've affected refuse our attempts. It would be like the beautician saying, "No thanks, you already blew it" when I tried to complete the tip.

That incident showed me the importance of making things right with others when we have opportunity to do so. I was not at peace until I compensated for my lack. Maybe that's why Paul encourages us to live at peace with everyone. It not only frees them, it frees us as well.

Everyday redemption doesn't always happen. Sometimes people walk away angry. But Paul encourages us to do what we can "as far as it depends on [us]." That means never seeking revenge but always looking for a way to bring good out of a situation. We extend second chances when asked to forgive, and we ask others' forgiveness when we fail.

Were it not for the redemptive love and power of Christ, it would be futile to try and "live at peace with all men." But he's in the business of making all things new. Even you. Even me. Be on the lookout for opportunities to show everyday redemption.

October 19th

Now that I, your Lord and Teacher, have washed your feet, you also should wash one another's feet. —John 13:14 NIV

Dirty Feet

Cheap grace says, "I don't care if you drink that poison. I love you anyway."

True grace says, "I love you enough to tell you the truth—that poison is going to kill you. Don't drink it!"

Costly grace, the kind Jesus offers to each one of us sinners, says, "I drank the poison so you don't have to."

Cheap grace lacks the power to save. Oh, it makes us feel good about our nonjudgmental selves, but it does nothing to rescue the ones we say we love. Far be it for us to make anyone feel uncomfortable. Or heaven forbid, offend someone. We muddle the truth and become misguided soothsayers.

When Jesus washed his disciples' feet, he told them although they were all clean except the one who would betray him, they would still need to have their feet washed. These disciples believed in Jesus. They had been cleansed from sin. Saved. But they still lived in a world covered with the grime and dust of sin. Everyday living put them in the midst of it. Their feet were bound to get dirty. So, Jesus told them to help one another by washing each other's feet.

Enter true grace.

True grace doesn't ignore the dirt. *Hey brother, I think you stepped in a little pride along the way. Let me help you get rid of it. Sister, that rejection is poisoning you with bitterness. Let me help you shake off the dust.* Being the body of Christ means helping one another get rid of any sin that sullies us. It requires a readiness to both give and receive correction.

We can't offer this true grace unless we first experience the costly grace of Christ. Jesus drank the poison intended for us. When Satan said, "I got him!" Jesus said, "Not so fast." His victory on the cross authorized him to come to our rescue. To clean us up. When we experience it, we can't help but want others to find the same kind of freedom. So, with gentleness and the consciousness of our own dirty feet, we offer grace.

True grace, not the cheap substitute.

October 20th

Therefore encourage one another and build each other up, just as in fact you are doing. —1 Thessalonians 5:11 NIV

Sour Spots or Sweet Spots

You've probably heard the term "sweet spot." Everything flows together at just the right time and just the right place to produce the maximum effect. We're in the groove. We're in harmony with the universe. Who doesn't love to experience sweet spots? But might there be such a thing as "sour spots?" I think so.

Usually when I'm writing or preparing for a talk, all is flowing well, when suddenly—and almost always—I hit a wall. It seems all my work to this point has been worthless, my efforts good for nothing. I feel like tossing it all aside and quitting. That's what I call a "sour spot." I suspect I'm not alone.

Sometimes sour spots can be remedied with a good night's sleep or a walk around the block. But sometimes they linger long and start to paralyze us. What do we do then? Scripture calls us to encourage one another and build each other up. C. S. Lewis serves as a clear example.

Had it not been for C. S. Lewis, *The Lord of the Rings* by J.R.R. Tolkien might never have been completed. After the success of *The Hobbit,* Tolkien wrote the opening chapter to the trilogy. Then he stopped. Bogged down with details and overwhelmed with a busy academic and home life, he lost confidence in the project and stalled. His sour spot lasted seven years. The only one in his life who urged him on in the project was Lewis. Lewis served as encourager extraordinaire, convincing Tolkien his work was meant for a larger audience. Lewis relentlessly pursued his friend to the point Tolkien himself said, *"But for his [Lewis's] interest and unceasing eagerness for more I should never have brought **The L. of the R.** to a conclusion."*

Never underestimate the power of encouragement. Scripture says as the body of Christ we should be encouraging one another, building each other up. When we see a brother or sister ready to throw in the towel, we can help them complete their mission. Our support can help them get back to a sweet spot.

I have an inkling life would be much richer for all of us if we did.

October 21st

One thing I do know. I was blind but now I see!   —*John 9:25 NIV*

Society Pressure

Are you sometimes ashamed to be aligned with truth when those around you are trapped in the pressure of society's opinions? Reluctance to speak truth—especially truth that may jeopardize our social standing—has been around for centuries.

Jesus, the way, truth and life, stands in sharp contrast to the whims of societal pressure. In the ninth chapter of John, Jesus spits on the ground, stirs up a little mud, and puts it on a blind man's eyes. He then instructs the man to go wash it off.

When he does, this former beggar—for the first time in his whole life—can see.

This did not go over well with the religious authorities, to say the least. The healing took place on the Sabbath, which was neither religiously correct nor popular. The Pharisees refused to even believe the man had been blind since birth, so they hunted down his parents and began an inquisition. You might have thought the parents would be so thrilled over their son's miraculous healing nothing could have silenced their praise. But if so, you would be underestimating the chilling effect of societal pressure. They were afraid if they acknowledged Jesus as their son's healer they would be thrown out of the synagogue. So, they circumvented the truth. They admitted their son's healing took place but professed not to know how or by whom. Their brave words: "He is of age; ask him" (John 9:23).

But as for the man, no amount of society's pressure could stop him! "I was blind but now I see!" And the bolder he spoke the truth, the greater the revelation. He progressed from identifying his healer as the man they call Jesus to a prophet to one from God to worshiping Jesus as the Son of Man.

Friend, don't fold to pressure stemming from any segment of society, whether the culture at large, friends or even family. It's not worth your soul. Choose to align yourself with courageous believers in every century who care more about God's approval than man's. Align yourself with Jesus Christ. The One who opened your eyes.

October 22nd

He has made everything beautiful in its time. —*Ecclesiastes 3:11 NIV*

Backstory

I'm a firm believer beauty has a way of stimulating us toward a more generous thought life. It lifts us above the petty and connects us with Something bigger. I think that accounts for what happened to me in the checkout line.

We were at Acadia Nation al Park in Maine. The rugged pink granite summit of Cadillac Mountain displays God's extravagant handiwork to me as do few other places. After taking it all in, we stopped at the grocery store to pick up a few things. My husband was already in line when I joined him with a couple more items. It meant going ahead of the woman behind him. I realized immediately my action did not set well with her. She grumbled something under her breath. I could almost feel the darts piercing my back.

In situations like this I try to just brush off the negativity. Not this time. When our turn came to check out, I turned to this angry, disgruntled woman and insisted she go before us. She initially refused, but then she placed her two quarts of milk on the counter ahead of us and said, "I'm just in a lot of pain." It was then I noticed her leg brace. "I was struck by a drunk driver. My leg shattered in fifteen places, and I'm still recovering after numerous operations." As we empathized with her, she continued to tell us her story. We no longer saw her as an irritable customer accusing us of cutting in line, but as a hurting woman in need of grace. She had a backstory.

Everyone we meet has a backstory. A story that explains why they're grumpy or bossy or controlling. And although our past experiences never justify sin, taking the time to discover someone's backstory goes a long way in diffusing conflict and promoting peace.

You see, I had my own backstory that day. Being immersed in the splendor of Acadia had connected me with the backstory behind all beauty—with God, the God "who has made everything beautiful in its time." It prepared me to meet a bit of ugliness with a gracious spirit.

Beauty. A gift from its producer. Soak it in. Then extend something beautiful to those around you who might have a not-so-pretty backstory.

October 23rd

I know that there is nothing better for people than to be happy and to do good while they live.
—*Ecclesiastes 3:12 NIV*

Happier than a Bird with a French Fry

"Today I will be happier than a bird with a french fry." Maybe you've heard that slogan. My daughter has a print of it hanging in her house. Wouldn't it be nice if we could simply choose to be happy each day? What if we could bring that happiness into a very sad world? Do you know God intends for us to do just that?

Happy people are contagious people. Who isn't affected by a hearty belly laugh? Remember the laughing Chewbacca mask lady? The video of her uproarious laughter while wearing the Star Wars mask went viral on the internet. At last count, she had over 159 million views! Such responsiveness to someone enjoying a simple pleasure in life should tell us something about our natural quest for happiness.

God did not create us to be *les misérables.* He desires us to be happy, even when surrounded with suffering and pain. We can't make sorrow go away with plastic smiles and insensitive platitudes. But neither can we lessen it by setting up camp in deserts of despondency. Sadness and happiness are intricately interwoven in the human experience. We ought not be afraid of either.

My personality tends toward melancholy. The idea of being happy while others suffer stirs up my guilt machine. And while I consider sensitivity to the hurting a beautiful gift from God, sympathy on steroids helps no one. If we have nothing to practically relieve another's pain, sometimes the best medicine we can offer resides in a cheerful heart (Proverbs 17:22).

The writer of Ecclesiastes combined being happy with doing good. Now, isn't that interesting? Contrary to what some may think, happiness is not inconsistent with holiness. In fact, holiness produces the only happiness that lasts. Happiness pursued out of greed and selfishness evaporates as quickly as it arrives because it has no solid connection.

The world needs to see your smile. To watch you enjoy all the goodness of God. So, go ahead and laugh. Choose to be "happier than a bird with a french fry!"

October 24th

He [Abraham] lived in tents.... For he was looking forward to the city with foundations, whose architect and builder is God.
—Hebrews 11:9–10 NIV

Temporary Tents

Some of my sweetest memories surround camping vacations when our kids were young. I always felt a sense of freedom from perfection when we camped. What if the food got a little charred over the coals—we had a campfire! A little more dirt or sand than we were used to? A few more insects? Didn't matter. We didn't expect normalcy; we expected the unexpected. Things didn't have to be "just right" to be enjoyed. We knew our sacrifices of convenience were short-lived, so we pitched our temporary tents and made the most of the moment.

I think we would experience more happiness in life if we cultivated a "temporary tent" mindset. If we viewed our short span here on earth as a privilege to enjoy rather than a chore to get "right." If we modeled Abraham, who refused to get trapped into giving permanent status to impermanent things.

When his wife Sarah died, Abraham took her body to be buried in Canaan (Genesis 23). This meant he had to buy land from the Hittites. They exploited Abraham's grief (and wealth), charging him an exorbitant amount of money for the tract of land he wanted. But rather than bickering over the injustice, he simply paid their asking price. He didn't fear being momentarily taken advantage of because his eyes were set on something more lasting. He knew his destiny resided in the eternal God— *El Olam*—not the hands of men (Genesis 21:33–34).

How much unnecessary stress would we be spared if we walked in that kind of faith? We have the opportunity to place our fleeting moments of inconvenience and day-by-day encounters with imperfection in the broader perspective of eternity. If you're at all like me, you may find it a hard mindset to maintain. We must be reminded occasionally not to take life— or ourselves—too seriously. Remember not to let impermanent things swallow up the permanent.

So how about it? Ready to break out the sleeping bags and Coleman stove and set up a "temporary tent?" Figuratively speaking, of course!

October 25th

This expression, "Yet once more," denotes the removing of those things which can be shaken, as of created things, so that those things which cannot be shaken may remain. —Hebrews 12:27 NASB

Whole Lotta Shakin' Goin' On

The thought of a frog invasion makes my skin crawl. Can you imagine? You turn on the sink; out hops an army of frogs. You open your cupboard; more frogs. You pull back the sheets on your bed to the insidious croaking of *ribbet, ribbet, ribbet.* The slimy amphibians swarm over everything in sight. Ugh!

The Egyptians had already experienced one bloody plague. The waters of every lake, well and cistern had turned to blood. The life-giving streams of the Nile River became a cesspool of dead fish. It was only the beginning. Eight more plagues would follow in a miraculous display of the power and supremacy of the almighty God (Exodus 7–12). Clearly, Egypt was being shaken. And how did the Pharaoh of Egypt respond? He doubled down. Rather than repenting and relenting, he hardened his heart.

Fast-forward to present day. Would you agree there's a whole lotta' shakin' goin' on in our world today? Like a giant wrecking ball hovering in the distance, the shaking threatens to smash everything from political parties to countries to the church itself.

The question: How will we respond to the shaking? Will we be like Pharaoh and simply deny the truth? Will we cling to idols we've created to rescue us? Or will we hold fast to what cannot be shaken? Only things glued to the truth will remain standing (Hebrews 12:27).

Truth matters. Perhaps more than anything in times of shaking. And the truth is that nothing can shake God's faithfulness to us. The whole earth may shake, the foundations be destroyed, but the God of truth remains unshakeable. When it seems everything is falling apart, don't be plagued with hopelessness. God faithfully brought his people out of a chaotic Egypt. In fact, he used the chaos to secure their deliverance.

We don't have to be afraid of the looming wrecking ball. No matter how much shaking goes on, our God remains firm, steady, secure. Who knows? Maybe all this shaking will cause some unwanted sediment in our own lives to surface so we can get rid of it.

Now that would be a really good shaking!

October 26th

Yet I hold this against you: You have forsaken the love you had at first.
—Revelation 2:4 NIV

Labor of Love or Love of Labor?

They worked tirelessly without growing weary. They endured hardship after hardship for the sake of Christ. They persevered when others folded. They fearlessly exposed hypocrisy in the church, unswerving in their dedication to truth. What a résumé! The early church at Ephesus set an example for all of us who would be a part of the body of Christ in future years. Except for one little glitch.

They forgot why they were doing what they were doing. Their initial love for Jesus waned to the point they loved the work of being a Christian more than they loved Christ. Turns out it was more than a small glitch. The Lord warned them if they didn't repent they would lose their light.

Forgetting our first love is a slippery slope. It can happen in almost any area of life. It occurs in marriages when husbands and wives become so engrossed in the duties of family life, they no longer cultivate the love that first drew them together. The relationship begins a slow death but they hardly notice.

It happens in causes we fight for. We begin with a deep concern for victims of injustice, poverty or abuse. We work hard to see wrongs righted, but if we're not careful, the cause itself consumes our love. It happens to politicians, to missionaries on the mission field, to teachers, to social workers, to nurses. It happens whenever our motivation moves from being a labor of love to loving the labor.

Does any of this describe you? If so, the apostle John brings good news. You can get off that slippery slope. Repent! Then intentionally go back and do the things you used to do to reignite the flame. If your love for Jesus is fading, return to the Word that once breathed life into your faith. Pray with the simple intention of drawing near to him. Forgive those you've begrudged. Tear down the idols of your good works and lay them at the cross of grace.

Love your labor, yes—but love the One you labor for more.

October 27th

Take delight in the LORD, and he will give you the desires of your heart.
—Psalm 37:4 NIV

The Last Desire

"Won't he be surprised when I live to be ninety!" That was my eighty-eight-year old mother's reaction when the doctor who discharged her from the hospital suggested she get hospice care. Her congestive heart disease and pulmonary problems had sent her to the hospital three times over the past couple years. It didn't look like her desire to reach her ninetieth birthday would become a reality.

But two years later, on January 26, 2015, we partied hearty. Mom even received a citation from her state legislator for reaching such a milestone! Her desire in life had been realized. Or so she thought. My daughter discovered she was pregnant, and Mom embraced a new goal—live long enough to hold her first great grandchild.

My grandson was born September 8. Since my daughter and her husband live over seven hours away, they planned to come home for Thanksgiving. But as the weeks progressed, Mom's breathing became more and more labored. After two years of being hospital-free, we once again had to admit her. She was discharged a week later—this time under hospice.

As I cared for her at home, hopes she would make it to Thanksgiving grew dim. But we prayed fervently God would grant Mom this last desire of her heart. On Saturday evening, October 24, that desire was met when our daughter made it home and placed her firstborn in Mom's frail arms. Yet God's mercies didn't stop.

On Monday, my brother and his family hastily arranged to drive in from Ohio. More prayer they would make it in time. More rejoicing when they arrived. My son found a flight from Nashville that would get him in around midnight. More prayer. More rejoicing when he walked in the door and said, "Hi, Grandma." Mom conversed with each of us at the breakfast table the next morning. When she died later that afternoon, my brother and I were both at her side.

My mom was one of the most flexible people I've ever known. She learned how to be content no matter what life handed her. Her life—and death—exemplify Psalm 37. She delighted in the Lord, and he granted her the desires of her heart. Even the last one.

Quite a finale, Mom!

October 28th

When all the people saw this, they fell prostrate and cried, "The LORD—he is God! The LORD—he is God!"   *—1 Kings 18:39 NIV*

Big "G" or Little "g"?

If I were to ask if you believed in God with a capital "G" or god with a small "g" you would no doubt say God with a big "G." I would too. But sometimes I wonder if my life actually demonstrates some capitalization confusion.

A big "G" God can do anything. He's not confined by nature; he established nature. He breaks its rules whenever he wants. Little "g" gods are restricted. They must operate within the bounds of the natural. Their hope extends no further than man's best efforts.

One of the most vivid contrasts between the two occurs when Elijah challenges the prophets of Baal to a showdown (1 Kings 18). Both Elijah and the Baal-ists present sacrifices—Elijah to the Big "G" God; the prophets to Baal. All day long the prophets cry out to their little "g" god. They scream. They rave. They cut themselves. But receive no response. Elijah taunts them. "You'll have to shout louder than that," he scoffed, "to catch the attention of your god! Perhaps he is talking to someone, or is out sitting on the toilet!" (v. 27 from the colorful *Living Bible* paraphrase). Then Elijah's God sends a supernatural fire from heaven and reveals himself as the only true deity.

Nothing lies beyond possibility for the Big "G" God—even death (John 11). Lazarus had been in the grave four days. With untouched certainty he was dead. No little "g" gods could change that. But then God with a Big "G" enters the scene. The God who exists beyond time and space calls "Lazarus, come forth!" (v. 43 NASB). And he does.

When we face impossible situations, I wonder if we're more like those little "g" prophets than we realize. We get in a frenzy. We seek out every solution known to man. Our hopes for restored marriages, rebellious children, faltering health, lie buried in a grave marked Lazarus. We forget about a Big "G" God.

Ah, friend, let's not waste our time with little "g" gods. They will die. Believe with me in the eternal, sovereign, awesome capital "G" God.

October 29th

My sheep listen to my voice; I know them, and they follow me.
—John 10:27 NIV

The Voice

My voice. When I arrived at Lakeside for my annual time-away-to-write venture, my voice turned out to be the one thing

I was missing. All my futile attempts to speak resulted in no more than a pitiful squeak. Then when my three pens ran out of ink while writing in my journal, I thought, "Oh no, they have laryngitis too!" I was alone, so technically I didn't need my voice, and it was easy to secure another pen; but the situation made me aware of the universal need we have to express ourselves. Voice is a part of who we are as image-bearers of our Creator.

God's voice, Scripture tells us, brought the universe into existence. "And God said, 'Let there be light,' and there was light" (Genesis 1:3). His voice echoes with power and majesty. It strikes with lightening, shakes the desert and breaks the trees (Psalm 29). Hearing his voice keeps our hearts from hardening and helps us resist temptation (Psalm 95:7–8). It's tough to imagine a more formidable means of expression than the voice of God.

Yet every believer on earth is given access to hearing this voice. That's what Jesus says in John 10. How profound! You and I have the ability to hear, as Francis Schaeffer would say, "the God who is not silent." So how do we hear his voice?

Jesus says his sheep know his voice. So, the first prerequisite in hearing him, is knowing him. The better we know him, the more likely we are to hear his voice. We grow to know him most through Scripture. His Word speaking to us lays the foundation for hearing. Once we do hear, we'll find our sensitivity to his voice increasing every time we obey what he directs us to do. At least that's been the case in my life.

Today, above all else, no matter where you are or what you do, take time to listen for his voice. It may come directly through your thoughts or it may come through a friend or circumstance. Don't miss the opportunity to develop the ability of hearing the voice of the Lord. Make no mistake. He wants you to listen.

October 30th

No, in all these things we are more than conquerors through him who loved us.
—Romans 8:37 NIV

We are...Winning!

The roar of "We Are ... Penn State" boomed across the whole commonwealth. Our unranked football team was up against Ohio State, positioned as number 2 in the nation, but that only intensified the electric atmosphere. You would have thought the Super Bowl was at stake. One announcer remarked that the crowd at Beaver Stadium served not just as the "12th" man, but the 13th, 14th and 15th man. This means the fans make so much noise in support of their team, it's like having an extra player on the field.

Penn State's football program had been crippled by NCAA sanctions since 2012, and many thought they would never recover. Add to that a year of unprecedented injuries. It wasn't surprising to find them as 19-point underdogs. The Nittany Lions entered the fourth quarter behind, 21–7. Then a touchdown followed by a field goal put Penn State within striking distance to catch the lead. With a little over four minutes left in the game, Penn State blocked the Buckeyes' field goal attempt and Penn State scooped up the ball and sprinted 60 yards for the deciding touchdown. Penn State won, 24-21. In no time, it seemed all 107,280 fans covered the field in wild celebration. It was the happiest *Happy Valley* had been in a long time.

But I must admit, I couldn't get excited until the last minute of the game when we had final possession of the ball. I kept imagining somehow Ohio State would get the ball back and score. No one, even ardent supporters, thought PSU would beat Ohio State. But the team didn't get the memo. Throughout the whole game, they looked like a team who knew they were winners.

I see in this a spiritual parallel. Scripture says we who are in Christ "are more than conquerors." In trouble, hardship, persecution and famine, victory belongs to us. No matter what it looks like—even going into the fourth quarter—God purposes us to win. Our opponent, the devil, will try everything to convince us we don't have a chance. Don't listen to his false predictions! If you are a believer, be assured of this: *We are winning!*

October 31st

I felt compelled to write and urge you to contend for the faith that was once for all entrusted to God's holy people.   —Jude 1:3 NIV

Hey Jude

Contend for the faith.

Jude urged the early church to fight against every smidgen of apostasy. It was a time when attempts to pervert grace into sin-filled license appeared to be succeeding. It was a time when attacking the deity of Christ proved fashionable. It was a time when moral compromise masqueraded as something noble. And it was a time of division when believers were incited to follow their own natural instincts instead of the Holy Spirit.

The relevancy of Jude's message resonates with me. As I view the world, it reminds me I'm called to do more than wring my hands in worry or shrink into a corner of defeat. My job— and the job "entrusted to all God's holy people"—remains unshakeable, no matter how turbulent the times. Contend for the faith. So just how do we do that?

We can't contend for the faith if we allow problems to gut it. We can hardly contend for a faith if fear and disappointment has emaciated us. Jude encourages us to build ourselves up in our faith (v. 20). It's not a once-and-done occurrence. We daily buttress ourselves by relying on the Word of God to nourish us in the truth so we won't be deceived. And we keep "praying in the Holy Spirit" (v. 20). Let's face it. We need supernatural help to contend for the faith.

Jude also makes it clear contending for the faith includes keeping ourselves in God's love (v. 21). Without God's love we have no mercy. Mercy to those who doubt. Mercy to those about to fall. Mercy to those whose sins appall us (vv. 22–23).

If you haven't read the book of Jude recently, I'd encourage you to check it out. May it inspire you in troubled times to not stop contending for the faith. Who knows but that Jude might help you "take a sad song and make it better."

November 1st

So they gathered them and filled twelve baskets with the pieces of the five barley loaves left over by those who had eaten. —John 6:13 NIV

God's Economics: Two Plus Five Equals Thousands

Two fish and five loaves of bread feed five thousand people with food left over (John 6:1-13). An impoverished widow saves her sons from being sold into slavery with a small jar of olive oil (2 Kings 4:1-7). Mustard-seed size faith moves a mountain (Matthew 17:20). In God's economy, less is more when we give him the less.

Mother Theresa once remarked she was a little pencil in the hand of God, sending a love letter to the world. What an impact that little pencil made! When we offer all we have to God, he uses our gifts to enlarge us and multiply our effectiveness in a needy world. All it requires is willingness.

My brother works long hours to support his family. In the last few years, helping my sister-in-law care for her aging parents has required more from him than he ever thought he could give. But his willingness to let God use his *little* has produced a profound deepening in who God has called him to be. When our dad died a few years ago, we both were given the opportunity to care for him in his last days. As I watched my brother tenderly attend to Dad's needs, I asked him, "Where did you learn to do this?" He simply smiled. Far from restricting him, God's economy has expanded him and enabled him to move far past his two fish and five loaves.

When we give the Holy Spirit our meager offerings, he always gives back more. When we bolster our efforts with faith and gratitude, he produces in us an excess beyond our imagination. God wants all his children to experience the most we can in this life. His economy makes it a reality.

How about you? Are you experiencing God's economy or do you feel like you are running on empty? Don't hold on to things that already belong to him anyway. You will never regret giving him your loaves and fish. You may think it cannot amount to much. But in an economy where two plus five equals thousands, nothing is impossible!

November 2nd

Now when Jesus heard this, he withdrew from there in a boat to a desolate place by himself. But when the crowds heard it, they followed him on foot from the towns. When he went ashore he saw a great crowd, and he had compassion on them and healed their sick.

—Matthew 14:13–14 ESV

Savior Interrupted

Jesus had just heard the sordid story of John the Baptist's beheading. Herod's act was as unjust and revolting as it gets. The grief Jesus felt was real. He sought to be alone. But the crowd followed him, and his compassion for them interrupted his plans. Putting his grief on hold, he stopped to heal them, teach them and feed them before he found solitude for himself.

The Savior of the world embraced interruptions. A woman suffering from a twelve-year blood disease interrupted his pursuit of healing the synagogue ruler's daughter (Luke 8:40–48). Friends of a paralytic interrupted his teaching (Luke 5:18–19). Fear-driven disciples interrupted his sleep (Luke 8:24). A Samaritan woman interrupted his need for rest (John 4:1–24). Jesus never complained when compassion called for a change in his plans. Unlike me.

I'm not always so welcoming of interruptions. A day doesn't go by that I don't ask God to have his way in me, but then, if I'm not careful, I get so engrossed in my plan, I miss his. The other day I was asked to cover for someone's negligence. It irritated me. The diversion was not a part of my day's schedule. The task was not my responsibility. But God knew I needed to be pulled away from my manmade structure for a while. In the end, the interruption took far less time than I imagined. And I experienced something far more important than reaching my day's goals.

When I realize how many times I've interrupted Jesus, how many times his compassion has made room for my needs, it puts my little inconveniences in a clearer perspective. It makes me want to lay down my agenda and more readily pick up his—

in whatever shape, form or fashion those divine interruptions arrive.

I'm so thankful I have a Savior who doesn't mind being interrupted. How about you? Ready to have him interject something new in your day?

November 3rd

Jesus, full of the Holy Spirit, left the Jordan and was led by the Spirit into the wilderness, where for forty days he was tempted by the devil.
—Luke 4:1-2 NIV

The Root of Temptation

Temptation seems like such an easy thing to resist—until we are tempted. Whether it comes in the form of denying ourselves a cookie or refusing to taste morsels of gossip, the spectrum of enticements ranges wide and deep. In a culture that thrives on indulgence, we are bombarded on every side. How can Christians possibly resist?

Much of our temptation stems from some form of doubt. Each one of Jesus' encounters with the devil hinged on doubt. First, the devil tried to make him doubt himself. "If you are the Son of God ..." (Luke 4:3). He wanted Jesus to question what God had spoken to him only forty days earlier. Doubts as to who Jesus was would undercut his whole mission.

Second, the devil tried to get him to doubt the plan. He showed him all the kingdoms of the world and offered to give them to him if he would worship him instead of God (v. 5). In other words, bypass the cross, bypass suffering. Satan could take him to the same place as God, but in a much easier fashion.

The third temptation cast doubt on God's faithfulness. The devil even used Scripture to entice Jesus into "proving" God would rescue him if he threw himself off the temple (vv. 9–11). If Jesus had taken up the offer, it would have revealed doubts about God's character. Most people do not usually trust what they must test.

Any of these forms of temptation sound familiar to you? Has the devil ever caused you to doubt who you are as a child of God? Has he tempted you to doubt God's plan in your life, and deceived you into thinking your suffering is unnecessary? Has he tried to convince you if God does not act in a certain way, then he can't be for you?

I have met that crafty serpent in each of these areas on more than one occasion. The Word of God enabled Jesus to resist him, and the Word of God enables me. If believers hope to defeat doubt and not fall to temptation, let's wield his Word that proves to be, as it says in Hebrews 4:12, "sharper than any double-edged sword."

November 4th

Forget the former things; do not dwell on the past. See, I am doing a new thing! Now it springs up; do you not perceive it?"
—Isaiah 43:18–19 NIV

No Encore

There's no do-over in life, is there? Someone once said "encore" is a useless word when it comes to living. I must confess, I enjoy ruminating over the sweet spots in life. Everything from studying in Switzerland, to our children's weddings, to Christmases at Mom's and women's conferences. Reminiscing takes me to a different place. Sometimes I'd like to go back in time and live those experiences all over again. But I can't.

And even if I could, I doubt it would be fruitful. Isaiah warns us about dwelling too much on the past. If we are planted in the "former" things we might miss seeing the new things God wants to do. The Lord promised a new future for Israel, but if they remained stuck in the *what-was* they might miss the *what-could-be*.

One of my favorite spots is Acadia National Park in Maine where we often vacationed. After our kids left home, I couldn't imagine going to Acadia without them. *No way could it be as much fun!* But then, a couple of years ago, we decided to go back to Acadia, just my husband and me. We rummaged through the attic and found our old tent and camping gear, packed up, and guess what? We had a wonderful time! The memories of past trips enriched our visit, rather than detracting from it. God took us to an "old" place, but let us experience a "new thing." It happened because we weren't looking for an encore.

How about you? Do you ever get so entrenched in the good things of the past you miss both the present and the future? Do you realize you have opportunity every day to draw near to God and begin a new adventure? An adventure suited to now, not yesterday.

We ought always to be thankful for everything God has done in the past, but it ain't over yet. So, let's not waste our time longing for an encore. Who knows but that the best is yet to come.

November 5th

When the time drew near for Israel to die, he called for his son Joseph and said to him "...Do not bury me in Egypt, but when I rest with my fathers, carry me out of Egypt and bury me where they are buried."
—Genesis 47:29–30 NIV

I Love You the Most

"I love you the most." My mom finished almost all of her goodbyes and goodnights with those words. Whenever we said, "I love you," she always responded with that signature phrase of her affection. She enjoyed having the last word. And we enjoyed hearing it. The last word—little did I know.

Mom lived with us for the last twelve years of her life. At seventy-eight years old, she moved from southern Ohio to become a Pennsylvanian. She adapted amazingly well, but as the saying goes, "You can take the girl out of Ohio, but you can't take Ohio out of the girl." When she died, it seemed fitting to take her ashes back home to Ohio for burial. My desire to bring her full circle made me think of Jacob's story in Genesis 47:28-31.

Before Jacob died, he had one request of his son. He asked Joseph to swear he would not bury him in Egypt. He wanted his bones to be carried home, back to the land where his fathers were buried. His request reflected more than a desire to come full circle; it indicated his deep faith that God's promise to him would be fulfilled. One day the now fledgling nation would return and carry out their unique purpose in God's plan.

As we approached Mom's gravesite, I carefully laid flowers on the grave before we prayed, read Scripture and sang a hymn. But I was drawn to the back of the headstone directly in front of Mom's grave. I could hardly believe my eyes. There, etched clearly were the words, *"I love you the most."*

Like Jacob, Mom's burial brought her full circle. And like Jacob, those simple words let me know God's purpose for her life had been completed as well. Her legacy of loving others more than herself lives on. God had a unique plan for Israel and for Mom, for nations and for individuals. For you. For me. May we let him complete it.

November 6th

Moreover, the LORD your God will send the hornet among them until even the survivors who hide from you have perished.
—Deuteronomy 7:20 NIV

The Hornets Are Coming!

Hornets. They sting. No one likes them. Most people try to avoid them. Hornet hunting is not a favorite pastime of anyone. Yet, here we find these wicked wasps in the book of Deuteronomy as instruments used by God to *help* Israel.

God promised Israel he would deliver them from all the enemies they encountered in the Promised Land. The seven nations inhabiting the land, although "larger and stronger," did not stand a chance because God would give his people the ability to drive them out, destroy their gods, and wipe their names off the face of the earth (Deuteronomy 7:22–25). Is anyone talking about the Hittites, Girgashites or Amorites today? For those who tried to escape Israel's wrath by hiding—

God would send hornets to surface them from every cleft and cave in Canaan. Once exposed, Israel could take them down. God kept his promise.

But I am thinking of other kinds of enemies, other kinds of hornets. The psalmist said, "Forgive my hidden faults" (Psalm 19:12). We are human, fallen people. Christians are redeemed, human, fallen people. Weaknesses, faults and sins lay buried sometimes so far below the surface we don't even detect them. Yet, they have a profound effect on keeping us from walking in the full victory of the Lord. Hidden enemies like prideful-ites, selfish-ites, begrudging-ites, jealous-ites, must be rooted out before they can be destroyed. So sometimes God sends in the hornets.

I am sure you have met them. You're feeling pretty good about yourself, then someone treats you disrespectfully. It stings as painfully as those hornets in the Judean desert. But what surfaces in our reaction can be even more painful. Self-righteousness? Anger? Condemnation of the contempt with our own cache of the very same thing? We can either welcome the hornets for exposing our hidden enemies or wallow in the pain.

Make no mistake. We need help to root out the enemies of our souls. Do not be surprised when God sends hornets in the form of husbands, wives, sons, daughters or friends as well as the person who cuts in front of us in the passing lane.

When those hornets come, don't try to squish them. They may just make it possible for you to enter the Promised Land.

November 7th

What great love the Father has lavished on us, that we should be called children of God! —1 John 3:1 NIV

Thine Indeed

I have been a high school cheerleader and a Colorado flower child. I have been a stay-at-home mom and a low-key professional, a born-again Christian as well as the worst of sinners. Our roles and self-assessments can vary from year-to-year and sometimes from day-to-day. Maybe, like me, you have at times found yourself wondering if the "real you" would please stand up.

The sense of identity and security we long for is discovered not in what we do but in whose we are. It begins with the deep-down awareness that we are, as it says in 1 John, God's child. We belong. We fit in the universe because the universe belongs to him. We are his in our victories, but no less his in our failures. We are his when everyone loves us and his when they reject us. His, for richer, for poorer, for better, for worse. His in sickness. His in health. He has made a place for us in this life as well as the next. "If it were not so, I would have told you" (John 14:2 NASB).

John describes God's lavish love for us. Lavish love is pouring, heaping, showering, smothering love. Our Father's extravagant love assures us we are not now who we will be, but as we let ourselves be soaked in this great love, our true identity will surface. When we see him, we're going to be like him (1 John 3:2).

Dietrich Bonhoeffer describes his struggle with identity in his poem, "Who Am I?" written while he was in prison awaiting execution for opposing the Nazi regime. It has inspired me numerous times when questions of my own identity have troubled my thoughts. He concludes with these lines:

> "Who am I? They mock me, these lonely questions of mine. Whoever I am, Thou knowest, O God, I am thine!"

Thine indeed! May you never forget the source of your true identity. You are a child of God.

November 8th

For out of the abundance of the heart his mouth speaks.
—Luke 6:45 ESV

Turn Up the Volume

"Turn up the volume ... live your faith out loud!" These were the words spoken by the conference speaker as he challenged the audience to bring God into our conversations.

Scripture says our words reflect our hearts. Whatever lives within us will eventually spill out of our mouths. So, if we hope to turn up the volume and live our faith out loud, it begins with examining our heart's content. Hearts that do not dwell on the goodness of God have mouths with little to say. We speak with as much resonance as a "resounding gong or clanging symbol" (1 Corinthians 13:1). The first step in turning up the volume lies in increasing our intimacy with the Lord.

Recently, the ladies in my small group conducted an experiment. For one week, we decided to "turn up the volume" on gratitude. We decided to be more intentional in giving thanks to God. Not just in our prayer times or before meals, but we would say thank you to him before everything we did as much as we could. It made a difference in each of us. I found it's hard to focus on the things that do not go right while preoccupied with thanking God for the things that go well. Turning up the volume of gratitude not only deepened our intimacy with him, but filled us up. We wanted to talk about him in the overflow.

It also takes courage. If we have been reluctant to turn up the volume in the past, we are not alone. The apostle Paul asked the Ephesian church to pray he would speak fearlessly about the gospel as he should (Ephesians 6:20). Although his heart overflowed with God, he still asked for courage to turn up the volume. He knew he should be bold, but he also knew he needed God's help. If Paul asked for prayer to speak more courageously, maybe we should too.

I've been trying to live my faith out loud since attending the conference. I've been filling my heart with thoughts of God's goodness. And I've been asking him to give me courage to talk about it.

How about you? Are you ready to turn up the volume?

November 9th

And they exceeded our expectations: They gave themselves first of all to the Lord, and then by the will of God also to us. —2 Corinthians 8:5 NIV

A Glut of Generosity

"Your bill has been taken care of," the waitress said. My husband and I were having breakfast with another couple when we heard those unexpected words. Although surprised, we immediately knew the responsible party. We had noticed a mutual acquaintance when we first arrived at the restaurant. We exchanged our hellos, and he left soon after. I didn't think much about it until we asked the waitress for our check. The man who picked up our tab left without any indication of his generous deed. But his simple gesture stopped me in my tracks. It felt like a glut of generosity had just landed on me.

His kindness made me want to emulate his big heart. Something, I must admit, I'm a little clumsy at. Like the time I tried to pick up the tab of some servicemen at a restaurant, only to discover they had already paid their bill. Going beyond what is expected can feel awkward at times. Even something as small as helping someone load groceries in the parking lot or letting a harried mom cut in line can make us feel uncomfortable. But a willingness to get out of our comfort zone is the first step.

The Corinthian church was certainly no stranger to "glut generosity." Although they lived in extreme poverty under great pressure, Paul commended them for exceeding every expectation of giving. What was their secret? "They gave themselves first to the Lord." Then they gave to others as God directed them. Not to get anything in return. Not to be looked upon as the world's greatest philanthropists. They gave in response to what they first received even "beyond their ability" (v. 3).

Unpretentious generosity demonstrates outrageous love. Whether manifest in resources, time or talents, giving of ourselves reveals the heart of a generous Father God.

Many things remain out of my reach. But living a life of generosity isn't one of them. How about you? How about if we commit ourselves to flooding the world with glimpses of what a generous God looks like. It may seem awkward at first, but I have a feeling all it takes is a little bit of practice.

November 10th

Lord, Son of David, have mercy on us!"   —*Matthew 20:31 NIV*

The Expectation Society

Our lives are packed with expectations. Daniel Boorstin's book *The Image* describes it well: "We expect anything and everything. We expect the contradictory and impossible. We expect compact cars which are spacious; luxury cars which are economical. We expect to be rich and charitable, powerful and merciful, active and reflective, kind and competitive." When expectations aren't met, even the contradictory ones, we can fall anywhere between disappointment and downright depression.

All too often I find expectations getting me into trouble. I image something happening in a specific way and when it doesn't, I look for someone to blame. It can make me wish I didn't have expectations in the first place. But in giving up all expectations, I also relinquish hope.

The biblical perspective of dealing with expectations points us to the heart of the issue: where we base our expectations. In Matthew 20:1–16 Jesus relates the parable of the workers. Those who worked longer in the vineyard expected to be paid more than those who had worked fewer hours even though they were given exactly what they had agreed to. Further in the chapter (vv. 20–28) the mother of James and John approaches Jesus. She, too, is expecting more. She asks that her sons be elevated above the other disciples. Both situations bring mild rebuke from Jesus.

But there is a third story in the chapter (vv. 29–34) that goes beyond expectation. Two blind men cry out to Jesus. They ask for mercy to receive their sight. Mercy means "undeserved." These men knew they had no right to expect anything. Unlike the previous situations, where expectations were based on merit, the blind men's request was based solely on the compassion of the "Lord, Son of David." And they received.

So, don't let expectations trap you. We're allowed to have them, but if we want to avoid a life of constant dissatisfaction, let's make sure we base them on the right foundation: we deserve nothing. From God or from man.

November 11th

As has just been said: "Today, if you hear his voice, do not harden your hearts as you did in the rebellion."
—*Hebrews 3:15 NIV*

Purple Heart Christians

How many of you have been wounded by unmet expectations? Hit by a mischaracterization of who you are? Have you ever had a relationship explode in front of you?

Everyone needs encouragement, but wounded Christians need a special infusing of courage to remain loyal to their Commander-in-Chief. When the shrapnel of rejection, betrayal or disappointment hits, we can choose how we will respond. Will we let the wounds calcify our hearts, or will we allow the suffering to propel us on to moral excellence?

Those who receive Purple Hearts in the military are soldiers who have been killed or wounded in battle. Most who receive this Medal of Honor exhibit the same mindset as my father-in-law, when given the Purple Heart in WWII: "I was just doing my duty." They do not particularly view themselves as heroes. They know the risks involved in war and accept them. It goes with the territory. They are strangers to bitterness and self-pity.

And so it is in our spiritual battles. The psalmist cautions us about not hardening our hearts like Israel did. When the shrapnel of disappointment and discouragement hit them, they chose to rebel rather than listen to the Lord's voice. In their bitterness, they complained against God and with each grievance their hearts grew harder. They refused to carry out their duty of trusting God in the wilderness.

God intends the wounds we receive in life to not harden us but "purple" us as we listen to his voice and simply "do our duty" during battle. If we have not been wounded in one way or another we have probably spent most of our time in the barracks or on KP. If we are truly engaging, we will get hit at some point or another, many times. When this happens, remember that no damage is permanent. If we steadily listen to his voice, we will keep our hearts soft. We'll become Purple Heart Christians.

November 12th

Set your minds on things above, not on earthly things.

—Colossians 3:2 NIV

Live Your Story

The results of a study conducted on senior citizens captured my attention. When asked whether there was anything they would change if given the opportunity to live their lives over again, three answers dominated the responses: they would be more reflective, they would take more risks, and they would focus less on the impermanent.

These seniors fell to what Donald Miller describes as the lure of the easy life. It stole their stories. But God intends to use our stories to transform the world. Our part begins when we allow him to edit, revise, expand and complete the manuscripts of our lives. It can be grueling at times, painful, costly. We will most certainly encounter a great deal of uncertainty. But isn't that true of all stories worth reading? You will never find themes of comfortable predictability on the *New York Times* bestseller list.

Scripture warns that if we hope to live a meaningful life, we must set our minds on things above the earth. Since our life is "hidden in Christ," it's in Christ where we find our story. We set our eyes on him and discover there's no longer room for our earthly nature (Colossians 3:5).

Once we meet the Author of the real story of our lives, we can never again find satisfaction in just living for ourselves, focusing on the temporary things in life. We discover a sense of meaning derived from realizing we are a part of a tale that is bigger, a tale more fulfilling, a tale eternal. The dots connect. The grains run deeper. Our clear purpose emerges. So, do not be like those senior citizens in the study. Don't get to the end of your life and wish you had reflected more, risked more and tried harder to resist the momentary.

The world needs your story. Embrace the Author's call. Let him help you complete those sentences and add those exclamation points!

November 13th

Now faith is the substance of things hoped for.   *—Hebrews 11:6 KJV*

More Than a Feeling

One of the biggest misconceptions about faith assumes it is a feeling—a flood of positive mental energy we must drum up. If we "drum it up" enough, we'll get what we ask for, but if we don't, we won't. Obviously, this is not a scriptural perspective.

A truer notion of faith became clear to me as I was returning home to Lancaster, Pennsylvania, after visiting my daughter when she lived in Fairfax, Virginia. I planned to ride the metro from where she lived to Union Station in D.C. and then take an Amtrak train home. My ticket was reserved for 5:30 p.m., so we left in plenty of time for me to catch the train. But something happened on the way to D.C.

The metro stopped. I mean a total halt. All you could see out the window was a mass of concrete block, immoveable concrete block. I kept looking at my watch. As the time ticked away, it became clear I was going to have a hard time making my connection. I did the only thing I could do at the time. I prayed.

Finally, the metro started moving. It was 5:30 p.m. My mind told me it was now impossible to make the train. But undaunted, as soon as the metro pulled in, I dashed off, running as fast as possible through the crowd, all the while searching for Amtrak signs. After finally making it to the ticket counter, I hastily got through the line and was directed where to go. I was still running full bore when I reached the train. The door had already closed, but the conductor—somewhat miraculously—motioned me on. In a second we were off.

What caused me to run like a madman even though I felt all hope was gone? Had I relied on my feelings, I would have given up. Something deeper than emotion was activated when I prayed. That something was faith. The kind of faith described in Hebrews 11. It proved to be the substance of what I was hoping for. Beyond my sight, beyond my understanding, beyond my feelings.

Are you relying more on feelings than faith to get you through? I can't think of a better time than now to switch trains.

November 14th

What should we do then?   —*Luke 3:10 NIV*

One Small Act

Never underestimate the significance of small acts of obedience. One response to God's voice triggers a chain reaction that can change the world.

In preparing the people for the coming Messiah, John the Baptist exhorted the crowd to repent and produce fruit in keeping with their repentance. They questioned him, "What should we do then?" He directed them to start with small acts. If you have an extra coat or food, share it with someone in need. If you've been cheating on your job, stop. Their small decisions to do what was right would make them ready for the "one who would baptize with the Holy Spirit and fire" (Luke 3:16).

When Jesus told Peter to take his fishing boat back into the deep waters and cast his nets again, the soon-to-be disciple was not filled with inspiration. He'd been fishing all night and caught nothing. Common sense would say it's a waste of time to go back, a fool's errand. Yet, despite his exhaustion and skepticism, Peter responded to Jesus with these words, "because you say so, I will let down the nets" (Luke 5:5). He did what Jesus told him to do, and the astonishing catch of fish that resulted changed his life forever. It began with that one small act of obedience.

I remember the first time the Lord asked us to open our home up to someone. A friend of my mother-in-law was seeking temporary refuge from her abusive husband. We had no idea at the time our yes would be the beginning of many others who would come to live with us as they sought a deeper walk with the Lord. It changed the course of our lives.

When I was first asked to teach a writing and speech class to homeschool students, I resisted. What did I possibly have to offer? Evidently, more than I realized, as the Lord used that small beginning to extend my teaching to college students and beyond.

How about you? Have you been asking the Lord, "What should I do?" Don't be surprised if he directs you in something small. You might not understand it or even desire it, but I pray you will respond as Peter did, "because you say so, I will." It might be the start of something big!

November 15th

Peter answered him, "We have left everything to follow you! What then will there be for us?"
—Matthew 19:27 NIV

What Do You Have to Lose?

I was engrossed in morning devotions when I looked outside the window at our farm and spotted a deer a few yards away. This was far from an everyday occurrence. I knew my husband would be thrilled, so I ran to the bottom of the steps and yelled up, "You've got to see this. There's a deer in the backyard!"

He hurried down, mesmerized, as he stood staring at the buck. It was hunting season, but his archery equipment was in the barn, about 30 yards from the house. He assumed if he moved toward the barn, he would spook the deer. So, he just kept watching ... and watching ... and watching. The deer hadn't moved for about 15 minutes. Finally, I said, "Why don't you at least try to sneak down to the barn? What do you have to lose?"

Turns out, those words were all he needed. He managed to make it to the barn without the deer noticing him. He secured his bow and arrow, and shot. Before I knew it, the buck was strapped to the jeep and my husband was headed to the butcher. It almost didn't happen. He could have literally watched his opportunity slip away. But he decided to take a risk. What did he have to lose?

Many of us are quick to assess certain situations as "impossible." We calculate the risk, and dare not go beyond our limited perspective. I'm not advocating recklessness, but I can't help but wonder if we too often box ourselves into a world bordered with unwarranted caution.

When Jesus warned his disciples about the difficulty the wealthy encounter in entering the kingdom, they expressed astonishment. They failed to understand with God "difficulty" is not synonymous with "impossible." When Peter questioned what would happen to them, Jesus assured them that leaving everything to follow him would prove well worth the risk. What did they have to lose?

How about you? Are there opportunities you're watching float by? In the words of Theodore Roosevelt, don't be afraid to "dare greatly." Don't be afraid to trust our impossible God. What do you have to lose?

November 16th

Love never fails.   —*1 Corinthians 13:8 NIV*

Sidebar Christianity

Author Bob Goff says the way we love people we don't agree with is the best evidence for an empty tomb. The love of Jesus should be the headline for all believers.

But I'm afraid love is being pushed to the sidelines. Division is running rampant in our country, shredding everything in its wake. The presidential election of 2016 drove people to different sides and positions, unearthing divisiveness with a force. I'm all for having strong opinions. Demonstrating the courage to stand up for what one believes elicits my admiration. Paul even says disputes in the church are needed to discover the truth (1 Corinthians 11:19). But when, as believers, we allow ourselves to identify more with our positions than we do with the love of Christ, we've succumbed to what I call "sidebar Christianity."

You're familiar with sidebars. In newspapers, websites and magazines, they're the little boxes that appear alongside the main article. They add supplemental information to the headline to increase interest. They were never intended to be more than complementary.

Sometimes I can let my Christianity become like one of those sidebars. It happens when I allow my opinions overshadow the main thing. The eternal thing. The beautiful thing. The right or wrong of an issue consumes not only my thinking, but my heart. I begin to harden toward those with a differing position. If I'm not careful, my dislike becomes stronger than my love for God. This should not be. When we can't love the people we disagree with, we let the headline be stolen.

Paul never let his love for Jesus be reduced to a sidebar. Whether addressing people within the church or opponents who tried to kill him, he never let differences stop Jesus' love from being the headline of his life. His first letter to the Corinthians shows us what that love looks like. It's kind, patient, humble, forgiving, hopeful, trusting, persevering (chapter 13). It infused every aspect of his life. And it ought to in ours.

I don't know if your love and faith are becoming sidebars, if secondary issues are crowding them out. Ah, don't let that happen. Immerse yourself again in Jesus' love. Don't let anyone or anything steal your headline.

November 17ᵗʰ

Now instead, you ought to forgive and comfort him, so that he will not be overwhelmed by excessive sorrow. —2 Corinthians 2:7 NIV

"All We Are Saying Is..."

"All we are saying ... is give peace a chance...." The song from the musical *Hair* has been running through my mind. Not because I'm feeling nostalgic for the 60s. I'm thinking about it in a slightly different context: people who dismiss God because they think they know about Christianity—or think they've tried—and found it wanting. They've been there, done that, or so they believe. As a result, they close themselves to any possibility their experience could be faulty. To them, I am saying, *Give God a chance.*

I have some young friends who fit that category. "Although they knew God, they neither glorified him as God nor gave thanks to him, but their thinking became futile and their foolish hearts were darkened" (Romans 1:21). They did not thank God because they didn't recognize what he was doing in their lives.

So, their picture of him became incomplete and distorted. They gravitated to sin and self-indulgence to replace the God they rejected. The process of knowing God—really knowing him—became tragically interrupted.

How do we respond to those who are struggling with their faith? How can we shine light into darkened hearts? Christianity is about more than crime and punishment, sin and consequences. It goes further. It holds hope for repentance and with repentance comes forgiveness. Paul encouraged the church to be gentle with fellow believers caught in sin. He exhorted them to confront the sin—that's the mark of true love—but after the brother or sister repents, the church ought to offer comfort, forgiveness and reaffirmation. To the church, Paul was saying, *Give grace a chance.*

I believe when we let ourselves be permeated with the grace of God, we position ourselves to pierce the darkness of an injured heart. There is no conceivable situation the grace of God cannot cover. If you, like me, are grieving over loved ones who are drifting from the truth, take heart. Let God's love and grace fill you with renewed hope as you pray they would hear what we are saying, and *Give God a chance.*

November 18th

"Now then," said Joshua, "throw away the foreign gods that are among you and yield your hearts to the Lord, the God of Israel."
—Joshua 24:23 NIV

Beware of Trojan Horses

Do you detect any Trojan horses in your life? They are subtle, sneaky and sly.

I'll never forget the graduate psychology course I took years ago at a local university. When I shared about my journey in life, the professor could not understand why I credited God with bringing me through the challenges I'd faced. The idea of not attributing my accomplishments (victories) to myself was to him a foreign concept. His worldview left no room for dependence on a deity.

Sometimes I forget how differently Christians think from the rest of the world. And because of this, we let down our guard on how much we allow the world to influence us. The world, including my professor, says it's good to boast in our accomplishments. But boasting in ourselves negates the Scripture which admonishes our "boast should be in the Lord" (2 Corinthians 10:17).

Joshua knew the lure of compromise would be an ongoing threat to Israel. Before his death, he warned the fledgling nation to remember the Lord as the source of their many victories. Not him. Not their own strategy (Joshua 23–24). In fact, he built no less than seven memorials to remind future generations of God's power and love for his people. Joshua cautioned them about the choice looming ahead of them. They could shift their allegiance to the gods of the nations they were demolishing. Or they could remain faithful to the God who called them. You would think the choice was a no-brainer. But history reveals they fell again and again to the stealth influence of their surroundings.

Let's be on guard. The voices from an unbelieving world will try to lure us into compromise. *Be like us! Fit in! Worship our gods!* Let's not listen to them. Let's not allow the influence of the world to invade our souls like a Trojan horse. Let's fight the temptation by intentionally remembering the Lord's love and faithfulness to us and never stop giving him the glory! He's the only One who deserves it.

November 19th

And behold, I am with you always, to the end of the age.
—*Matthew 28:20* ESV

How Do You Spell " Oblivious"?

Oblivious: B-e-c-k-y T-o-e-w-s. That's how I wound up spelling the word.

When we picked our son and his girlfriend up at the airport for Thanksgiving, the first thing I looked for was a ring on her left hand. My husband and I both suspected he would announce their engagement. But no ring.

The night after Thanksgiving the whole family went out for dinner. Josiah told us he and Lauren were going for a hike and would meet the rest of us at the restaurant. When we all finally arrived, I noticed how unusually animated they both were. They couldn't stop smiling. I took a picture of everyone at the table, not giving a second thought as to how Lauren held her left hand predominately to the camera. Nor did I take notice when she helped me pour water with her left hand. She sat next to me throughout the whole meal, but I was oblivious until the end. When I at last noticed the beautiful rose gold ring on her left hand, I looked at my son. He nodded and we all broke into cheers and laughter.

So how could I be so oblivious? Because the announcement didn't take place when I thought it would, I assumed it wasn't going to happen. Evidently, I locked into that mindset. So much so that I missed the obvious.

I do the same thing with God at times. I develop a mindset that blocks me from seeing him. I limit my perception to what I view with natural eyes, and I miss his presence. Yet, the last promise Jesus made before he ascended to heaven was that he would always be with us, even to the end of the age. He didn't want us to think because we couldn't perceive him, he had left us alone. There is never a time when his presence is not near—whether we catch it or not.

Do you ever limit the presence of God to preconceived ideas? Look for him in all your circumstances. Don't let your name spell o-b-l-i-v-i-o-u-s.

November 20th

You need to persevere so that when you have done the will of God, you will receive what he has promised. —Hebrews 10:36 NIV

What About Those Pilgrims?

What comes to mind when you hear the word Pilgrim? You probably think immediately of Thanksgiving. How about pioneers? Maybe religious fuddy-duddies? Overcomers? Whatever comes to mind, one word stands out—if the Pilgrims were anything, they were perseverers. They possessed a perseverance rare in today's culture.

They joined together in sixteenth century England when people could be burned at the stake for possessing a Bible. Forced underground for fear of being condemned for treason, they planned to escape England to freely pursue their faith. By the time the Mayflower set sail in 1620, the Pilgrims had encountered one slammed door after another. Their first attempt at escape resulted in getting caught and thrown into prison. The second attempt took them to Holland where they spent twelve years in abject poverty. When they finally boarded for America, one of their vessels sprung a leak. Some of them were forced to abandon their dream while the remaining 102 passengers crammed into the Mayflower.

Conditions on the voyage were deplorable. But the situation when they landed in Plymouth was not much better. Within three months, the harsh winter would take almost half of these brave folks. Yet, when given the opportunity to go back to England on the returning ship, not one Pilgrim said yes. What about those Pilgrims?

What made them so brave and uncompromising? They believed they had a call from God. They took seriously the admonition from Hebrews that persevering in the will of God would eventually be rewarded. When circumstances turned for the worse, time and time again, they didn't throw in the towel and consider their hardships as a sign from him to turn back.

Perhaps this Thanksgiving we would be wise to remember our forefathers, the Pilgrims. To be grateful for all the sacrifices they made to establish a country where freedom to worship God would be at its very core. To be inspired by their unconquerable persevering spirit. And imitate it!

November 21st

Enter his gates with thanksgiving and his courts with praise; give thanks to him and praise his name. —Psalm 100:4 NIV

The Grateful Instead

Thank goodness! Thank my lucky stars! Thank heaven! Expressions we often hear from those who experience something good in their lives. We humans are designed to give thanks. Gratitude surges as an instinctive response when all goes well—even if directed to an impersonal source. This compulsion to thank something for our good fortune should lead us to the conclusion that there is, indeed, Someone to thank.

Connecting our impulse of gratefulness to that Someone increases our sense of satisfaction exponentially. It unlocks the gate to God's presence and draws us inside. We're no longer waifs with our noses pressed against the window. No wonder the psalmist encourages us to enter his gates with thanksgiving. There is no other way. The greater our awareness that God is the source of "every good and perfect gift" (James 1:17) the fuller our joy.

So, gratitude to God makes good things better. But it also makes sad things, well, good.

Nothing combats the isolation of depression more than gratitude. Thankfulness peels back the distortion we have nothing for which to be grateful, even in the worst of circumstances. Job understood this. When he was stripped of everything, he humbly declared, "Naked I came from my mother's womb, and naked I will depart. The LORD gave and the LORD has taken away; may the name of the Lord be praised" (Job 1:21). Maintaining an attitude of gratitude throughout his ordeal released the strength Job needed to persevere to the other side. It will do the same for us.

I've read the 60s rock group, *The Grateful Dead,* acquired their name via a random opening of the dictionary. I would like to propose something more intentional. What if we who love God would be known as *The Grateful Instead?* Grateful instead of whining. Grateful instead of complaining. Grateful instead of self-pitying. Grateful instead of self-congratulating.

We are created to be thankers. Every day. In every situation we face, we can choose the greatness of gratitude. We can decide to be grateful instead!

November 22ⁿᵈ

My Father will love them, and we will come to them and make our home with them. —John 14:23 NIV

Thanksgiving at L'Abri

One of my fondest memories of Thanksgiving occurred while I was living, ironically, in another country when my husband and I were students at L'Abri. Nestled in the tiny Swiss village of Huemoz, we gathered in our chalet with fellow Americans to give thanks. We were in a foreign land where Pilgrims and Indians and Plymouth Rock seemed light years away, but gratitude's seamless nature transported us beyond borders.

The day after Thanksgiving remains indelible. My husband and I, along with three fellow students, pooled our money together, rented a car, and became tourists. We visited a cheese factory, gawked at the lavish countryside, and learned how cow bells were manufactured. That evening we dined at Le Fox, a quaint Swiss café whose specialty was raclette, a type of cheese melted over boiled potatoes. As the snow fell quietly outside, the warmth of friendship and the delight of a new adventure forged into something unforgettable—a Thanksgiving memory that has become a family tradition for us. Every year on Thanksgiving Eve we gather around our very own Swiss raclette machine and enjoy the moment.

I am thankful for the tradition our Thanksgiving at L'Abri spawned over thirty years ago. I am thankful for the beauty, the friendships, the excitement during that season of our lives. But that's not all. That year—the year when we were so far from all things familiar—I became aware of a profound truth. For the first time in my life I realized no matter where we were, God was with us. We may have been strangers in a foreign land, but I discovered home was anywhere he was. It's just as Jesus promised when he said he and his Father would make their home inside all who believe.

How about you? Are you distant from loved ones this holiday? Or is discontentment separating you from gratitude? Don't let it. Whatever your circumstances might be, as you release a spirit of thankfulness, God will lead you to himself ... to home.

November 23rd

For although they knew God, they did not honor him as God or give thanks to him, but they became futile in their thinking, and their foolish hearts were darkened. —Romans 1:21 ESV

Killing Gratitude

It's supposed to be a season of Thanksgiving, but evidence we live in a fallen world surrounds us. The shadow of the fall touches us through another's insensitivity and mocks us when we try to live righteously. It screams through nightly news broadcasts and social media posts. So how can we give thanks when we're engulfed with so much trouble? How do we keep from killing gratitude?

Gratitude comprises an indispensable part of life. When we fail to give God thanks, more dies than gratitude. Thank*less*ness plunges us into a sea of decadence. It eventually kills sound thinking, morality, love and virtually everything that makes life worth living. That's what Scripture says (Romans 1:21–31). On the other hand, thank*ful*ness protects us from deception and helps us stay upright when the waves of disappointment and uncertainty threaten to throw us overboard. You would think by now we would know that, wouldn't you?

Jesus maintained gratitude even when he knew a disruption of seismic proportions would be occurring within the next twenty-four hours. Fully aware he was about to be betrayed, deserted and crucified, he didn't let the approaching darkness distract him. In the intimacy and quietness of that upper room

Jesus took the bread, then the cup and he "gave thanks" (Mark 14:22–23).

Jesus allowed no second-guessing of the plan. Second-guessing always stirs discontentment and kills gratitude. Jesus knew his Father. He trusted him to fulfill his purpose and refused to dishonor him by withholding his thanks, even when life took an unpleasant turn.

As followers of Jesus, let's honor God and never stop giving him thanks. Even when trouble knocks on the door, let's seek to remain thankful for a God who has a plan for our good. This Thanksgiving, maybe more than ever before, may you be intentional about giving thanks. Don't bury it under a rubble of complaint and worry. Don't let anything kill your gratitude.

November 24th

Give thanks to the Lord, for he is good. His love endures forever.
—Psalm 136:1 NIV

Thanks, Thanks, and More Thanks

Gratitude—it's simple but profound in its power. It rouses generosity. It expresses faith. It initiates a chain reaction that could end in a miracle. And it plain down makes everyone feel good.

How do you react when someone shows appreciation for a gift or an act of kindness? Doesn't it usually make you want to give more? Or someone thanks you for your prayers. Don't you feel like getting right back on your knees? The genuine expression of gratitude moves us. It makes us want to keep giving.

When Jesus healed the ten lepers, only one returned to thank him (Luke 17:11–19). The lack of gratitude in the other nine seems to have surprised Jesus. It contrasted sharply with the humble praise of this one grateful man—a foreigner no less. Not only was the leper cleansed, the faith he displayed in his thankfulness resulted in his salvation. A miracle occurred in the healing of diseased skin, but more importantly, in the healing of a diseased soul.

I always begin my day with thanksgiving. Gratitude is like a key that opens me up to the presence of God. I guess I take Psalm 100:4 quite literally: "Enter his gates with thanksgiving and his courts with praise." Any of you familiar with the children's book, *Goodnight Moon* may think like I do ... that it is the specificity of the *room*, the *moon* and the *red balloon* that makes it so delightful. *Goodnight stars, goodnight air, goodnight noises everywhere.* I see giving thanks like that. I believe it pleases God when we get specific in our thankfulness.

This morning I thank him for coffee with cream and iced sugar cookies, for letting me get back from my walk five minutes before the deluge of rain, for Internet connection at the laundromat, for thoughts and words—words that encourage me, and words that I hope encourage you. To give thanks.

November 25th

For now we see in a mirror dimly, but then face to face; now I know in part, but then I will know fully just as I also have been fully known.
—1 Corinthians 13:12 NASB

Interrupting Cows

When our son was young he loved to tell jokes. One of his favorites was the interrupting cow joke. Maybe you know it:

"*Knock knock*"
"*Who's there?*"
"*Interrupting Cow.*"
"*Interrupting Co...*"
"*Moooooo!*"

Our family got so in to this joke that we expanded it to interrupting pig, interrupting chicken, even interrupting walking stick! We never failed to laugh hysterically.

I was thinking about that joke recently and the tendency some of us have to finish others' sentences. We anticipate what they are going to say, so we interrupt, somehow thinking that if we complete the sentence, we are helping along the communication. The problem comes when we end their sentence or interpret their words in a separate way than they were thinking. Rather than aiding the discourse, it disrupts it and causes confusion.

Although these kinds of interruptions are commonplace and harmless, I wonder how many times I do the same thing to God. How many times do I finish his sentences? I think I know the direction he is leading, but rather than patiently waiting for him to complete his phrase, I'm off and running. I fill in the blank spaces with my thoughts. Sometimes it's hard to realize where I go wrong.

Even though Scripture warns that we see through a glass darkly, we tend to forget we only know in part. When things don't work out the way we expected, it's helpful to remember we are only given a part of the picture. Yet, knowing in part is better than not knowing at all. Because I sometimes fail to get the whole message, I don't want to stop learning how to listen, how to separate his thoughts from mine. A day is coming when the glass will no longer be dark.

There are few things in life dearer than hearing the voice of the Lord. He speaks to us in many ways if we pay attention. May we be more intent on listening, and less on adding our own two cents. Let's not let our thoughts turn into interrupting cows.

November 26th

After the wind there was an earthquake, but the Lord was not in the earthquake. After the earthquake came a fire, but the Lord was not in the fire. And after the fire came a gentle whisper.

—1 Kings 19:11-12 NIV

God Whispers

Sometimes the voice of the Lord seems almost audible. We pick up the Bible and it's as if certain words are italicized. We hear a preacher and conclude God must have told him our secrets. The message comes across clear, direct, unmistakable. Other times, to hear the Lord speak, it is necessary to come closer and lean in because he is whispering.

You're probably familiar with the story in 1 Kings where God communicates with Elijah. The prophet expected God would speak in shock-and-awe—in the howling wind, the earthquake or the fire. But he didn't. Instead God spoke in a still small voice—a whisper. Maybe Elijah had to silence his expectations of how God would speak before he was ready to listen. Hmmm ... could our expectations be causing us to miss his whispers? Predetermined expectations as to how God wants to speak can cause us to miss his voice.

But it's also hard to catch whispers in noisy environments. We get distracted by the clamor of busyness, of endless to-do lists shouting we don't have time for quiet. The worries of life scream for our attention. Before long we develop a habit of not listening.

But Matthew 13 describes the saddest hearing impairment of all. In the parable of the sower Jesus spells out one specific reason why the people cannot hear—they don't want to. "For this people's heart has become calloused; they hardly hear with their ears" (v. 15). It is as if they put on their own private headphones to conveniently filter out sounds they might find confrontive or uncomfortable. They become desensitized to God's voice, deaf to his whispers.

Let's not let any of these factors cause us to miss the whispers of God. Let's be alert, always listening for his voice, wherever we are, whatever we are doing. Let's lean in close so we don't miss a syllable.

November 27th

As the LORD commanded his servant Moses, so Moses commanded Joshua, and Joshua did it; he left nothing undone of all that the LORD commanded Moses. —Joshua 11:15 NIV

Nothing Left Undone

I love those days when everything falls into place. Items on my list checked-off, all tasks completed. To the best of my awareness I've finished whatever God assigned, whether critiquing students' speeches or enjoying coffee with a friend, picking up groceries or working on the computer. The lines have fallen "in pleasant places" as the psalmist describes (Psalm 16:6 ESV).

But sometimes, those pleasantly-placed lines become blurred. It seems more like I'm swimming in a sea of frustration. I begin to compare myself with myself. *I'm not doing as much as I used to do. Am I committing sins of omission? Am I not giving where I should be giving? Am I sacrificing enough time, money, effort?*

When Joshua and his army began the conquest of Canaan, God promised to be with them. After only seven months of fighting, and forty years of preparation, they subdued over thirty-one kings, securing enough land to begin the distribution to the twelve tribes. God was pleased with Joshua. He had followed all of his commands. Scripture says Joshua "left nothing undone." Yet there remained large tracks of land to be taken. Battles yet to be fought. Victories yet to be won. The tribes were given the task of fortifying their own borders. Not Joshua.

Have you heard of the Peter Principle? Joshua did not suffer from it. He stayed in his lane throughout life, not burdening himself with jobs unassigned to him. He simply, yet profoundly, followed what God told him to do.

I think that is the key for us if we hope to live satisfied lives. When we yield to God's will and not let it be diluted with either our own agenda or others' expectations, when we accept that different seasons in life carry different responsibilities, and when we trust God will show us if more is to be done, we can, as did Joshua, find "rest."

That is what God desires for each of us. When my weary soul gets hold of that and I recognize such grace, mercy and goodness, the only thing left undone is me.

How about you? Are you resting in God's plan?

November 28th

The LORD gives strength to his people; the LORD blesses his people with peace.
—Psalm 29:11 NIV

Hurricane Resistant

Do you need some fortification in your spiritual life?

Shortly after my husband and I were married, we moved to Florida where he and his brother teamed together to begin a business. Their first project entailed buying and clearing land to build a house which they would in turn sell. We spent every waking hour in August and September—the hottest, most humid time of the year—working on that house. I remember times when I prayed for a breeze. It was my introduction into the construction world, and despite the physical challenges, I learned about a few things. Things like rebar.

Rebar, short for re (enforcing) bar, consists of steel rods placed in concrete to help the structure withstand outside pressure, such as that in hurricanes. Rebar was a mandatory requirement in Florida buildings due to the frequent occurrences of gale winds. I think rebar of a different kind is needed in the Christian life.

Psalm 29 describes the power and strength of the Lord. He is King of the Universe, the source of all strength. He wants to give that strength to his people so that when the hurricanes of life come against us, we will be able to stand our ground.

God's supremacy in our lives not only fortifies our faith but buttresses us against the weaknesses of others. Just as rebar allows concrete to carry "tensile loads," so our relationship with God enables us to deal with the "loads of tension" that at times come with our interactions with people. When battered by others' judgments and rejections, our security doesn't crumble because it's built on the strongest force in the universe—the love of God.

So, how's your rebar? Has some brokenness in a relationship whipped you around? Are you making every effort to keep the Lord as your first love? Are you letting him reconstruct the areas in your life that need some overhaul? Don't let anything dilute, dislodge or dismantle your rebar.

November 29th

Surely the LORD is in this place, and I did not know it.

—Genesis 28:16 NIV

Unlikely Places

Jacob knew it was time to get out of Dodge. He had deceived his brother Esau and stolen his blessing as the firstborn. Esau vowed to kill him. So, Jacob fled. He headed for his mother's homeland in faraway Paddan Aram. But his journey brought some unexpected twists—like encountering God.

God does that at times, doesn't he? Shows up at places when we least expect it, or deserve it. Jacob, alone and anxious, stopped on his journey to rest. That's when God appeared to him in a dream. God promised to someday bring him back to build through him a great nation. Jacob, filled with awe, named the place Bethel—the house of God—and proclaimed, "Surely the LORD is in this place, and I did not know it."

I believe God appears in a lot of places. But like Jacob, we just don't know it. We are not expecting him, so we don't look for him. Sometimes, however, I get a glimpse.

On summer Sunday nights, I used to take my mom to community lawn concerts. She loved music, no matter what the venue. She would tap her toes and clap her hands, mouthing the words to anything from "God Bless America" to "Moon River." Those Sunday nights proved to be special times. The first time I went back after her death I was struck with her absence. I missed her.

During the break, the lady next to me struck up a conversation. Turns out, the ninety-three-year-old woman came every week. Although she looked nothing like my mom, her eyes twinkled with that familiar octogenarian gratitude for another day of living. She engaged me until the band opened the second half when she, like Mom, started to move with the music. Her presence brought me a comfort I didn't even know I needed.

How likely that out of the hundreds of people at the concert I would have happened to be sitting next to a woman who reminded me of Mom? Not very. You might call it coincidence, but I believe it was a "Surely the Lord was in that place and I did not know it" moment. He showed up in an unlikely place to speak to me in an unlikely way.

He will do the same for you. Don't miss him.

November 30th

Not so with you. Instead, whoever wants to become great among you must be your servant. —Matthew 20:26 NIV

The Secret of Greatness

Jesus turned the definition of greatness on its head when he said the greatest would be the servant. Not the person with the top position, not the highest skilled athlete, not the one whose face graces the most magazine covers. The creator of the universe says the mark of true greatness lies in serving. Why? What is so important about serving?

When we serve others, we open a window to give them a glimpse of the God who took the nature of a servant when he walked on the earth (Philippians 2:7). We help what had been a hazy picture of God come into focus. Eugene Peterson writes our whole purpose in life involves serving others because when we serve, "we represent to one another the address of God." In other words, we lead people to the place where he lives—in us! All this when we serve someone.

No one had a clearer picture of servanthood demonstrated to them than the disciples. Day in and day out they observed how Jesus lived to advance his Father's agenda, never his own. Even as thoughts of his pending crucifixion weighed heavily on his mind, he still served. The disciples didn't get it.

When the mother of James and John asked Jesus if he would place her boys on his right and left after he entered his kingdom, the other disciples were "indignant." After all this time with Jesus, they still jockeyed for position. His response laser-beamed right into the heart of the issue. Place and position are man-centered trappings that have nothing to do with what it means to be great. Greatness can only be found in serving (Matthew 20:24–28).

Let's get it. If we want to learn the secret of greatness, we must first learn what it's not. We let the culture's definitions slip away and take seriously the Lord's description. We decide to serve his agenda before our own. It might mean being interrupted by a call from "one of the least of these" or washing some smelly feet.

God calls you and me to walk in greatness. Greatness defined by serving. So, what's holding us back?

December 1st

Brothers and sisters, I do not consider myself yet to have taken hold of it. But one thing I do: Forgetting what is behind and straining toward what is ahead I press on toward the goal to win the prize for which God has called me heavenward in Christ Jesus. —Philippians 3:13–14 NIV

The Power of Self-Condemnation

In *Prayer: Conversing with God* Rosalind Rinker writes: "And you, my tender-hearted, overly conscientious friend, can rest in Him too, so that your prayers will be answered and so that you do not need to continue condemning yourself." Her words penetrate my heart and expose a kind of low-grade guilt lying right below the surface. Maybe you're like me—at times aware of self-condemnation's presence but perhaps not of its power.

If we hope to impact the world with the love of God, it's time to get over it. Condemning ourselves for past weaknesses and mistakes shifts our focus from what God can do to what we have done. It blinds us from seeing a trustworthy redemptive God. And when our confidence in God blurs, our faith diminishes. Our prayer life withers.

Paul knew the importance of self-forgetfulness. The man who referred to himself as the "chief of sinners" is the same man who refused to give his past the time of day. He chose to focus on what lies ahead, to put forth every effort toward the heavenly goal found in Christ. What if he had been consumed with the innocent people he'd persecuted? With his ugly Pharisaical pride? With his ill-directed influence on fellow Jews? Paul knew he had been forgiven and that his past had been redeemed. There was no reason to look back. To beat himself up. He took full responsibility for his sins, repented, and left his past where it belonged—at the cross of Christ.

We should do the same.

Don't let low-grade guilt sabotage your confidence in God and divert his plan for your life. We all sin. But each day presents a clean slate, a new beginning. Press on. Look *heaven*ward, not *in*ward. Strip the power of self-condemnation from your life and find the rest that accompanies prayers of faith. It's what the God you so long to please wants you to do.

December 2nd

Jesus answered, "If I want him to remain alive until I return, what is that to you? You must follow me." —John 21:22 NIV

"Grandma! Grandma! Grandma!"

I could hardly contain my excitement as we set out on the six-hour drive to Rhode Island. We hadn't seen our nineteen-month-old grandson for what seemed like years (four months). Although my daughter dutifully skypes with us weekly, how can you take stroller rides, play in sandboxes and cuddle up with books across the computer screen?

I had a habit of saying "Grandma, Grandma, Grandma" every time we skyped. You know, just to make sure he didn't forget who I was. Much to my delight, my daughter told me the week before our visit he had finally been able to formulate the words ... *Gam-maw.* YES!

We arrived at their home right before his bedtime, and just as I hoped, he exclaimed, "Gam-maw, Gam-maw!" The only problem was he ran straight for my husband! After all my attempts at indoctrination! Throughout the week, we tried to help him make the distinction between *Gam-maw* and *Gam-paw,* but we both continued to carry the esteemed nomenclature of *Gam-maw.*

We all had a big laugh. Well, my laugh probably wasn't as hardy as everyone else's, but it's tough to feel slighted in the company of such grandson adorableness.

It did get me thinking, though, of times when I've experienced being overlooked or someone else getting the credit for my work. It happens to all of us, doesn't it? We respond by either letting the hurt consume us or shake it off and move on.

When Jesus appeared to his disciples after the resurrection, he singled out Peter. Jesus wanted to reassure him he still had a place in the kingdom of God, even after his infamous denial. When Peter asked Jesus about John's destiny, he made it clear there was only one thing Peter should concern himself with: was he following Jesus?

It's the answer for us as well. We don't measure ourselves by other people's responses or how their walk compares to ours. If we focus on doing what the Lord is calling us to do, and if we do it with all our heart, nothing else matters.

Don't get caught in the comparison trap. "You must follow" Jesus.

December 3rd

Keep your servant also from willful sins; may they not rule over me.
—Psalm 19:13 NIV

Don't Let Us Blow It

"Don't let us blow it, Lord!" How many times I've whispered that desperate prayer! I doubt I'm alone. Those of us who believe in Christ desire, perhaps more than anything, to be found faithful in the hour of testing. Like the psalmist, we pray willful sins won't rule over us. We don't want to let God down by failing to trust him in a crisis. As Edith Schaeffer writes in *The Tapestry*, we hope in those times our love for God will prove to be "solid oak, not a thin veneer." No matter how big or small the trial, we long for the grace and peace of our Savior to be revealed, not some half-hearted acquiescence to our sinful nature.

I find myself praying "Don't let me blow it" whenever I'm faced with making decisions I consider above my pay grade. Like when we brought my mother home to care for her in the final days before she died. I became acutely aware of my inadequacies. *Am I getting her medications right? Is she receiving enough oxygen? Would she be better off in the hospital?* I wanted to be a help, not a hindrance, as she finished the last miles of her race. *Could I maintain her dignity as her body grew weaker and weaker? "Don't let me blow it Lord!"*

Inevitably, I made mistakes. At times I surrendered to fear and doubt. But you know what I discovered? God covered me. The God whose strength is made perfect in my weakness had my back. He knew where I would fall short, and at the same time, he knew my prayerful cry. He knew all this before the foundation of the universe and wove it into the tapestry of Mom's life and mine.

I am human. So are you. We will blow it. So, although it's good to ask for God's help in not messing up, our ultimate hope lies in redemption, not perfection. I like how author Bob Goff puts it in *Love Does*. He sees the book of life "about people traveling in the direction of Jesus, trying to follow Him.... People like me who made lots of mistakes and midcourse directions [but]...who stayed within the large circle of His love and grace."

Amen.

December 4th

When he lies, he speaks his native language, for he is a liar and the father of lies.
—John 8:44 NIV

Dial Up Truth

Things in Egypt went from bad to worse. In asking Pharaoh's permission for Israel to go to the desert and worship God, Moses had taken one step forward. Pharaoh pushed back with three. He refused their request to go, commanded them to keep making bricks at the same quota, and now required them to supply their own straw. Adding insult to injury, he denounced them as "lazy" (Exodus 5:3–8).

Lazy? It was a lie, of course. The nation proved anything but lazy. The heartless slave drivers made sure of it. But isn't that a primary scheme of the father of lies? He launches a false accusation against us, which is often the exact opposite of the truth, and hopes we'll bite.

Rejecting his lies is vitally important, no matter how they're packaged. A tragedy occurs and Satan whispers—*you deserved it!* Our child falls short of our expectations—*you're a failure as a parent.* Sometimes the accusations are so outrageous that we're knocked off our feet before we know what's happening. I have a friend whose co-worker reported him for "religious harassment" because he simply asked if she was going to a Christmas Eve service. She labeled him with our society's sin of all sins—if society believed in sin. She said he was intolerant.

Satan's most insidious lies come in those accusations pointing to who we were before we became a new creation in Christ (2 Corinthians 5:17). He wants to make us think we're essentially the same as we used to be. But we're not!

When we reject who Satan says we are and by faith embrace who God says we are, the transformation of a new creation begins. Just like when Jesus called Peter the Rock. Not much in Peter's life evidenced the kind of stability such nomenclature indicated. But Peter believed what Jesus said about him and became it. He refused to listen to the language of Lie.

So, the next time the Father of Lies hurls false accusations your way, silence him. Put on your earbuds and dial up truth.

December 5th

Your troops will be willing on your day of battle. —Psalm 110:3 NIV

Pick Your Battles

Do you ever feel you have more losses than wins?

Although we face defeat for many reasons, one of the less appreciated causes lies in a lack of discernment. We don't pick the right battles. We fight when we should be standing still in faith. We retreat when we should be advancing in confidence.

Israel was no stranger to this. You're familiar with how Joshua and Caleb's advice to advance into the Promised Land after leaving Egypt was spurned. Israel rebelled against God's promise to lead them to victory. Their lack of trust in fighting the giants resulted in a forty-year delay of God's plan. It's a battle they should have picked.

Years of wandering in the desert taught them a few things about tactics. They learned the only stratagem that worked: reliance on God. From the food they ate, to the shoes they wore, to the very water they drank—they discovered God could be trusted. When time came to take the land, it was necessary for them to follow God's directives. He told them not to engage in battle with Seir, land given to Esau's descendants, or with the Moabites and Ammonites, descendants of Lot. They obeyed when they were told to stand down. It was a battle not to be picked.

Sometimes I think we exhaust ourselves by skirmishing in areas where God has not directed us to fight. Then when it's time to engage in the real conflicts, we're torn, worn and depleted. This plays out in areas from parenting to the national stage. We have to know when God says, "That's worth fighting for." But we also need to discern when he says, "Shake the dust from your feet."

If we hope to experience more wins than losses in life, it may well begin with increased discernment—discernment based on the fact we are called to fight for God's glory; God is not called to fight for ours. Victory comes as we embrace the truth: the battle is the LORD's (1 Samuel 17:47).

December 6th

I have said all these things to you to keep you from falling away.
—John 16:1 ESV

Overlook It

What were those things Jesus said to his disciples to keep them from falling? After walking with him for three years, seeing his miracles, hearing his teachings, experiencing his compassion, who would have thought anything could have jeopardized their faith? Who would have thought any words would be necessary? Who would have thought? Jesus.

Jesus was not about to let them go into the dark unprepared. He knew his impending crucifixion would be earth-shattering to his disciples. All they hoped and longed for would come to a screeching halt. They would not, could not, understand at this point why. Rather than letting them flounder in confusion and doubt, he warned them of what was to come. He compared his death to a woman in childbirth. Although the process of childbirth brings great anguish, all the sorrow turns into unspeakable joy once the mother delivers the baby. He assured them their intense grief over his death would birth the same kind of happiness. He encouraged them to overlook the coming pain by looking over it when it arrived.

No one likes going through pain, especially when we don't see an end in sight. How do we keep from getting stuck in our hurts and letting disappointment cement us into a mentality of hopelessness? How do we keep unmet expectations from shipwrecking our faith?

We overcome by embracing the same wisdom Jesus gave to his disciples: look over the pain. Look beyond it with the deep, gut level assurance God stands on the other side. As we overlook our current struggle and cast our vision to the promised joy, we find strength. The night of weeping will give way to a morning of joy (Psalm 30:5). Either in this life or the next.

Are there circumstances in your life right now you need to overlook? Don't get fixated in your pain. Let Jesus peel your eyes from the momentary sting and focus on the permanent peace (John 16:33). Listen to his words and let him walk you right straight through the hurt.

Look over, my friend—over to the good that lies ahead.

December 7th

We instructed you how to live in order to please God, as in fact you are living. Now we ask you and urge you in the Lord Jesus to do this more and more.

—1 Thessalonians 4:1 NIV

The Spirit of the Age

What was up? The Thessalonians were already living in a way that pleased God. But Paul, ever mindful of the spirit of the age, urges them to press into even more holiness. Maybe he was recalling Israel's penchant for soaking in the surrounding culture. Time and time again, they felt the pull to be like "other nations." It almost destroyed them. Paul didn't want the church to fall prey to the same fate. So, in his first letter, he instructed them in three major areas: avoid sexual immorality (4:3-8), increase their love for each other (4:9-10) and live responsibly (4:11-12). I can't think of three areas more relevant in today's culture.

Sexual immorality continues to flourish. Those who oppose trendy lifestyles find themselves labeled as narrow-minded. As far as increasing our love for one another, the church seems to have fallen in lock-step with a society saturated by divisiveness. Can we honestly say the world recognizes us by our love for one another? And as our country becomes increasingly dependent on government programs, can we resist the pull toward personal irresponsibility?

These three areas all have a common denominator. Each pose a danger to the dignity of manmade in the image of God. Sexual immorality, divisiveness and irresponsibility play to our selfish nature and peck away at who God designed us to be.

Author Flannery O'Connor once wrote, "Push back against the age as hard as it pushes against you." Friends, if there ever was a time when the spirit of the age was pressing hard, it is now. If we hope to live as salt and light we would do well to listen to Paul's admonition. Let's not be afraid to take a stand against sexual activity that contradicts the word of God. Let's refuse to withhold love from fellow believers who disagree with us. And to the extent we can, let's be diligent and productive in whatever work we're called to do. Let's bring truth and grace into every aspect of our lives ...

More and more ... more and more ...

December 8th

So may all your enemies perish, LORD! But may all who love you be like the sun when it rises in its strength. —Judges 5:31 NIV

Photovoltaic Christians

Is anything overshadowing your light?

A few years ago, we installed solar panels on our farm. It has been amazing to see our electric meter actually move backward as the energy generated from the sun gets "credited" to our account. The solar panels work most effectively in direct sunlight, free from obstructions that could cause shade. The more sunlight, the greater the production of electricity.

Like loving God.

Judges 5 records the "Song of Deborah." It recounts the great victory God had given to Israel when Deborah led them against the Canaanites. Victory was completed when Jael, a Kenite woman, ran a tent peg through the commander of the Canaanite army. The song concludes with praise to God and the request that those who love him would be like the sun rising in its strength.

It's an apt description of the way God's love works in us. The more we love him, the stronger we become. It necessitates letting go of those parts of ourselves that would "shade" love— self-interests, judgmental attitudes, criticalness, unforgiveness. As long as those traits remain, the power in which we could be walking diminishes.

So, when victories seem to escape our grasp, maybe it's a good time to consider whether we've been allowing shadows to block the light. *So, what if I hold on to this little grudge. It's not hurting anyone. Who do they think they are?* Even a little negativity deflects God's love from pouring into us the strength we need.

As we make a conscious decision not to let anything in us obstruct the light of love, a three-fold phenomenon occurs. We find renewed strength for ourselves, the love streaming through us reflects on other people, and God is glorified (Matthew 5:16).

Want to have a "photovoltaic effect" emanating from your life? Commit to absorbing the love of God.

December 9th

For if you remain silent at this time, relief and deliverance for the Jews will arise from another place. —Esther 4:14 NIV

Complete Confidence

I wish my confidence in God stood as strong as Mordecai's.

The book of Esther illustrates the power of his unflinching trust in God. An edict had been given that all the Jews living in the Persian Empire were to be slaughtered. It seemingly came out of nowhere. An incensed official, angered at Mordecai's refusal to bow to him, persuaded the king to set a date for Jewish annihilation. Kings' edicts in those days proved irreversible. The Jews were exiles. They had no power or means of defending themselves. They didn't even have a country at this point in which to escape. If anyone had reason for pessimism, Mordecai did.

But rather than giving in to the quite formidable circumstances, Mordecai put all his trust in the Sovereign God. He beseeched his adopted daughter, Esther, who happened to be the queen, to go before the king and plead for her people. Knowing that going before the king unsummoned could mean her death, she resisted. That's when Mordecai spoke some of the most powerful words of faith recorded in the Bible, "If you remain silent at this time, relief and deliverance for the Jews will arise from another place."

His complete confidence in God never faltered. He knew God would rescue them whether Esther chose to be a part of the undertaking or not. His resolve proved to have such an effect on her that she willingly put her life on the line. "And if I perish, I perish" (v. 16).

Esther didn't perish. Neither did Mordecai. Neither did *any* of the Jews. God, indeed, delivered his people.

It makes me wonder how different the world would be if we took the kind of bold, no-holds-barred approach Mordecai displayed. His unabashed confidence affected not only Esther, but a whole nation. It stirred heaven. It moved earth.

Whatever circumstances you or someone you know may be facing right now, don't be afraid to trust God. And trust him boldly. Believe he has a plan to bring you through the darkest night, the most dangerous threat. Who knows but that your faith and steadfast confidence in his sovereign goodness is not but meant "for such a time as this."

December 10th

Do not take a purse or bag or sandals; and do not greet anyone on the road.

—*Luke 10:4 NIV*

Traveling Light

How much room do you have in your heart for Jesus?

When experienced travelers fly, many jam all their belongings into a carry-on. They want to avoid the time and hassle of baggage claim. Their years of flying have taught them the importance of "traveling light."

Jesus, in sending out the seventy-two disciples, warned them to "travel light." No wallet. No bags. No sandals. Evidently, they would not be able to accomplish the mission if they were carrying excess baggage. But I think Jesus may have been including some other kind of "baggage" when he further instructed them on how to deal with the people's response to their message.

Jesus told the disciples when they encountered towns that did not welcome them, they were to dust their feet and move on (Luke 10:10-11). He knew rejection of the gospel was inevitable, and he didn't want them to be hindered by feelings of resentment. The same applies to us. If our bags are weighed down with attitudes of insecurity and self-consciousness, it will be near-impossible to face rejection. Rather than being able to travel on, the heaviness of negative responses will add unwanted weight to our luggage. Instead of dusting our feet we will more likely sink in the mud.

On the other hand, what if we meet success? What kind of baggage can cause us to get bogged down when "even the demons submit to us"? (v. 17). How about conceit? Self-reliance? Jesus warned his disciples to drop any notions of self-advancement. They were to keep their focus. Rather than succumbing to the vacillating assessments of man, they were to humbly rejoice that their names were written in heaven (v. 20). Pride in our accomplishments—no matter how noble—turns into bulky garments of self-righteousness that are way too heavy for travels that advance God's kingdom.

So, how does your suitcase look these days? Do you have some excess baggage you want to discard? Need to leave some attitudes at the security gate? I've been doing some unpacking these days, trying to prepare more room for him. Feels pretty good to "travel light."

December 11th

Jesus answered her, "If you knew the gift of God and who it is that asks you for a drink, you would have asked him and he would have given you living water."
—*John 4:10 NIV*

Knowing God Part 1: Knowing Immanuel

Jesus basically tells the Samaritan woman if she knew, she would have asked, and he would have given. That passage makes me wonder how well I know the gift of God. I don't want to someday look back on my life with the regretful mourning of if I'd only known—if I'd only known the intensity of his love; if I'd only known the accessibility of his power; if I'd only known the certainty of his faithfulness. I want more than to just touch the hem of his garment.

This Christmas season as we observe his entry on earth, I'm making it my aim to recognize him in the celebration. When I sit next to my Christmas tree in the early morning hours, I want to let him remind me of his beauty. When I receive a Christmas card, I want to realize that it's his grace that has given me dear friends. When I light my Yankee candle, I want to remember how prayer is a sweet fragrance to him. When I hear the strains of "Come, Thou Long Expected Jesus," I want to be made aware that he has been here all along.

God went to a lot of trouble to make himself visible so we would know the one we worship. And even though the incarnate Christ no longer walks among us, he still delights in making himself known. The charge against the Samaritan woman was that she worshiped what she did not know (John 4:22). May that not be said of us. I'm praying that we detect him in the midst of our holiday activities. Maybe in a candlelight service, maybe in a child's delight on Christmas morning, maybe in the warmth of an unexpected act of kindness.

Immanuel has come. So we might know.

December 12

Jesus answered her, "If you knew the gift of God and who it is that asks you for a drink, you would have asked him and he would have given you living water."
—John 4:10 NIV

Knowing God Part 2: Asking Immanuel

Jesus wanted the Samaritan woman to ask. He also wants us to ask, so much so that he tells us that whatever we ask in his name we will receive. The caveat, of course, is in his name, which takes us back to the beginning of the verse. Asking in his name comes from knowing the One to whom the name belongs. We are more prone to ask when we realize the One we're asking not only has the power but also the heart to answer. Confidence in his character becomes the basis for all our requests.

Paul Miller, in his excellent book *A Praying Life: Connecting with God in a Distracting World,* describes prayer as a "moment of incarnation—God with us involved in the details of our lives."

We will never realize how interested he is in all those details if we don't ask him about them. When we ask, we not only see his interest, we see him. We see Immanuel.

So, don't be discouraged by your needs. Perhaps they are intended to lead you to that divine place of entreaty. One writer comments we "need our needs" because of the drive they give us toward prayer. And don't give in to the mentality of "drive-thru" prayer where you place your order and immediately pick it up at the next window. If you've asked and not yet gotten an answer, ask again and again and again.

I think it's interesting Christmas carries with it such a strong element of asking. Right now, thousands of people are inquiring of loved ones, "What do you want this year? What's on your list?" I hate the commercialization of the season as much as anyone, but maybe there's a message hidden in the endless sales fliers and early bird specials.

I want to encourage you to *ask*. Ask God. And as Paul Miller urges, "Ask boldly. Ask boldly but surrender completely." That's advice I'm taking to heart this Christmas. I hope you will too.

December 13th

Jesus answered her, "If you knew the gift of God and who it is that asks you for a drink, you would have asked him and he would have given you living water." —John 4:10 NIV

Knowing God Part 3: Receiving Immanuel

Jesus told the Samaritan woman he would have given her even more than she was asking for. He would have given her something substantial, something beyond her wildest dreams, something eternal.

A. B. Simpson once remarked that we may pray much over a promise and yet never obtain it because asking is not taking. If God has given us a promise, it is up to us to receive it. But how do we receive what we can't see?

It is far easier to take the tangible requests. Things we can touch, taste, or hear aren't hard to ascertain. This Christmas, squeals of delight will be offered over games and toys, gift cards to favorite restaurants, and long-desired items. Nothing too difficult about receiving those Ugg boots or latest tablet.

Receiving what we can't grasp with our five senses requires something more. Asking moves to taking when our requests ignite with faith. We believe in the one "who is able to do immeasurably more than all we ask or imagine" (Ephesians 3:20). We believe our Father in heaven gives "good gifts to those who ask him!" (Matthew 7:11). We believe "every good and perfect gift is from above, coming down from the Father of the heavenly lights" (James 1:17). What was once intangible bubbles up into "living water," and our deepest thirst is quenched.

If I could give you a gift this Christmas, I would encourage you to take God at his Word. Drink deeply of the truth: The unseen God who so longed for us to be with him, came in visible human form to show us the way.

Receive Immanuel. God with us.

December 14th

Then he said to them, "The Sabbath was made for man, not man for the Sabbath."
—Mark 2:27 NIV

Tunnel Vision Christmas

I'm going for "tunnel vision" this Christmas. I want my mind to be wrapped around one overriding thought: Christmas was made for us, not us for Christmas.

Of course, I'm paraphrasing what Jesus said about the Sabbath. The legalists in Jesus' day had turned the Sabbath into a burdensome set of rules to be strictly followed, a tradition-laden weight impossible for anyone to carry. The consequences of demanding such strict adherence to the regulations cancelled any sense of the rest and refreshment God intended when he said, "on the seventh day you shall rest" (Exodus 34:21). The peripherals had replaced the main event. Jesus restored the true meaning of the Sabbath by shifting the focus back to its original intent: God gave the Sabbath to man as a gift, as a time to pause, to regroup, to reflect on our relationship with him. I believe it applies to Christmas as well.

God gave us Christmas as a time to celebrate, to stop and contemplate his incomprehensible gift. A time to simply respond to the miracle of the incarnation, not tie ourselves in knots trying to "make the season bright." I'm afraid we all too often get caught in peripheral vision.

Don't get me wrong. I love the peripherals of Christmas as much as anyone. I love the songs, the smells, the decorations, the memories of past seasons, even the shopping. But I must admit, I sometimes fall prey to worn-out frenzy. I make my list and check it far more than twice. When my traditions move from peripheral vision to the center, my focus gets distorted. I no longer see Christmas as my response to his gift. Somehow all my activity feels like my gift to him.

Christmas. God created it to remind us of a gift so profound it stimulates our own generosity and goodwill toward others. To remind us every time we say his name, Immanuel, we are not alone. To remind us we have reason for hope in a world stained with tears.

Will you join me this Christmas and ask God to give you some "tunnel vision" and fix your eyes on this one truth: Christmas was made for you, not you for Christmas. Enjoy!

December 15th

"I am the Lord's servant," Mary answered. "May your word to me be fulfilled."
— Luke 1:38 NIV

On the Road to Bethlehem: Against the Flow

No one could ever accuse Jesus of maintaining the status quo.

From the outset of his birth, the long-expected Messiah came to the world in the most *unexpected* of ways. The smelly cow's stall, the lowly manger, the swaddling clothes barely wrapping his newborn body, the humble audience who received him—all were eons away from what one would anticipate for the birth of the King and Savior of all men.

His life and death were just as shocking. His complete abandonment to God, his miracles and his message of forgiveness rocked the religious establishment. He overturned "tables" of all kinds. The cross broke the power of evil's darkness just at the moment when it looked like all was lost. As lyricist Mark Harris puts it, "It was a strange way to save the world."

But save us he did. And he remains in the business of shaking up our positions of shallow comfort and false security. He wants to upset our apple carts from time to time lest we fall into a gradual state of spiritual entropy where the light purposed to shine before all men barely flickers.

Certainly, those God chose to entrust with his birth displayed a willingness to abandon the status quo. Virgin births weren't any more common in those days than today. When the angel announced to Mary she would be giving birth to the Messiah, she responded with absolute abandon. And what of her response after riding hours on a donkey only to reach their destination and find no provision for the night? Status quo thinking would have reasoned since she had so radically obeyed the will of God, he would have come through at least with a room. But nothing in Scripture indicates Jesus was born to a disappointed, disillusioned mother. No way. She wasn't a status quo thinker.

So, where are you this season on the road to Bethlehem? Has God been turning over some of your tables? Have you been disappointed he hasn't met some expectations? May you and I escape status quo mentality. May God look on us and deem us vessels to which he can entrust the radical, unorthodox, sweeping nature of his Son.

December 16th

In the beginning was the Word, and the Word was with God, and the Word was God.
—John1:1 NIV

A Christmas Gift

Gifts. Gifts. Gifts. They come in all sizes and packages, but at Christmas we focus on the one gift that surpasses them all.

The best gift ever given to the world—the incarnate Word of God, Jesus!

He is a gift wrapped like no other under your tree. This gift is wrapped in light (Psalm 104:2) and is adorned with ribbons of truth (John 14:6). The tag on this gift bears your individual name and is signed with love ... the kind of love written in indelible ink, indelible because it's engraved in the palms of his hands (Isaiah 49:16). If ever there was "a gift that keeps on giving" this gift fits the bill (Matthew 28:20).

You can refuse to open this gift. You can choose to simply gaze at it, to "wonder as you wander." You might possibly touch it, but that's a lot different than letting it touch you. Who knows what might happen if you get too close to this gift. Could cause some major upheaval in your life. And what if the instructions are too hard to follow?

Or you can try to ignore this gift altogether. Christmas season will soon be over and you can slide back into normalcy. Store it in the attic along with the rest of your decorations. There will be other Christmases. Maybe next year.

God went to a lot of trouble to give us this gift. The price he paid can't be measured by human standards. Its pricelessness gives value to every other gift known to man. Every single one. So, if I could give you a gift this Christmas, it would be one of encouragement. Open this gift, embrace it, live in it. Friend, let this be the year you take God at his Word. The year you believe his promises. The year this Word who became flesh finds a home in you.

December 17th

Who has believed our message and to whom has the arm of the LORD been revealed? —Isaiah 53:1 NIV

Expecting the Unexpected

There are two types of people in the world: those who love surprises and those who don't. I fall into the first category, especially around Christmas.

My husband likes to tell the story of the time he and my cousin were working in our attic. I was running up the stairs when suddenly, I froze. "Don't look," they warned, "your Christmas present is right here!" Immediately I closed my eyes and let them navigate my steps for the next few minutes until I retrieved whatever it was I needed. I wasn't even tempted to peek. But as it turns out, my eyes could have been as wide as a deer's in a headlight. They were just messin' with me. There was no Christmas present. No imperiled surprise. Took a while to live that one down—much to their amusement.

I believe God loves to surprise us. To teach us how to expect the unexpected. From Jesus' birth to his resurrection, few expected him to either come to the earth or leave it in the way he did. The Everlasting Father born to a young, poor virgin? The good news of his birth announced first to shepherds instead of religious clerics? The Savior of the world "like one from whom people hide their faces" possessing no physical beauty or majesty to hint of his heritage? (Isaiah 53:3). A crucified Creator who rose from the dead and infused breath into lifeless hope? Jesus did not meet anyone's expectations.

Nope—he surpassed them. He touched untouchables. He healed unhealables. He loved unlovables. He forgave unforgivables. Like you. Like me. Why then do we keep trying to hem him into all our preconceived notions?

Let's allow God to surprise us with the unexpected. Let's respond to Isaiah's ancient question of "Who has believed our message?" with a resounding, "We do!" It will take trust. Might have to walk through the attic blindfolded at times. But in this case, something greater than a Christmas present awaits us. So, go ahead—start expecting the unexpected from our faithful loving God.

December 18th

And the angel said to them, "Fear not, for behold, I bring you good news of great joy that will be for all the people." —Luke 2:10 ESV

Resounding Joy

Sometimes my mind feels like a pinball machine. Spring-loaded thoughts dart, spin and flip everywhere searching for a place to land. Emotions, ranging from ecstasy to grief, rise and fall like those little raucous silver balls. The last three months has been one of those "sometimes."

Within the last three months, my daughter gave birth to our first grandson, my ninety-year old mother died, and my son got engaged. Some of the most significant milestones in life were squeezed into this small segment of time. Oh, and did I say Christmas was coming?

Christmas. The advent of Christmas causes those pinballs to spin even more. Traditions, plans, parties and programs; trees, decorations, lights and candles; presents—thinking of presents, buying presents, wrapping presents and giving presents. Into this flurry of activity an angel of the Lord comes and says, "FEAR not ... I bring you good news of great joy."

News so big it overshadows every other human experience in life from the monumental to the mundane. News with the capacity of turning a road of self-destruction into a freeway of freedom. News of reverberating, resonating, resounding joy ... *A Savior has been born to you.*

Weary world, full of darkness, hopelessness and fear ... *A Savior has been born to you.*

Faithful woman who's discovered her husband's unfaithfulness ... *A Savior has been born to you.*

You who have just received a diagnosis of cancer ... *A Savior has been born to you.*

Even you who think you are rich but are soon to discover your spiritual poverty ... *A Savior has been born to you.*

"The kingdom of this world has become the kingdom of our Lord and of his Christ" (Revelations 11:15 ESV). That timeless message has a way of putting everything else in perspective. Nothing we face in life can diminish its power.

I don't know your circumstances this Christmas season. Maybe you are enjoying a period of peace. Maybe, like me, you're running for pinball wizard of the year. Wherever you are, I pray you will hear as if it was for the first time, the great news of resounding joy.

A Savior has been born to you.

December 19th

For unto you is born this day in the city of David a Savior, who is Christ the Lord.   —Luke 2:11 ESV

" O Holy Night" Revisited

Taxes. Lots of taxes. Political power on steroids. A religious establishment frayed and fragmented. Misguided zealots fueling chaos and violence. Life in the twenty-first century has obviously advanced since the days of Jesus' birth, but I find it hard to dismiss the similarities between the two. The world described in Adolphe Adam's classic "O Holy Night" could not be more applicable than in the present.

Ours is a world that still lies in sin and error. We pine, we long, for something to appear offering us a sense of worth. We yearn for the dawning of a new and glorious morning. Because we're a weary world, just as they were two thousand years ago.

Two thousand years ago, an ordinary night became a holy night. Something revolutionary took place. Thrilling hope replaced dim despair; good news overcame strife. And a weary world rejoiced at his appearing. He appeared then, and he appears now. Not by the light of a shining star or in the confines of swaddling clothes, but yes, he comes, and his divine intervention brings great joy.

Like the woman in Ferguson, Missouri, who invests her life savings to open a bakery gets caught in the crosshairs of racial tension and loses everything in the riots. People across the country hear about her plight and within two weeks over $178,000 is donated to help her rebuild. *And a weary world rejoices.*

A bomb threat that would have killed hundreds of innocent people is exposed. *And a weary world rejoices.* Prodigal children who have left their faith to find something sexier in the world realize their folly and return to the truth. *And a weary world of parents rejoices.* Crowded malls filled with exhausted, package-laden customers are invaded with holiday flash mobs to the tune of "The Hallelujah Chorus." *And a weary world of shoppers rejoices.*

Let's look for his appearing this season. And as they did on that first holy night, let's rejoice. Let's fall on our knees and rejoice.

December 20th

And this will be a sign for you: you will find a baby wrapped in swaddling cloths and lying in a manger. —Luke 2:12 ESV

This Will Be a Sign

When the angel appeared to the shepherds, they certainly had no forewarning. They were quietly watching over their flocks when the glory of the Lord appeared. The angel calmed their fears by bringing them good news—the Savior Messiah had just been born in Bethlehem! They would recognize him by a sign: he would be wrapped in swaddling clothes lying in a manger. The sign would assure them this baby was indeed God in flesh.

I believe God still gives us signs. Like the Christmas season when God gave a sign of certainty to our family that in spite of the circumstances, Immanuel was with us.

The call came most unexpectedly. My husband's youngest brother was being rushed to the emergency room. His Down's syndrome, dementia and decreasing physical functioning all seemed to be crashing in. Unresponsive, the nurse speculated he'd had a stroke. Now, my sister-in-law was trying to reach the other three siblings. No small task.

The sister who lives about forty-five minutes away "happened" to be in town at a theatre ten minutes away from the hospital. The oldest brother also "happened" to be at the same show. Getting in touch with the middle brother is sometimes next to impossible unless he's at work. That night he "happened" to be working late, and when the phone rang at the office, he picked it up. Within the hour, we were all gathered at the hospital. We were together, surrounding his hospital bed, when Danny took his last breath.

The fact that within such a short span of time in the middle of a busy holiday season we were all there was not lost on any of us. It was nothing short of a miracle. God graced us with a sign that even though he was taking our beloved brother, he was in control. He was with us.

We probably miss God's signs more often than not. We get busy. We rely on our natural instincts. But when we recognize the signs, peace replaces fear. So, don't miss those hints of God's presence in your life. Remember this Christmas season and always: Immanuel has come.

December 21st

Glory to God in the highest, and on earth peace among those with whom he is pleased! —Luke 2:14 ESV

Bethlehem and Beyond

The contrast could not be sharper. Jesus' arrival and departure on earth paint stark differences.

Mary's kiss of affection on her baby's cheek is replaced with Judas' greedy kiss of betrayal. Adorned in swaddling cloth at his birth, a makeshift purple robe and twisted thorns clothe him at death. Instead of being lovingly laid in a manger, he is cruelly laid on a cross. A brilliant star illuminates the night sky at his birth. A piercing darkness shrouds the noon day sun when he dies.

The air fills with the sound of jubilant angels in the city of David, "Glory to God in the highest!" A lone shattering cry of "My God, my God, why have you forsaken me" resounds from Calvary. The myrrh offered as a gift in happy celebration of his coming mixes with wine to deaden the excruciating pain at his crucifixion.

He entered the world and left it with acknowledgement that he was the king of the Jews—the first time in homage by three foreign kings, the second in mockery by hardhearted soldiers.

In his birth, heaven came to earth. In his death, earth returned to heaven.

So, what are we to make of such contrasts in the two most important events in human history? Until we understand the humanity of Jesus found in the Nativity we cannot embrace the divinity revealed in his resurrection.

At Christmas we have the opportunity, each year, to embrace the incredible truth that God came to us in human form. He came to show us who he is. In Jesus, God revealed what the highest form of his creation would look like were it not for the ravages of sinful self-will. Maybe this season is a good time to linger at the manger a bit longer, to soak in the humanity of the King of Kings and Lord of Lords, then rise with renewed determination to follow him all the way to the cross and beyond. The Savior born in Bethlehem is indeed Christ the Lord. The Resurrection and the Life. Now that's cause for celebration!

December 22nd

And all who heard it were amazed at what the shepherds said to them.
—Luke 2:18 NIV

"Do You Hear What I Hear?"

"Do You Hear What I Hear?" You're probably familiar with this seasonal melody. It was written in 1962 by Noel Regney and Gloria Shayne. With names like "Noel" and "Gloria" how could they *not* write a Christmas song? It describes how hearing about the birth of Jesus brings "goodness and light."

Isn't that what so much of our celebration is about? Believers asking the world to see what we see, to hear what we hear? It's probably the only time of year when the message of the gospel can be heard resonating from department stores, radio stations and even *(gasp)* public buildings through the sounds of the season.

I will never forget my first Christmas away from home. We had moved to Florida—away from all the familiarities that triggered the season. Our landlords invited us to join them Christmas Eve to go caroling. We packed into the back of their Camino and headed to the town trailer park occupied primarily by retirees. As we drove through the rows of mobile homes and people came to their doors offering us candy and smiles of appreciation, something began to happen in my heart. Maybe it was because many of the things that had previously defined Christmas were stripped away. Perhaps it was just the grace of God. But as we belted out "Hark the Herald Angels Sing," "O Come All Ye Faithful" and "Joy to the World," I sensed the message of those timeless choruses overtaking me. I *knew* I was preaching the good news, unabashed, unashamed and unforgettably.

We never know when heaven might invade earth. I certainly wasn't expecting it that night. It's clear the shepherds were caught off guard when the heavenly hosts made their entry on that first Christmas. So maybe some people in your sphere will be surprised this year. You don't have to be part of a flash mob in the mall to let the carols transform you into a bringer of good tidings. Who knows? Maybe a few of your friends and acquaintances just might hear what you hear!

December 23rd

When the angels had left them and gone into heaven, the shepherds said to one another, "Let's go to Bethlehem and see this thing that has happened, which the Lord has told us about." So they hurried off.
—Luke 2:15–16 NIV

"Rise Up, Shepherd and Follow"

"Leave your sheep and leave your lambs.... Follow the star to Bethlehem." The Christmas carol, "Rise Up, Shepherd and Follow," describes both the challenge and opportunity the shepherds faced that first Christmas. If they wanted to see where the Savior of all mankind was born, they had to abandon their flocks. It appears they realized something bigger was at stake than their livelihood, for the Scripture says, "they hurried off." They literally left everything on the field.

The term "lay it all on the field" is used often during football season from players, coaches and even sportscasters. It's a call to hold nothing back, to give your very best in order to win the game. It implies if you give everything, there will be no regrets at the end of the season.

Christmas is about laying it all on the field. It applies to more than the shepherds. Mary left her fear, security and reputation on the field. "I am the Lord's servant ... May your word to me be fulfilled" (Luke 1:38). Joseph forfeited his need for answers and clarity. "He did what the angel of the Lord had commanded him" (Matthew 1:23). But no one laid it all on the field more than God. "He who did not spare his own Son, but gave him up for us all" (Romans 8:32). The splendo of absolute goodness and perfection was surrendered to secure our victory.

That same challenge and opportunity to lay it all on the field exists for us today. If we're to follow the star to Bethlehem and discover the Messiah, we can't be double-minded. Following means first fleeing from all that would hold us back—people, places and things.

So, are there areas in your life that need to be laid on the field? Don't hesitate. This Christmas—rise up mothers, fathers, grandparents and follow. Rise up teachers, mechanics, cashiers and follow. Rise up secretaries, businessmen, beauticians and follow. Wherever God leads you, follow. He promises that in the end you will have no regrets if you lay it all on the field.

December 24th

And a sword will pierce your own soul too. —Luke 2:35 NIV

"Mary, Did You Know?"

At the annual Christmas concert at the college where I teach, the joy of the season emanated through every song. But one arrangement especially touched me. "Mary, Did You Know?" written by Mark Lowry, has been recorded by numerous artists since its release in 1992. You're probably familiar with it. The lyrics ask whether Mary realized her baby boy would someday walk on water, heal the blind and calm storms. Did she comprehend that this one who she delivered would soon deliver her? Did she know she was holding the "great I am?"

The Lancaster Bible College choir's rendition was accompanied by beautiful slides of Mary tenderly caressing the baby Jesus. Then, in stark contrast to the lovely Nativity scenes, a picture of Michelangelo's Pietà appeared—the exquisite sculpture of a grief-stricken Mary cradling the dead body of Jesus after his crucifixion. The juxtaposition of these two slides penetrated my blissful appreciation.

Christmas without a clear understanding of why Christ came may instill hopes for peace on earth and goodwill toward men, but hopes based on what? I love the manger, the shepherds, the angels and wise men. I treasure the small crèche that sits on my mantle. But without the Pietà, it's all reduced to no more than a romantic tale. Did Mary know? Did she understand when Simeon told her Jesus would cause a sword to pierce her own soul?

Jesus came to the earth to die.

> He was pierced for our transgressions, he was crushed for our iniquities; the punishment that brought us peace was on him, and by his wounds we are healed. We all, like sheep, have gone astray, each of us has turned to our own way; and the Lord has laid on him the iniquity of us all. —Isaiah 53:5-6

Without his sacrifice, there would be no hope for anyone.

This year I want to move beyond tradition and sentimentality. I want to remember, as Lowry so poignantly writes, that this baby boy, "heaven's perfect Lamb," has come to make me new. That is the power of Christmas.

December 25th

God has visited his people! —*Luke 7:16* ESV

God With Us

A number of years ago we received a calendar from some missionary friends living in France. The December Scripture was taken from this passage in Luke 7: *"Dieu a visits son peuple."* To me, that verse captures the essence of Christmas! *God came to visit his people.*

He never left. The gospel of Matthew begins with a declaration that he is here: "'and they shall call his name Immanuel' (which means, God with us)" (1:23 ESV). It ends with the same assurance: "surely I am with you always, to the very end of the age" (28:20). This profound assertion meets one of man's most basic needs—knowing we're not alone in the universe. Christmas crystalizes the hope Someone is here. The incarnation lets us see that in the midst of a world characterized by broken relationships and isolation, there remains a God who is both sovereign and near.

But the message of Christmas goes further. It heralds the tidings that incalculable good can emerge from the most unlikely of circumstances. Brennan Manning notes Christmas is a promise that in the end everything will be all right. I like that. I like knowing that nothing—*nothing*—can harm us permanently. Neither losses nor defeats last indefinitely. Jesus is born as the Redeemer who buys the wreckage of our lives and puts us back together.

One of my favorite Christmas carols ...

> *Come, Thou long expected Jesus,*
> *Born to set Thy people free;*
> *From our fears and sins release us,*
> *Let us find our rest in Thee.*

God has come through Jesus. He remains through the Holy Spirit. The most unimaginable has become a tangible reality. He is with us! It's cause for great celebration.

Happy Birthday Jesus!

December 26th

Why do you pass judgment on your brother? Or you, why do you despise your brother? For we will all stand before the judgment seat of God.
—Romans 14:10 ESV

It's All How You Look at Things

Do you ever find yourself judging people who don't look at life the way you do?

While waiting for my flight to board, the couple sitting next to me at the airport caught my attention. They had in hand a recent purchase from Starbucks. A Caramel Macchiato? Skinny Peppermint Mocha? Eggnog Latte? Nope. It was none of these. I heard them refer to it as a Puppuchino as they lovingly let their dog lick up the whipped cream from the hand-crafted treat.

Now I love our little dog, Beau, but clearly my perspective of four-footed creatures differed from theirs. And theirs from the next dog family to enter the gate. Imagine an exquisitely groomed white French poodle, complete with pink bow and jewel-studded leash prancing by. She leads her proud owners who trail behind pulling two poodle-printed carry-ons. It wouldn't have been quite so funny had I not heard the Puppuchino lady remark, "Well, that's over the top!" One person's over-the-top is another's normal.

Paul warns us about not judging others. He reminds us we will all stand before the judgment seat of God. Those who deal with life differently than we do in the nonessentials ought not have to be the brunt of our criticism. The truth is, we usually don't know why people see things the way they do. But in a culture marked with increased negativity, we have the opportunity to shine a brighter light. As we choose to live our own lives to full capacity, we can let others do the same.

I don't think I'll be getting Beau a Puppuchino any time soon. And I'm sure I won't be getting him a fancy doggie carry-on. But if you do, that's fine with me. It's all how you look at things. I'm heeding Paul's directives. I'm going to let God do the judging. How about you?

December 27th

If I have the gift of prophecy and can fathom all mysteries and all knowledge, and if I have a faith that can move mountains, but do not have love, I am nothing. —1 Corinthians 13:2 NIV

Love's Victory

The battles that count in life are the ones raged in the soul. Whether those battles are won or lost pivots upon the undefeatable mark of Christianity: love. Theologian Frederick Boehner writes in the *The Magnificent Defeat:*

> "The love for equals is a human thing...love for the less fortunate is a beautiful thing...love for the more fortunate is a rare thing... love for the enemy.... This is God's love. It conquers the world."

Sometimes my love can seem puny. It's far from world-conquering, especially when I meet rejection, betrayal or indifference. Christ knows better than anyone how ill-prepared we fallen creatures are for such encounters. Yet he calls us to live in overflowing love. To help us, he not only shows us how, but also imparts a bit of himself—in us—to carry out the task.

It costs something, though. It cost God everything. The One who made all things became nothing so we could become something. For as the Scripture says, even if we have mountain-moving faith, mystery-solving knowledge and body-surrendering sacrifice, without love we are *nothing.* He spared not one thing to bring us into this life of love.

We face a choice: let the sins of the world and weaknesses of others incite us to react in kind, or access the love Christ embeds in us and shine light in the darkness. We don't have to wear ourselves out with endless mental arguments as to why we're in the right and therefore justified in our judgments. Instead we can lay our wounded, depleted souls at his feet for healing and replenishing.

And what of our cost? Pride. Selfishness. Insecurities. Fear. Rationalizations. Bitterness. We lose something of ourselves every time we choose love. But in the words of Buechner, what a *magnificent defeat!*

December 28th

I have fought the good fight, I have finished the course, I have kept the faith.
                                                        —2 Timothy 4:7 NIV

Finishing Well

Do you ever feel like a recovering failure?

It seems like no matter what your role—wife, husband, mother, father, daughter, son, friend, mentor—you're missing the mark? Maybe you consider your challenges too hard. The disappointments too devastating. You're afraid your supply of faith will never get you to the finish line. You may think you're alone, but we all come to crossroads that force us to decide whether we will forge ahead or shrink back.

Regarding these crossroads, Madeleine L'Engle writes in *Walking on Water,* "It is in our responses that we are given the gift of helping God write our story." We are not predetermined robots, actors playing fixed roles. As long as we have breath, we will be confronted with choices determining how we finish our story. Whether in Scripture, politics, business, sports, or the church, there is no want for examples of people who start out with good hearts, determination and a clear perspective only to end up lost. When they reached the crossroads, they took the wrong turn.

The apostle Paul was not one of those. He met every crossroad with one factor in mind: will my decision bring glory to God. It put him in more than a few rough places, but as his life drew to an end, he experienced no regrets. He had fought every obstacle that tried to stand in the way of his call. He completed his story. He maintained his faith. He understood the great battle every believer faces. And he wrote to encourage us to finish well.

So, about those crossroads you're facing—let the grace of Christ meet you there. He will ask you at times to do more than you can do, but he promises to help you. In the process, he will grow your faith—no matter what the circumstance—if you call on him. Never throw up your hands in defeat and premature quitting. The only finishing line that matters is the one that ushers you into his presence.

The one where you hear him say, "You fought the good fight, you finished the race, you kept the faith." That, my friend, will be finishing well.

December 29th

"I'm going out to fish," Simon Peter told them, and they said, "We'll go with you."
                                                              —John 21:3 NIV

Back to Normal

My Christmas tree is down. Rather than sitting next to its warm glow, I'm having morning devotions back in my little porch room. Half & half foams my coffee instead of eggnog. No more sound of Manheim Steamroller to complete my daily Christmas ritual. New photos—photos reflecting a year of transitions—grace the family room. I've even spent all my Christmas money! We're back to normal.

As much as I love the Christmas season, normalcy actually feels pretty good. Normal connotes ordinary, maybe even a bit boring. But normal for followers of Christ means anything but boredom. In him we find life to be a stable, albeit unpredictable, *caper* (to use Bob Goff's term). Every day God offers us opportunity to infuse the ordinary with his extraordinary.

The disciples seemed to be seeking normalcy after the excruciating sorrow of Jesus' crucifixion. They had spent the last three years literally walking with God. They witnessed health restored to the sick and sanity to the demoniacs. They saw violent winds quieted by his command. They watched him set the hypocrisy of the religious establishment on its heels. For the first time in their lives, they experienced pure, holy, unconditional love. Now it was gone. Abruptly. Inconsolably. So, Peter decided to do the only thing he knew to do. Go fishing. Back to normal.

He didn't realize life after encountering Jesus would produce a new normal. The disciples—and all future disciples—would be given the opportunity to take the torch Jesus lit and shine up the world. "Truly, truly, I say to you, whoever believes in me will also do the works that I do; and greater works than these will he do, because I am going to the Father" (John 14:12 ESV).

Peter wasn't expecting a miracle when he went back to normal. But one came. And so it is with us. God intends to use our big events, our non-normal experiences to transform us.

Have you been experiencing the overflow of new-normal-living? Jesus wants you to. He wants to infuse all your normals with his extraordinary presence. Go ahead. Ask him.

December 30th

There is a time for everything, and a season for every activity under the heavens.
                                                    —Ecclesiastes 3:1 NIV

Times, Seasons and Purposes

We only have one life, don't we? A life filled with fruitful seasons, barren seasons, happy, sad, exciting, mundane. The writer of Ecclesiastes assures us a purpose exists for the myriad of conflicting experiences we encounter. Sometimes I feel like a Dodge Ram commercial. I'm ready to "grab life by the horns." Other times I can't even find the horns. Thankfully, the value of life doesn't rest on fleeting feelings. Significance lies in every season—all of the "a time to's" listed in the book of Ecclesiastes. If we let it.

I like Florence Nightingale's perspective, "Live life while you have it. Life is a splendid gift—there is nothing small in it." Her experiences on the battlefield taught her the harsh reality of death and made her aware of the dearness of each of life's moments.

We've had seasons of tough losses, having to walk through "a time to mourn." Grief can overshadow everything else. Depression tends to freeze us in time, tricking us into thinking we'll never be truly happy again. But in truth, sadness will not last forever. It's only a season, a "time to embrace" God's grace. Until we hope once more.

Times to "dance, laugh and love." Ah, those are the seasons we wish would last forever. But I guess life would be pretty lopsided if the good times never ended. Their transience should cause us to not take them for granted, but to be thankful. Our pure gratitude for the good seasons creates a bank of strength to draw from when times "to tear down" or "uproot" or go to "war" descend on our souls.

We will never understand why some seasons come our way. But knowing every season has a purpose can bring us tremendous peace, even satisfaction. For the Sovereign God who makes "everything beautiful in its time" (Ecclesiastes 3:11) created us to live life fully.

As we close in on the end of another year, what season are you experiencing? No matter what the "time" might be, may you remember this ageless advice. Live life while you have it. It's a splendid gift. There is nothing small in it.

December 31st

Your word is a lamp for my feet, a light on my path.
—*Psalm 119:105 NIV*

And Miles to Go

As a new year approaches, you have new miles to travel. How will you navigate them?

I'm not exactly a whiz at directions. Even with a GPS. One time a friend and I were driving to a retreat center only to discover the friendly voice on the navigation system spoke only German. Neither of us spoke German! And there have been several times when I've carefully followed the directions only to pull up to a dead end as the voice says, "You have reached your destination." Once, well actually twice, I thought my morning trip was leading me east on Interstate 80. After about sixty miles I realized something must be wrong because the sun was at by back. I had to turn around and go back with the refrain *east not west, east not west* running through my disoriented mind.

No matter how many miles I have left to go in life, my goal is to travel them well until I reach my destination. So, how can I be assured in light of the truckload of decisions I make every day that I'm on the right road? By following the Word of God.

No better case could be made for relying on the Word of God as our navigation system than that found in Psalm 119. The psalmist says God's Word is a "lamp for our feet, a light on our path. (v. 105). It leads us through the dark patches in our journey (vv. 25, 28). It keeps us from running into potholes of shame (vv. 6, 46). Promises in the Word not only guide us, they comfort us when other travelers reject and ridicule us (vv. 50–51). God's Word protects us from getting off at the wrong exits (vv. 9–10). It instills us with hope and happiness to keep going (vv. 47, 49).

One of my favorite poems, "Stopping by the Woods on a Snowy Evening" by Robert Frost, inspires me to make my miles count.

> *The woods are snowy, dark and deep.*
> *But I have promises to keep,*
> *and miles to go before I sleep.*
> *And miles to go before I sleep.*

As we let the Word of God guide us, we can be assured of finishing our miles. Keeping our promises. Arriving safely ... HOME.

References

Introduction

Mrs. Charles E. Cowman, *Streams in the Desert* (Grand Rapids, MI: Zondervan, 1965), p. 100.

January

2nd C. S. Lewis, personal correspondence with Rev. David R. Jones, June 3, 1959.

Max Lucado, *Fearless* (Nashville: Tomas Nelson, 2009), p. 20.

8th Annie Dillard, *Teaching a Stone to Talk: Expeditions and Encounters* (New York: Harper & Row, 1982), pp. 40-41.

16th Martin Luther King, Jr., *Letter from a Birmingham Jail*, April 16, 1963, https://www.theatlantic.com/politics/archive/2013/04/martin-luther-kings-letter-from-birmingham-jail/274668/

Henri Nouwen, *Bread for the Journey: A Daybook of Wisdom and Faith* (New York: HarperCollins, 1997), p. 291.

18th Abbott Iscu story found in *Jesus Freaks* (Minneapolis, MN: Bethany House, 1999).

23rd Gary L. Thomas, *Authentic Faith: The Power of a Fire-Tested Life* (Grand Rapids, MI: Zondervan, 2002), p. 29.

24th Oswald Chambers, *My Utmost for His Highest* (New York: Dodd, Mead & Company, 1963), p. 137.

February

2nd Arthur C. Brooks, *Gross National Happiness: Why Happiness Matters for America—and How We Can Get More of It* (New York: Basic Books, 2008), pp. 180-181.

5th Max Lucado, *Out Live Your Life: You Were Made to Make A Difference* (Nashville: Thomas Nelson, 2010), p. 157.

6th Brett McCraken, "The Perils of 'Wannabe Cool' Christianity," *Wall Street Journal,* https://www.wsj.com/articles/SB10001424052748704111704575353531112264810 0, August 15, 2010.

C. S. Lewis, *The Voyage of the Dawn Treader* (New York: Collier , 1952).

10th Tim Keller, *Counterfeit Gods: The Empty Promises of Money, Sex, and Power, and the Only Hope that Matters* (New York: Penguin, 2009), xvii.

11th C. S. Lewis, *Mere Christianity* (New York: Macmillan, 1960), p.174.

15th Peter Wood, *A Bee in the Mouth: Anger in America Now,* (New York: Encounter Books, 2007)

Ravi Zacharias, *The Grand Weaver: How God Shapes Us Through the Events of Our Lives* (Grand Rapids, MI: Zondervan, 2007), p. 39.

17th Francois Fenelon, *The One Year Book of Encouragement: 365 days of Inspiration and Wisdom for Your Spiritual Journey,* ed. Harold Myra (Wheaton, IL: Tyndale, 2010). March 9.

19th Quoted by Mrs. Charles E. Cowman, *Springs in the Valley* (Grand Rapids, MI: Zondervan, 1968), p. 231

23rd Max Lucado, *Great Day Every Day: Navigating Life's Challenges with Promise and Purpose* (Nashville: Thomas Nelson, 2012), p. 74.

March

11th C. S. Lewis, *Out of the Silent Planet* (New York: Scribner, 2003).

17th St. Patrick's Prayer
http://www.crosswalk.com/devotionals/your-daily-prayer/a-prayer-of-blessing-for-st-patrick-s-day-your-daily-prayer-march-17-2017.html

20th Randy Alcorn, *Happiness* (Wheaton, IL: Tyndale, 2015), p. 230.

30th Billy Graham,
https://www.c-span.org/video/?198399-1/billy-graham-library-dedication&transcriptQuery=%22too+much+billy+graham%22

April

2nd Oswald Chambers, *My Utmost for His Highest* (New York: Dodd, Mead, 1963), p. 53.

5th Ibid., p. 31.

16th Matthew Henry,
https://urbanfaith.com/2011/11/what-did-matt-w-henry-say-when-a-man-stole-his-wallet.html/

19th C. S. Lewis, *The Last Battle* (New York: Collier, 1970), p. 184.

24th Dinesh D'Souza, *What's So Great About Christianity* (Tyndale Online, Google Books, 2013), p. 253.

25th Tim Keller, *The Freedom of Self-Forgetfulness: The Path to True Christian Joy* (UK: 10Publishing, 2012).
Billy Graham, *The Secret of Happiness* (Nashville: Thomas Nelson, 2011), p. 10.

30th G. K. Chesterton, *Orthodoxy,*
http://www.pagebypagebooks.com/Gilbert_K_Chesterton/Orthodoxy/The_Paradoxes_of_Christianity_p13.html

May

11th Brother Lawrence, *The Practice* of *the Presence of God,*
https://www.goodreads.com/author/quotes/66573.Brother_Lawrence

16th Dr. Keith Ablow,
http://www.foxnews.com/opinion/2013/01/08/are-raising-generation-deluded-narcissists/#ixzz2HXRcU3GP.

18th Greg L Hawkins and Cally Parkinson, (2011-07-15). *Move: What 1,000 Churches Reveal about Spiritual Growth* (Kindle Locations 234-237). Zondervan. Kindle Edition.

27th C. S. Lewis, *The Abolition of Man* (New York: Macmillan, 1973), p. 35.

June

8th Oswald Chambers, *My Utmost for His Highest* (New York: Dodd, Mead, 1963), p. 193.

23rd Elisha A. Hoffman, "What a Fellowship, What a Joy Devine," Public Domain.

25th Francis Chan and Chris Tomlin, *Crazy Love: Overwhelmed by a Relentless God* (Colorado Springs: David C. Cook, 2008), p. 42.

July

2nd C. S. Lewis, *God in the Dock* (Grand Rapids, MI: Eerdman's, 1970), p. 155.

George McDonald quoted in C. S. Lewis, *The Great Divorce* (New York: Harper One, 1973), iii.

5th Pope Benedict XVI , "Do Not Give In To Temptation To Instrumentalize God," *The Catholic News*, 2013, http://catholicnews.sg/index.php?option=com_content&view=article&id=8421:pope-do-not-give-in-to-temptation-to-instrumentalize-god-&catid=196:vis-vatican-information-service&Itemid=530&lang=en.

13th Timothy Keller, *Walking with God through Pain and Suffering* (New York: Penguin, 2013), p. 123.

18th C. S. Lewis, *The Great Divorce* (New York: Harper One, 1973), p. 38.

28th C. S. Lewis, *Mere Christianity* (New York: Macmillan, 1960), p. 118.

August

5th Brené Brown, *Daring Greatly: How the Courage to be Vulnerable Transforms the Way We Live, Love, Parent, and Lead* (NewYork: Penguin, 2012).

16th Story cited in Dean Nelson, *God Hides in Plain Sight: How to See the Sacred in a Chaotic World* (Grand Rapids, MI: Brazos Press), p. 42.

18th William W. Walford, "Sweet Hour of Prayer," Public Domain.

21st Kerry Patterson, et.al., *Crucial Conversations: Tools for Talking When Stakes Are High* (USA: McGraw-Hill, 2002).

22nd Dean Nelson, *God Hides in Plain Sight: How to See the Sacred in a Chaotic World* (Grand Rapids, MI: Brazos Press, 2009), p. 19.

25th Mark Buchanan, *The Holy Wild: Trusting in the Character of God* (Grand Rapids, MI: Multnomah, 2003), p. 56.

September

5th Corrie ten Boom, *The Hiding Place* (Minneapolis, MN: Chosen, 1984), p. 25.

13th Brennan Manning,
https://www.youtube.com/watch?v=0iaZp3CzUXk

20th C. S. Lewis, *Mere Christianity* (New York: Macmillan, 1960), pp. 104-108.

October

2nd W. H. Lewis, ed., *Letters of C. S. Lewis* (New York: Harcourt, 1988), p. 86.

11th Quoted in James C. Hume, *Speak Like Churchill, Stand Like Lincoln: 21 Powerful Secrets of History's Greatest Speakers* (New York: Three Hills Press, 2002), p. 164.

20th Alister McGrath, *C. S. Lewis—A Life: Eccentric Genius, Reluctant Prophet* (Wheaton, IL: Tyndale, 2015), p. 199.

November

1ˢᵗ Mother Theresa, *The Joy of Loving: A Guide to Daily Living* (New York: Penguin, 2000), p. 92.

7ᵗʰ Dietrich Bonhoeffer, "Who Am I,"
http://www.dbonhoeffer.org/who-was-db2.htm.

10ᵗʰ Daniel J. Boorstin, *The Image: A Guide to Pseudo-Events in America* (New York: First Vintage Books Edition, 1992), p. 4.

30ᵗʰ As cited in Dean Nelson, *God Hides in Plain Sight: How to See the Sacred in a Chaotic World* (Grand Rapids, MI: Brazos Press, 2009), p. 199

December

1ˢᵗ Rosalind Rinker, *Prayer: Conversing with God* (Grand Rapids, MI: Zondervan, 1959), p. 66.

3ʳᵈ Edith Schaeffer, *The Tapestry: The Life and Times of Francis and Edith Schaeffer* (Waco, TX: Word, 1981), p. 615.

Bob Goff, *Love Does: Discover a Secretly Incredible Life in an Ordinary World* (Nashville: Thomas Nelson, 2012), p. 158.

7ᵗʰ Flannery O'Conner,
https://lifeondoverbeach.wordpress.com/2012/06/07/flannery-oconnor-push-back-against-the-age-as-hard-as-it-pushes-against-you/

12ᵗʰ Paul Miller, *A Praying Life: Connecting with God in a Distracting World* (Colorado Springs: NavPress, 2009), p. 109.

25ᵗʰ Charles Wesley, "Come Thou Long Expected Jesus," Public Domain.

27ᵗʰ Frederick Buechner, *The Magnificent Defeat* (San Francisco: Harper Collins, 1966), p. 105.

28th Madeleine L'Engle, *Walking on Water: Reflections on Faith and Art* (Colorado Springs: Waterbrook, 2001), p. 233.

30th Florence Nightingale, https://www.goodreads.com/quotes/840036-live-life-when-you-have-it-life-is-a-splendid

31st Robert Frost, "Stopping By Woods On A Snowy Evening," https://allpoetry.com/Stopping-By-Woods-On-A-Snowy-Evening

About the Author

Becky Toews lives in Lancaster, Pennsylvania, with her husband, Chip, who pastors New Covenant Christian Church. They have served in ministry for over forty years after studying under Francis Schaeffer at L'Abri in Switzerland. They have two grown children and one grandson. Becky also teaches Public Speaking at Lancaster Bible College.

She is passionate about helping people draw closer to God and fulfill His purpose in their lives. If you would like to see what she's up to, visit her website @ **www.beckytoews.com**. Check out her weekly devotional thoughts on the Fresh Tracks page.

You can also follow her on Facebook @ **https://www.facebook.com/authorbeckytoews/** and on Twitter and Instagram @**Becky_Toews**.

She would love to hear from you!

If you would like to order additional copies of *Between the Lamp Posts*, go to Amazon.com where it is available in print and e-book form or you may order directly from Becky by contacting her at **beckytoews@newcovcc.us**

Read Becky's Book!

Virgin Snow: Leaving Your Mark in the World

Fresh tracks moving through uncharted territory saying, "I was here"—identifiably here. Like leaving footprints in fresh snow, we all leave marks in life. *Virgin Snow* shares a biblical perspective of how to develop marks that last. In our pursuit of fulfillment, only the character of Christ, distinctly engraved on us and shared with others, will produce the meaning we long for.

Virgin Snow offers a fresh outlook concerning the everyday challenges we face and does so in an understandable, practical way that is ideal for personal or group study.

If you would like to order a copy, go to **www.beckytoews.com** or **Amazon.com**. Also available as an e-book on Amazon.